BAR MITZVAH, A HISTORY

University of Nebraska Press | Lincoln and London

BAR MITZVAH
A HISTORY

Rabbi Michael Hilton

The Jewish Publication Society | Philadelphia

♾

Library of Congress Cataloging-in-Publication Data

Hilton, Michael.
Bar mitzvah, a history / Michael Hilton.
pages   cm
"Published by the University of Nebraska Press
as a Jewish Publication Society book."
Includes bibliographical references and index.
ISBN 978-0-8276-0947-1 (paperback: alk. paper)—
ISBN 978-0-8276-1167-2 (epub)—
ISBN 978-0-8276-1168-9 (mobi)—
ISBN 978-0-8276-1166-5 (pdf)
1. Bar mitzvah. I. Title.
BM707.H53 2014   296.4'42409—dc23   2013050487

Set in Minion Pro by L. Auten.

For Samuel, Jacob, and Benjamin, benei mitzvah
Shabbat Lekh Lekha, 5761
Shabbat Bereshit, 5764
Shabbat Aharei-Mot Kedoshim, 5770

CONTENTS

LIST OF ILLUSTRATIONS   viii

ACKNOWLEDGMENTS   ix

INTRODUCTION   xi

1. How Bar Mitzvah Began   1

2. How Bar Mitzvah Became Popular   35

3. The Spread and Regulation of Bar Mitzvah   54

4. Jewish Confirmation   74

5. Bat Mitzvah   106

6. Into the Modern Age   135

7. Current Issues and Trends   160

8. The Evidence Assessed   192

NOTES   227

GLOSSARY   261

BIBLIOGRAPHY   267

INDEX   295

ILLUSTRATIONS

1. Earliest account of bar mitzvah ceremony,
   thirteenth century   15

2. Ignaz Goldziher delivering his
   bar mitzvah speech, 1863   50

3. Program for first confirmation service
   at Tifereth Israel, Cleveland, 1896   75

TABLE

Introduction of confirmation, including
first coming-of-age ceremonies for girls   86

ACKNOWLEDGMENTS

This account could not have been written without the help and support of many scholars, libraries, and friends who have been kind enough to share personal reminiscences. In particular my thanks are due to my supervisor and guide, Dr. Sacha Stern at University College London (UCL); to scholar and academic Dr. Klaus Herrmann in Berlin; to my friend and fellow history researcher David Jacobs; and to my tireless editors at the Jewish Publication Society and the University of Nebraska Press, Carol Hupping and Elizabeth Gratch.

My thanks also to the many people who have assisted greatly by offering advice, finding sources, translating difficult texts, and reading drafts, especially Rabbi Marc D. Angel, Dr. Helen Beer, Rabbi Jeff Berger, Dr. Annette Böckler, Rabbi Barbara Borts, Vanessa Freedman, Rabbi Amanda Golby, Dr. Claire Hilton, Rabbi Yuval Keren, Yoav Landau-Pope, Rabbi Dr. Abraham Levy, Rabbi Josh Levy, Dr. Naftali Loewenthal, Miriam Rodrigues-Pereira, Rosita Rosenberg, Rabbi Professor Marc Saperstein, Dr. Jeremy Schonfield, Rabbi Dr. Michael Shire, Rabbi Daniela Thau, and Victor Seedman.

Help with photography has been kindly provided by Rabbi Frank Dabba Smith and help with finding illustrations by Fabian Graham and by the Temple Museum of Religious Art, the Temple-Tifereth Israel in Beachwood, Ohio. Figure 3 is reproduced with its permission, and figure 1 with the permission of the Bodleian Libraries, University of Oxford. The archives of West London Synagogue were consulted and are here quoted with permission.

Every library where I have conducted my research has been helpful, but the library of Leo Baeck College in London surpasses them all for being willing to obtain and even purchase rare material. I have also learned a great deal from comments made by those attending my lectures and seminars at Kol Chai Hatch End Jewish Community, the Liberal Jewish Synagogue, Leo Baeck College, Limmud, and elsewhere.

I owe a very special debt of gratitude to Kol Chai for generously allowing me time to study and sharing so many fascinating reminiscences. This book was researched and written in its entirety while I was serving as rabbi to Kol Chai. Bar mitzvah and bat mitzvah have been vital parts of its community life, as they have of mine.

INTRODUCTION

Laura Jean from Dallas, Texas, was twelve years old when she told her parents in 2003 that she would like a bat mitzvah: "She loved bat mitzvahs: the singing was "inspiring"; the parties were exciting; the attention, no doubt, was flattering. Why couldn't *she* have one?"[1] The problem was that she was Methodist, not Jewish. But she went ahead anyway and held a party for 125 friends and relatives. The writer who reported this story commented: "In the United States, bar mitzvahs (for boys) and bat mitzvahs (for girls) get more attention than first communions, baptisms or confirmation *combined*, even though Christians outnumber Jews 590 to 1. They're the summit, the zenith, the tops when it comes to teenage rites of passage."[2] The popularity of the celebration has led to the phenomenon of many Christian teenagers wanting a bar mitzvah in order to emulate their Jewish friends. From 2004 onward in the United States there have also been reports of "black mitzvah," a party celebrated by African American boys and girls. One blogger wrote of the so-called black mitzvah: "I love the warmth and respect shown by the adults to these kids. They made these young men feel special and I believe they will be successful in life."[3] The suggestion is that the African American parents want to express the same kind of pride in their children that they notice among Jewish families.

How did bar and bat mitzvah come to be so popular? What is it that appeals to Jews with totally different beliefs and lifestyles from each other and even to non-Jews? How did the ceremony start, and why is it that a higher proportion of Jewish children celebrate it today than at any time in the past?

The original ceremony, which was only for boys, was invented by fathers for their own sons. *Bar mitzvah*, many books tell us, means "son of the commandment."[4] But the first meaning of the term was "someone who has the responsibility for carrying out a particular duty." That is the way the term was used in ancient times, before anyone had thought of celebrating a boy's coming of age. The meaning of the term changed as the ceremony became important; it came to mean a Jewish boy aged at least thirteen and one day who from now on had the responsibility of carrying out all the religious duties of a Jewish man. In the twentieth century *bar mitzvah* changed its meaning again and came to refer to the celebration, rather than the child. In English today this is what the phrase means, and the child is called "the bar mitzvah boy" or "the bat mitzvah girl."

If you attend a boy's bar mitzvah today, you are likely to see some or all of four traditional elements that have been combined into a single sequence for the last four hundred years. First, during the synagogue service the boy is called up to the Torah to say the traditional blessings and, if he is able, to read or chant his own portion from the Torah scroll, instead of the usual weekly practice of it being read by a skilled volunteer or professional. In the main Ashkenazic tradition followed today in Israel, much of Europe, and in English-speaking lands, the boy is called up for *maftir* and haftarah on Shabbat morning—that is to say, on a Saturday morning in the synagogue, after the whole of the week's section has been read and seven adult men called to the Torah, the bar mitzvah recites the blessing before reading the Torah, repeats the prescribed last few verses that have already been read, recites the blessing after reading the Torah, and then reads the prescribed reading from the Prophets, with blessings said before and after.[5]

The blessings recited by the bar mitzvah are the same ones said by everyone called up to the Torah. Before the reading the boy says, "Bless the Eternal whom we are called to bless." The congregation responds, "Blessed is the Eternal whom we are called to bless forever and ever." The boy repeats the response and then carries on, "Blessed are You, our Eternal God, Sovereign of the Universe, who chose us from all peoples to give us your Torah. Blessed are You, Eternal One, who gives us the Torah."

After the reading the boy recites another blessing: "Blessed are You, our Eternal God, Sovereign of the Universe, who gave us the teaching of truth and planted eternal life within us. Blessed are You, Eternal One, who gives us the Torah." After the bar mitzvah boy has read from the Torah and recited the second blessing, the boy's father recites a five-word Hebrew blessing: *barukh she-petarani mei-onsho shel zeh*, "Blessed be the One who has freed me from punishment because of him." This is the second traditional element of the ceremony. These words were first recorded fifteen hundred years ago and later incorporated into bar mitzvah.[6] In Sephardic and some Ashkenazic communities the blessing is recited on the occasion of the boy's first wearing tefillin, leather boxes worn for prayer on the head and arm for weekday mornings. Some traditions have not used this blessing.[7]

A celebration meal or party held for the family and other invited guests is the third element of the traditional ceremony. It is an essential part of the celebration. Finally, the boy delivers a *derashah* at the meal, that is, a speech explaining some aspect of Torah. This aspect of bar mitzvah still exists in Orthodox circles but has long been in decline. Today it is more common to hear the boy give a brief *derashah* as part of the synagogue ceremony.

Other elements such as a special prayer for the occasion and a speech and/or blessing given by parents and/or a rabbi grew up in the nineteenth century and have become common practice. There are many other modern additions to the ceremony, such as physically passing the Torah scroll from grandparents to parents to the child, symbolizing the handing on of the tradition.

There are many variations in the way bar mitzvah ceremonies are performed. In particular, an additional ceremony (or sometimes the only one) may take place when the Torah is read on a Monday morning, a Thursday morning, or on a Shabbat afternoon, in which case there is no haftarah for the boy to read. On a Monday or a Thursday the boy will wear tefillin. In many traditions, but not all, the boy will wear tefillin for the first time on the occasion of his bar mitzvah. In many Sephardic and some Hasidic traditions, the tefillin ceremony is regarded as the actual bar mitzvah, and the calling up to the Torah on the following Saturday is secondary.

WHY I WROTE THIS BOOK

I have stated that the bar mitzvah ceremony is universally popular among Jews, but there have been curious exceptions. I never had a bar mitzvah. The synagogues in the British Liberal movement had abolished bar mitzvah completely and replaced it with what they called "confirmation," a group ceremony held for both boys and girls at the age of fifteen or sixteen. My ceremony took place at Wembley and District Liberal Synagogue on the Sabbath before the festival of Shavuot, Shabbat *Bemidbar*, May 21, 1966. The confirmation class conducted the service, and we, the students, then had separate family parties.[8]

By the time I began to train as a rabbi at Leo Baeck College, London, in 1982, every Liberal synagogue had reintroduced bar mitzvah and, alongside it, an identical ceremony for girls, bat mitzvah, both held at the age of thirteen. The reintroduction was largely because of pressure from parents, who managed to convince a number of reluctant rabbis that the traditional ceremony could still be meaningful. In my work as a student rabbi in East London, my single most important task was to take family after family through the ceremony; indeed, in the smaller and younger communities these events were their principal activity and reason for existence. And yet, although universally popular among the parents, many children began their bar mitzvah year motivated mainly by parental pressure and the prospect of getting presents and having a party. It was my job and that of the other teachers to try to ensure that by the time the big day came around, the students' understanding was a little deeper and their love of Judaism enhanced by the process. I wondered if it had always been like that—a ceremony driven by parents, like most things in children's lives. I wondered, too, about the incredible popularity of the ceremony and how it began. This book is the result of my personal quest to find out. What I discovered is a fascinating story, especially because of hundreds of years of attempts by Jewish communities in Europe to limit the size and extravagance of the celebration and at the same time to improve the educational standards of the children. I came to realize that the dilemmas and tensions that surround bar and bat mitzvah today are by no means new. It was not so surprising after all that the ceremony was mainly driven by parents because it had always been like that. Bar mitzvah was invented by Jewish fathers for their own sons.

This history describes the origins and growth of the synagogue coming-of-age ceremonies known as bar mitzvah (for boys), bat mitzvah (for girls), and Jewish confirmation (for boys and girls). Before 1800 there was only one ceremony, bar mitzvah for boys, and it was rarely heard of outside Ashkenazic and Italian Jewish communities. I explore why confusion exists about the date of the first bar mitzvah and the first bat mitzvah and offer my own solutions to the puzzle of the evidence. I trace the growth, spread, and development of the celebration across Ashkenazic Europe and beyond; most of the earlier sources come from France, Germany, Poland, and Italy.

For the medieval period the sources refer to two elements of the ceremony, the blessing said by the father and the celebration meal. From the sixteenth century onward the sources also mention the readings and the speech and, beginning in the seventeenth century, the bar mitzvah test. Jewish confirmation was an invention of Reform Jews in Germany at the start of the nineteenth century, and bat mitzvah is said to have begun in 1922, a claim that I examine in detail. I have chosen to emphasize those sources that illustrate the origin of the ceremonies, their social and educational aspects, and particularly the tensions between the educational and social elements, many of which are still relevant today. The individual stories given are examples from the many thousands available to illustrate the story of these very popular ceremonies. My emphasis has been on the synagogue ceremonies, the family celebrations, and issues that affect them. I have included Jewish legal aspects when they are relevant to the origin, growth, or shape of the ceremony. Readers not familiar with Hebrew terms will find brief explanations in the glossary at the back of the book.

Tensions between religion and culture, between synagogue officials and families, between faith and practice, are not new. Understanding the history helps today's debates about Jewish identity. Every bar mitzvah boy is aware that he is taking his place in a long tradition. Today girls are also part of that tradition. The popularity of bar mitzvah and bat mitzvah among such diverse communities of Jews can best be understood by exploring the history of the ceremony. The four traditional elements described earlier include both religious ceremony and party, both parent and child. The "people of the book" created a ceremony that has at its heart the reading from its most holy book. Yet within the Jewish community there is a wide range of views on whether it is the social or the religious aspects that are more important. A Jewish family today could regard the ceremony as marking a birthday, as marking an important transition on the way to adult life, as an educational achievement, as a simple step along the path of life in a religious community, as an excuse for a party, as a time for family nostalgia, or in many other ways. The traditional elements allow for any or all of these motives to be highlighted, explored, or even thrown out.

Ritual undoubtedly has the power to transform lives. But often it does not. Not every bar mitzvah is a deeply meaningful experience. A wide range of writers has explored this issue. Arthur Magida described his own bar mitzvah as "being yelled at a lot and wearing a suit that never stopped itching." You did it because it is what you were born into.[9] The memoirs recounted in his book show that bar mitzvah or bat mitzvah can be an unpleasant chore for the child. Undoubtedly, much of the celebration's high profile has come from the hype and glitz of very lavish parties. Many people never see beyond that. But thoughtful children are able to see past the glitz and to realize that the most successful celebration is not the most expensive but one that the child puts the most into.

For four hundred years there have been battles between families who want the minimum educational import and synagogues who demand the most they can get. Bar mitzvah began as an unusual ceremony probably indicating a special degree of piety. As soon as it became popular, inevitably there were those who wanted to cut corners. Regulations from Krakow in 1595 limited the number of guests who could be invited to the party. No doubt then, as now, there were families who considered the party more important than the synagogue service. And within one generation of the invention of the bar mitzvah speech, we find Leon Modena in Venice supplementing his income by composing speeches for the boys. For the less learned and less observant, the studying was a chore to be avoided if possible. But the emotional content for Jewish parents and grandparents has remained high. In *Putting God on the Guest List: How to Reclaim the Spiritual Meaning of Your Child's Bar or Bat Mitzvah* (1992), Rabbi Jeffrey Salkin encouraged parents to devote time to exploring the meaning of the ceremony, understanding the concept of mitzvah, and finding suitable charity projects.

This history makes clear that the tensions surrounding the ceremony have had a real and important purpose in preserving and enhancing the popularity of bar mitzvah. For those living in a non-Jewish environment, bar mitzvah has played a huge part in the survival of Jewish life. Take away the effort of learning, and the ceremony loses its sense of achievement, its value as an educational tool on the path of Jewish life; take away the hype, and the ceremony loses its luster in an age when celebrity status often counts most of all.

Many accounts of bar mitzvah suggest that it has now become a burden imposed on a reluctant child by families, communities, and rabbis. That interpretation fails to explain why it is more popular now than at any time in the past. The ceremony grew and became popular only because people wanted it—there is nothing in the Torah or rabbinic law to say that a child has to celebrate a bar mitzvah. It may be that children in the past were just as reluctant as some are today. It is the parents and grandparents who so often shed tears at a bar mitzvah, and it may well be the case that it has marked an emotional stage in their lives more than in the child's life. The older sources only tell us what was done, not how people felt about it. But we can speculate. The origin of bar mitzvah was when Jewish fathers began to thank God with the words "Blessed be the One who has freed me from punishment because of him." Whose feelings are described here? The father's, not the son's.

The emphasis then was on the emotional experience of the parents, not the child. Family tensions and feelings are built into the ceremony. Bar mitzvah has provided an opportunity for parents and children, families and community, to act out their relationships in a secure environment. Rites of passage are imperfect but valuable ways of enacting meaning.[10] Rites of passage are performances that help us make sense of our daily lives.[11] In our time many Jews have lost the monthly and seasonal rhythms of Jewish life. But they retain the sense of a journey through life, in which important steps can be marked and celebrated. Bar and bat mitzvah have bucked the trend, growing in popularity even while other celebrations have declined.

In a world in which family life has become difficult and often troubled, such celebrations have taken on an added importance for many people. By creating the myth of an unchanging tradition that can be passed on in its entirety, bar and bat mitzvah require participants to act as if their family lives were stable, in the hope of modeling and even creating permanence amid the fragility of existence. For a fleeting moment everything in the world becomes as we would like it to be, and hopes and plans for the future can be expressed, publicized, and celebrated. Some children and parents begin the process with a degree of skepticism, but very few emerge from it unmoved.

This book has been shaped and inspired by questions asked by students, especially the many boys and girls whom I have taught and encouraged through the time leading up to their own bar/bat mitzvah ceremonies. Many of their parents, too, have awakened my interest about the origin of particular customs. Among my past students are my own three sons, Samuel, Jacob, and Benjamin, whose constant questioning and curiosity have for many years led me on the quest for answers. To them, with great affection, this book is dedicated.

BAR MITZVAH, A HISTORY

CHAPTER ONE

How Bar Mitzvah Began

> The Bible records twenty as the age of majority, but in rabbinic times it became twelve plus one day for girls and thirteen plus one day for boys.

> In the midrash, as Esau at the age of thirteen went off to worship idols, his father Isaac was relieved of responsibility for him. Therefore, at that age and onward, a boy's father should say, "Blessed be the One who has freed me from punishment because of him."

> The synagogue ceremony was first recorded in thirteenth-century northern France. The boy was called to the Torah, and the father added the blessing. The ceremony may have been held before he left home for study in the schoolhouse. One of the sources for the synagogue ceremony also mentions that a father should make a party for his thirteen-year-old son.

THIRTEEN AND A DAY

Abraham's father, Terah, kept a shop to which customers would come to buy idols. When Terah was away, Abraham was left to mind the shop. One day he took a stick, broke up the idols, and put the stick into the hand of the largest one. When his father asked what had happened, Abraham replied that the big idol had smashed up all the little ones. Terah said this was impossible, and his son, Abraham, pointed out that his father had revealed himself to be a fool who believed that man-made objects could be worshiped. This story is not found in the Bible but comes from Jewish literature known as "midrash." Early versions do not say how old Abraham was at the time, but later retellings say he was thirteen years old,[1] suggesting that this age had over time become recognized as the age of adult understanding.

There was no bar mitzvah in ancient times, no ceremony and no party. Many modern customs are not as old as we imagine them to be; children's birthday parties, for example, were invented in the nineteenth century,

1

yet many people assume they have always existed. Bar mitzvah is not a modern invention, but it is not as old as people think it is; many Jews and non-Jews imagine it has always been part of the Jewish faith. But in the ancient world not only was a boy's thirteenth birthday not celebrated, but none of his other birthdays were either. In the Hebrew Bible the only person who celebrated a birthday was the pharaoh who rescued Joseph from prison.[2] He would hardly have been taken as an example by the small group of Hebrews who were destined to become slaves to his successor.

People had good reason to fear the birthdays of kings: in the story of Hanukkah the desecration of the Temple by the wicked King Antiochus is said by some to have taken place on the date of his birthday celebration, which he insisted was observed every single month.[3] In the Christian Scriptures King Herod threw a birthday party at which John the Baptist was beheaded at Salome's request.[4]

Ordinary people could not have held birthday parties, even if they had wanted to. Although most people were aware of their age, precise dates of birth for most people were simply not recorded. Even weddings originally had no ceremony or party; the only ceremonial event connected with the marriage of Isaac and Rebekah, for example, was the formal negotiations between their parents. When he met her, Isaac simply "brought her into the tent of his mother Sarah, and he took Rebekah as his wife. Isaac loved her, and thus found comfort after his mother's death."[5]

It was Isaac's birth, not his marriage, that provided a reason for a family party. Abraham threw a party for Isaac's weaning onto solid food as a young child. The Bible gives no details of this party, mentioning only Sarah's jealousy of Abraham's concubine Hagar and their son, Ishmael. But the Hebrew words used to describe the party, *mishteh gadol*, are significant. The word *mishteh* implies drinking rather than eating—what we would call a "party" rather than the normal translation "feast." The only other mention in the Bible of a *mishteh gadol* (a big party) is the wedding banquet of Queen Esther and King Ahasuerus in the story of Purim.[6] So, not surprisingly, the rabbis elaborated the story of Abraham's weaning feast, imagining that he had invited all the great kings and chieftains of the time. The medieval commentator Rashi (1040–1105) explained that it was called "big" because all the important people of the time were there, such as Shem and Eber and Abimelech.[7]

Unable to find any evidence for bar mitzvah in the Bible, some came to believe that Isaac had been thirteen years old at the time of the party, that he had been weaned from his "evil inclination" (that is to say, acquired his adult impulse to do good), and that this had been the very first bar mitzvah party. In the minds of those who thought up this idea, the bar mitzvah party was a more ancient practice than the synagogue ceremony celebrating the occasion.

The Torah insists that parents have a duty to teach their children and also mentions the son asking his father the meaning of the Passover offering and other laws.[8] Apart from these details we know almost nothing about how children were educated in biblical times. Even later, in the time of the Romans, it is by no means clear that most boys would have been able to read from a Torah scroll. The literacy rate among Jews in Roman Palestine is thought to have been somewhere between 3 and 15 percent. Culture and traditions were largely handed down orally.[9] Until Jewish literacy began to flourish in the Middle Ages, bar mitzvah remained a ceremony whose time had not yet come.

Although people did not know their exact date of birth, they would certainly have been aware of the changing seasons and kept count of how many years they had lived. The Torah tells us that Abraham was ninety-nine years old when he was circumcised. And, it goes on, his son Ishmael was circumcised on the same day, and he was thirteen years old at the time.[10] At this point in the story Abraham has just been told by God that Isaac, the son who is yet to be born, will be his true successor, rather than Ishmael. So, Ishmael's circumcision was *not* regarded as a precedent for the descendants of Isaac, and when Isaac was born, he was circumcised at the age of eight days. The ancient historian Josephus mentions, however, that the Arab peoples of his day circumcised their sons at the age of thirteen.[11] Rashi stated that Ishmael's circumcision took place on the very day he was thirteen.[12] This comment was part of a train of thought suggesting that age thirteen could mark an important moment of transition.

BECOMING AN ADULT AT TWENTY

When were boys thought of as adults? The Book of Numbers begins as follows:

On the first day of the second month, in the second year following the exodus from the land of Egypt, the LORD spoke to Moses in the wilderness of Sinai, in the Tent of Meeting, saying:

> Take a census of the whole Israelite community by the clans of its ancestral houses, listing the names, every male, head by head. You and Aaron shall record them by their groups, from the age of twenty years up, all those in Israel who are able to bear arms.[13]

Only men are to be counted in this census, and only those aged twenty and above; this was the age at which they were able to go to war because they would be strong enough by then.[14] No other age requirement for being an adult is mentioned in the Bible, even for marriage.

In the Mishnah, which gives us our first insight into rulings made by rabbis, there are different functions assigned to various ages.[15] Anyone old enough to walk holding his father's hand was not to be considered a "child" when it came to making the three annual pilgrimages to Jerusalem:

> Everyone has an obligation to appear on the festival pilgrimage, except for a deaf mute, a mentally disadvantaged person, and a child . . . Who is considered a child? Anyone who is too small to ride on his father's shoulders and to ascend from Jerusalem to the Temple Mount, according to the School of Shammai. But the School of Hillel say: anyone who cannot take hold of his father's hand and ascend from Jerusalem to the Temple Mount, as it says,[16] "three *foot* festivals."[17]

According to the School of Hillel, even young children just able to walk were obligated to participate in rituals and abide by established rules.

In the Christian Scriptures the young Jesus is described as twelve years old when he went to Jerusalem with his parents for Passover. We are not told whether or not this was the first time he had accompanied them. According to the story, as told by Luke, Jesus got lost, and it was three days before his parents discovered him in the Temple precincts, in enthusiastic dialogue with the teachers. A few Christian commentaries and some Christians today describe this as "Jesus' bar mitzvah," even though the story itself has no such suggestion.[18]

TAKING A VOW AT TWELVE OR THIRTEEN
—PLUS ONE DAY

The first mention of the age thirteen in the first rabbinic book of rules, the Mishnah, comes in a completely different context, that of taking a vow. In traditional Jewish law the act of speaking a vow or an oath out loud gives it binding value.[19] Jews are familiar with this idea from the *Kol Nidrei* prayer recited on Yom Kippur eve, when God is urged to cancel any vows or promises made to God in error. The Mishnah discusses the question of the earliest age at which a girl or a boy could be considered responsible enough to make a vow:

> If a girl is eleven years old plus one day, her vows are examined [to make sure she is old enough to know what she is doing]. If a girl is twelve years old plus one day, her vows are valid. They examine them for the whole of her twelfth year.
>
> If a boy is twelve years old plus one day, his vows are examined. If a boy is thirteen years old plus one day, his vows are valid. They examine them for the whole of his thirteenth year. Before the requisite age, even if they say "We know in whose name we have made the vow" or "we have made the dedication," their vow is no vow and their dedication is no dedication. But after the requisite age, even if they say "We do not know in whose name we have made the vow" or "we have made the dedication," their vow is indeed a valid vow and their dedication is a valid dedication.[20]

Even though this text has nothing to do with having a bat mitzvah or bar mitzvah, and even though the ceremony was invented many centuries later, it remains to this day the foundation for the "correct age"—twelve years plus one day for a girl and thirteen plus one day for a boy.

The Age of Puberty

The Mishnah goes on to describe the physical changes that take place in a girl at puberty, thus making it clear that the age of twelve has been chosen because this is when her physical development normally occurs. She is therefore now able to take responsibility for her actions, as is a boy at the age of thirteen. The phrase "plus one day" seems to have been added simply to make absolutely certain that the correct age had been reached. It can be found in bar mitzvah regulations even today.

The Mishnah mentions girls before dealing with boys. That is not surprising, as this text comes from the section called *Niddah*, which deals with menstruation and family purity. But it may also be because girls mature at a younger age, so the Mishnah is able to proceed logically up the scale from age eleven to twelve and then to thirteen. So, even though the ceremony of bar mitzvah for boys is much older than bat mitzvah for girls, the correct age for a girl can be found listed first, followed by the age for a boy.

The Presumption of Rava

Once the age of responsibility was established, it became a fixed law for all girls and boys. Thus, there has been no need to quiz each child on his or her physical maturity or intellectual ability. It is similar to the way we may think of a child as being part of a particular school year, regardless of the intellect or growth rate of that individual child. A general rule was fixed, based on the majority, and it was then applied to everyone.

The Babylonian Talmud makes clear that this specific rule could be applied to fix an age of majority for girls: "Rava said: a girl who has reached the required number of years need not undergo a physical examination since we can make a presumption that she has produced the marks of puberty."[21] This rule became known as the "presumption of Rava" and was applied to boys as well as to girls. It later became part of the rules for bar mitzvah. The age of thirteen plus one day became a sufficient measure, without any test or physical examination required.

"Thirteen for the Commandments"

Another mention of the age of thirteen for boys comes from the well-known section of the Mishnah known as "Sayings of the Fathers" (*Pirkei Avot*) and follows a saying given in the name of a rabbi who lived in the second century CE, Judah son of Temah: "He used to say: a son of five years old for Bible: of ten years for Mishnah: of thirteen for the commandments [mitzvot], of fifteen for Talmud."[22] The list suggests that these are the best ages for boys to start learning about the particular subjects. But none of the ages given here had legally binding status.[23] They were merely suggested ages rather than definite rules, for the passage goes on, amusingly: "eighteen for a wedding, twenty for a job, thirty for authority, forty for intelligence, fifty for giving advice, sixty for being an elder, seventy for grey hairs, eighty for special strength, ninety for being bowed back, and at a hundred, a man is as one that has died and passed away from the world."

Yet not all ancient texts are what they seem. Although the saying appears in the Mishnah, it is in fact a later addition. The famous twelfth-century scholar Maimonides (1135–1204) did not include this paragraph in his edition of the Mishnah and did not use it when drawing up his own educational curriculum for the study of Torah. Some manuscripts even place it in a different place.[24]

The paragraph that precedes this text ends with a short prayer,[25] indicating the original ending of the section. There is no clear evidence that the saying was considered part of the Mishnah until the twelfth century.[26] The whole chapter gives lists based on various numbers—the ten items created on the eve of the Sabbath, the seven indications of a wise man, the four kinds of student, and so on. The paragraph noted here, on "the ages of man," was modeled on the same pattern. The use of the word *Talmud* apparently referring to a specific book or books proves that this paragraph was written later. *Talmud* was a general word indicating "study," but obviously one could not study "the Talmud" until it had been written, meaning no earlier than the year 500 CE.[27] So, the famous saying "thirteen for the commandments" does not suggest that the tradition of bar mitzvah existed in ancient times.[28]

But thirteen was nevertheless an important age. It is mentioned in rabbinic literature as the time when the "impulse to do good" is acquired.[29] It also came to be the time when a boy could be considered a man. In the Book of Genesis we are told that Simeon and Levi, two of Jacob's sons, took revenge on the people of the town of Shechem for the rape of their sister Dinah: "Simeon and Levi, two of Jacob's sons, brothers of Dinah, took each his sword, came upon the city unmolested, and slew all the males."[30] The Hebrew literally means "they took each *man* his sword," and that additional and unnecessary word *man* led to this comment: "Rabbi Shimon son of Elazar said: They were then thirteen years old."[31] His comment was taken up in an anonymous twelfth-century commentary, which discussed the importance of the age of thirteen and added: "They introduce him to the fulfillment of the commandments." The Hebrew word used here for *introduce* can also have a more physical meaning: "they bring him in."[32]

Much more recently, in nineteenth-century commentaries, this story was linked with the bar mitzvah ceremony and used as evidence that at that time a boy becomes a man. Even though Simeon and Levi were aggressive and vengeful, and even though their actions were condemned, the idea that at thirteen a Jewish boy becomes a man has become part of modern Jewish popular consciousness, so much so that to this day bar mitzvah boys use the phrase "Today I am a man" in their speeches to their guests. In North America, it has become the traditional way such a speech begins and was particularly popular in the mid-twentieth century.[33]

Since the 1950s some boys parodied the phrase by saying "Today I am a fountain pen," because for thirty years fountain pens had been popular gifts for the occasion. At his bar mitzvah in July 1946 Barry Vine, of New Haven, Connecticut, received sixteen fountain pens as gifts.[34] Perhaps the facetious "Today I am a fountain pen" was intended by bar mitzvah boys to discourage well-meaning relatives from giving this little-appreciated gift.

More recently, the phrase "Today I am a man" was parodied in an episode of the TV series *The Simpsons*. In it the character Krusty the Clown is the son of a rabbi, but he did not have a bar mitzvah as a child because his father thought he would make fun of the ceremony. He decides to learn Hebrew and have a bar mitzvah as an adult. During the preparation period Krusty has to give up doing shows on a Saturday and is replaced by Homer Simpson. The episode was called "Today I Am a Clown."[35]

READING THE TORAH
AND LEADING THE SERVICE

At what age did boys take an active part in synagogue services? The Mishnah tells us that a boy may read from the Torah and translate.[36] It does not state any age and does not suggest that this was a common practice. The Jerusalem Talmud raises the question of whether the boy really understands what he is doing.[37] By the time the question was discussed in medieval Europe, it was common, as it is now, for a skilled leader to do the actual reading and for others simply to come up and say the blessings before and after.

A twelfth-century prayer book from France, the *Machzor Vitry,* rules that a boy is permitted to read from the Torah;[38] others insisted that at least three men be called up as well.[39] Rabbi Joshua Falk (Lvov, 1555–1614) mentioned the practice of a boy being called up as *maftir* (an additional call up to the Torah and reading the haftarah as well). But he objected to boys below the age of thirteen being included among the first seven men called up on Shabbat morning. The *Mishnah Berurah*, a rule book commonly used today by Orthodox Jews, confirms this ruling, that a boy under thirteen may *only* be called up for *maftir.*[40]

An exception is made on Simchat Torah, an autumn festival with many colorful customs deriving from medieval Ashkenazic Europe, when all the children in the synagogue can be called up as a group to the reading of the Torah. But that very custom marks an exception, a special day of rejoicing when the boys could be offered a taste of the life of an adult Jew.[41]

It may well have been a substitute for the earlier practice of allowing a boy to be called to the reading on an ordinary Shabbat or weekday, an honor from which boys under thirteen have gradually been excluded, so that the bar mitzvah boy comes up on his own for the first time in his life at his own celebration. This ruling applies whether or not he actually reads from the scroll or just comes up to say the blessings. Today it is common for the bar mitzvah to be called up for *maftir*, an honor permitted even for younger boys, but it is not a universal practice and was not the norm when bar mitzvah first became popular.

Leading the Prayers

In the Jerusalem Talmud we find that a man should be fully grown—that is, twenty years old—before leading prayers.[42] During the medieval period the age was lowered. The ninth-century Rav Natronai Gaon stated that in an emergency someone younger than twenty could lead the prayers, provided he had reached the age of thirteen and one day.[43] The first full Jewish prayer book, *Seder Rav Amram*, was written by one of Natronai Gaon's students. It quoted his ruling but went on to criticize the custom of those places where a thirteen-year-old could be chosen to lead prayers, preferring someone fully grown.[44] Clearly, this was happening.

Most of the rules we use today about Jewish prayer come from the book known as "Tractate *Soferim*," originally compiled around the year 750 CE. It states that a boy has to be at least thirteen to be included in the quorum for a service.[45] It goes on to say that the age itself is sufficient and no physical examination is required. But this section of *Soferim* is now thought to be much more recent. It is a huge complication in the history of Jewish customs that we cannot simply accept the traditional dates for a great deal of the evidence. In medieval times copying and revising a manuscript was every bit as effective as saving a new version on a computer today; the older version has gone forever.[46] The *Machzor Vitry*, a later prayer book, rules that in order to lead the part of the service including the *Shema*, a boy must be age thirteen and one day *and* have the beginnings of physical maturity.[47]

So, we have traced a fall in the minimum age from twenty down to thirteen. But it seems that even younger boys were sometimes allowed to lead prayers in medieval Europe. Although the general rule was thirteen, not everyone obeyed it. In practice it became quite common after the Crusades for boys who had lost a parent to lead the *Kaddish* for those who had died and often to lead the last part of the service. Rashi's prayer book, discussing the end of morning service on Mondays and Thursdays, states, "And the boy rises to say *Kaddish*."[48]

Joseph Caro (1488–1575) wrote about this custom disapprovingly. A child was not obliged to pray regularly and so could not lead the prayers on behalf of adults. Caro mentioned that the custom of a boy leading prayers had even spread to Spain, and he knew about it from the rabbis who opposed it.[49] And so he ruled in the Shulchan Arukh, as did his contemporary Moses Isserles for Ashkenazic Jews, that age thirteen was the demarcation age and specifically that age alone was the defining moment, regardless of physical maturity: "At thirteen years old . . . they can make a presumption that he is like an adult . . . This is the custom and there is no need to change it."[50] Similarly, Isserles added that the prevailing custom was for a boy not to wear tefillin "until he becomes bar mitzvah, that is, thirteen years old and one day."[51] Thus, we see that Jewish boys younger than thirteen in medieval Europe were at times allowed to lead prayers and read from the Torah, but both practices were gradually prohibited, except for the remaining custom, still practiced in some communities, of a younger boy being called up for *maftir*.

Keeping All the Commandments

Even in medieval Europe, not every rabbi thought that the age of thirteen on its own was sufficient to make it compulsory for a boy to perform all the commandments. The earliest indication of its importance can be found in an eleventh-century comment about the wearing of fringes on the corners of a garment: "Just as a man has to perform this command, so when he reaches the age of thirteen years and one day he becomes obligated for all the commandments of the Torah."[52] The statement was quoted with approval by the great commentator Rashi. Some claimed that it showed a very clear definition of the age of majority.[53] But nevertheless the debate was not over.

Since that time there has been considerable disagreement among rabbis, some of them insisting on there being physical signs of puberty in the boy, not just his arrival at the correct age. This issue came to be important when the new idea arose of celebrating bar mitzvah by means of a special meal.

We have traced a very clear change, from an age of male majority of twenty in the Bible to an age of thirteen during the Middle Ages. The change reflects changes in Jewish history and life. The original age of twenty was considered a suitable age to join the army; the new age of thirteen was suitable for leading and performing rituals in the synagogue. Because thirteen marks the onset of puberty, a modern writer has explained the bar mitzvah age in rather discouraging terms: "The Rabbis treated all sexuality as fraught with danger. They evidently believed that the most difficult task of a grown-up human being (or at least a male) is controlling the sexual urge: so to insist that all the *mitzvot*—commands or precepts—were operative at puberty meant that the community was bracing itself to govern those urges."[54] Some scholars have linked the popularity of bar/bat mitzvah today to the fact that it takes place at puberty, a common time for coming-of-age rituals in many societies, when young people can be guided toward becoming adults supportive of the wider group and formally inducted into a particular faith or culture.[55]

"A BEAUTIFUL CUSTOM"

The next pieces of evidence lead directly to the origin of the bar mitzvah ceremony. Tractate *Soferim* contains a description of "a beautiful custom in Jerusalem."[56] Boys and girls, we read, were trained to practice fasting before the age when it became compulsory. They would fast for a half-day at age eleven, a full day at age twelve, and "afterwards" they were taken round all the elders of the town to receive congratulations and a blessing. The word *afterwards* could mean at the age of thirteen,[57] and if so, it certainly indicates a marking of that age with congratulations. Even if this text comes from the later part of *Soferim*, which reflects European practice, it could still be early evidence for celebrating the coming of age.[58]

One obvious stumbling block to linking this text to the history of bar mitzvah is that girls are here included along with the boys. But far more problematic is the likelihood that the text from *Soferim* as normally printed is wrong. Some texts read that the story is not about children aged eleven or twelve at all but about children aged one or two.[59] It is easy to dismiss this detail on the grounds that babies could not possibly have been trained to fast. But it is not as impossible as it at first appears. The twelfth-century northern French scholar Rabbeinu Tam criticized an overly pious practice of not feeding very young children on the fast day of Yom Kippur.[60] For those who disagreed with him, inventing or finding a story that even babes in arms would fast back in Jerusalem was a good way of encouraging people to be more pious.

The Origin of the Father's Blessing

The foundation text for the father's blessing later used at the synagogue celebration of bar mitzvah comes from the book *Bereshit Rabbah*. The core of this book has traditionally been thought to have been put together by Rabbi Hoshaiah, who lived in the land of Israel in the third century CE. The book was probably expanded and edited in the fifth century, and some parts possibly even later. It is a commentary on the stories of Genesis, the book that recounts the history of Abraham and his family. In Genesis 25:27 we are told of the twins Esau and Jacob: "When the boys grew up, Esau became a skilful hunter, a man of the outdoors; but Jacob was a mild man who stayed in camp." For thirteen years, says *Bereshit Rabbah*, the two boys went to school. But from that age onward one of them, Jacob, went to the house of study ("stayed in camp"), while the other, Esau, went to houses of idolatry ("a man of the outdoors").[61]

So, at the age of thirteen the twins Esau and Jacob made their own decisions about their lifestyle. Therefore, comments *Bereshit Rabbah*: "Said Rabbi Elazar: 'A man must take responsibility for his son up to the age of thirteen years, and from then on he needs to say "Blessed be the One who has freed me from punishment because of him."'"[62] This means that up to the age of thirteen the punishment for any misdeeds done by the son will be inflicted on his father, but from then on the boy takes the blame on his own, and the father cannot be punished for anything his son does. Rabbi Elazar may have been thinking of Esau in particular. Esau's father, Isaac, he suggests, is entitled to declare, now that the boy is thirteen and making his own way in life, that he as his father is not responsible for the misdeeds that will be done by him in the future and even by his descendants.

But Rabbi Elazar is not only thinking of Isaac and his twin sons, who turned out to be so different from each other. He suggests that any father should consider uttering such a blessing when his son reaches thirteen or at any suitable time after that. Rabbi Elazar does not suggest a definite time or occasion when the blessing is to be used. The phrase *from then on* indicates that it is something a father might say at various points in the future, particularly perhaps if the young man misbehaved. In the case of Esau *from then on* could carry the implication of "for all time."

Saying the Blessing Out Loud

"Blessed be the One who has freed me from punishment because of him." Perhaps some fathers, discovering this blessing in *Bereshit Rabbah*, may have said it privately or muttered it under their breath when their teenage sons got into trouble. But then one day someone decided it would be a good idea to recite it out loud in the synagogue, in front of the congregation. But on what occasion would one do this? If it were to be done when a thirteen-year-old boy was called up to the reading of the Torah, it would be a declaration to everyone present that the boy was destined to grow up as a pious Jew, like Jacob, not as a good-for-nothing, like his brother Esau. The first time this was done can be thought of as the very first bar mitzvah ceremony, even though nobody called it a "bar mitzvah" at the time.

THE SYNAGOGUE CEREMONY

We have access to more knowledge about the origins of bar mitzvah than was available to previous generations. Some of the first accounts of the synagogue ceremony come from manuscripts first printed late in the twentieth century which are examined here very carefully, in chronological order from the time each one was written. The early accounts have a French background and reveal that what we now call "bar mitzvah" became a French Jewish custom in the thirteenth century.

In his book *Sefer HaIttur* Rabbi Isaac the son of Abba Mari of Marseilles, Provence (c. 1122–c. 1193), wrote: "When he says the blessing on the redemption of the firstborn, the priest says 'Just as you deserve this mitzvah, so may you deserve to fulfill all the commandments (*mitzvot*) of the Torah.' And there are places where, when he reaches thirteen, one recites the blessing: 'Blessed be the One who has freed me from punishment because of him.'"[63] The life cycle of a Jewish boy is under discussion here. The prayer being quoted is that said for a firstborn son, in which the hope is expressed that the boy will grow up to be able to fulfill God's commandments. At thirteen he is able to do so, and the father is then free of his responsibility. This is the first evidence we have that the blessing composed by Rabbi Elazar was actually being used; moreover, it was not used by one particular person but is given as a general rule, and it was not used for a boy at any time after the age of thirteen but now specifically at that age.

The text does not say that the prayer was said in synagogue or that the boy was bar mitzvah, but there are suggestive associations. It does not say here who actually recites the blessing—in *Bereshit Rabbah* it was the boy's father, but here it could mean any member of the family or anyone who knew that the boy had just become thirteen. Most likely, it was his father, as we can see from our next source.

Rabbi Judah the son of Yakar, who was born in Provence in the mid-twelfth century, made a similar brief mention of the custom. He had studied in northern France, which is where he may have heard of the new custom. From 1175 he was known to be living in Barcelona, Aragon. He wrote: "If someone has a son and he grows up to the age of thirteen, he says 'Blessed be God (*ha-makom*) who has rescued me from punishment because of him.'"[64]

There are two variations—*God* and *rescued*—from the traditional text of the blessing, perhaps suggesting that as the custom of using it became more common, people remembered it wrongly or else deliberately varied the words. The phrasing "who has rescued me from punishment" really does make it sound as if the father thus becomes free of his responsibilities for his son.

These two sources from southern Europe do not mention any synagogue ceremony. But two sources from northern France do. One of them was not published until 1973. Several manuscripts survive that give teachings from Rabbi Yehiel of Paris, a famous scholar who defended Judaism in a public disputation in Paris in 1240. At the end of his book of teachings, in two of the manuscripts, there are a few pages giving an anonymous tiny collection of Ashkenazic customs and rules entitled *Horaot MiRabbanei Tzarfat* (Teachings of the Rabbis of France):

> If someone has a son and he reaches the age of thirteen years, the first time that he stands up in the congregation to read from the Torah, his father should recite the blessing "Blessed are you, Eternal God, who has redeemed me from punishment because of him." And the Gaon Rabbi Judah the son of Barukh stood up in the synagogue and recited this blessing the first time his son stood up to read from the Torah. And this blessing is obligatory.[65]

Figure 1 shows four paragraphs from the Oxford manuscript. Rabbi Judah (Yehudah) the son of Barukh, sometimes given the title Gaon, lived in Mainz and Worms in the middle of the eleventh century. This places him in the second generation of Ashkenazic rabbis, after Rabbeinu Gershom (c. 960–1040) but before Rashi (1040–1105).[66]

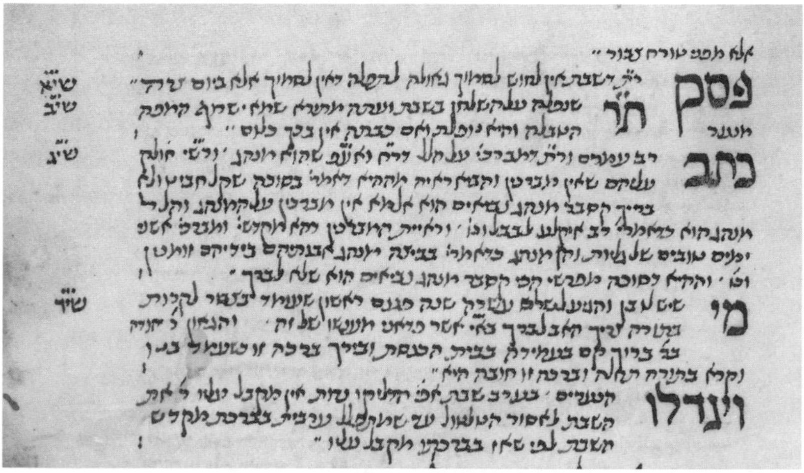

Fig. 1. Manuscript account of the earliest bar mitzvah synagogue ceremony containing a specific name (thirteenth century). Reproduced with permission from the Bodleian Libraries, University of Oxford, Manuscript Opp Add 4° 127, fol. 62a. The illustration shows the top half of leaf 62a, and the account is in the third paragraph, numbered 314.

A FATHER'S NAME IS RECORDED

Despite being called "Teachings of the Rabbis of France," the little collection contains many rulings of German rabbis,[67] indicating that German customs were spreading to France. Here we have the first boy whose father's name is mentioned, along with the age of the child, the nature of the synagogue ceremony (reading from the Torah), the role of the father, a particular instance of the blessing being said, and a ruling for the future. What it does not say is that the little ceremony necessarily took place close to the boy's birthday. And from the wording it was not necessarily the first time the boy had read from the Torah, only the first time after his birthday that he had done so. As we have seen, younger boys sometimes read from the Torah in synagogue at that time.

The wording of the blessing here has two changes from the traditional wording. First, the introductory words "Blessed are you, Eternal God" were added. This might appear unimportant, but it was an absolutely crucial change for the history of bar mitzvah. A declaration or blessing that does not include the name of God could be said as often as you wanted at any time. But a Hebrew blessing that included God's name could only be said in particular circumstances. By adding the name of God to the father's blessing and then stressing that the blessing is compulsory, the "Rabbis of France," whoever they were, were making a rule that these words should *only* be said on the first occasion that one's son is called to the Torah after he reaches the age of thirteen. Unlike our first account, this one states that saying the blessing was obligatory. This meant, in effect, that having a bar mitzvah (as it was later called) was here thought of as compulsory for the boy, so that his father could say the blessing.

The second change is strange. Instead of "Blessed be the One who has freed me from punishment," Rabbi Judah said, "who has redeemed me from punishment." The word *redeemed* brings to mind the "redemption of the firstborn," for which a ceremony is mentioned in ancient sources and by our first medieval source, *Sefer HaIttur*.[68] The new synagogue ceremony is here likened to a second "redemption." *Redeemed* is a stronger word than *freed*, suggesting the father has really been saved from danger. But this variation in the text of the blessing did not catch on, so the phrasing "freed me from punishment" became the norm.

THE EUROPEAN ORIGIN OF BAR MITZVAH

Only when the story of Rabbi Judah son of Barukh was published in 1973 did it become really clear that bar mitzvah had a European origin. The simple story does not explain why this new custom began. Very little is known about this Rabbi Judah, but one of the few reports we have about him tells us that he used to fast for a second day after Yom Kippur. This may seem extraordinary, but it was a known practice among the group known as the Hasidei Askenaz, a pious group in twelfth-century Germany, and among their French contemporaries known as the tosafists.

So, this new custom that we now call bar mitzvah may have started off as another pious practice, a public acknowledgment by the father that his son will be responsible for his own actions and do his religious duties.[69] But is this report correct? Can we be sure that Judah was the first to do this, if the only account we have was written two hundred years later?

We do not know, but what we can be sure about is that this little ceremony was recorded as a French custom in a collection of sayings added by a scribe to a book by Rabbi Yehiel of Paris, who left France for the Holy Land in about the year 1260.[70] This first report was therefore before 1260 but not necessarily a long time before that. Until further evidence comes to light, the best way to interpret this evidence is to say that the synagogue ceremony was first recorded in thirteenth-century northern France.

AVIGDOR THE FRENCHMAN

In 1996 another unusual text was printed for the first time, and it gives us further information. It was published under the name of an otherwise unknown Rabbi Avigdor Tzarfati ("Avigdor the Frenchman"). His report of the same thirteenth-century French custom has not been noticed by previous studies of the history of bar mitzvah:

> In *Bereshit Rabbah* it says that on the day when his son was thirteen Isaac stood up and recited "Blessed are you, Eternal our God, Sovereign of the Universe, who has freed me from punishment because of him." **And this is the ruling**: it is a duty to recite this blessing over one's son when he is thirteen years and one day old, when he stands up to read from the Torah, and one needs to stand over one's son to place one's hand on his head, and to recite the blessing as expressed here. **And this is the French custom.**[71]

Here for the first time it is ruled that the little ceremony should take place on the exact day the boy reaches the required age. As the Torah is not read in public every morning, it follows that the ceremony might have to be postponed for one or two days but not longer. The instruction is very precise.

This account of what was later called bar mitzvah adds the fascinating new detail of the father placing his hand on his son's head. This was a time-honored Jewish gesture, traditionally done with two hands.[72] Jacob had placed his hands on the heads of his grandsons when blessing them, using a text that was taken up by Jewish families.[73] Moses placed his hands on the head of Joshua, and this became a key text for rabbinic ordination.[74] But this simple act has not elsewhere been connected with the father's bar mitzvah blessing until modern times, when it is sometimes done by the father and sometimes by the rabbi.

Christians had introduced an individual laying on of the hands by the bishop as part of the Roman Catholic confirmation rite in the twelfth century.[75] This practice was modeled on an account in the Christian Scriptures,[76] and its reintroduction by the Church in the twelfth century followed the thinking of Hugh of St. Victor (1096–1141),[77] a scholar known to have studied the Bible with Jewish teachers.[78] Hugh taught at the Abbey of St. Victor in Paris.

Avigdor's account suggests that the father's blessing went back to Isaac, who "stood up and recited it," as if he had been attending synagogue with his son Jacob. According to one account, Rabbi Avigdor's own father was called Isaac, and in his youth Avigdor had traveled with his father and two teachers to Paris to witness the famous public disputation between Rabbi Yehiel of Paris and the convert Nicholas Donin (1240).[79] Perhaps his own father had recited the blessing for him according to the ruling preserved among the French customs. Perhaps, too, a party was held afterward because Avigdor's book is also an important source for that.

THIRTEENTH-CENTURY FRANCE

The two earliest reports of the synagogue ceremony were both recorded in French sources. One comes from a book of French customs, and the other says explicitly that bar mitzvah was a French custom. Paris was the largest city in Europe, and important centers of Jewish scholarship developed there and across France. Born in Troyes in 1040, the famous scholar Rashi studied in Worms on the Rhine and traveled frequently between the two towns. Following Rashi, the innovative twelfth-century scholars known as tosafists were a group based in both countries. The best known was Rashi's grandson, Rabbeinu Tam (1100–1171). They adopted a very distinctive approach to the study of rabbinic texts, refusing to depart from tradition but finding skillful ways of adapting the texts to the time and the culture in which they lived.

In thirteenth-century Normandy the age of thirteen marked a real practical transition in a boy's life. An Oxford manuscript dated 1309 preserves a rule book for the education of children.[80] The third stage of the child's education is that of the *perushim* (separated):

> The rabbis said, "A thirteen-year-old for [the performance of] precepts." Their words are supported by [the verse], "I have formed this people for myself, they shall relate my praise" [Isa. 43:12]. The *gematria* equivalent of the word "this" (*zu*) is thirteen. They are worthy of being counted in a quorum of the community and to pray, and they can be counted among the numbers of the *perushim*. The father shall take his son the *parush* and encourage him with good words, "You are fortunate that you have merited to do the holy work," and he shall be

entered into the house that is designated for the *perushim*. The obligation of separation (*perishut*) does not begin until he reaches the age of sixteen. [The father] brings him before the head of the academy and he lays his hands upon him saying, "This is consecrated to the Lord." And he says to his son, "I am directing to here that which you would have consumed in my house, for I have consecrated you to Torah study." And he will remain there for seven years.[81]

There is a contradiction here between the ages of thirteen and sixteen for the boy going off to the house of study, but the quotations used support the age of thirteen. This would mean the young man would remain in the school until the age of twenty. It has been suggested that this rule book comes from Normandy. Archaeological remains of what may have been used as a boys' high school (yeshiva) were discovered in the Jewish quarter of Rouen in Normandy in 1976.[82] Our text may well be linked to the remains of this building in Rouen.[83] One relevant point is that this rule book also specifically mentions a "French custom."[84]

At the enrollment of the boy in the high school, there was a ceremony in which the father's hands (or the director's hands) were placed on the boy's head.[85] This act echoes Avigdor's account of bar mitzvah. So, this is one place where the ceremony could have developed, with the first part (which we now call bar mitzvah) taking place in the family town synagogue before the boy left for school and the second ceremony taking place on his arrival at the school. We now have not only a time and place for the ceremony but also a possible reason for it taking place, as boys became separated from their parents and went off to school on their own.[86]

Christian Cultural Influences

The culture in which the small Jewish communities of France lived was a Christian one, in which Jews only survived when royal rulers and the Church allowed them to. Attacks on Jews were frequent during the first Crusade (1096–1099) and King Philip Augustus had all Jews expelled from those areas of France under his control in the year 1182. In 1198, however, they were allowed to return and resume their lives. But although life was hard for medieval Jews, this does not mean that every Jew and every Christian hated each other; the small Jewish communities would never have survived if Jews had been hated by all their Christian neighbors. Some Jews studied with Christians and knew how they interpreted the Bible.

There are many examples of Jews taking up Christian customs, provided they were consistent with Judaism. When Avigdor described the custom of the father placing his hand on the boy's head, he may well have known that this was also done in church. But because it was in the Hebrew Bible, it was acceptable. It was precisely this kind of innovative approach that allowed new rituals, such as bar mitzvah, to be developed and accepted.[87]

The recital of *Kaddish* by mourners was another new French custom from the same period and was particularly associated with boys who had lost a parent.[88] So, a boy who had a father could celebrate the new ceremony later called bar mitzvah—while a boy without a father could take part in another new tradition, that of saying *Kaddish*. It is easy to imagine two friends, one celebrating and one mourning.

The poignant juxtaposition of the two innovations brings to life the hazards and joys of medieval French Jewry. A boy would say *Kaddish* to plead for mercy for the soul of his dead father, who had been righteous and pious enough to teach his son. A father would say the bar mitzvah blessing to give thanks for the righteousness and piety of his son, whom he had taught and who was now responsible for his own actions. The two innovations mirror each other. One was a sad way, one a happy way, of marking the separation of a son from his parents and the transfer of responsibilities in an era of danger and persecution.

Bar Mitzvah in Medieval England?

Over two hundred manuscripts left by the tosafists have never been published, so there are very likely further early accounts of bar mitzvah waiting to be discovered.[89] Because of the closeness of the Norman French and medieval English Jewish communities, it is quite possible that bar mitzvah was also celebrated in thirteenth-century England, though we have no local evidence.[90]

I have described how the spread of bar mitzvah may have been linked to the high school in Rouen, with the recital of the blessing by the father in synagogue implying a wish that the son would go on to further study, like Jacob in the midrash from which the blessing was taken. Rouen has been described as a model for the medieval London community. King John of England proclaimed the Jew Jacob of London "king of the Jews" in a document he issued at Rouen in 1199. But within a few years King John lost control of Normandy, and thereafter Jewish links were not so close.

Evidence from the South of France

An account from the south of France in the fourteenth century comes from the *Orhot Hayim* of Rabbi Aaron the son of Jacob HaCohen of Narbonne. Jews were expelled from France and from Provence in 1306, and Rabbi Aaron fled to Majorca, where his book was completed around the year 1327. It is a code of Jewish law that reflects the practices he knew in Narbonne. The book was published in 1752 and contains this fascinating account: "If someone has a son who reaches the age of thirteen years, the father needs to say 'Blessed is the One who has freed me from punishment because of him.' And there are those who say the blessing the first time their son goes up to read from the Torah. And the Gaon, Rabbi Yehudai, of blessed memory, stood up in the synagogue and recited this blessing the first time his son read from the Torah."[91]

Who was the "Gaon Rabbi Yehudai?" Yehudai the son of Nahman lived in the town of Sura in Iraq (called "Babylon" in Jewish tradition) in the eighth century.[92] But quite how an account of an event in Babylon could have surfaced in Narbonne five hundred years later is unclear. We do know that Yehudai Gaon wrote his rulings in the form of letters to communities across the then known Jewish world, and no doubt these letters were cherished and handed down by their recipients.[93] But this account states that "there are those who say the blessing," indicating that this had become a custom in Narbonne.

It is not clear why an innovation of a specific Babylonian rabbi would have been adopted in this place at this time. Furthermore, this account makes it clear that it was at the age of thirteen that boys read from the Torah for the first time. The wording seems to follow the older account and was therefore very likely a French custom.

Before 1973, when the story about Judah the son of Barukh was published, many thought this was an account of the first bar mitzvah and that it took place in Babylon. But now we can see a more probable explanation. It seems likely that here we have another account of the same story. The older account spoke of Judah the son of Barukh, known as Gaon ("distinguished"). This account speaks of Yehudai Gaon, which in the Hebrew is only one letter different. Probably the account had been handed down by word of mouth, and a slight change of name was the result. It is not surprising that before the other account was known, Yehudai Gaon of Babylon was thought to be the inventor of the synagogue ceremony.[94] But we should not regard either account as accurate. The Jewish tradition valued oral legend and loved to think of every custom as old. The sensible way to suggest a date for a custom is by the date it was recorded.

By the time the new ceremony reached Narbonne, it was normal practice that on the occasion of the bar mitzvah, the boy had never read from the Torah before. Huge importance was attached to local custom among European Jews of the time—so much so that French and German rabbis made no effort to collect their own writings because they did not expect or intend them to carry authority beyond the immediate case at hand.[95] This helps to explain how it is that we have these obscure references indicating the existence of a synagogue ceremony for bar mitzvah, even though the custom is nowhere mentioned by the major authors of Ashkenazic Jewry.[96] In these early stages of the ceremony the custom existed but was only rarely practiced.

THE CEREMONY SPREADS TO GERMANY

The next account takes us from France to Germany, as the custom of the father's blessing spread. It comes from the *Tashbetz Katan*, written by Rabbi Shimshon the son of Tzadok, who lived in Germany during the thirteenth and fourteenth centuries: "From *Bereshit Rabbah*, reported by Rabbi Shimon [*sic*] son of Rabbi Tzadok. A man has to take care of his son until he is thirteen years old, and from then on he needs to say, Blessed are You, our Eternal God, Sovereign of the Universe, who has freed me from punishment because of him."[97] This would simply be a quotation of the ancient source of the blessing, had not the author changed it by adding the full introductory formula. This indicates that the blessing was by now seen as a highly significant marker of a particular date.

The First Boy Who Was Called "Bar Mitzvah"

More detailed evidence for the recital of the blessing comes from Rabbi Jacob the son of Moshe Moellin (c. 1365–1427) of Mainz, known as the "Maharil," in his "Hilkhot Keriat HaTorah": "Maharil the Levite. At the time when his son was made bar mitzvah and he read from the Torah, he said the blessing over him: 'Blessed are You, our Eternal God, Sovereign of the Universe, who has freed me from punishment because of him.' And this is found in Mordecai HaGadol, with the name of God and his kingship mentioned."[98]

This adds a very important detail. Here for the very first time the term *bar mitzvah* is associated with the blessing. The phrase replaces the one in the previous accounts "when his son reached the age of thirteen years." This is close to the use of *bar mitzvah* in its modern sense and with reference to some kind of synagogue ceremony. Maharil wrote in the third person, but he was writing about his own son. This boy was the first we know of to be called a "bar mitzvah."

Exactly what happened, however, is not clear. It does not say this was the first time he had read from the Torah. Indeed, it is not even clear that it was the boy who read from the Torah—perhaps it was his father. Maharil cites the full form of the blessing in the name of the Mordecai HaGadol, that is, Rabbi Mordecai the son of Hillel HaCohen (c. 1240–98). Yet the passage mentioned has not been found in Mordecai's writings. But we do know that Mordecai was a collector of the decisions of Rabbi Yehiel of Paris, whose name is linked to both of the two earliest accounts of the synagogue ceremony.[99]

The term *bar mitzvah* as used by Maharil indicates one who is now responsible for his actions and not, as the words literally might indicate, a "son of the commandment." The phrase has been taken from the Talmud to correspond to the father's blessing: just as the father is released from punishment, so the responsibility passes to the son; as the father recites the blessing, his son is *made* bar mitzvah, and the ceremony is an act of transfer of responsibility. It appears close to the colloquial modern English usage of *barmitzvah* as a verb, as if the father "barmitzvahed" his son.

In a sense this is what happens, though this is purely an interpretation of the symbolism of the ceremony. The son is responsible for his actions when he reaches the required age, whether or not his father says the blessing.[100]

Maharil lived at a time of appalling persecution. Jews became victims of atrocities in over three hundred towns in Germany in the fourteenth century. "We are an orphaned generation," he wrote, "without anybody who knows the difference between right and left."[101] In his day orphans flocked to the synagogues to recite *Kaddish*. Throughout history Jews have affirmed their faith in the face of tragedy. But Maharil insisted that the new practice of saying *Kaddish* was not compulsory. He had a different way of expressing his own hope in the future, by referring to his son as a "bar mitzvah." He could not know how popular that ceremony and that term were to become.

Bar Mitzvah in Austria

As time went on, the bar mitzvah custom spread.[102] Another important text, missed by previous histories of bar mitzvah, comes from Austria. Rabbi Isaac Tyrnau was a contemporary of Maharil, who was known to have been in contact with him. The text is from his book *Sefer Minhagim*: "If they call to the Torah a lad who was made bar mitzvah, after he reads from the Torah, his father says the blessing 'Blessed are You, our Eternal God, Sovereign of the Universe, who has freed me from punishment because of him' (*Bereshit Rabbah, Maharil*)."[103]

Maharil described what he did personally, but Tyrnau was an avid collector of contemporary custom. So, he must have had another source or seen it himself or heard of the custom spreading. In this account the father says the blessing after the boy has concluded his reading, at the point where the blessing can be found to this day in Ashkenazic prayer books.

The Full Formula

In reading these accounts today, we want to know what happened and how the custom of bar mitzvah spread from place to place. But the books that contain the accounts are books of customs, not books of history, so the interest of the authors was in the technical details. Much of the early legal discussion about bar mitzvah was about whether or not the father's blessing should contain the full introductory formula or simply its original short form.

The blessing with the full formula "Blessed are You, our Eternal God, Sovereign of the Universe" came to be seen as an indication that it was a meritorious deed, if not an obligation, to arrange for a son to have a bar mitzvah, for otherwise it would not be permissible for his father to recite a blessing using God's name. Those books that approve the full formula were giving a rabbinic stamp of approval to the whole notion of a bar mitzvah ceremony. Yet the original reason for upgrading the blessing may have been rather different. Some thought that even boys under thirteen were responsible at least in part for their own actions. Those who promoted the recital of the full blessing thought that the father alone carried the full legal responsibility for how his son acted until he was thirteen.

The debate was taken up by Moses Isserles of Krakow (1520–72) in his comments on the Shulchan Arukh: "There are those who say that somebody whose son is made bar mitzvah says the blessing 'Blessed are You, our Eternal God, Sovereign of the universe, who has freed me from punishment because of him' (Maharil in the name of Mordecai and *Bereshit Rabbah Toledot*), but it is best to say the blessing without referring to the name of God and God's kingdom."[104] In downgrading the father's blessing, Isserles is in effect downgrading the whole ceremony. In his time bar mitzvah had ceased to be the preserve of a few pious families, and was beginning to become a widespread practice across the Jewish community. Tyrnau says "*If* they call to the Torah . . . a bar mitzvah," but Isserles has "somebody whose son is made bar mitzvah," as if this was the norm.

From Austria the ceremony of bar mitzvah moved to Poland—not yet to Sephardic lands. There is no mention of the custom in the main text of the Shulchan Arukh or the other works of Joseph Caro. As we will see, the increasing popularity of bar mitzvah raised the question of whether introducing a major new ritual was permitted. Not everyone was happy with the idea. The rulings of the Shulchan Arukh with Isserles's comments became authoritative for Ashkenazic Jewry, so to this day the shorter form of the father's blessing preferred by Isserles is the one that is used.

THE FATHER'S BLESSING IN PRAYER BOOKS

The father's blessing has frequently been printed in prayer books, after the blessings for reading the Torah, at the point in the service where Tyrnau indicated it should be recited. But instructions often added to the books reveal different customs about when the blessing was actually said. To this day most Ashkenazic traditions follow Tyrnau's Austrian practice. But a few prayer books printed in Vilna and elsewhere, following a Chabad custom, say that the father recites the blessing as his son comes up to read.[105]

The symbolic resonance is quite different. In this tradition the blessing is recited before the boy reads, so his reading is his first act as an adult. The implication is that his real bar mitzvah has taken place a few days earlier, at his tefillin service. But in the main Ashkenazic tradition the blessing is recited after the boy reads, so his reading is his last act as a child. This pattern fits with the common practice today among Ashkenazic Jews of the boy reading *maftir* and haftarah, a duty permitted to a younger boy.

A daily prayer book published by the Jews' Free School, London (1819), added a Hebrew rubric to indicate that the father says the blessing either "when they call his son to the reading of the Torah or when his son prays in the congregation."[106] This wording suggests that the boy might celebrate by wearing his tefillin at school on a Tuesday, Wednesday, or Friday when there is no Torah reading, and in that case the father would still say the blessing.

THE PARTY

As we have seen, the idea of a bar mitzvah party was imagined to be even older than that of the ceremony and went back to Abraham's weaning feast for his son Isaac, described as a *mishteh gadol*, a "big party." On this party the midrash *Bereshit Rabbah* comments: "Rabbi Hoshaiah Rabbah said he was weaned from the evil inclination. The Rabbis said he was weaned from his mother's milk."[107] Rabbi Hoshaiah was traditionally said to be the author of *Bereshit Rabbah*, and his title, "Rabbah," might hint at this. Here it is the rabbis who give the simple plain meaning of the verse, while Rabbi Hoshaiah gives a spiritual interpretation.

The main biblical commentators all followed the plain meaning of the story, and none of them picked up on Rabbi Hoshaiah's interpretation. Other midrashim link the "big party" to Isaac's circumcision.[108] But the later *Midrash Aggadah* states, "There are those who say he was weaned from an evil to a good inclination, and he was then thirteen years old."[109]

Many have taken this statement to refer to a bar mitzvah—and not only that but one celebrated by a meal. In *Torah Shelemah*, for example, Menachem Mendel Kasher (1927) writes that "from here we have a source for the custom of holding a meal on the day of the bar mitzvah, as is explained in *Zohar Hadash*."[110] The *Midrash Aggadah* has therefore been taken to give at least a hint of the existence of a bar mitzvah feast at the time it was written, probably in the twelfth century.

The introduction to the Zohar expands on the story.[111] Satan, says the Zohar, hates those who do not give to the poor on festive occasions. Abraham held a big party when Isaac was weaned and invited the great of that generation. Satan, the accuser, stood at the door disguised as a poor man, but Abraham did not invite him in; he busied himself serving his guests, while Sarah suckled their children. Satan complained to God, who punished Abraham by making him offer up his son.[112] Sarah died in sorrow for her son, and it all happened because Abraham did not give to the poor.[113]

This is an unusual story about Abraham and Sarah, who are generally regarded as the prime examples of good hospitality to strangers.[114] The later popularity of the Zohar meant that this story was taken seriously. Its influence can be seen in the later tradition, first recorded in Krakow in 1638, that the father of the bar mitzvah should make donations to the community fund on the occasion of the party. Here we have a clear source for the origin of the very popular charity projects that are so much part of bar mitzvah today.

All this tells us only that at the time when bar mitzvah spread across France from the thirteenth century, families might perhaps have held a party. It does not tell us that they did. As with the ceremony, a good deal of detective work has to be done to find out whether or not bar mitzvah parties were really held in those days.

A Convert to Christianity Tells His Story

Judah the son of David the Levite was born around 1107 to a Jewish family in Cologne. He appears to have had little or no Jewish education and became a messenger sent out to collect loans for his father's business. Judah became a Christian at the age of twenty, when he was sent to collect a loan from Bishop Ekbert of Münster and found himself spending several days with the bishop's servants and followers. He wrote as if these were the first people really to have taken any interest in him. Later in life, using his Christian name of Herman, he wrote an autobiography in Latin,[115] and at the start of the book he recalled a dream he had when he was thirteen years old. In this dream the Roman emperor Henry V appears to him and gives him gifts he had confiscated from a dead prince: a muscular white horse, a golden and beautifully crafted belt, and a silk purse containing seven heavy coins. Judah receives the gifts, makes a speech of thanks, and accompanies the king to his palace, "where, as he dined splendidly with his friends, I recline next to him, as if his dearest friend, and from the same bowl as he I ate with him a salad concocted from many herbs and roots."[116] At the end of his "little book" Herman gives his own interpretation of this dream, full of Christian symbolism, the white horse meaning baptism, the belt representing the strength of chastity, and the seven coins the gifts of the Spirit. The table is the altar and the salad the gospel of Christ.

In 1981 a London historian suggested that perhaps this meal was a bar mitzvah party. His thinking was that the meal consisted of a salad because Jewish dietary laws were observed at the feast. He went on to suggest that this could be the earliest evidence for a bar mitzvah party in Germany— "we find the banquet, the presents, and maybe even the speech."[117] There are certainly many realistic autobiographical details in Herman's account.

But the way he tells the banquet story shows that every detail is designed to give a particular Christian message. The feast stands for knowledge. The dream is a fiction composed for the purposes of the autobiography.[118]

Herman's sad life story has a fascination of its own but tells us nothing about bar mitzvah parties. But it is of interest for the history of the bar mitzvah in quite a different way. It is quite possible that the education reforms made by the Jewish community in medieval France were a defense against conversion. In medieval Europe, including England, the Church was eager to approach Jews wavering in their faith to tempt them to baptism. A lad such as Herman, who seemingly had little or no knowledge of his own faith, was a prime target. Conversion to a full Christian life was regarded at that time as a lifelong process.[119] And so a lifelong process of Jewish education was an appropriate response, with the new ceremony of bar mitzvah marking an important transition along that path. The new marker of legal liability, bar mitzvah, needed to be accompanied by a growth in religious education.[120] Herman's story helps us understand why bar mitzvah became necessary.

A Party for His Son

From the mid-thirteenth century comes a very brief comment from the *Perushim Ufesakim* thought to be by Rabbi Avigdor Tzarfati. It reads simply: "to make a party for his son when he is thirteen years old."[121] This text has been taken as clear evidence for the existence of a bar mitzvah party in those days,[122] but these few words are not easy to interpret. In the printed edition of Avigdor (the work was first published in 1996), the comment is enclosed in square brackets. The reason is that the entire text of the paragraph is missing from the manuscript, and the sentence has been inserted from an index in the back of the book. In the index it comes under the heading for the section of the Torah known as *Vayera*, which includes the story of Abraham's feast for his son. The Hebrew phrase *mishteh livno*, "party for his son," denotes more than an ordinary party; it is a common phrase in rabbinic literature and is most frequently used to describe parties held by non-Jews that Jews should not attend for fear of participating in pagan practices. The most common occasion for such a party would have been a wedding or betrothal, and this is the usual interpretation of the phrase.[123]

But although it was most often used of non-Jewish parties, the phrase was occasionally used for Jewish family events. Rabbi Akiva gave a "party

for his son" at which the wine flowed freely.[124] In Maimonides there appears
to be a distinction between the party for his son and the wedding feast that
follows, perhaps indicating that the party for his son is a betrothal.[125] If
Avigdor was referring to a bar mitzvah party, it suggests quite a different
kind of celebration from the bar mitzvah meal (se'udah) of later centuries.

On the other hand, party (mishteh) was the word used in the Bible itself
(Gen. 21:8), so it would be natural to use it in an index of customs based
on that story. We know that Avigdor was aware of bar mitzvah because he
mentioned the synagogue ceremony, and in his account he suggested that
the patriarch Isaac was the author of what was to become the bar mitzvah
father's blessing.[126] The implication is that Isaac's father, Abraham, gave
him a party when he was thirteen, and he in his turn later instituted the
blessing for his own sons. Thus, the custom began to be handed down
from father to son.

If the party was not for a wedding, perhaps it was for a boy leaving for
boarding school. I have already mentioned a link between Avigdor and a
medieval rule book for the education of children. Both mention the father
placing his hands on the boy's head in blessing. We now come to another
link, for both texts also mention a party (mishteh). The educational text
describes "a party and rejoicing for the covenant and for the separation
(perishut)," though it is not clear if this is one or two separate parties and
whether it means separation as a boy over thirteen leaves for school or a
commitment made at a younger age, as it mentions Hannah dedicating
her son Samuel to the Temple.[127]

A FEAST AMONG THE MYSTICS

The famous book of Torah interpretation known as the Zohar is the central text of the Kabbalah, the Jewish mystical tradition that developed first
in Provence and then in northern Spain in the twelfth and thirteenth centuries. Because the Zohar is set in ancient times, it was thought to be an
ancient work, and so many of the customs it records were incorporated
into later rule books. Its narratives provide early evidence for many popular Jewish customs, including the tikkun leyl Shavuot, the all-night study
session held by many communities at the Shavuot festival.

The term bar mitzvah does not occur in the Zohar, and there is no mention of any ceremony. But four times the Zohar uses a previously unknown
phrase, bar onsha, to refer to someone old enough to be liable to punishment if he does something wrong; the phrase is used three times about

Ishmael and once about Isaac.[128] It is based on the midrashic blessing the father says at a bar mitzvah, "Blessed be the One who has freed me from punishment (onsho) because of him." In addition, there are three paragraphs in the section of the Zohar known as *Zohar Hadash* that have been thought to be influential for the history and development of the bar mitzvah party. The first one describes how Rabbi Shimon the son of Yohai, the central teacher mentioned in the Zohar, threw a party for the thirteenth birthday of his son Elazar:

> Said Rabbi Elazar, Up to the age of thirteen, the human being is occupied by an animal soul. From the age of thirteen and over, if he seeks to be worthy of it, they give him a holy and elevated soul . . . Rabbi Shimon the son of Yohai invited the scholars of the Mishnah to eat at a great meal which he made for them, and filled all his house with expensive vessels and seated the scholars on one side and he sat on the other side, and he was very happy. They said to him, "Why are you happier on this day more than on all other days?" He said to them, "Because on this day a holy and elevated soul descended on four winged creatures to Rabbi Elazar my son, and at this party my happiness is complete."[129]

There are two background sources for this story. The first is the statement in the Talmud that as soon as someone becomes obligated to wear fringes on the corners of his garments, he also becomes obligated in all the other commandments of the Torah.[130] This was read with the eleventh-century comment that the obligation begins at the age of thirteen and one day.[131] The Talmud goes on to state in the name of Rabbi Shimon the son of Yohai that whoever is careful to observe the duty of wearing fringes is worthy to receive the Divine Presence.

The second background source is the midrash from *Bereshit Rabbah*, the original text for the father's blessing. In some manuscripts it is attributed to Rabbi Elazar, who was the son of Rabbi Shimon the son of Yohai. In view of this report that he composed the blessing that was now being used in the synagogue, what could be more natural than for the authors of the Zohar, writing in Spain toward the end of the thirteenth century, to expand on the midrash by imagining that the young Rabbi Elazar had himself had a bar mitzvah?

The Zohar here draws on the idea that at Abraham's "big party" Isaac was released from his evil inclination. In the language of the Zohar, he was now *bar onsha*, and the event is represented by the image of a purer soul being brought down from heaven. The *Zohar Hadash* consists of sections of the Zohar that were not included in the first two printings of 1558–60. The work we now call *Zohar Hadash* was compiled in Safed from many manuscripts and first printed in 1597. Because the Zohar was thought to be an ancient work, it soon became very influential on the spread of customs, which means that this story about Elazar's party could have helped the rapid spread of the bar mitzvah parties in the seventeenth century. What is much more difficult to decide is whether Rabbi Shimon's party for his son reflected any thirteenth-century custom.

Although composed in Spain, there is ample evidence that the authors of the Zohar knew of contemporary Ashkenazic customs from traveling scholars who took French and German customs to Spain.[132] They could well have known of the blessing offered by Rabbi Judah the son of Barukh for his son or of the report of Avigdor. If celebratory meals did take place for bar mitzvah, a narrative like this is how one would expect them to find a place in the Zohar.

Weddings and Bar Mitzvah

Two other sections of the Zohar texts mention the thirteenth birthday as a cause for celebration. They are not specifically about Elazar the son of Shimon but talk in more general terms about the importance of a boy reaching the age of thirteen. When a boy becomes thirteen, it is a joyous time for the righteous: "What is a wedding? It is on a day when he is fit to perform the commands of the Torah, which is the joy of the righteous. And when does he become fit? Said Rabbi Yitzhak, from thirteen years old and upwards, and on that day it is an obligation for the righteous to be joyous of heart, like the day when he comes up to the bridal chamber."[133] This passage certainly refers to some kind of celebration when a boy is thirteen, but the nature of the celebration is not immediately apparent. The text undoubtedly influenced much later developments in eighteenth- and nineteenth-century Poland, when the bar mitzvah was sometimes celebrated at the same time as a wedding.[134]

A third Zohar text is from a well-known section in which the "old sage of *Mishpatim*" offers advice about how to live. It begins: "Any one who merits the age of thirteen and over is called a son of the community of Israel, and everyone who is twenty years old and over, and merits them, is called a son of the Holy One, Blessed be He."[135] The text goes on to describe the first thirteen years of life as *orlah*, a word used in the Torah for fruit trees during their first three years, when the fruit was not allowed to be eaten.[136] The word *orlah* literally means "foreskin," which in the language of the Zohar indicates a state of impurity from which the boy is gradually cleansed by attending school and synagogue. The text may be hinting at the story of Ishmael, whose foreskin was removed at the age of thirteen.

But here when the boy becomes thirteen, he reaches only a halfway stage. He is "a son of the community of Israel"—that is to say, in kabbalistic terminology, under the influence of the *Shekhinah* (indwelling presence of God), the female *sefirah* (aspect of God) through which God's presence enters the world. But the boy is capable of more, and so at the age of twenty he comes under the influence of the Holy One, a higher mystical level. In the Zohar the term *Holy One* refers to some of the male *sefirot*.[137]

The text goes on to describe the arrival at the age of thirteen using a variety of mystical images, culminating in this one: "What does the Holy One Blessed be He do to that soul? He brings her to His room, and gives her gifts and many presents, and adorns her with adornments from on high, until the time when he brings her to the wedding chamber (*chuppah*) in that son, when he is thirteen years old and over."

Most translators take the word *chuppah* to mean "wedding canopy," which is incorrect for this period. The portable canopy on poles now familiar at Jewish weddings was an Ashkenazic innovation in the sixteenth century.[138] At the time of the Zohar the word could have indicated a head covering, or tallit, spread over the bride and groom, but more likely the word retained its biblical meaning of "bridal chamber."[139] So, here the Holy One conducts the soul from His own chamber, corresponding to the chamber of the groom, to the chamber of the bride, corresponding to the body of the thirteen-year-old boy. If these texts are about a bar mitzvah, then the bar mitzvah is like a spiritual wedding, to be celebrated with as much pomp and ceremony.

INTERPRETING THE EVIDENCE

The evidence given so far for the origin of the party is very difficult to interpret. Each text on its own gives away very little. The Zohar texts and Herman's dream provide very faint hints that perhaps gifts were given to a bar mitzvah boy, but put the texts together, and perhaps there is a hint of something real. Add in the midrashim on Abraham's feast, the blessing given by Rabbi Judah the son of Barukh to his son, the report of Avigdor, and finally the feast given in the Zohar by Shimon the son of Yohai for his son, and there is some evidence for bar mitzvah celebrations having been arranged for sons by single pious individuals in the early centuries of Ashkenazic Jewry. But the suggestion that this means that bar mitzvah parties did exist in those days is not without its problems.[140]

The first problem is that only one of these early sources for a home celebration, the one from Avigdor, can be linked to evidence about a ceremony taking place in synagogue. Otherwise, it is as if the synagogue and the home celebration were known to different people in different places; the only thing they have in common is the link to the boy's thirteenth birthday. This reading places huge importance on Avigdor's evidence, of which only the heading has come down to us.

A second problem is that these texts describe the party in very different terms from the modest bar mitzvah meals of the sixteenth century onward. The Hebrew term *mishteh* (party) is not the same as the later term *se'udah*, meaning "meal." The Zohar does use the Aramaic equivalent of *se'udah*, but the party described is wonderfully extravagant and is also described as a *hilula*, a term that normally refers to a wedding feast.

The possibility must be considered that all these texts that are said to give early evidence for bar mitzvah parties are in fact describing wedding or betrothal celebrations. Child marriages were common in the Jewish communities of France, Germany, and England from the eleventh to the thirteenth centuries. Although the ages are younger than average, it was not at all rare for the bride to be eleven and the bridegroom thirteen.[141] During the period under discussion it was common for Jewish girls to be betrothed before the age of twelve, which suggests that the boys were not much older. Maimonides ruled that it was proper to be married as soon as possible after puberty, once the age of thirteen had been reached.[142]

The evidence of the texts could fit a wedding feast as well as a bar mitzvah—except for Herman's sad story, in which no biographical interpretation can really be anything other than conjecture. Later in his "little book" Herman describes how he bowed to pressure from the Jewish community and married a Jewish bride and was miserably unhappy.[143] He was around twenty or twenty-one at this time. But Herman was writing as a Christian who had left Judaism.

All the texts from Jewish sources could easily be about weddings. The text from *Midrash Aggadah* is a comment on the biblical phrase *mishteh gadol* (big party), the same phrase used for Queen Esther's wedding feast. Avigdor uses the term *mishteh livno* (party for his son), a phrase almost invariably associated with a wedding. The Zohar texts are full of explicit wedding imagery. Ashkenazic marriage customs are just as likely to have found their way into the Zohar as bar mitzvah customs. The spiritual wedding described at the age of thirteen could mirror a real wedding on earth.

The only reasonable conclusion, then, is that the early evidence for the home celebration of bar mitzvah is open to different interpretations. It is all too easy to assume that a Jewish boy having a party on his thirteenth birthday was celebrating his bar mitzvah, but it is wrong to read this modern assumptions into medieval texts. There is no text from earlier than the sixteenth century that unambiguously mentions a bar mitzvah party. But if the parties for thirteen-year-old boys began as wedding celebrations, they could have continued simply as bar mitzvah parties when the age for marriage rose.

This marks the end of this description of the origins of bar mitzvah in medieval France, and its later spread to Germany. Although described as a "custom," bar mitzvah, in medieval France and then Germany, seems to have been a custom taken up by very few people and consisted only of the father saying a blessing to his thirteen-year-old son. There may well have been important reasons to mark the age of thirteen—perhaps a boy was beginning a new school, leaving home for the first time, or getting married. However unusual bar mitzvah was, a new tradition had been established, and in the fourteenth century the term *bar mitzvah* began to be used. But it would not become popular or widespread until the sixteenth century.

CHAPTER TWO

How Bar Mitzvah Became Popular

- A key text from Solomon Luria indicates that by the late sixteenth century: bar mitzvah was now a popular custom; it was celebrated in Germany with a party; and a speech made by the boy at the party was recommended.
- By the late 1500s tutors could earn extra income by writing boys' speeches for them.
- From 1617 comes evidence that the minimum age of thirteen plus one day for the bar mitzvah was being strictly enforced.
- The peculiarities of the Jewish calendar make it occasionally possible that a younger boy will be entitled to his bar mitzvah before an older one.
- Since 1759 it became common for the bar mitzvah to read *maftir* and haftarah (sometimes known as "muff and huff").
- Many pocket books were published in the United States containing a selection of standard speeches for the boy to choose from.

THE MISSING YEARS

There is not even a hint of evidence of a celebration meal for the bar mitzvah from the 1280s until the mid-sixteenth century, a gap of nearly three hundred years. There are isolated reports of the synagogue ceremony but no mention of any kind of party. But we do know that bar mitzvah must have continued as a social occasion, for when we hear about it again, it reappears as an established custom, found for the first time among ordinary Jewish families.

The missing years in our story were bleak times for European Jewry, when scholars were few and persecutions many. Jews had been expelled from many European countries, and were blamed for the Black Death, which killed twenty-five million people between 1347 and 1352. Ashkenazic Jews placed great emphasis on the importance of custom but felt little need to write their customs down.[1] The extraordinary creativity of Ashkenazic Jewry, which has bequeathed to today's Jews Simchat Torah, the *Purim-spiel*, yahrzeit candles, two Sabbath candles, the mourner's *Kaddish*, the chuppah and broken glass at a wedding, as well as bar mitzvah—all this was developed and handed down within local communities.[2]

During the years of missing evidence we can assume that bar mitzvah did not become a popular custom. It was little more than a synagogue blessing and perhaps a family party celebrated by a few pious individuals from time to time. Suddenly, in the second half of the sixteenth century, it emerged as a widespread custom in Germany and Poland. It is worth asking why.

BUILDING A TRADITION

Bar mitzvah marks a birthday, and at this time people in Europe were beginning to celebrate their birthdays. The celebration of the birthdays of kings was common in the Roman Empire, and both Jews and Muslims frowned on the ordinary celebration of birthdays as an idolatrous custom.[3] Most people could not have celebrated even if they had wanted to. Before the keeping of clear records, most people would have been aware of the season, but not the precise date, of their birthday.

Among peasant societies in Europe many people were unaware of their precise birthdays until the early twentieth century.[4] Even the date of Shakespeare's birth in 1564 was not recorded, as his baptism marked the significant date. There are many examples from that time of vagueness about the age of a child.[5] Jews as well as Christians began to enter birth dates in family Bibles from the fifteenth century.[6] Annual birthday celebrations among Jews did not become popular until modern times,[7] but once birth records existed, the celebration of bar mitzvah was at least possible. New education arrangements in Europe made it important to know your age because schools started to be organized in year groups according to age.[8] Such changes encouraged people to mark the passing of the years of a child's life. Seen against this background, it is not surprising that bar mitzvah began to become more popular.

The key piece of evidence comes from the *Yam Shel Shelomoh* of Solomon Luria (Poland, 1510–74), known as Maharshal, and suggests how bar mitzvah came to be observed as we understand it today. It is the first undisputed evidence of the bar mitzvah meal as an established custom and indeed the first clear evidence of any *home* celebration for the bar mitzvah. The bulk of this work has not survived, and so it is by a lucky chance that we are able to read what Luria wrote about the bar mitzvah meal.[9] The existence of a bar mitzvah party as a widespread custom also informs us that the synagogue ceremony was itself popular by this time.

The form the bar mitzvah party took from the sixteenth century onward was that of a se'udah, a "meal" to which family and other guests were invited. Celebratory meals are common to all cultures and a part of Jewish practice since ancient times. The Hebrew word se'udah does not indicate in general that the meal had to include a festive menu or a large group of people. The word was commonly used in the ancient rabbinic sources, specifically to designate the meals held on the Sabbath—domestic meals, as opposed to those marking a national event, such as the Passover seder. Maharshal included bar mitzvah in a paragraph about the se'udat mitzvah, the meal that celebrated a happy occasion involving a religious obligation, such as the arrival of a new baby (circumcision and redemption of the firstborn), the completion of a Torah study program, or the dedication of a new house. He defined se'udat mitzvah as a meal held to publicize the performing of a happy duty.[10] Its earliest usage was to describe the Sabbath meals, but among the Jews of Europe the term was extended. It was the obligation, rather than the menu, that has been the essence of the occasion among the most pious. In the eighteenth and nineteenth centuries among the Hasidim, the minimum requirement for a se'udat mitzvah might well have been a simple meal consisting of "herring, potatoes and liquor diluted with water."[11]

After describing the meal held for the dedication of a new house, Maharshal continued: "The bar mitzvah meal which the Ashkenazim make—apparently there is no greater meal of obligation than this, and its name proves it."[12] Maharshal was writing from Poland, where the word Ashkenazim meant the Jews of Germany, living to their west. He had heard reports of the new custom but does not appear to have seen it himself. The word here translated apparently is the Hebrew word likhora, which Maharshal always used to indicate a degree of doubt. We could use the English allegedly, indicating that what follows is part of the report he had received about what was happening in Germany. What he had heard is that it had to be an important "mitzvah" (obligation) because its name (bar mitzvah meal) showed it to be so. This does not mean that he approved. The word apparently suggests that he had his doubts about it.[13]

Maharshal went on to explain that the purpose of the meal was to give thanks to God that the boy has the merit of becoming bar mitzvah. He then gave his own suggestion about the reason for the celebration. He drew on a story from the Talmud discussing a ruling that people who are blind are exempt from having to perform many of the commands of the Torah.[14] Rav Haninah expressed the view that it is better to do something one is obliged to do than to do something voluntarily. Thus, a sighted person who has to perform the commands would earn more merit than a blind person, who does not have to. Rav Yosef was blind and thus exempt. He replied to Rav Haninah that he would love to be in the position of having to do those commands he only does voluntarily because doing so would give him more merit. He would celebrate it with a special banquet for the rabbis. The view of Rav Haninah is characterized as one that discredits a blind person—Rav Yosef's view is the one that prevailed. The Talmud allows the blind person to speak for himself.[15] Maharshal argued that this is a precedent for celebrating that one has the obligation to carry out God's commandments. It is by this precedent that bar mitzvah parties came to be accepted.

Maharshal then went on, however, to express a reservation. He worried that a thirteen-year-old boy might not yet have the physical signs of puberty and therefore the party celebrating his obligation to carry out God's commands would then have been held too soon; he does not have to perform the obligation because physically he is too young. According to Maharshal:

> This "bar mitzvah" does not appear right to me, for most of them do not have two (pubic) hairs, and therefore they cannot fulfil the obligations for others, for prayer and for grace after meals . . . As soon as he reaches the age of thirteen and one day, they make the meal, and train him to recite the grace after meals, and to pray for the occasion. But if this was not done at the proper time, and now it is not even known what his right time is, why is it called a "meal of obligation"? It is not like the meal for a circumcision or for the redemption of a son. Even when the first time for it has passed, nevertheless all their days they are mandated, and it is still their proper time, so they should not delay the obligation. That is not so in this case, because maybe his time has not arrived, except on the strength of relying on a presumption. [Otherwise, as soon as he was physically mature enough] he would have to train him at once, and to make a meal. In any event it appears that where they train the lad to

make a speech of Torah at the meal for the sake of the occasion, it is
no worse than a meal for the dedication of the house, and all those
are meals of obligation which we permit. However, one should not
make too many of them, lest they threaten to eliminate, God forbid,
one's regular Torah learning completely.[16]

The passage is not easy to follow. At a circumcision or at the redemption ceremony for a firstborn son, it is obvious why the celebration meal
is being held, and the tradition lays down a fixed time. If it is delayed,
the obligation remains. But for a bar mitzvah the proper time is when
the boy is physically (and thus intellectually and spiritually) ready. The
"presumption" that Maharshal mentions comes from the Babylonian Talmud, an opinion expressed by Rava but not universally accepted.[17] It is
only on the presumption that at thirteen he will be mature enough that
the celebration can proceed. Even though it is permitted to proceed, the
best custom is to train the boy to make a *derashah* at the meal, a speech
explaining some aspect of Torah. Doing so provides an extra safeguard
just in case the event were held too early because the meal now becomes
an occasion to hear words of Torah. And this is permitted—permitted
but not necessarily recommended. That is because if bar mitzvah parties
were to proliferate, they would take away from regular time for study.

Maharshal's stringent view about the physical signs of purity disagreed
with many earlier rulings. He ignored the acceptance of Rava's presumption by Rashi that a boy automatically becomes obligated to perform all
the commands at the age of thirteen and one day. But Rashi's ruling did
not settle the matter. Many different opinions were expressed, and it was
only Maharshal's Polish contemporary Moses Isserles who finally ruled,
quoting earlier precedents, that the age alone was the defining moment,
regardless of the physical signs: "There are those who say that they do not
join up with him at all (to form a group to say grace after meals) until he
is thirteen years old, and at that age they make a presumption that he is
like an adult and has two (pubic) hairs. And this is the custom and there
is no need to change it."[18]

Maharshal's statement suggests that he was trying to fend off a new idea
that was spreading eastward from Germany. News of it had reached him,
and perhaps the practice was even beginning to be celebrated locally. There
are frequent references in his book to "Ashkenaz" (Germany), and although
Maharshal did not openly criticize the customs apparently spreading from

the West, he used the term in a way that distanced himself from them. In this case he clearly did not feel able to prohibit the custom, and so he very grudgingly accepted it. But his acceptance was circumscribed with doubts, particularly regarding the physical maturity of thirteen-year-old boys. Had his stricter view prevailed, bar mitzvah would never have become such a popular custom. The preparation and inviting of the guests presupposed a date fixed well in advance. Waiting for the "right time" would not have been a popular option. The right to make an assumption that any thirteen-year-old had the physical signs solved the problem. Isserles's clear ruling has been generally accepted,[19] a ruling very important for the future of bar mitzvah in Ashkenazic lands. Now that bar mitzvah was becoming established, it was being marked not just as the first time the boy was called to the reading of the Torah but also as a clear demarcation time for other ritual practices. Isserles commented that the best custom was for a boy not to put on tefillin for daily prayers "until he becomes bar mitzvah, that is, thirteen years old and one day."[20]

JUSTIFICATION FOR THE PARTY

When Maharshal used the story about the blind Rav Yosef to justify holding a bar mitzvah party, he had no access to the story from *Zohar Hadash* about the party Rabbi Shimon son of Yohai threw for his thirteen-year-old son, Elazar. That story was first published in 1597 and came to replace the story about Rav Yosef as a source for the bar mitzvah party. At the time it was believed to be the clearest ancient source for the custom.[21] It was first referred to in a work published in 1648, *Yalkut Hadash*: "It is obligatory on a man to make a meal at a bar mitzvah just as when he comes under the bridal canopy, and great is the reward (see *Zohar Hadash*)."[22] Maharshal had mentioned the bar mitzvah party almost as an afterthought to his discussion about a celebration meal upon moving home. This new reason for holding a party upgraded it significantly because now it was being compared to the most important celebration in Jewish life—the wedding feast. The same comparison was taken up by another seventeenth-century scholar, Avraham Gombiner (1633–83), who added: "Bar mitzvah—this is when a boy reaches the age of thirteen years and one day, and in our time the custom is to say a blessing when the lad prays or reads on Shabbat for the first time, and then everyone recognizes that he is bar mitzvah."[23]

Noteworthy here is the ambiguous use of the term *bar mitzvah*, which could mean either the boy or, like the common modern usage, the actual occasion. Gombiner continued by clarifying the customs of his day, with the four now traditional elements all present in his description—the calling to the Torah on Shabbat (or the leading of prayers), the blessing (to be said by the father, though this is not explicitly stated), the party (which can be of considerable size, like a wedding), and the *derashah*, which is still regarded as constituting an appropriate reason for the party: "It is a duty for a man to make a meal on the day when his son becomes bar mitzvah like the day when he comes under the wedding canopy . . . if the boy makes a speech, it is a meal of obligation." Since Gombiner there have been many rabbinic rulings amplifying and clarifying the legal and technical aspects of bar mitzvah, but that line of inquiry is not part of this history.

From this time thirteen and one day became strictly the minimum age for the bar mitzvah, and the prevailing custom has been for the celebration to take place as soon as possible after that. Rabbis were soon beginning to use their authority to be very strict about the correct minimum age. In the *Minhagbuch* of Rabbi Juspa, the shammash of Worms, he recalled the preparation for his own bar mitzvah in the town of Fulda in 1617 and noted a change to the expected date:

> The following incident occurred when I reached the age of thirteen on Shabbat, Section *Tetzaveh*, 13 Adar I, 5377 [February 18, 1617]. I was taught to chant the Torah portion, but when the rabbis were informed of the situation, they did not permit me to read Section *Tetzaveh*. Instead, I was required to read Section *Ki Tissa* on the following Sabbath, for they decreed that the one who chants the Torah portion must have reached the age of thirteen years and one day. This incident occurred in the community of Fulda.
>
> Similarly, I observed that the members of the Yeshiva in Worms prevented the lad Barukh the son of Zekli from Alsace from chanting the Torah on the Sabbath on which he turned thirteen. He read the portion on the following Sabbath; by then, he had already attained the age of thirteen and one day.[24]

Juspa no doubt remembered the incident because it must have been extremely upsetting. The boy was the victim of a disagreement between his teacher and his rabbi. The teacher instructed him on the portion to celebrate on his birthday, but the rabbi refused to let him have his bar mitzvah on that day, as he had to wait the extra day. As the custom in his town was to celebrate on the Shabbat, he had to wait a full week and relearn his portion so as to be able to chant the portion for the following Shabbat morning. Once bar mitzvah had become established, it was already the subject of disagreement between a formal and an informal approach. The boy's feelings were not taken into account at all.

We can see here that Juspa had to prepare the chanting of his portion in advance. We do not know whether or not boys read their own portion before this time; they may have just come up to say the blessings. For those who devote their lives to Torah study, then, as now, reading Torah is not difficult. But once bar mitzvah became popular, it spread also to the less learned, who needed to practice. Juspa had his own teacher, no doubt paid by his parents, as is still the norm.

Rabbi Juspa, the shammash of Worms, presented other information about bar mitzvah in his day. The custom in Worms was for the boy to put on tefillin every day for a month before his bar mitzvah so as to be correctly trained. This practice contrasts with the ruling by Isserles that tefillin should not be worn before the correct age. To this day there are different customs about this practice. On the Shabbat, after the boy reached the required age, those able to sing acted as cantor for part of the Shabbat morning service, leading one of the songs in a special tune used only on the occasion of a bar mitzvah. The father came up and recited the father's blessing in a whisper and then returned to his place in the synagogue: "And there are bar mitzvah boys whose voice is pleasant and skilled to pray in the congregation and they lead the morning service and the additional service, either all of it or as much as they are able . . . And they make for the bar mitzvah boy two blessings, the second to promise a pound of beeswax oil for lighting."[25]

Juspa relished curious details and explained how, because of the extra month inserted into the Hebrew calendar in a leap year, it was possible for a younger boy, or a younger twin, to celebrate his bar mitzvah before an older one: "If a boy is born on the 29th of Adar I during a leap year, and another boy was born on the first of Adar II, and the year when they are 13 is not a leap year, the one who was born on the 29th of Adar I needs to wait until the 29th of Adar in the year when he is 13 for his bar mitzvah, and the one who was born after him, on the 1st of Adar II, will be 13 on the first of Adar in the year when he is 13."[26]

FOLLOWING THE RULES

Individual synagogues or particular towns developed their own rules for bar mitzvah. Sometimes rules were made to cover a whole area, the most well known being "The Council of the Four Lands," which operated in Poland from 1580 to 1764.[27] In northern Germany the Jewish communities' three towns of Hamburg, Altona, and Wandsbeck were combined from 1671 to 1811. Elsewhere the rule books covered a single town or, from the eighteenth century, a welfare society, such as those for Jewish orphans established in Amsterdam and Fürth.

Occasionally, individual synagogues printed and published their constitutions, as happened in Amsterdam and London. The availability of such printed constitutions gives a bias in this information to the wealthier communities that were able to publish them. Changes in the way the regulations were drawn up reflect changing social and cultural conditions. The "Rules of the Great Synagogue" in London, for example, were published in three different languages within eighty years—in 1791 the rules were in Yiddish, the 1827 edition was in Hebrew and English, but the 1863 publication was in English only.[28] This was the principal Ashkenazic synagogue in Britain, whose rabbi was considered "Chief Rabbi" for the whole country. The building was destroyed by German bombing in 1941. In 1870 the Great and other London communities banded together to form the United Synagogue, and the rules from the Great Synagogue formed the basis for the bylaws of the United Synagogue, which laid down rules about bar mitzvah that are followed to this day.

Juspa the shammash has provided us with the first story about a boy preparing for his bar mitzvah (1617). In the centuries that followed, it came to be one of the duties of the synagogue cantor to make the arrangements. In the regulations from Hamburg and Altona from 1685 onward, permission was given for the bar mitzvah boy to read only on condition that the cantor taught him properly, for which there was a fee of five marks. If someone else taught him, the cantor would have to test him, for which there was also a fee.[29] Various rules show how provisions came to be made for the poor who could not afford their own tuition. At Krakow they decreed in the year 1595: "For the male poor up to age thirteen, the community servants (*gabbais*) take care of payments to assist with their learning, but over thirteen they do not pay out anything at all; the father has to pay for the high school (yeshiva) by a payment deducted from his pension." The society for the provision of orphans in Amsterdam, founded in 1738, and the similar society at Fürth in Germany, founded in 1763, made similar provisions.[30]

In order to make sure that the boy read his portion properly, it was often necessary to restrict the amount he was allowed to do. In Hamburg-Altona (1700) it was ruled that the boy must not read more than one section (that is, one seventh of the reading for that Shabbat) and that it had to be certified in advance by the cantor, to make sure that he could do it correctly with the proper melody. The regulation was designed to ensure that the performance on the day matched the ability and application to learning of the individual child:

> A bar mitzvah may not take the Torah scroll out or return it to the Ark. But he may read from the Torah on Shabbat and undertakes the duty of being called up. But not on a Shabbat which falls on a festival and especially not on the High Holydays. And the junior cantor must teach him the reading. And he must pay him five marks. And if he does not have membership of the congregation he may not read from the Torah and there is no obligation at all [to call him up]. In the year 1700 it was added that a bar mitzvah may not read more than one section and then only if the cantor bears witness that he is skilled in the chanting of the whole Torah and if the cantor does not so witness, he may not read even one section.[31]

If he failed the test, this would have meant that his bar mitzvah would consist simply of coming up to say the blessings.

In the Ashkenazic synagogue in Amsterdam (1815), the boy was allowed to read one section only. But nearby in The Hague (1800) there was no limit on how much the boy was allowed to do; on the contrary, the leaders of the congregation saw an advantage in it. If there was more than one bar mitzvah on the same Shabbat, the boy who claimed it was easy would be asked to prepare the whole portion for the week, except for one section each for the other boys. So, there was value in making the exercise somewhat competitive. In the Great Synagogue, London, a rule was laid down in 1827 that the official Torah reader had to stand next to the bar mitzvah boy the whole time he was reading the Torah, on penalty of a fine. In the Western Synagogue, London (1833), no boy was allowed to read from the Torah on the Saturday morning unless he had read from the scroll on the

Thursday beforehand in the presence of the regular reader, who had to be convinced his reading was accurate.[32]

After all the preparation, the great day dawns. In many places the bar mitzvah has become the first occasion on which the boy will wear a tallit for attending synagogue, a custom that in our time has spread to girls in those synagogues that practice equality. Ever since bar mitzvah became popular, the tradition has been that this will also be the first time the boy is called to the Torah. In Krakow in 1595 the boy took priority over any other claims to be called on that Shabbat, even that of a bridegroom.[33] This custom was also followed in most communities in Germany. In Prague (1609) a bridegroom had the first claim, followed by a bar mitzvah. In Posen (1612) local people had priority—perhaps a boy and his family had come to celebrate from a nearby village, but those who lived in the town had the first claim to be among the seven men called up. In Hamburg-Altona the boy was second in the list, but in Amsterdam he was fourth.[34] But in the Great Synagogue, London, the boy was the first priority, following the German custom. Large and busy synagogues had tight timetables. So, in London the bar mitzvah was expected to come on a Shabbat morning. At other times, such as Shabbat afternoon, the High Holy Days, or festival days, the bar mitzvah had no claim to be called up.[35] The British United Synagogue retained until the 1970s the provision that a bar mitzvah had the first priority to be called to the Torah.[36] Other sources give the bridegroom and the bar mitzvah an equal claim.[37]

In some communities nuts were thrown when the boy came up to the Torah: where that custom exists today, the nuts have been replaced by sweets (the original meaning of the word *confetti*). The throwing of nuts and sweets was borrowed from wedding customs. The strewing of nuts before a bridal pair is mentioned in the Talmud.[38] In the eighteenth century special prayers and poems, often set to music, were composed to accompany the boy as he came up. After the boy completed his reading, the father would say the blessing, "Blessed be the One who has freed me from punishment because of him." There were different customs concerning whether he said it out loud or under his breath or whether he would include the full introductory formula. Afterward, the cantor would intone a blessing for the boy and his family. Some communities had rules about how this should be worded and who from the family should be included.[39]

Since the eighteenth century it has been common for large crowds of people to attend synagogue for a bar mitzvah, both invited guests and others. Some communities found it necessary to make rules to ensure good behavior in the synagogue. In the days when the rule books were written exclusively by men, such rules often targeted women and children. In Hamburg-Altona it was the custom to lead the bar mitzvah in a group procession from the boy's house to the synagogue. But by 1715 so many boys were joining in, no doubt some of them uninvited, some even bringing presents, that it was causing a disturbance and public resentment, with the result that strict fines had to be imposed. In the Ashkenazic community of Amsterdam in 1717, rules were made to prevent women from getting up from their seats in the ladies' gallery to shout *mazel tov* (good luck).[40]

"Muff and Huff"

Clearly, the variety of regulations about the boy's reading shows us that the widespread practice that exists today in Ashkenazic synagogues was not the norm in the eighteenth century. For today we find most often that the boy reads *maftir* and haftarah only—the brief last section of the Torah reading, which is in fact a repetition of the last few lines, and the reading from the prophets. There has been a long-standing custom of allowing a boy *under* the age of thirteen to participate in this way, and this is mentioned in many codes of Jewish law.[41] But it is not the general practice today, except in Sephardic communities. Instead, we find that the bar mitzvah, on the day he declares "I am a man," is given the very same duty theoretically permitted to younger children. It has been suggested that this is because he is "really" still a child. But that is not the case. Hasidic practice is concerned about the same doubts that troubled Maharshal— perhaps the boy has not matured physically and so is not entitled to read or lead prayers on behalf of others. But this is not the norm. The clear ruling of the Shulchan Arukh has been generally accepted: at the age of thirteen and one day the boy is to be regarded as an adult for the purpose of reading from the Torah.[42]

So, why has it become so common for the boy to have this particular duty of *maftir*? There was only one early precedent: the fourteenth-century account by Maharil, the first one to use the term *bar mitzvah*, was included in his rule book under the instructions for the *maftir*.[43] But it did not become the norm until much later. It was mentioned in the Amsterdam Yiddish rule book of 1759 that there were a few haftarah readings each year that should not be offered to a bar mitzvah—suggesting it was becoming common for the boy to do this.[44] No reason was given, but it seems likely, considering where and when it was introduced, that it was simply to enable the boy to prepare the shortest possible Torah reading and then to learn to chant the haftarah. This practice is much easier than learning a Torah portion because the haftarah is read from a printed book with the vowels and musical signs included.

Yet the custom of assigning *maftir* and haftarah to the bar mitzvah raises a real issue. If the rule is that a younger boy is permitted to do this, how does this duty mark out the bar mitzvah as an adult? The traditional answer is that it his tefillin service on a weekday morning that marks the moment of transition, not the haftarah on a Shabbat morning. The Portuguese community of Amsterdam (Sephardic) has long had a rule that the bar mitzvah must be called to the Torah on the Shabbat afternoon because younger boys can also read the haftarah in the morning.[45]

Today it has become so widely accepted in many communities that the bar mitzvah reads the haftarah that rabbis have found it necessary to publish rulings, and synagogues to lay down rules, on what to do if there are two boys who are celebrating on the same day. In the past they would simply read separate sections from the Torah, but now both their families are likely to expect them to have the duty of *maftir*.[46]

THE BAR MITZVAH SPEECH

The rise and decline of the *derashah*, as the speech was generally called, is an excellent way of charting the growth, popularity, and change in function of bar mitzvah itself. Bar mitzvah gradually developed from a religious to a more social occasion as it ceased to be the preserve of the learned and gradually came to attract less observant members of the community. Clearly, many of these boys were not in a position to compose their own speeches.[47]

The bar mitzvah speech well may have been Maharshal's invention: "However it seems to me that they should train the lad to make a speech of Torah at the meal for the sake of the occasion."[48] The speech is a device to enable a new celebration to take place. Maharshal was concerned that the boy might not have the physical signs of puberty and thus the celebration would be in vain. The speech would make it kosher. Maharshal's proposal suggests that a boy of any age was permitted to make a speech explaining an aspect of Torah. It is known from other sources that boys younger than thirteen years old were allowed to preach.[49] In the well-organized communities of Poland a good system of education already existed, and boys were trained in the hairsplitting method of argumentation known as "pilpul." It was thought that suitably trained guests would interrupt the bar mitzvah speech with challenges to details of the boy's argument,[50] a procedure surely designed to intimidate all but the best trained and most confident boys. In contrast with other centers of Jewish life where preaching remained firmly in rabbinic hands, *pilpul* was open to every student able to understand its subtleties. Five books of bar mitzvah speeches were published between 1585 and 1600, the earliest being by Rabbi Abraham Halperin (1585) and Rabbi Aaron Cohen Rapaport (1598).[51]

It is clear that composing a bar mitzvah speech of this nature was not for the fainthearted. So, it did not take long before teachers started writing speeches for the students. The earliest such speech that survives is by the Polish rabbi Efraim Solomon, the son of Aaron of Luntshits, a student of Maharshal.[52] His method of elaborating details was scorned by one nineteenth-century historian of bar mitzvah: "The most tasteless allegory became the most shining finery."[53] Yet Luntshits himself rejected mere elaboration of detail and wanted preaching on the Sabbath to be about ethical matters and Torah laws, not rabbinic homilies.[54]

Rabbi Leon Modena of Venice, in a letter of 1593, mentioned attending a synagogue service at which a bar mitzvah boy made a speech,[55] and his own book of sermons included two such speeches that he had written for boys to deliver. Modena constantly needed funds to support his gambling habit and was able to charge to write speeches for the boys and then make more by publishing the finished results in his book.[56] His speeches have a simpler style than Luntshits used; he chose verses of ethical value from the Torah reading of the week and elegantly combined commentary on the Scripture with homilies stressing the importance of the occasion.[57] Modena did not approve of the trend for having technical legal discussions in sermons.[58]

The bar mitzvah speech reached its peak of development in the midseventeenth century, at which time it would have been between thirty and sixty minutes in length.[59] In effect, it was the culmination of eight years of learning since the age of five, with the teacher choosing the subject. Even when the teacher was responsible for writing the speech, as occurred often, the boy would have to be thoroughly familiar with the points made so that he could respond to objections. Although the speech frequently focused on the *mitzvot* to be performed from the age of bar mitzvah, such as the daily wearing of tefillin, it was not a requirement, and the choice of subject was less important than the technical brilliance displayed.

Inevitably, as bar mitzvah spread to the less intellectually gifted and those with less formal education, such a system could not last. Not only did the technicalities of the speech become beyond the range of most students, but poorer members of the community also had difficulty affording teachers' fees, either for training an able boy to make his own speech or for writing one for him. A rule enacted by the Fürth society in 1763 for the bringing up of orphans stipulated that no fee could be charged by the teacher.[60] Elsewhere teachers would be able to waive a fee only in exceptional instances. Moreover, the Polish communities where the bar mitzvah speech was born suffered terribly in the seventeenth century, particularly at the time of the Chmelnitzky massacres of 1648. Most of those who survived the Cossacks left for Lithuania or Western Europe.

Gradually, the Talmudic *derashah* lasting thirty to sixty minutes was replaced by a shorter and clearer *mamar* (speech) of perhaps ten minutes, and this kind of speech was particularly favored by the Hasidic movement, which became popular in the eighteenth century. Toward the end of the eighteenth century, under the influence of the Enlightenment, the *mamar* was in turn replaced by a "sermonette," or *devar Torah* in the vernacular.[61] This remains the most popular form of speech today; it is often delivered in the synagogue as part of the ceremony.

An unusual surviving photograph of Ignaz Goldziher (1850–1921) shows him standing at a podium in Hungary in 1863 delivering his bar mitzvah speech (fig. 2). In a black cloak with black hat, looking up from the book he is holding in his left hand and gesturing with his right hand to make a point, Goldziher is the very image of youthful self-confidence. Even though this picture was mocked up in a photographer's studio, it is nevertheless a reminder that although many must have dreaded the moment, some young intellectuals must have reveled in it. Later in life Goldziher became a pioneering Western scholar of Islam.

SPEECHES OFF THE SHELF

In the late nineteenth and early twentieth centuries in the United States it was no longer necessary to pay a teacher to write an individual speech. Small pocket books were published containing a selection of standard speeches for the boy (or his parents) to choose from. The earliest examples are in Yiddish, then in both Yiddish and English, and finally in English

Fig. 2. Ignaz Goldziher delivers his bar mitzvah speech, 1863. Photo reproduction by Frank Dabba Smith.

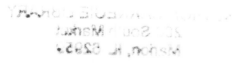

alone. The speeches given did not link to particular Torah readings but offered only general sentiments, so the boy could articulate the importance of the occasion, rather than show off his learning.

One such book was *The Jewish American Orator*, over five hundred pages in Yiddish, English, and Hebrew, compiled by George Selikovitch, first published in New York in 1907, and frequently reprinted. The bar mitzvah speeches were short, around five to ten minutes in length, and consisted of thanks by the boy to his parents and remarks on the importance of keeping the commandments from that point on, in particular the wearing of tefillin. Here is a sample:

> In the presence of my dear parents, teacher, friends and honored assembly, I pledge my word to-day that I will be a reliable soldier in the army of the Jewish people. My only wish be that the Almighty Architect of the universe may shed light upon my path. I hope to succeed in this wish as our sages assured us that God always helps the one who desires to lead a pure life. My only striving is to give honor to my parents who have done so much for me, to give honor to my people, to participate in its joys and woes, and do all there is in my power to honor the name of the Jew.[62]

It must have been all but impossible for a boy to sound sincere when uttering sentiments like this that he had not written himself. The publication of such books continued until 1954.

The system of paying a teacher to write a boy's speech persisted in Europe into the twentieth century. Writing of his childhood in Berehovo, Rabbi Hugo Gryn recalled his bar mitzvah in 1943 and how he had faithfully learned by heart the speech provided by his teacher, Mr. Schwartz, which was full of quotations from the Talmud in Hebrew and Hungarian. At the same time the young Hugo secretly wrote his own speech, based on Psalm 114, "When Israel came out of Egypt." When the time came to deliver the speech, Rabbi Gryn recalled:

> I stepped forward and spoke as eloquently and feelingly as only a middle-aged thirteen-year-old who had picked up some of the most dramatic habits of a provincial theatre company could speak. There were pauses and gestures—and a deep seriousness as well—and the words that I had written and practiced so painstakingly came tum-

bling out. There were nods and smiles of encouragement from grand-parents, aunts and uncles, but gradually I became aware that my mother's face was getting darker and darker . . . she was looking not at me but through me.[63]

When Hugo finished, his mother hissed in his ear, "That was not the speech we paid for."

In the final years of Eastern European Jewish life before the Nazi destruc-tion, preparing the speech took precedence over learning to read from the Torah. Daniel Bertram's bar mitzvah was in Krakow in 1933. He recalled:

That rebbe prepared me a droshe. And I had to talk about tefillin, in Yiddish, which I had never spoken. I learnt it by heart. And I said it. Granddaddy understood, my uncle understood, I don't know if my aunt spoke Yiddish. Then I translated into Polish. Instead of prepar-ing me for something else, to read the Torah on Saturdays, he made me translate a speech like that. But I was allowed up to the Torah, of course.[64]

COMMON LINES FROM BAR MITZVAH SPEECHES

Today the formal speech has often been replaced by a speech of thanks made at the party, often following numerous other speeches by family and friends. A humorous book published in 1981 gives common lines that might well have been used in such bar mitzvah speeches at that time:

1. "The first candle will be lit by . . ."
2. "Today I am a man, no matter *what* my mother says."
3. "If only my Uncle Yitz could be here . . ."
4. "I'd like to thank my teachers, without whose persistence and tone deafness . . ."
5. "Today I am an Israeli bond."
6. "If the band could stop playing already, I'd like to thank . . ."
7. "Unaccustomed as I am to public speaking . . ."
8. "I'd like to thank Dad for that roasting of his only son. But seri-ously, folks . . ."
9. "I'm especially flattered that my Aunt _____ is here, all the way from _____."

10. "It's a great thrill to finally be Bar Mitzvahed, because now I can finally drop out of Hebrew school and play in the little league like the other kids in the seventh grade."

11. "I can hardly wait to get home and see what's in these envelopes so many of you have handed me."[65]

The Parent's Speech

A speech given by a parent, in praise of the child, is a familiar part of contemporary bar/bat mitzvah parties. In many American Reform and Conservative congregations the parent's speech has been made more formal, and given a spiritual value, by being given as part of the synagogue service. Such parental talks may be offered at the presentation of a special tallit or before or after the Torah service. A guide book entitled *Bar/Bat Mitzvah Basics*, first published in 1996, gives examples of such speeches, which include a parents' thoughts about family history, growing up, the meaning of the ceremony, wishes for the future (perhaps expressed in poetry), and especially the handing on of the tradition:

> I want you to remember that you come from a family that for countless unbroken generations has held the Torah close to its heart. We have cherished it and tried to live by it. We found wisdom and comfort in it. We were protected and directed by it. During the Holocaust, many members of our family were killed because they clung to it. But through it all, the Torah was passed on from generation to generation. We never dropped it. It is my wish and your grandfather's wish that you never forsake the Torah. That you live by it, that you find your direction through it, and most importantly, that you pass it on to your children so they may pass it on to theirs.[66]

We have seen how, in the sixteenth and seventeenth centuries, bar mitzvah developed into a popular ceremony with all four traditional features, a call up to the Torah, the father's blessing, a party, and a speech. In the next chapter we will look at how the ceremony and the party spread geographically and in particular how the party developed set rules.

CHAPTER THREE

The Spread and Regulation of Bar Mitzvah

> At Krakow in 1595 and Berlin in 1730 the maximum number of bar mitzvah guests was limited to ten men.
> At Frankfurt in 1715 the boy was not allowed to wear a wig or give out honey cake to the guests.
> At Prague in 1767 no music was allowed at the party.
> In Ancona in 1793 only coffee and biscuits could be served at the party.
> At Hamburg-Altona in 1712 parties in synagogue were banned because of boys' misbehavior.
> At Metz in 1769 a requirement for a minimum of two years' Jewish education was laid down in an attempt to stop boys from stealing or running wild in the streets.
> Benjamin Disraeli, the British prime minister, never had a bar mitzvah.

THE SPREAD OF THE CELEBRATION

In spite of Maharshal's doubts about the celebration, within a single generation there is clear evidence that bar mitzvah had become an established custom. This was important because during the seventeenth century Poland had developed into the largest and most important Jewish community in the world. The system of self-government enabled a flourishing cultural life, and the appointment of rabbis and synagogue officials laid the foundation for the well-organized Jewish communities that have existed ever since.

The Spread of Rules

The community records of this time have a totally different tone from the rabbinic rulings of earlier years. The gradual spread of the celebration across Europe was accompanied by controversy and tension between those who thought of it as a purely religious celebration and those who promoted its social aspects. Indeed, the subsequent history suggests that

Maharshal's doubts about holding a party were justified. As soon as the party became a common practice, bar mitzvah ceased to be the preserve of the pious. In spite of the obvious joy and pride in the occasion that shines through the sources, the legislative record and surviving anecdotes describe problem after problem—extravagant banquets, inappropriate dress, and boys with an insufficient knowledge of Hebrew. As bar mitzvah spread across the community, large parties sometimes overshadowed the religious reason for the celebration. A paradox began to emerge. The new institution of the *derashah*, the boy's speech apparently invented by Maharshal, enabled the bar mitzvah to show off his educational achievements. But the manner of celebrating those achievements became dependent on the wealth and influence of the family, not the intelligence and speaking skill of the boy.

The oldest Jewish community rule book from Poland is written in a mixture of Yiddish and Hebrew and comes from Krakow, 140 miles from Maharshal's principal city of residence, Lublin. Most of the rules come from 1595.[1] Here bar mitzvah takes its place alongside other life cycle events marked in the synagogue on Shabbat. On these occasions a set payment had to be made by the family to the cantor officiating at the service, plus an additional 25 percent to charity. The *takkanot* (community rules) seek to regulate the customs of the time, which required the sending of presents, often of food, by the host of the party to neighbors and community leaders. In order to prevent extravagance, taxes were payable to the synagogue for permission to send the gifts, the tax increasing according to the size of the gift.[2]

The first of these regulations that mentions bar mitzvah is a list of priorities for being called to the Torah in the synagogue: "bar mitzvah, birth, circumcision, anniversary of a death, or a groom on the first Shabbat after his arrival, or when he comes here, or on the Shabbat of a pre-wedding celebration a call up (*aufruf*), and he gives a quarter of one *złoty* to the above mentioned charity."[3] Bar mitzvah, although an innovation, is listed first, suggesting that the boy even had priority over a bridegroom. Donations to charity were the norm for those being called to the Torah in the synagogue, and the bar mitzvah was no exception.

The rule book goes on to discuss the party. Invitations for a bar mitzvah were to be sent on the Thursday, two days before the event, "so he can accept fish." Fish such as carp would have been available in the markets on a Thursday because the local Catholic population ate it on Fridays.

It is not clear from the wording whether the fish was sent by the host to the guests with the invitation or by the guests to the host with the reply.

Invitations had to be limited to a "bare quorum" of ten men. Wealthier members of the community, defined as those who paid more tax to communal funds, could seek permission to be allowed to invite more. One who gave as much as two gold coins in tax could invite whomever he wanted.

Gifts such as *ein gemakht* (preserved foods) were permitted to be sent by the host but only to close relatives, the rabbi, and the head of the study house (*yeshiva*). Other permitted gifts were a quart of wine or a pot of mead. It is clear that in those days such delicacies were sent to the guests by the family, not by the guests to the boy.

The rules were amended in 1610 to allow an increase in the number of guests on an incremental scale but only in order to invite the extended family. A tax had to be paid to the community for every five extra guests. Those who failed to pay the tax were described as "stealing from the charity fund."

Thus, within a single generation after Maharshal, bar mitzvah had thus become a social occasion with community expectations and set rules. The Krakow ordinances are merely the oldest of many such decrees, from which we can trace the spread of bar mitzvah across Europe.

In the Krakow rules no reason was given for the need to regulate family parties. But a rationale for the whole system was given in the decrees from Lithuania of 1637: "Inasmuch as people are spending too much money unnecessarily on festive meals, every Jewish community and settlement . . . is expected to assemble its officers and rabbi to consider the number of guests which it is suitable for every individual, in view of his wealth and the occasion, to invite to a festive meal. And nobody is to turn up for a meal to which he has not been invited."[4]

THE *PINKASIM* ARCHIVES

Seventy-nine extracts from Jewish community rule books limiting private expenditure were made available online, providing a rich resource that was not available to earlier historians.[5] Most of the regulations are in Hebrew or Yiddish, but some were written in local languages or published in translation. Bar mitzvah is mentioned in about one in three of the rule books. Such rules were often preserved as part of the local *pinkas*, or community records. The primary purpose of the early *pinkasim* was to record the community's property and other business transactions. Their growth was parallel to an increase in bureaucracy and record keeping in surrounding non-Jewish societies. In most cases the communal ordinances were written by the rabbi or scribe of the community. Yet neither the style nor the content of the many laws on expenditure support a claim of rabbinic authorship. The frequent use of Yiddish or the local language, the concern to raise revenue for the community, and the frequent changes of rules in response to social expectations within the community all suggest that for the most part the rules were the work of paid officials or voluntary committees. The *pinkas* was "a tool of government and an arbiter of power" that revealed "both democratic tendencies and social tensions within the Jewish communities."[6]

For the historian of bar mitzvah the rule books serve a dual purpose, charting not just the restrictions placed on the celebration but its geographical spread across Ashkenazic Europe and Italy. Through those parts of the *pinkasim* that regulate expenditure, it is possible to trace the popularity of the celebration through Alsace, Germany, and Poland in the seventeenth century to Italy and beyond in the eighteenth century. These rule books specifically mention bar mitzvah parties:

Krakow, 1595, 1610
Posen, 1617, 1639, 1645, 1647
Council of the Four Lands, 1659
Głogów, 1688
Altona, 1686–1725, 1782
Metz, 1690, 1692, 1769
Schnaittach, 1690
Frankfurt, 1715
Boskovitz, 1720–28
Fürth, 1728, 1770, 1786
Berlin, 1730
Runkel, 1749
Sugenheim, 1756
Nikolsburg, 1760
Lithuania, 1761
Modena, 1765, 1793
Prague, 1767
Aschaffenburg, 1774
Mantua, 1783
Ancona, 1793

Normally, bar mitzvah is mentioned after circumcision celebrations and before the regulations on weddings. Where the decrees pass directly from circumcision celebrations onto weddings, without any mention of the bar mitzvah, it does not mean that bar mitzvah did not take place in that community. But it does indicate either that bar mitzvah was not considered sufficiently important for expenditure rules to be made or that, as often happened, parts of the rule book had been copied from an older one and so was not up-to-date.

Those decrees that do mention the bar mitzvah most commonly limited the number of guests at the party, the clothes that could be worn, the foods that could be served, or the permitted gifts. Such decrees are known as "sumptuary laws," rules designed to limit lavish expenditure. Such laws have long been a feature of traditional societies and were particularly common in ancient Rome. The Jewish examples often give specific reasons for their stipulation, most commonly the fear of exciting the envy and hatred of the non-Jewish world.[7] One such example comes from Metz (1692): "It has come to our knowledge that many women have their veils embroidered by non-Jews which may arouse great jealousy and animosity because formerly non-Jews were under the impression that the gold which Jewish women wore on their dress was imitation and now they know that it is real."

The remedy proposed was immediately to prohibit sending out garments for non-Jews to embroider. The regulations state that consideration had been given to exempting brides and the mother of a bar mitzvah. Yet there could be no such exemptions because "a large number of honorable merchants of this City are astonished at the display of luxury and wealth and their jealousy is greatly aroused against the Jews."[8]

But this stated reason may not have been the only one. Considering the clear lack of will of sections of the community to observe such laws, as is apparent in some communities by their frequent repetition, cynics must have considered many of them to be revenue-raising decrees used by synagogue and community officials. Drafting required great care to ensure that the rules remained worthy of respectful attention and were not held up to ridicule by wealthy members of the community, as this sentence from the same rule book may well indicate: "It will undoubtedly be necessary to make many further restrictions under the present circumstances but it has not been considered advisable to prohibit everything at one time."[9]

Although many of the laws about costume were aimed at the wealthy, some sumptuary laws were clearly designed to protect poorer members of the community from feeling that they had to spend beyond their means. This was a particular issue at the end of the seventeenth century, a time when much of central Europe was engulfed by war. The rule book of Schnaittach in Bavaria (1690) highlights the issue: "An ordinance so that they should not incur great expenditure for no especially good reason in these days when small coins go from the pocket, and Israel is very impoverished in many provinces, and especially in provinces where war increases: so some individuals have requested that decrees be made for them to reduce expenditures incurred for no good reason."[10]

Among the published decrees this one is unusual in that it came from a smaller rural community, where problems were very different from those caused by urban prosperity. The decrees from Carpentras (1738), where rich and poor lived side by side, particularly emphasized the need to control the envy of Jews for each other: "and how each one endeavors to show his superiority over his neighbor . . . all desiring to appear men of eminence and of wealth in their apparel and in the adornments of their women, without being able to sustain the expense: in consequence whereof they are brought low, and borrow needlessly from Gentiles, and become impoverished."[11]

The most common restriction on expenditure for bar mitzvah limited the number of guests, as at Krakow. A decree from Posen from 1617 restricted the number of guests at a bar mitzvah party to fifteen. The Council of the Four Lands in Poland (1659) insisted that at least one of the guests should be a person in need.[12] In Głogów, in southwest Poland (1688), the numbers depended on income, as at Krakow: "And similarly for a bar mitzvah as for a wedding meal: a person in reduced circumstances may not invite more than thirty men and the community servants, and somebody in between not more than forty men and the community servants, but for the rich there is no limit."[13]

A similar decree from Fürth (1728) allowed ten men for an ordinary family celebration, twelve for the middle-income group, and twenty-four guests for the wealthiest. The general tendency was for bar mitzvah and other celebrations to increase in size over the years, as evidenced by subsequent rules from the same community. Yet the original basic restriction of ten guests, as in the 1595 Krakow rule book, persisted in various places for a long time. At Berlin in 1730 invitations were restricted to ten men "without their wives," plus close relatives and the rabbi and cantor of the community.[14] At Runkel (1749) the limit was twenty-one. No distinction was made between different classes because "rich and poor are as one."[15]

In most cases only men are mentioned among the number permitted. This does not necessarily mean that women did not attend with their husbands and perhaps children as well; Berlin was exceptional in ruling explicitly that the party was to be for men only. In the eighteenth century much would depend on the ethos and culture of a particular locality and community. In those places where women went with their husbands and took the children as well, the total guests at the party would have been considerably more than the number of men mentioned. By the mid-nineteenth century the cultural norm was for men and women to attend celebrations together and even to sit at mixed tables.[16]

The decrees also provide evidence for a gradual growth in the nature of the celebrations. In Krakow (1595) a meal held on Shabbat, and with a limit of ten guests, must have been little different from a large family weekly meal. In Worms during the seventeenth century the celebration was held on Saturday afternoon, after the synagogue service. The bar mitzvah boy himself, dressed in the new clothes he had been wearing for that Sabbath, would enter the houses of the guests to summon them to eat the third Sabbath meal with him, and he would lead grace after meals.[17] By the early eighteenth century in Frankfurt (1715) two celebration meals were held, one on the Sabbath and one the following day. Johann Jacob Schudt, a non-Jew who published the regulations, added a comment of his own: "On the Sunday after the bar mitzvah meal another banquet is held, which is even better, because one can now serve hot dishes which were not allowed on the Sabbath. The regulations for this meal are the same as the ones concerning the meal held on the third day after a circumcision."[18] This is the earliest known reference to today's common practice of holding the synagogue ceremony on Saturday with a small family gathering and a larger party the following day.

The regulations also laid down rules about what was permitted to be worn for the ceremony of bar mitzvah or on reaching that age. In 1715 in Frankfurt the rules stated: "No bar mitzvah boy may stand before the Torah scroll wearing a wig. He should not distribute nor send round honey cake nor distribute shirts and collars. To the cantor, who has taught him his portion, he may give a collar, and nothing more."[19] It was common practice at the time for men to shave their heads and wear a wig. The regulation suggests that this custom was inappropriate for one so young. Both costume and the gifts being sent by the child, even the fashionable large men's collars, were considered too ostentatious. In the same year (1715), in the "three towns" of Hamburg-Altona-Wandsbeck, the local regulations decreed that a boy aged thirteen or older was permitted to wear a black hat.[20]

In the decrees from Prague (1767) a bar mitzvah meal is mentioned first, before other family celebrations, perhaps indicating that by this time it was considered the life cycle event that demanded the most restrictions. The rules include a "server" among those who could be invited and further extended the potential number by allowing guests from outside Prague without limit. Aside from the host's daughters and daughter-in-law and his mother and mother-in-law, however, women were not invited. The decree continues with a ban on entertainment that really does suggest that steps were now necessary to stop the banquet from becoming as significant as a wedding: "Under absolutely no circumstances are musicians (klezmer) or entertainers to be allowed at a bar mitzvah meal."[21] Taxes were levied both on the food ("any fish other than carp, but no meat other than beef, or poultry either goose or turkey, but not both") and on the drink ("three pints and not more"). Coffee was prohibited.

REGULATIONS IN ITALY

None of the Italian decrees have rulings about bar mitzvah parties until the second half of the eighteenth century, which suggests a later date for the arrival of the celebration. The absence of bar mitzvah from the Rome communal regulations of 1702 has been taken to mean that it had probably not yet arrived there.[22] But such deductions may be wrong. In Venice at least, the synagogue ceremony of bar mitzvah arrived much earlier. Leon Modena (1571–1648) did not mention having a bar mitzvah in his autobiography,[23] but in a letter written in 1593 he gave an account of attending a bar mitzvah. He mentioned that the boy gave his speech as part of the Shabbat service in the synagogue, which may suggest that there was no party on this occasion.[24]

The rules from Mantua, Italy, were discovered in an unpublished manuscript in the 1940s. Bar mitzvah is not in the earlier regulations but first appears in the rules dated 1783. Thirty-six guests were permitted. For the banquet a choice had to be made between fish or meat dishes, but not both, and desserts set in order round the table were forbidden, as were brandy and sweets. Later the bar mitzvah boy would be brought in, and coffee, Savoy biscuits (sponge fingers), and sugared almonds would be served.[25]

Other decrees from Italy mention meals of a different kind, more like a tea party or cocktail party. In Ancona (1793) one states: "During the ceremony of 'the entry of the male sons to their fourteenth year' (bar mitzvah), any banquet is prohibited, except for the serving of coffee and a Savoy biscuit for everyone who comes to the house to offer congratulations."[26]

Establishing Expectations

As the institution of the bar mitzvah became firmly established in European towns, gradually the expectation arose that a Jewish boy would definitely have a bar mitzvah. This can be shown from the eighteenth century from the rule books of the societies for the bringing up of orphans from Amsterdam (1738) and Fürth (1763). Both of these make special provision for the bar mitzvah of an orphan boy. At Fürth one of the members of the society for the bringing up of orphans would be chosen by ballot to arrange the party. He was expected to pay a set fee to the caterer from his own pocket and to find two relatives of the orphan boy to do the same. The teacher and a synagogue official would have a place at the meal free of charge, but if they turned down the invitation, they, too, would have to pay a fee, which went to the funds of the society.[27]

This very small sample of the surviving Ashkenazic and Italian regulations is sufficient to indicate that in the minds of communal officials bar mitzvah in the seventeenth and eighteenth centuries was as much a social occasion as a religious one. The abundance of regulations does not mean that every family celebrated, but it does mean that among the wealthy the celebrations had to be restricted in order to avoid communal tensions. The detailed legislation about permitted menus shows how, in different regions of Europe, Jews adopted the social customs of the wealthy among whom they lived. This system created the paradox that the distinctive celebration of a maturing boy's Jewish identity became at the same time an indication of a family's standing in the wider community and a possible gateway to assimilation.

AMONG THE SEPHARDIM

As the *pinkasim* cover only European Ashkenazic and Italian communities, they do not tell us how bar mitzvah spread to Sephardic communities or outside Europe. The best place to begin that story is in the New World because the first communities of the Caribbean, the American colonies, and Canada were Sephardic. The early Sephardic communities had to work out systems to facilitate bar mitzvah for Ashkenazic Jews who arrived in town and became part of their communities.

BAR MITZVAH REACHES AMERICA

The first bar mitzvah boy whose name is known to us in the lands that now form the United States was Mordecai Sheftall, who reached the age of thirteen in Savannah, Georgia, in 1748. Whether there were sufficient numbers to celebrate the occasion properly is not clear. A group of forty-two Jews had settled in Savannah in 1733, after arriving aboard the ship *William and Sarah*. Of them thirty-four followed the Spanish and Portuguese (Sephardic) ritual, so the congregation they founded, Mickve Yisrael, naturally followed that rite, as did earlier congregations in New York and Philadelphia. Many of the Sephardic Jews left in 1742, concerned about an impending Spanish attack from nearby St. Simon's Island, leaving behind only a few Ashkenazic Jews, who held services in private homes.

The congregation was kept going largely through the efforts of one Benjamin Sheftall. When his older son, Mordecai, was coming up toward the age of bar mitzvah, he sent for books and tefillin from London, which unfortunately failed to arrive in time for his son's birthday. He wrote to a friend in London to try to find out if the ship carrying the items had been lost at sea: "I leave your Honour to guess in what grief I am in to be misfortenable, my oldest son being three months ago thirteen years of age, and I not to have any frauntlets nor books fit for him."[28] Mordecai Sheftall grew up to become not only a leader of the congregation in Savannah but also the highest-ranking Jewish officer on the American side during the Revolutionary War.

Apart from Mordecai Sheftall there is sparse evidence of bar mitzvah beyond Europe in the eighteenth century. Among Ashkenazic Jewry it was an established custom but not yet a universal one. Whether at this time it was celebrated by Sephardic Jews in Europe has proven difficult to determine. We find stated in the communal regulations from Altona of 1747:

> At a bar mitzvah meal, dinner is not to be served for more than ten men without their wives, except for fathers and mothers and grandfathers and grandmothers, brothers or sisters and their wives, the host and his wife and the teacher of the speech, and the presiding offi-

cer for the month and his wife, and the head of the rabbinical court and the rabbis, and the cantor who is on duty for that week, and the principal warden of the community (may it continue for ever) and the cantor of his synagogue, and Sephardim and guests from other places are not counted in the number.[29]

This statement would have been a commonplace regulation were it not for the mention of Sephardim. There was a large Sephardic community in the area, and it appears there was no limit on inviting them to an Ashkenazic bar mitzvah party. No reason is given. Perhaps Sephardim were here equated with people from out of town because they were less likely to attend an Ashkenazic bar mitzvah party at this time. There may even be a touch of humor in this regulation, as if to say "We don't need to count up the Sephardim because they hardly ever turn up for an Ashkenazic bar mitzvah." In the Sephardic rule books from Hamburg of the seventeenth century, I have found no mention of bar mitzvah, but that does not mean that simple weekday ceremonies did not take place.[30] The reason why the precise origins of the bar mitzvah celebration among the Sephardim of Europe are difficult to trace is because it took a less public form. The general custom arose of teaching a twelve-year-old boy how to wear tefillin. There was no need to wait for the thirteenth birthday for the ceremony. When he was ready, he would attend synagogue on a Monday or a Thursday, don his tefillin, be called to the reading of the Torah, and deliver his *darush*, as the speech was called in many places. A celebration meal would be held at home.[31] In many places it was not the custom for the boy to read his own portion from the Torah—in some Sephardic communities this was not done even in the mid-twentieth century.[32]

Perhaps the first place in Europe where a Sephardic Jew might have been able to witness the new ceremony of bar mitzvah was Venice. After 1580, when the community of Ferrara was broken up, Venice became the place of preference for Marranos to reveal their identity and to revert to Judaism. Within a generation the Portuguese congregation, known by the name *Talmud Torah*, had a position of primacy in the European Sephardic world. David Nieto went from Venice via Livorno to become *haham* (the spiritual leader) in London, and Saul Levi Morteira and Joseph Pardo left to take up the leadership of congregations in Amsterdam. The Amsterdam Portuguese congregation modeled its laws (*ascamot*) on those of Venice, and those in London were based on the *ascamot* of Amsterdam.[33]

A letter written by Rabbi Leon Modena (1571–1648) gives an account of attending a bar mitzvah at a synagogue in Venice. It mentions that the boy gave his speech as part of the Sabbath service in the synagogue.[34] Many customs developed in a different way in Italy. In Poland and Germany the boy's speech was made at the party. Modena indicates that the bar mitzvah took place at the *Beit HaKnesset HaGedolah*, which was the Ashkenazic synagogue.[35] It is interesting to note that when Sephardim did begin to celebrate bar mitzvah, the same custom of the speech being given in the synagogue was followed. This practice suggests that Sephardic bar mitzvah may have spread from Venice.

In Livorno, a community that followed Spanish and Portuguese customs, the sumptuary regulations from 1655 and 1687 give rules for the clothing permitted to be worn by children "up to the age of 13." But the rules for parties pass directly from circumcision to weddings, implying that there was as yet no need to regulate the celebration of bar mitzvah.[36] The rules do indicate that age thirteen marked a change of lifestyle.

The first Western Sephardic congregation to introduce bar mitzvah was probably Shearith Israel, New York, whose origins go back to the arrival of the first group of Jews in 1654. It served the whole Jewish community of New York until 1825 and therefore had many Ashkenazic members. Eighteenth-century minute books of the congregation refer to bar mitzvah by the term *bar minyan*, which was an alternative name for bar mitzvah used by Leon Modena in Venice. Modena worked with Joseph Pardo before Pardo left for Amsterdam. One of Pardo's grandsons, Saul Pardo, arrived in New York in 1685 and became the first cantor of the congregation, which worshiped in a rented house on Mill Street. He is known to have taken many Italian melodies and other customs with him, so it is possible that the Italian term *bar minyan* came from him. Saul Brown (as he became known) died in 1702 or 1703, so if he did introduce bar mitzvah to New York, that would have been a half-century before Mordecai Sheftall celebrated his bar mitzvah in Savannah. No individual name of a bar mitzvah boy from Pardo's time in New York, however, has yet been discovered.[37]

An Ashkenazic visitor to the Sephardic community of Amsterdam around 1680, Rabbi Shabbatai Sheftel Horowitz, noted that the boys studied Bible and Mishnah until the age of thirteen and only then began the study of Talmud.[38] Here, too, the age thirteen marked an important demarcation, but there is no evidence that the occasion was marked by a ceremony or ritual. If there was one, it was not significant enough for Horowitz to think it worth mentioning.

We do not know precisely when bar mitzvah was introduced to the Portuguese Synagogue in Amsterdam, but we do know that the custom was for the bar mitzvah boy to read from the Torah on Saturday afternoon and that he would be escorted to the reading desk by two sponsors (*padrinhos*).[39] This is mentioned without source or date of origin, but the custom is known to survive to this day: the *padrinhos* are now two younger boys.[40]

An autobiographical sketch written by Rabbi Hayyim Yitzhak Mussafia (b. Jerusalem 1760, d. Split 1837) describes the dramatic events around the time of his bar mitzvah in Sarajevo, Bosnia, in 1773. His father's capital was in Jerusalem, which was under siege, and after three years of not having access to his funds, he decided to make the journey there. Unfortunately, he never reached the port of Acre. News of the father's death reached his son, who reported that "in a few days I became bar mitzvah, and my rejoicing was turned to sorrow."[41] This account is early evidence for bar mitzvah among Sephardim, but here, too, it is more a demarcation date than a public ceremony.

From the Spanish and Portuguese Synagogue, London, we find this laid down in the *Ascamot* in 1785 concerning the duties of the presiding warden, known as the "Parnas Presidente": "that he do not give a Misva [duty or honor during the service] to any person under thirteen years of age, except it be to say Aftarah [haftarah, a reading from the service], Ashem-melech [singing the line beginning 'Adonai Melech'], or Kadish."[42] The text shows the age of thirteen as marking a ritual boundary but does not state that this age was yet marked by any formal ceremony. When the congregation's cantor, David Aaron de Sola, published a comprehensive guide (1829) to Hebrew blessings said both on everyday and special occasions, there was no mention of bar mitzvah, but perhaps no special blessing was said on that occasion.[43] But in 1852 formal permission was given in London for the bar mitzvah boy to address the congregation.[44]

The precise date when bar mitzvah was introduced by the London Sephardim would be a trivial detail were it not for the fact that historians have sought the extent of the Jewish education of Benjamin Disraeli, who became British prime minister in 1868 and again from 1874 to 1880. When he was nine or ten, the young Benjamin was sent to Potticary's boarding school in Blackheath, where he was allowed to "stand back" at prayer time and where he and another Jewish boy, Moses Saqui, had Hebrew lessons from a visiting teacher on a Saturday after school.[45] According to more than one biographer, the lessons must have been in preparation for his bar mitzvah, but it seems very unlikely that the London Sephardic community celebrated the occasion at that time.[46] In Benjamin's case his Jewish education was cut short by the death of his grandfather in 1816. Benjamin's father, the writer Isaac D'Israeli, had had a dispute with the community some years earlier and no longer felt any ties to Judaism. Once his own father had passed away, he felt free to leave the synagogue. Benjamin Disraeli was baptized a Christian at St. Andrew's Holborn in July 1817, shortly before he became thirteen.[47]

Among the London Sephardim it was still customary in the second half of the nineteenth century for the boy not to read his own portion, so Haham Benjamin Artom published a special prayer for him to recite instead as well as a prayer to be said by the officiating rabbi. On a Shabbat morning the boy was called fifth to the reading of the Torah, and the traditional father's blessing was not said.[48] The boy's prayer has been frequently reprinted in prayer books from both Sephardic and Ashkenazic congregations and has inspired similar compositions by others.

ACCOUNTS OF BAR MITZVAH
FROM NON-JEWISH SOURCES

Accounts by non-Jews and Jewish converts to Christianity have contributed to the information we have about the celebration of bar mitzvah in the seventeenth, eighteenth, and nineteenth centuries. These accounts add interesting details not always recorded in Jewish sources. Jewish converts to Christianity and Christian Hebrew scholars often criticized each other's accounts of Jewish life,[49] but Christians who had taken the trouble to study Hebrew offered sympathetic accounts.[50]

One of the earliest such accounts to mention bar mitzvah is *De Synagoga Judaica* (1603), by Johannes Buxtorf (1564–1629), professor of Hebrew at Basel, Switzerland. Buxtorf considered that his monumental work would reveal customs and ceremonies practiced by Jews in secret, away from Christian eyes.[51] On bar mitzvah he wrote:

> the father invites a Minjan, ten Jews, to witness that his son is thirteen years old and that he has learned the laws, that he learned the customs of Zizis [fringes worn on the four corners of a garment] and Tephillin, that he can say his daily prayers and that the father wants

to be free of his sins and punishment, and from now on he should
be a Bar mitzva and bear his own sins. After the other Jewish men
witness that, the father says a prayer in which he thanks God that he
has freed him from his son's sins and he prays that he should grow
up to a long life and good deeds.[52]

Buxtorf makes no mention of the ceremony taking place on the Sabbath
or of a party being held. His account shows that the blessing said by the
father was a prominent part of the ceremony in his day. He interprets the
ceremony not so much as a ritual performance by the boy but as an oral test
of his knowledge, like a Christian child reciting catechism. In the church
such summaries of doctrines in a question-and-answer format had long
been handed down orally. Luther's catechism was published in 1530 and
the first Catholic catechism in 1566, authorized by the Council of Trent.[53]
It is not possible to tell whether there really was an element of an educational test in the ceremony or if this was simply Buxtorf's interpretation.

Buxtorf's was not the only non-Jewish account to mention a test of
the boy's knowledge. From Venice comes a report by a Jewish convert to
Christianity, Giulio Morosini, once a student of Rabbi Leon Modena.[54] In
1683 Morosini described a bar mitzvah in a synagogue, and this is also the
first Italian source to mention a party. In his account the test of knowledge
is carried out prior to the ceremony. According to Morosini, the father
had to present his son to the rabbi at the synagogue to testify that he was
of age and that he had mastered the speeches and benedictions and the
precepts of the Law, which it was his duty to learn. Noteworthy in Morosini's description of the ceremony are the public congratulations the boy
received from the congregation both before and after his reading and his
public announcement of donations to charity, to the community, and to the
synagogue officials. The father's blessing is not mentioned in this account,
suggesting a lower priority given to this element of the ceremony among
Italian Jews. When the boy completed his own thanks to God that he had
become bar mitzvah, he kissed his father's hand and that of his teacher.[55]

Johann Jacob Schudt (d. 1722), whose comments on the Frankfurt party
regulations have been noted, compiled a huge collection of documents
from Jewish communities that he called "Jewish Peculiarities." Like a modern anthropologist, he based his work on detailed research, both in the
library and in the field.[56] He was open about wanting to convert Jews to
Christianity,[57] but it is not clear precisely how the detailed mass of infor-

mation he provided about Judaism would have served his purpose. There is a parallel today in the huge amount of accurate information on the world's religions available on atheist websites.

As soon as bar mitzvah became a social occasion, it ceased to be an occasion celebrated only by the pious. Leon Modena of Venice lamented the current low standards of Jewish education in his *Riti Hebraici* (1637). Modena was writing in order to emphasize the biblical and rational roots of Judaism and to give a more sympathetic account of Jewish ritual than Buxtorf.[58] He also wanted to portray Judaism sympathetically to a non-Jewish readership, and indeed his book was translated into English by a non-Jew, Edmund Chilmead. The translation, published in 1650, aroused interest in England in Jewish ritual just a few years before Menasseh the son of Israel petitioned Cromwell to allow Jews to live openly in London:

> But now, in these daies, there are very few, throughout the Whole Nation of the Jews, that take so much care, about the Education of their Children, as to make them so Learned: and, for the most part, they use to read, speak, write, and compose, whatsoever businesse they have to do, merely out of Practice, and use; and especially the *Dutch.* . . . When a Son is now come to be Thirteen years, and a day old, he is then accounted a *Man*, and becomes bound to the Obser-vation of All the *Precepts of the Law*: and therefore he is now called *Bar mitzvah*, that is to say, *Filius Mandati*, a Son of the Command-ment: although some call him *Bar de minian*; that is to say, one that is of age to do any businesse, and may make One, in the number of the *Ten*, that are required to be present at any of their Publick Acts of Devotion. And whatever Contracts he makes, they are of force; and if he were formerly under *Tutors*, he is now Freed from their Juris-diction over him: and, in a word, both in Spirituall, and Temporal Affaires, he is Absolute Lord and Master of Himself.[59]

Modena did not explicitly link the poor standards of Jewish education with bar mitzvah, but that seemed to be in his train of thought, as he moved straight on to bar mitzvah in the next sentence. In his description in the book of an ordinary Shabbat morning, Modena mentioned that the haftarah, the reading from the prophets, "is read by some Child, for the most part, to exercize him in Reading the Scripture." The boys who did this would have been proficient in Hebrew and unlikely to be among those whose poor education Modena lamented in his discussion of bar mitzvah. The implication is that in Venice at the start of the seventeenth century some of the boys who were celebrating bar mitzvah were not from families regularly attending the synagogue.

Similarly, in the seventeenth-century *Minhagbuch* of Rabbi Juspa, the shammash of Worms, he complained that not every boy was able to read from the Torah: "There are those who do not know how to read [the portion in public], so they do not read in public; however, they call them up to the scroll of the Law."[60]

Bar mitzvah was now attracting even the less learned and less well-educated families in the community. The decline in Jewish educational standards in Western and central Europe from the seventeenth century onward has been well documented. Many communities were short of elementary teachers, especially in rural areas: "In a small community near Worms, a Christian missionary asked about the teacher and was told: 'There are only a few Jews here, and they don't have enough money to hire a teacher.'"[61]

In a poignantly written anonymous biography from Moravia, later in the seventeenth century, a boy described his father's neglect of his education after his mother died in 1671, when he was only four. He was sent from teacher to teacher and learned little. Eventually, at the age of thirteen, he was sent to a teacher in Hermanitz, near Meseritsch, who "noticed that I could not read properly through the fault of my first teacher, who had not instructed me well. The little I had known I had forgotten, and I was in great trouble." Over time the teacher taught him the melodies for the Torah and haftarah, and he "went to Minyan" (i.e., became bar mitzvah) with new clothes on Shabbat *Nahamu*. No party was mentioned.[62]

Many boys in the seventeenth and eighteenth centuries celebrated with little or no party. *The Life of Glückel of Hameln* (1646–1724) contains extensive information about her family but no mention of bar mitzvah.[63] The autobiography of Jacob Emden (1698–1776) does mention his bar mitzvah in Amsterdam in 1711 but only as a time of family and public troubles, not as a time of joy: "At that time I became a bar mitzvah . . . [but] the time was not conducive for diligent study nor to achieve perfection because of the lack of a teacher or companion, mentor or guide, to bring me blessing . . . it was a period of gloom, distress, and darkness; a time of anxiety, sorrow and worry."[64]

But a number of boys did have large celebrations. An account by Rabbi Yair Hayyim Bacharach (1638–1702) describes how he was invited to attend a bar mitzvah celebration at a community in Worms by a well-known teacher in the town. He was reluctant to break off his studying to attend—

> but when in his letter he constantly pleaded with me to come, and even hinted at "dowry and gift" (Genesis 34:12), then I "made his speech nothing worth" (Job 24:25) [i.e., by refusing the invitation]. He wrote again to me bragging about the big party which had taken place, and the important people from the community who were there, and how not one of them had been left at home, but all of them had gathered for the celebration, and "he did well to be angry" (Jonah 4:9).[65]

It seems that Rabbi Bacharach refused the invitation not because he was unable to attend but because he was put off by the pleading, the promise of a gift, and no doubt by a party, which he considered an unnecessary extravagance. When he received the second letter, however, Bacharach decided that he had to make amends and did so by means of sending a detailed reading list for the bar mitzvah boy's continuing study.[66]

In Worms large celebrations and an interest in bar mitzvah by the less well-educated can both be documented from the seventeenth century. By the eighteenth century the social nature of many celebrations could lead to bad behavior by groups of children, as a Yiddish regulation from Hamburg-Altona makes clear: "New regulation of 24th Sivan 5472 = 28th June 1712. Every time a lad is bar mitzvah there is a great commotion among the lads, which creates a bad impression. So from today onward no party may be held in the synagogue and no treats for the lads at all. Any transgression will incur a fine of 20 Reichstahler for the welfare fund, with no exceptions."[67]

By the end of the eighteenth century the popularity and demand for bar mitzvah among less-observant Jews was clearly creating educational problems for communities. The Jewish community of Metz introduced an innovatory system of compulsory education toward the end of the seventeenth century: school attendance was required up to the age of fifteen, with one hour a day for the following four years following. There was a severe penalty attached for truants—the loss of the right to reside within the community.[68] But even this measure did not solve the problem of ignorant bar mitzvah boys, so another rule was enacted in 1769:

We have come to understand that some parents do not supervise their children, so as to train them to study Torah. As a result, as soon as the boy reaches the age of six or seven, he walks around paths and the streets at his leisure and rejects his obligations toward God and ends up devoid of everything—he knows no Torah, no respect, he is good for nothing, unable to work, and because of this laziness, he gets bored and becomes a highway mugger. Because we know of many troubles, where through the intermediary of boys like this, people try to buy stolen or pirated goods, we ordain as a preventative measure that, if we discover that a boy is not studying permanently with a teacher for at least two years before his bar mitzvah, he will not be authorized to read the portion in either of the two synagogues of the Council when the time comes for his bar mitzvah.[69]

The situation here described is much worse than Juspa the shammash's complaint from the early seventeenth century. Then there were those who were simply unable to read. But here boys of eleven or twelve years old, or even younger, were playing truant from school and turning to a life of crime. It says much for the authority of the community that it could be imagined that the simple sanction of refusing a bar mitzvah would be sufficient to bring them back.

This ordinance is fascinating not just because of the social reality that it reveals but also because of the proposed remedy. Since the 1930s Jewish communities have set educational requirements for those hoping to celebrate bar/bat mitzvah, and two years attendance at classes is a common rule. Such rules are thought to be modern ones, but in fact the earliest known such enactment is this one from nearly 240 years ago. The modern dilemmas that surround bar mitzvah were being debated in Metz in 1769.

Meanwhile, in Poland, where the party as an established custom as well as the first community rules to mention bar mitzvah were first documented, bar mitzvah had changed because of early marriage. The Jewish population of Poland grew threefold between 1648 and 1765, to more than a half-million. In the census of 1897, 53 percent of the country's Jews were under twenty years old, a higher proportion than in the general population. One reason for this population explosion was early marriage. An examination of the biographies of several dozen writers shows that most of them were married by thirteen or fourteen. Because a two-year engagement was the norm, the matchmaking was often concluded when the boy was eleven. "The typical goal was to celebrate the *bar mitzvah* and the marriage at the same party."[70] This system of early marriage was hated by many young people and was an important spur to rebellion against traditional Judaism. The tensions were very different from those of Western Europe but just as real.

The growth in the popularity of bar mitzvah was never planned. From a simple marker of a boy becoming thirteen, it developed into a cause for celebration. The implications of its popularity have been illustrated here. First, the spread of bar mitzvah meant that educational targets had to be set and standards maintained. The 1769 rule from Metz that a boy could be refused a bar mitzvah if he failed to study would have seemed nonsensical two hundred years earlier, when the ritual was still simply marking a date and celebrated by families skilled at reading Hebrew. Second, the spread of bar mitzvah meant the spread of family parties, with all the rivalries, jealousies, and shows of extravagance that might entail. By 1800 the boy could easily become an object to be shown off, rather than the subject of the celebration. But in the nineteenth century much was to change, as bar mitzvah was abandoned in some circles and a new ceremony that included girls arrived on the scene.

CHAPTER FOUR

Jewish Confirmation

- ➤ In the nineteenth century Jewish confirmation ceremonies were based on a "catechism"—giving formal answers to formal questions about Judaism.
- ➤ Leopold Zunz was one of the first Jews to be confirmed; the ceremony took place in 1807 at his Jewish day school. He later became a famous scholar and recorded the date himself.
- ➤ Confirmation has often been held at Shavuot, going back to 1811. Protestant confirmations were held at the parallel Christian festival of Pentecost.
- ➤ From 1810 through the 1970s many rabbis and leaders promoted confirmation as more meaningful than bar mitzvah. Bar mitzvah was often abolished in favor of confirmation.
- ➤ Confirmation reached Charleston, South Carolina, in the 1820s and New York in 1846.
- ➤ In the twentieth century the age for confirmation rose from thirteen to fifteen or sixteen or occasionally even older.
- ➤ Confirmation has been in decline since bat mitzvah became popular in the 1970s.
- ➤ In 1981 the Liberal Jewish Synagogue, London, became the last known congregation to bring back bar mitzvah.

Early in the nineteenth century a new Jewish coming-of-age ceremony was invented in Germany, known as "confirmation." Originally a graduation ceremony for a Jewish day school class, this soon came to be a synagogue ceremony, often held for a group at the festival of Shavuot and involving both boys and girls. This was the first time in Jewish history that any coming-of-age ceremony had been offered to girls. In synagogues that adopted the new ceremony, it typically replaced bar mitzvah completely.

Confirmation Service,

SUNDAY, MAY 17, 1896,

10 o'clock.

Organ Prelude —Melodie—(*Liszt*).

Anthem—Except the Lord build a house—(*Gilchrist*) . . . . CHOIR.

Organ—March—(*Novello*).

Blessed be ye who come—(*Lob*) . . . . CLASS.

Welcome, ... BY THE RABBI.

Opening Prayer, ... BERTHA ZSUPNYIK.

Lord, what offering, ... CLASS.

Lord! what offering shall we bring,	Willing hands to lead the blind,
At Thine altars when we bow?	Heal the wounded, feed the poor;
Hearts, the pure unsullied spring	Love, embracing all our kind;
Whence the kind affections flow.	Charity, with liberal store.

Teach us, O, Thou heavenly King,
Thus to show our grateful mind,
Thus the accepted offering bring,
Love to Thee and all mankind.

The Offering of Flowers, ... FRIEDA GUGGENHEIM.

The Teachings of Judaism, ... CLASS.

The Scrolls of the Law, ... ETTA SAMPLINER.

Taking Out of the Scrolls, ... HARRY BRACKER.

Exaltation of the Law, ⎫
⎬ (*Ex. xx; 1-15*) . . . . MILTON EINSTEIN.
Reading from the Thorah, ⎭

The Ten Commandments, ⎫
⎬ . . . . EDDIE WEISENBERG.
Return of the Scrolls, ⎭

Happy who in early youth, (*Traditional*) . . . . . . CLASS AND CHOIR.

Fig. 3. Part of the program for the first confirmation service at Tifereth Israel, Cleveland, held on Erev Shavuot, 1896. The service was led by Rabbi Moses Gries (Weidenthal, "Confirmations in Cleveland"). Photograph courtesy of the Temple-Tifereth Israel Archive, Cleveland OH.

Although today it is offered mainly by Reform temples, in the past it was also popular in Conservative and even Orthodox synagogues.

A NEW CEREMONY FOR A NEW ERA OF FREEDOM

Confirmation began as a ceremony that differed from bar mitzvah in that it required a declaration of faith by the child and did not normally involve being called to the reading of the Torah. Passing an exam before confirmation was essential from the start. Unlike bar mitzvah, confirmation has never emphasized the rituals of Judaism but began as a celebration of an entry point to participation in the wider society—becoming an adult in the civic and public sphere. By the 1820s it was invariably a group ceremony, held annually at the age of thirteen for boys, at the age of twelve for girls, or for a mixed group. In the early twentieth century the age of confirmation rose from thirteen to fifteen or even higher, in parallel with the raising of school leaving ages.

Jewish confirmation has never had any set form. At first the children, as part of the ceremony, were expected to give rehearsed answers to questions about their faith. An early example from 1813 shows the nature of this exchange:

> Q. What does religion mean to you?
> A. To believe in God and to do His will . . . That there is an invisible and inexplicable being that has been there forever and that is the creator, the King and preserver of the whole world.
> Q. What does invisible and inexplicable mean?
> A. God is a being that we can neither see with our eyes nor understand with our senses . . . God is the originator of the whole world; He made everything out of nothing; He wanted it to be, and it was.[1]

This question-and-answer format had been used by Protestant and Catholic churches since the Reformation and was called a "catechism."

The first Jewish catechism was not written for synagogue use but as an educational manual for children. *Lekach Tov* by Abraham Jagel was published in Hebrew in Venice in 1595, around the time that bar mitzvah first reached Venice. It was soon translated into several languages. One edition was published in England in 1679 with the original Hebrew and a Latin translation on the facing page. Jagel provided simple questions and answers that a child or a non-Jew could easily understand. Although the Hebrew title means "good doctrine," the Latin title *Catechismus* suggests that already by this time the book was attracting a non-Jewish readership. Unlike the nineteenth-century examples, which are based on beliefs and principles, Jagel emphasized keeping the commandments and observing the Sabbath.[2] The book was often reprinted in the eighteenth century, until modern Jewish teachers and rabbis started writing their own. It is estimated that over 150 such manuals were published in the late eighteenth and the nineteenth centuries, mainly in Germany.[3] The first of these manuals to take up the title *Katechismus* was brought out in 1807 by the head teacher of a Berlin Jewish girls' school, Moshe Hirsch Bock.[4] He was followed by a Hamburg Reform preacher, Eduard Kley, in 1814.[5]

Such question-and-answer formulas continued to be part of Jewish confirmation ceremonies for many decades, but by the end of the nineteenth century the ceremony began to be based on the more traditional Jewish forms of prayer, Torah reading, quotations from Scripture, and speeches. A pamphlet by David Philipson (1862–1949) from 1891 offered these suggestions:

As a ritual for confirmation I would, therefore, suggest something like the following:

Opening hymn by the class.
Opening prayer.
Music by choir.
Floral prayer, according to the suggestion made by Dr. Wise in his hymn-book, that the children deposit their flowers on the pulpit; a very graceful act symbolical of the season of the year and the flower-like lives of the confirmants.
Recital of the Ten Commandments from the Torah, with appropriate prayers before and after.
Music by choir.
A few words by one of the confirmants telling of the significance of the day.
Music.
Sermon by rabbi to congregation, to close with admonitory address to children.
Music.

Short examination, to conclude with declaration of faith.
Blessing of children by rabbi.
Closing hymn, sung by class.
Concluding prayer.
Dismissal of children to parents.
Music.[6]

From 1811 onward confirmation was frequently celebrated at the festival of Shavuot, and this explains the recital of the Ten Commandments and the reference to the "season of the year." The association with the festival continues to this day. Shavuot, which celebrates the giving of the Torah to the Jewish people, was thought to be an appropriate occasion for a declaration of faith. In medieval Europe ceremonies to initiate very young children into formal Hebrew learning were held at Shavuot, but such ceremonies had long since died out.[7] More relevant to Jewish confirmation at Shavuot is the long-standing practice in many churches of holding Christian confirmation on Pentecost Sunday, a festival precisely parallel to Shavuot.[8] Jewish confirmation was copied from the Protestant rite, with its confession of faith and the invoking of God's blessing, its sermons preaching morality and virtue, and its equality for boys and girls.[9]

THE FIRST JEWISH FREE SCHOOLS

Confirmation grew out of a new Jewish day school movement in Germany. The idea of offering secular and religious education in a single day school curriculum, taken for granted by Jewish day schools today, began in the late eighteenth century in the German Jewish "free school" movement. The first Jewish Free School was founded in Berlin in 1778 by Isaac Daniel Itzig and David Friedländer to give opportunities for boys from modest backgrounds to have an education broad enough to enable them to obtain office work among the new German middle class. The school was guided by principles laid down by Moses Mendelssohn (1729–76), the "mediator between two cultures,"[10] who had promoted the idea that Jews could learn secular subjects and Judaism side by side.

Such a form of education, which seems completely familiar to us today, was not available in those days except for the wealthy, and German Jews were only just beginning to be admitted to the wider society.[11] The Berlin school has been described as "the first modern school in the world," but it never had more than one hundred students, some of whom were Christians. There was little support from the Jewish community at the time, but today it is recognized as a pioneering school that led to a permanent change in the education of Jewish children.[12]

The Jewish Free School movement soon spread to Breslau, Dessau, Seesen, Copenhagen, and other towns and is an important part of the background to the origins of Reform Judaism. The new ceremony of confirmation, which was often called in German *"Einsegnung,"* was originally a graduation ceremony for boys from the Free Schools. Leopold Zunz (1794–1886), who was to become a well-known academic and founder of what became known as the "Science of Judaism," has left us the earliest known account of how confirmation was introduced into the Free Schools. The son of a cantor, Zunz lost his father before he was eight years old; his mother had little choice but to send him away to school at Wolfenbüttel, where he could attend the free Talmud Torah. There were two ramshackle buildings, and the ten or so boys were badly neglected and often infested with vermin. The curriculum consisted almost entirely of Talmud, until a new director arrived, who had come to turn the Talmud Torah into the Samson Free School. He modernized not just the curriculum but the living conditions as well.[13] Zunz later wrote:

> On Sunday noon, the 5th of June in the year 1803 I arrived with my uncle in the [school] courtyard . . . The study of the Talmud now began straightaway from the very next day . . . There were no school rules, no protocol, to a certain extent no pedagogy . . . I think Inspector Ehrenberg turned up at the end of 1806 or January 1807 . . . In one day we literally moved over from a medieval age into a modern one, at the same time stepping out of Jewish helotism into bourgeois freedom. Just think, all that I had been deprived of until then, parents, love, instruction, and educational materials, was given to me . . . The first confirmation that Inspector Ehrenberg performed was my own, Sabbath 22 August 1807.[14]

This account by Zunz is very moving. The changes in his school were far more than a simple change of curriculum but began to give him an emotional security that up to then had been missing from his life.[15] For the first time he had a teacher and school subjects he could relate to. The new ceremony took place when he was thirteen and replaced his bar mitzvah; instead of reading from the Torah, he had to give rehearsed answers about his faith, Maimonides' thirteen principles of Judaism, and an original Hebrew prayer. Ehrenberg recited a blessing.[16] It must have been the happiest moment of his life. His earlier attempts to grapple with Talmud had only increased his loneliness, but now suddenly his grief and loss had been replaced by a brighter future. Accounts of confirmation repeatedly emphasize that it was an emotional experience for both students and congregations. Such statements of feeling are completely missing from accounts of bar mitzvah from that time.

Later in life Zunz wrote a very brief article in which he listed the first confirmation ceremonies in various towns. The first one on his list was Dessau, and the date he gives is 1803.[17] No contemporary evidence has been found, but that does not mean his date must be incorrect. The Jewish Free School in Dessau was founded in 1799 and headed by David Frankel, who was to become one of the pioneers of the new Reform movement. Zunz described the form of those early ceremonies: "a song, a prayer and speech by the teacher, test questions, an address and admonition by the teacher to the boys, the confirmation avowal and prayer, giving of blessing, prayer, song circuit."[18]

Throughout the nineteenth and early twentieth centuries the German and English term *confirmation* was also used to translate the Hebrew term *bar mitzvah*. Therefore, sources mentioning *confirmation* have to be treated with caution. Here I use the term to describe the kind of ceremony described by Zunz and later variations along the same lines, clearly very different from the ceremony of bar mitzvah.

Israel Jacobson

The spread and success of this new ceremony was in no small measure due to the tireless work of one man.[19] Israel Jacobson (1768–1828) was neither a scholar nor a rabbi but, rather, a successful businessman who devoted his life and his funds to promoting a new kind of Judaism. He did not invent the ceremony of confirmation, but its use in schools was entirely due to his promotion of it, and it was he who had placed Samuel Meyer Ehrenberg at the head of Leopold Zunz's school.[20] Later the ceremonies he organized attracted widespread press publicity. And in 1811 he became the first to link confirmation to the Jewish festival of Shavuot, a link that remains popular to this day.

Jacobson had become a millionaire banker by the age of nineteen. In spite of his success, he found himself ignored and sometimes insulted as a Jew and was determined to improve matters. On his business travels he met many of the Jewish intellectuals of his day and came to believe that Jews would be better accepted if they had the opportunity for secular education and a more modern style of worship. His own native language was Yiddish, and his accent in German was obvious to all. He decided to devote his life to Jewish education and synagogues.

Jacobson was responsible for the founding of the Jewish school in Seesen (a town in Lower Saxony) in 1801. Six years later that part of Germany fell to Napoleon's army, and Seesen became incorporated into the "Kingdom of Westphalia," a French vassal state ruled by Napoleon's brother Jerome Bonaparte. Jacobson moved to Kassel, the capital of Westphalia, and became a leading financier for the new government. In return King Jerome put him officially in charge of organizing the Jewish community. Jacobson convened an official council of the leading Jews of the nation in order to "bring a number of customs which have crept into Judaism, more into line with changed circumstances."[21] In January 1808 King Jerome officially granted the sixteen thousand Jews of Westphalia equal rights, and the "modernization of the Jew was now a matter of state legislation."[22] In March 1809 the council published "The Duties of the Rabbis" for the kingdom, establishing that "the rabbi must supervize the schools and charitable institutions of the Jews so that the good intentions of the state may be realized . . . He must prepare the young for confirmation and himself perform the act of confirming them."[23]

From 1810 we have the first description of the council's rule being put into practice in a synagogue confirmation:

In the synagogue, the children say their prayers shortened and alternating between Hebrew and German. They understand the prayers, which is why there is an exemplary silence and a holy atmosphere in the synagogue. One of the teachers says the words very clearly, and the children repeat them quietly . . . The Bible quotations are read one by one, without any vocal music, by some chosen teacher, and as soon as he is finished with his blessing, one of the students comes up and reads the German Mendelssohn translation of those Hebrew quotations . . .

The confirmation of the boys and girls (because also the daughters will be instructed in religion) will be done in a very festive way in the synagogues, in the presence of the rabbi. Recently the first confirmation of this kind was done here [Kassel, 1810]. After a speech on the purpose of confirmation, that was made by the Consistory's Councillor Heinemann on Sabbath in the school's synagogue, when the reading of the bible quotations was over, the boy talked about the basic truth of religion that he learned by means of God's legislation and he promised—but without a vow or handshake—to follow the religious moral laws and to always truly fulfil the federal laws. Then the venerable rabbi, Consistory's council Lob Berlin, gave him his blessing with most sincere emotions in presence of an important congregational gathering, using his own words.[24]

Unlike the bar mitzvah ceremony, which was initiated by Jewish fathers, confirmation was initially led by teachers, then by rabbis. In Westphalia the rabbis and teachers were under the control of Jacobson's council. But that did not mean that Jacobson always got his own way. Jacobson opened the so-called Seesen Temple, now considered to be the world's first Reform Synagogue, in July 1810, and the first confirmation there was held at Shavuot in 1811. Unfortunately, part of the ceremony had been partly written by a Protestant pastor, and a rebuke from the council followed.[25]

An Alternative to Baptism

Was confirmation an innovation borrowed from Christianity? As the name and form and date (Shavuot/Pentecost) of the ceremonies indicate, the Christian influence cannot be doubted. Jacobson wanted forms of Jewish worship more acceptable and understandable to Christian visitors, in the hope of improving access for Jews to wider society and improving their standard of living. But the introduction of choirs, the wearing of robes and clerical collars, and moves toward more formal, more decorous worship were common in mainstream communities across Germany in the first half of the nineteenth century. The boundaries between what was acceptable and what was not should not be judged by today's norms.

Furthermore, the new Jewish ceremony of confirmation provided a real alternative to the Christian ceremony. The early Reformers wanted to discourage baptism into the Church, which was becoming common among the wealthy, who wanted their children to succeed in the world. In Berlin, Lea and Abraham Mendelssohn had their son Felix baptized in 1816 at the age of seven, paving the way for him to become a famous composer.[26] The very next year, in London, Isaac D'Israeli had his twelve-year-old son, Benjamin, baptized into the Church of England, smoothing the way for his later parliamentary career. But baptism was never the end of the matter. Benjamin Disraeli had to endure anti-Jewish taunts throughout his public life, and there is evidence that, in England at least, schoolboys who had been baptized were bullied more than unconverted Jews.[27]

Meanwhile, in Germany, the Kingdom of Westphalia came to an end with the French retreat, and Israel Jacobson moved to Berlin, where he began again by starting a synagogue in his home. At Shavuot 1815 he held a confirmation service there for his own son. The new synagogue was so successful that in 1817 services moved to the nearby palatial residence of Amalie and Jacob Herz Beer, where the new style particularly appealed to the younger and wealthier sections of the Jewish community. Christian visitors also attended and participated in services.[28] It was at the "Beer Temple," as it came to be known, that the very first Jewish coming-of-age ceremony for two girls was held that year. Eduard Kley came from Hamburg to officiate in Berlin and took confirmation back to Hamburg with him. He held a ceremony for girls there on November 15, 1818, and one for boys on December 20, 1818. The sermons he gave on those occasions were published.[29] (Details of these and other confirmation ceremonies for girls can be found in chap. 5.)

In Denmark, as in Westphalia, confirmation came under government control. Liberal-minded Jews founded a modern boys' school in Copenhagen in 1805 and a separate school for girls in 1810. They invited a teacher from the Berlin Freischule to write a textbook for them outlining the basic tenets of the Jewish faith from a rationalist perspective. When in 1814 the Jews of Denmark were granted citizenship by royal decree, one condition was that boys and girls be instructed according to the new textbook and pass a public examination, to be known as confirmation. To obtain this concession, the modern-minded Jews allowed the Royal Commission to alter the text of their book and to remove references to the oral law.[30] This was one of several instances in which members of a Jewish community, in the struggle for emancipation, found themselves submitting to unwarranted government interference in matters of worship.

The first confirmation ceremony in Copenhagen

took place on May 19, 1817 in a spacious room that had once served as a concert hall. An organ had been placed on the east wall, a table bearing two candles stood on the west in front of a plaque displaying the

Ten Commandments. A large crowd gathered to hear Mannheimer conduct the examination and deliver a Danish sermon on the text from Job: "Wisdom, where shall it be found?" Some psalms were sung in the vernacular to musical accompaniment. The ceremony apparently made such a favorable impression on many Jews, and also on Gentiles present, that it prompted the community leadership to initiate regular devotional exercises in the same hall.[31]

This account does not state that an ark and scrolls were brought in or needed for this ceremony. The setting was a public hall, and the ceremony clearly resembled a school speech day more than a synagogue service. The gifted young preacher, Isaac Noah Mannheimer (1793–1865), was to go on to introduce confirmation in Vienna and to play a leading part in the formulation of the Reform Vienna program (1826) that helped to spread confirmation across Europe. But perhaps he found synagogue ceremonies less meaningful than those in a school because in Vienna he held only nine confirmations in thirty years.[32]

Criticisms of Bar Mitzvah

Those familiar with Reform confirmation services today will be able to imagine the kind of ceremonies that took place in the early nineteenth century. What is difficult for us today is to envisage the emotional impact that they had. This impact seems to have come from the freshness of the ceremony. Bar mitzvah had often become a ritual devoid of content, with Hebrew learned by rote. A statement made in 1810 in the journal *Sulamith,* founded by David Frankel to spread the new Reform ideas, articulated the problem:

> In the Jewish religion we presently find amongst many honored ceremonies some which can hardly pass the test of common sense. Among these latter we count the meaningless ceremonial at confirmation time (bar mitzvah) . . . Many are even ashamed of worship itself, and thus the celebration . . . is either neglected altogether or observed without enthusiasm. Thus the young man often enters the arena of life without any intellectual or moral education.[33]

Elias Birkenstein complained in 1817 that the boys undertook the traditional ceremony "without any acknowledgement of belief or duty, but instead only the Torah portion, and they bleat like sheep in the Hebrew language without understanding a single word of what they must prepare for the occasion with great accuracy."[34] Such criticisms of bar mitzvah help to explain the popularity of the new ceremony and also help us understand why girls were offered confirmation rather than a ceremony parallel to the boy's traditional call to the Torah.

A Setback

In Berlin the new temple soon found itself subjected to unwelcome attention from the government of Prussia. It was the price of success. In its eight-year history more than one third of the Jewish adults in Berlin had shown some kind of interest in the new prayer style.[35] The Beer Temple was officially closed in 1823, and religious reforms in synagogues were prohibited by government decree, a ruling that was not rescinded until 1844. Officials did not object to Jews imitating Christian practices, but when Christians attended regularly and seemingly were attracted to Jewish ceremonies, it was seen as a cause for concern. The emphasis on civic identity was also troubling to the authorities, who were anxious to avoid any gatherings that might help political dissidents to organize.[36]

Israel Jacobson retired to his country estate and never returned to his religious work. He died in 1828 at the age of sixty, a deeply disappointed man. It has recently been shown, based on genealogical research ordered by the Nazis, that the number of Jews in Berlin who became Christians decreased during the years Jacobson's temple was functioning there.[37] But discouraging Jews from joining the Church was only part of his aim. He had embarked on a personal campaign with his objective being nothing less than the reform of Judaism itself. The new coming-of-age ceremony of confirmation was central to his purpose.

CONFIRMATION SPREADS

After the government crackdown, Reform initiatives in the 1820s and 1830s centered on education, of which confirmation was a part. Even when there were Orthodox objections, they were generally happy if the ceremony was held in the school (as a graduation event) rather than in the synagogue.[38] From the 1820s onward the new ceremony spread rapidly across Europe and became popular in both Reform and Orthodox communities, as the table shows.

Introduction of confirmation, including first coming-of-age ceremonies for girls

In most cases the ceremony was introduced after the arrival of the rabbi or leader listed. In a few cases only the date of the rabbi's arrival is known, not the date of the ceremony. These are indicated by a plus (+) sign after the date. The word both indicates separate ceremonies for boys and girls.

DATE	PLACE	BOYS/GIRLS	PRINCIPAL OFFICIANT	MOST RELIABLE SOURCE FOUND
1803	Dessau	boys	—	Zunz, *Gessammelte Schriften*, 2:215
1807	Seesen School	boys	—	Zunz, *Gessammelte Schriften*, 2:215
1807	Wolfenbüttel	boy	Samuel Meyer Ehrenberg	Herrmann, "Jewish Confirmation Sermons," 91
1810	Kassel	boy	Jeremiah Heinemann	"Westphalen." *Sulamith* 3.1 (1810), 6–15
1811	Seesen Temple	boys	—	Marcus, *Israel Jacobson*, 95–96
1815	Berlin	boy	—	Marcus, *Israel Jacobson*, 109
1817	Berlin	girls	Eduard Kley	*Sulamith* 5.1 (1817): 279
1817	Copenhagen	boys	Isaac Noah Mannheimer	Weil, "Copenhagen Report," 94
1818	Hamburg	girls	Eduard Kley	*Sulamith* 5.1 (1817): 402; Kley, *Predigten*
1820 +	Karlsruhe	—	—	Meyer, *Response to Modernity*, 57
1820 +	Königsberg	mixed	—	Meyer, *Response to Modernity*, 50
1821	Posen	boys	—	Resnick, "Confirmation Education," 216
1825–30	Charleston	—	—	Wice, "Bar Mitzvah and Confirmation," 60
1826 +	Vienna	—	Isaac Noah Mannheimer	Rose, *Jewish Women*, 30
1826 +	Bamberg	—	Samson Wolf Rosenfeld	Meyer, *Response to Modernity*, 102

Year	City		Name	Source
1828	Frankfurt	—	Michael Creizenach	Philipson, *Reform Movement*, 111
1830s	Heidelberg	mixed	Karl Rehfuss	*Pinkas Hakehillot*, 2.309–17
1831	Brunswick	mixed	Samuel Egers	*Jewish Encyclopedia*, "Eger" and "Confirmation"
1831	Munich	girls	—	Wice, "Bar Mitzvah and Confirmation," 55
1831 +	Fürth	—	Isaac Löwi	*Jewish Encyclopedia*, "Löwi"; Philipson, *Reform Movement*, 77
1833 +	Strasbourg	—	Arnaud Aron	*Jewish Encyclopedia*, "Aron"
1837 +	Liegnitz	—	Asher Sammter	*Jewish Encyclopedia*, "Sammter"
1837 +	Prague	boys	Michael Sachs	Meyer, *Response to Modernity*, 154
1839	Worms	boys	Dr. Samuel Adler	*Pinkas Hakehillot*, 3.191–205
1840	Dresden	—	—	Meyer, *Response to Modernity*, 106
1840	Riga	girls	Max Lilienthal	Ruben, *Max Lilienthal*, 34–35
1842	Bordeaux	both	—	Fonséca, "Instruction religieuse"
1843	St. Thomas	mixed	Benjamin Carillon	*Occident* 1.10, Jan. 1844
1843	Paris	mixed	Salomon Ullmann	Löw, *Die Lebensalter*, 222
1843	Warsaw	—	—	*Jewish Encyclopedia*, "Medals"
1844	Breslau	girls	Abraham Geiger	Kober, "150 Years," 109
1844	Verona	girls	Joseph M. Cameo	Conigliani, "Iniziazione religiosa"
1845	Eperies	mixed	Solomon Schiller-Szinessy	Loewe, "Solomon Marcus Schiller-Szinessy," 150; and UCL archive papers
1845	London	mixed	David Woolf Marks	*Jewish Chronicle*, Oct. 2, 1846, 222–23 (mentions "the previous confirmation")

DATE	PLACE	BOYS/GIRLS	PRINCIPAL OFFICIANT	MOST RELIABLE SOURCE FOUND
1846	Lemberg (Lvov)	mixed	Abraham Kohn	Meyer, *Response to Modernity*, 157
1846	Schwerin	mixed	Samuel Holdheim	Baader, *Gender Judaism and Bourgeois Culture*, 71
1846	New York	mixed	Max Lilienthal	Ruben, *Max Lilienthal*, 85–86
1847	Leipzig	mixed	Adolf Jellinek	Jellinek, *Die erste Confirmations-Feier*
pre-1847	Lugos, Hungary	—	—	Philipson, *Reform Movement*, 476
1850	Marseilles	—	—	Löw, *Die Lebensalter*, 222
1851	Philadelphia	—	Jacob Frankel	*Occident* 9.4, July 1851
1852	Manchester UK	mixed	Solomon Schiller-Szinessy	Schiller-Szinessy, *Confirmation*
1853	Birmingham UK	boys	Abraham Pereira Mendes	Mendes, *Sermons*, 185–200
1855	Cincinnati	—	Isaac Mayer Wise	Wise, *Selected Writings*, 106–7
1861	San Francisco	—	—	Silverstein, *Alternatives to Assimilation*, 19
1864	Cleveland	mixed	Rev. G. M. Cohen	*Cleveland Plain Dealer*, June 13, 1864, 3
1867	Altona	girls	Jacob Ettlinger	Ettlinger, *Responsa Binyan Tziyon Ha-Chadashot* 2, no. 107
1899	Johannesburg	girls	David Wasserszug	*Jewish Chronicle*, June 2, 1899, 24
1900	Ancona	girls	Isaac Refael Tedeschi	'Fiducia,' "La maggiorità religiosa"
1900	Bologna	girls	Alberto Orvieto	'Fiducia,' "La maggiorità religiosa"
1901	Alexandria	girls	Eliahu Hazan	Miccoli, "Moving Histories"
1906	Sydney, Australia	mixed	Francis Lyon Cohen	*Jewish Chronicle*, Jan. 25, 1907, 14

We do not know whether or not family parties were held after such confirmation ceremonies. It is reasonable to assume that those rabbis who promoted confirmation as a point of entry to a surrounding non-Jewish society would not have wanted any excessive expenditure. Isaac Francolm, who introduced confirmation to Köningsberg in the 1820s, wrote that "the parents may invite friends, but they must take care that the religious act should not become a social function."[39] This piece of instruction suggests that the holding of individual parties was politely but firmly discouraged.

Europe

A dispute in Frankfurt in the 1840s helps illustrate how confirmation was viewed at that time. Leopold Stein, a moderate Reformer, was appointed rabbi of the community in 1844. His attempts to follow a moderate line pleased neither the conservatives who ran the synagogue nor the radicals who ran the school. Stein was firmly refused any role in the school, and throughout his tenure he protested against this prohibition. Matters came to a head over the confirmation ceremony. Articles in the local Jewish journal the *Orient* maintained that the rabbi had been excluded from religious instruction in the school, that the confirmation ceremony was essentially an examination, and that confirmation itself had been inaugurated by Jewish schools. Stein insisted that the ceremony was incomplete without a rabbi.

Elsewhere in Europe, and shortly afterward in the United States, confirmation was to be established purely as a synagogue ceremony, but in Frankfurt and other towns in Germany it maintained its historic link with the Jewish day school.[40] Some provincial councils forbade confirmation in synagogues, while others instructed that it should take place on an annual basis.[41] Even Jacob Ettlinger (1798–1871), a fierce critic of Reform Judaism, found himself officiating at a synagogue confirmation service in the Great Synagogue of Altona in 1867. Later he published the text of his sermon. In it he took pains to emphasize that it was only because of the local regulations that the ceremony had to take place in the synagogue instead of in the school: "For Jews there is no need for a festive religious ceremony to mark the acceptance of belief, for a person is bound from birth by all the commands of the Torah, and there is no way to detach himself from that obligation. The activity in which we are engaged here is not a religious rite, but rather an examination in religious studies."[42]

Confirmation was in decline in its original homeland of Germany in the second half of the nineteenth century,[43] but it still had its enthusiastic supporters. Leopold Löw, who brought out the first book to contain a brief history of bar mitzvah and confirmation in 1875, was severely critical of the ritual nature of the bar mitzvah ceremony and preferred the confirmation ceremony.[44]

Meanwhile, confirmation had spread to neighboring countries. In Italy beginning in 1844, ceremonies were held specifically for girls,[45] while boys had individual bar mitzvah ceremonies, but in France boys and girls shared confirmation. A report from an Orthodox community in Paris in 1852 describes the French system:

> The ceremony of confirmation which is called *initiation religieuse*, takes place in the synagogue every year after the Shavuot festival. Even though confirmation has been in existence for only a few years, it has already made a place for itself in the life of the French Jews and has brought them many blessings. Between sixty and eighty children appear at the ceremony. Whether they are poor or rich, they are nicely dressed, and in the holy place confirm their entrance into the synagogue at the end of a meticulous examination.
>
> In this manner children of both sexes from families of the most diverse backgrounds obtain a thorough knowledge and love of their faith. By rearranging and reordering an old form, a need has been satisfied which our times demanded. Such reform is beneficial and after some time it will be firmly rooted in the congregation and among the people.[46]

Noteworthy in this account is the distinctive French name for the ceremony, the large number of children taking part, and the continued link with Shavuot.

These ceremonies in France and Italy took place in Orthodox synagogues because at that time many congregational rabbis had Reform sympathies but continued to work within mainstream synagogues.[47] Places that had Reform communities also introduced confirmation ceremonies for both boys and girls.

The United States

Confirmation reached the United States in the 1820s. The Jewish community of Charleston, South Carolina, exceeded in size that of New York at the time. The Reformed Society of Israelites began to hold monthly services in January 1825, with choir, hymns, and instrumental music. Their prayer book, which survives, was written in manuscript form in 1825 and published in 1830. It laid out details of the confirmation ceremony: "Mode of Confirmation. Anyone born of Jewish parents, not under the age of thirteen and desirous of expressing his belief in the Jewish faith may, on any Sabbath, make declaration of the same and be confirmed therein as follows. He advances to the minister's desk, and repeats the articles of faith of the Society."[48] The articles of faith were ten in number and were based on the traditional thirteen principles of the Jewish faith but omitted belief in resurrection, in the Messiah, and even in Torah apart from the Ten Commandments.[49]

The brief ceremony described here was a simple declaration of these principles, and no mention was made of any study or preparation needed beforehand. Although it was called a "confirmation," the ceremony was very different from the group graduation ceremonies common elsewhere at the time. It was more like a public way for new members to declare their allegiance. The Charleston congregation was a breakaway group that operated with no leaders and was in many ways different from any other Reform congregation before or since. It closed in 1833.[50]

In 1839 a Jewish catechism in English was brought out in Philadelphia by Isaac Leeser, based on Eduard Kley's German text but greatly expanded. The book is dedicated to Rebecca Gratz (1781–1869), the pioneer American Jewish educator, who had recently started a Hebrew Sunday school in Philadelphia. Leeser's introduction states: "It has been my endeavour to make myself understood by children of from eight to fourteen years old."[51] Although he does not specify how he expected the book to be used, the question-and-answer format on Jewish beliefs must have been designed for teachers to ask the questions and for children to learn the answers in a classroom. The book ends with a section on the "Jewish Creed," in reality the thirteen traditional principles of the Jewish faith, which the child was expected to "recite."[52]

In 1844 a report in the monthly journal *The Occident* stated that a letter had been received about a confirmation service held on the island of St. Thomas, in the Caribbean, at the previous Sukkot. At that time the island was managed by the Danish and was not part of the United States.[53] In 1846 the same journal reported that another confirmation service had been held at St. Thomas, this time on the eve of Shavuot. The journal gave the names of the three boys and six girls who took part and reported that the ceremony included a pledge of obedience to God, made with the hand on a Torah scroll. This report provoked a lively correspondence from an objector, who complained that it was highly inappropriate for young Jews to make such a pledge.[54] The criticism must have hit home because a further report from the island in 1847, when the confirmation was held at Passover, mentioned that no scrolls were taken out and no oaths or promises administered.[55]

Another report about confirmation in the same issue of *The Occident* was from New York, where the service was conducted by Rabbi Max Lilienthal (1815–82). Lilienthal was a German education expert who as a young man had been sent to Riga to found a modern German Jewish school there. Lilienthal introduced confirmation to that town in 1840, with separate classes for boys and girls. By the time the girls' ceremony took place at Shavuot, his original group of seven girls had grown to twenty-five.[56] Lilienthal arrived in the States in 1845 and held his first confirmation service at the Anshe Chesed Synagogue in New York at Shavuot in 1846. Lilienthal had planned a service for the first day of Shavuot that included the normal questions, answers, and declarations of faith, followed by a blessing by the rabbi. On the following day, the second day of Shavuot, all the confirmands were called up to the reading of the Torah.[57] There were five months of twice-weekly classes leading up to the ceremony.[58] In the event sixteen boys and girls participated, and a congregation of fifteen hundred assembled in all. A press report stated, "The Rabbi delivered an impressive sermon, which drew tears from all, and satisfied everyone, that far from being a destructive innovation, 'confirmation' was an earnest appeal to every Jew to rally with heart and soul round the standard of our holy religion."[59]

Max Lilienthal befriended Rabbi Isaac Mayer Wise (1819–1900) shortly after Wise arrived from Bohemia in July 1846. Wise conducted his first confirmation service at Albany, New York, at Shavuot in 1848.[60] After his arrival in Cincinnati in 1854, Wise introduced confirmation to the Benei Yeshurun congregation on his first Shavuot. There was a repeated pattern, both in Europe and in the United States, of rabbis introducing the new ceremony shortly after their arrival in town, which certainly suggests a degree of dissatisfaction with the traditional bar mitzvah and a desire to try something new. At that time Jewish education in Cincinnati was going through a similar process of change as that described by Zunz in Germany fifty years earlier, with the Talmud institutions closing down as Jewish children were admitted to public schools.[61] Confirmation was an ideal ceremony to reflect the new emphasis on faith, rather than on ritual, based on these "five principles of Judaism":

1. There is but one God . . .
2. Man . . . is the image of his Maker.
3. It is man's duty to do the will of God, attain human perfection, and to become God-like.
4. It is the will of God, that man should be happy here and hereafter.
5. The time will come, when truth will reign supreme, all men will be saved, united and enlightened in justice and love.[62]

Not only were traditional Jewish rituals missing, but there was not even any mention of Torah or revelation in the words used in Wise's confirmation ceremonies. The principles to be repeated by the confirmands were to be entirely consistent with those of the United States.[63]

After the first confirmation at Rodef Shalom, Philadelphia (1851), *The Occident* reported: "We cannot say that we are altogether in favour of confirmation; but if it does no good, it can do no harm; and if it produces a wholesome effect on one child even, and fixes its principles for life, there is something gained." [64] The following year the *Occident's* correspondent who had witnessed the confirmation at Rodef Shalom expressed more serious reservations about the new ceremony: "It may have its good effects; but, we fear, that, whilst parents are not as strict as they ought to be, it is folly and sin to demand a solemn pledge from children that they will obey truly to the last day of their life the dictates of the Lord, when the very next hour, perhaps, they have placed before them prohibited things, or are induced to violate the Sabbath and festivals."[65]

From 1857 onward, with the publication of Wise's prayer book *Minhag America*, confirmation was firmly associated with the growing Reform movement. Wise devotes a section of his book to confirmation, which he suggests should take place at the end of the Shavuot morning service. The ceremony there prescribed is remarkable for its clarity, scope, and detail. All the boys were expected to dress in black, the girls in white. They would process into the synagogue, each carrying a bouquet, and form a semicircle around the ark, the boys on one side, the girls on the other. After an address by the rabbi and declarations and scriptural quotations by the confirmands, the rabbi would declare them initiated into the congregation of Israel.[66]

Wise was not afraid to use the term *initiation*. There was no precedent at this time for a confirmation ceremony actually making someone Jewish, and its history was that of a school graduation ceremony, but by using the word *initiation*, Wise was in effect declaring a hope that in the future everyone would formally enter Jewish adult life in this way. It was to be a triumph of civic religion, with the institution of the synagogue taking the place of what had been the preserve of the family—the handing on of Jewish identity.

At the festival of Shavuot in 1864, the first confirmation service was held in Cleveland, Ohio. Twelve girls and four boys took part, and there was an enthusiastic report in the local newspaper about it. The ceremony was held in the synagogue of the Anshe Chesed congregation:

> Entering from the glare of the street, into its darkened aisles, lit by numberless jets of gas whose light fell upon the thronged assembly of dark-eyed, dazzling daughters of Judah, richly arrayed in honor of the festival: pausing a moment to watch the procession of young girls arrayed in white, with wreaths of flowers and ribbons, and the bright-eyed boys with rosettes following and wending their way through arches of evergreens and flowers, one could almost imagine a scene of oriental beauty. And, as if to add to the fascination, the rich volume of sacred music that flowed from the organ, carried still more lofty by the voices of the choir, fell upon the ear in all the solemnity of divine adoration.[67]

Decorating the synagogue with greenery and flowers was a long-standing tradition for the festival of Shavuot; the manner in which this traditional decoration had been used to enhance the confirmation service shows the great deal of planning and care taken for the first such event in the town.

Another American prayer book, Raphael Lewin's *American Jewish Ritual* (1870), describes the confirmands kneeling in front of the open ark during the ceremony and subsequently taking an oath with one hand raised: "I do, of my own free will and accord, most solemnly and sincerely swear and vow to cherish and defend my holy religion to live in that religion, to die in that religion, and through that religion alone to seek eternal salvation."[68]

From then on, confirmation was firmly associated with the Reform movement, as it is to this day. It soon spread across the United States. The first confirmation at San Francisco's Emanu-El Temple was held at

Shavuot in 1861. In 1875 the Sabbath School Committee of the UAHC laid down that synagogue schools should include in their curriculum "catechism in all the classes preparing for confirmation and in confirmation class." By the 1880s it was such a well-established part of Reform Jewish education that congregations began to conduct post-confirmation classes to take the young people forward into adult life.[69] By the end of that decade the ceremony had become widespread in both Reform and Conservative communities across the United States: "The ceremony has since gained so firm a foothold in America that there is now no progressive Jewish congregation in which the annual confirmation on Shebu'ot is not a regular feature of congregational life and one of the most inspiring ceremonies of the whole year."[70]

By this time bar mitzvah had become an anachronism because coming up to say the blessings on reading the Torah had been abolished in most American Reform congregations. Temple Emanu-El in New York, for example, had stopped boys from reading their portions when they introduced confirmation in 1848. At first they still continued to come up to say the blessings, even though nobody else did. Clearly, that was an anomaly that was not going to last, and eventually bar mitzvah was abolished as an "old fashioned, useless ceremony."[71]

The tradition of holding confirmation at Shavuot remained the norm at this time.[72] It was such an important part of the rabbi's year that in 1896 Isaac Mayer Wise described it as "closing the year's work for the Rabbi" and thus a proper time to advertise rabbinic vacancies for the coming year.[73]

Britain

In England confirmation was introduced to West London Synagogue (Reform) by its first rabbi, David Woolf Marks. In his inaugural sermon on the opening of the congregation's first building in January 1842, he declared: "It will be incumbent upon children of both sexes, connected with this synagogue, to be publicly confirmed in their faith at the age of thirteen years; the catechetical exercises joined with this important ceremony will embrace the whole of the principles of the Jewish faith."[74] A footnote in the printed text added three important words "if duly qualified," suggesting that, following the precedent set in Metz for bar mitzvah in 1769, the ceremony was only open to those who had attended classes and passed an appropriate examination. As confirmation had begun as a school graduation ceremony, this was not surprising.

The early confirmations at West London Synagogue took place at the Rosh Hashanah morning service, after the sounding of the shofar.[75] There is a surviving press report about the ceremony held at Rosh Hashanah in 1846. The report was at pains to emphasize the beauty of the ceremony, so much more meaningful than bar mitzvah, because the boys and girls, aged thirteen or fourteen, understood what they were doing:

> A catechetical examination takes place, embracing the leading articles of Judaism; and the confirmants having satisfactorily replied, the minister addresses them at considerable length, explaining each duty enjoined by their faith towards God, towards man, and their country. At the conclusion of the address, the children are required to say whether they are prepared to be confirmed, and to hold themselves from the present day responsible to God for all their actions; on their replying in the affirmative, they are confirmed by the minister, who pronounces upon them a solemn benediction . . . it is hardly possible to convey to anyone who has not witnessed it, the emotions awakened by this deeply affecting spectacle . . . Many members of the congregation being absent from town, their seats were eagerly sought after by a crowd of visitors.[76]

Rosh Hashanah, the Jewish New Year, was an unusual date to choose for the ceremony, with many synagogues already being full to overflowing, but West London clearly had empty seats, as the reference to members being out of town indicates. Perhaps David Woolf Marks sought to compensate for his congregation's reluctance to return to town by mid-September by filling his seats with the new ceremony.

The ceremonies at West London attracted the attention of Orthodox rabbis. A catechism "for the Period of Confirmation" was brought out by Benjamin Ascher, one of the rabbis of the Great Synagogue, London, in 1850. His introduction made the point that preparation for bar mitzvah on its own was insufficient. His catechism began with a series of striking questions and answers, indicating that this particular course of instruction was designed only for boys and only for those born in England:

Q. What are you my young friend?
A. I am a human being, like my fellow creatures.
Q. Of what nation are you?

A. By birth, an Englishman; in faith, a Hebrew.

Q. What are your duties as a man?

A. To regulate my life according to the principles laid down by reason.[77]

Soon after Ascher's catechism was published, confirmation was taken up by Orthodox synagogues in Birmingham and Manchester. It was introduced to Birmingham by Rabbi Abraham Pereira Mendes and to the Orthodox community in Manchester by the Hungarian rabbi Dr. Solomon Schiller-Szinessy.[78] At Shavuot in 1852 Schiller-Szinessy conducted a confirmation ceremony at what was then the only synagogue, in Halliwell Street. Eight girls and one boy were confirmed. Schiller-Szinessy described confirmation as "a genuine Jewish institution," giving examples going back to Joshua and Isaiah. His argument was, in short, that Judaism as a religion demanded not only faith but also knowledge and that the rabbis of old had not only permitted but encouraged the use of an oath to keep the Divine Commandment. And so he began the ceremony: "O, my children! Let not the declaration which you make be a mere word, a dead formula; but let it be the expression of a living and strong will to keep that which you are about to utter!"[79]

After the annual ceremony in Manchester in 1854, the *Hebrew Observer* reported:

> The children appeared to feel what they were undertaking, and what was said to them, very much, several of them could not refrain from tears. The proceeding was something more than a mere ceremony: to them it was a wholesome reality; and to others who witnessed it, not connected with the Jewish community, it afforded a sure evidence of the efficacy and faithfulness of that religious instruction which is provided by our Hebrew fellow-citizens for the children under their care.[80]

In 1856 Schiller-Szinessy was suspended as rabbi of the congregation, and the following year he and his supporters left and founded what was to become Manchester Reform Synagogue.[81] Confirmation was part of his published manifesto.[82] He thus introduced the ceremony into both an Orthodox and a Reform synagogue in the same town.

In London confirmation was taken up by the new Bayswater Synagogue in 1864 and the new Hampstead Synagogue in the 1890s.[83] In 1892 Chief

Rabbi Hermann Adler approved the holding of special services for children who had completed their religious education in all the synagogues under his jurisdiction, though he did not use the word *confirmation*.[84] In a letter to the British *Jewish Standard* in 1888 Schiller-Szinessy claimed that the ceremony had impeccable Orthodox credentials and that Hermann Adler had himself once officiated at such a service.[85]

The information and extracts presented here are just a very few of the many surviving sermons, service booklets, and press reports about confirmation. For the nineteenth century it is better documented than bar mitzvah, even though far fewer children were involved. The reason is simple: confirmation was a ceremony invented and promoted by rabbis, teachers, and leaders of congregations to serve specific educational and civic ends. They provided the surviving documentation that has survived. In the original duties for Rabbis and Synagogue Councils of the Kingdom of Westphalia (1809), it was laid down that careful records had to be kept of all confirmations.[86] The bar mitzvah ceremony, on the other hand, was invented and promoted by Jewish parents, and rabbis and communities were sometimes reluctant participants.

It is astonishing to note that until recently, synagogues rarely recorded and kept the names and dates of boys becoming bar mitzvah. For confirmation, service booklets often recorded the names of those taking part in the ceremony. The scant record reflects the relatively low esteem in which bar mitzvah has sometimes been held. There is no doubt that confirmation was often promoted as an alternative of superior moral and spiritual value. This preference can be seen by the numerous pamphlets, sermons, and other writings that promote confirmation and are very critical of bar mitzvah. Toward the end of the nineteenth century, however, some writers became critical of confirmation as an appropriate coming-of-age ceremony for girls, as we will see in the next chapter.

INTO THE TWENTIETH CENTURY

During the nineteenth century confirmation ceremonies were generally held at the age of thirteen, replacing bar mitzvah. David Philipson was among those who promoted the idea that confirmation should be delayed until later, writing in 1891:

> Every rabbi who has had confirmation classes under his instruction has felt that the age of thirteen, or even fourteen, is entirely too early

for a proper comprehension of the lessons taught and also that however deep may be the impression made on the day of confirmation the children are not old enough for a proper appreciation of the meaning and importance of the ceremony. We should have not an age test but a capability test. In the first place, no child that has not taken the full course of the Sabbath-school instruction should be permitted to enter the confirmation class . . . there is no reason why we should not confirm children at fifteen, sixteen or even older.[87]

The early-twentieth-century *Jewish Encyclopedia* noted that it was by then customary to delay the rite until the sixteenth or seventeenth year.[88] A 1931 report from American Reform communities shows that at that time about 40 percent of confirmands were age fourteen, and a similar percentage were fifteen. In 1958 only 22 percent were fourteen, and 64 percent were fifteen.[89] When the age rose from thirteen, it became possible to have both bar mitzvah and confirmation ceremonies. But Reform congregations were at first reluctant to offer both. The Responsa Committee of the Central Conference of American Rabbis, the rabbinical arm of the Reform movement, chaired by Kaufmann Kohler, declared in 1913 that calling up a thirteen-year-old to the Torah was not in harmony with the spirit of a Reform service.[90] In communities where the traditional blessings for reading the Torah had been abolished, bar mitzvah remained a complete anachronism.

But that did not mean that the ceremony that replaced bar mitzvah was always successful. The grand hopes that Isaac Mayer Wise had for confirmation were never achieved. David Philipson went on to say that just as bar mitzvah had become dry and unmeaning, so confirmation was now being threatened with the danger of pomp, show, display, and ostentation. In the synagogue there was too much theatricality, and printed programs created the impression that the ceremony was an entertainment or an exhibition. Parents were concerned with the beauty and brilliance of the day, not its inner meaning, and this emphasis led far too many good people to withhold their children from confirmation.[91]

Philipson was unable to stem the tide. Already in 1910 Rabbi Judah Magnes had called on the Reform movement to bring back bar mitzvah.[92] By 1930 confirmation had so lost its luster that an article in the *Yearbook* of the Central Conference of American Rabbis declared: "The religious significance of Confirmation was lost in gift-giving, formal pageantry, display of fine clothing and jewelry, elaborate receptions, etc."[93] Such public displays had never been the idea. The early reports say nothing about family parties, and indeed they give the impression that for the new and more meaningful ceremony to take root, the synagogue service should be the only focus.

BAR MITZVAH RETURNS

In the 1920s and 1930s, fifty or sixty years after many Reform Temples had abolished it, bar mitzvah began to return as confirmation declined. Keneseth Israel in Philadelphia brought back bar mitzvah in 1924,[94] and Shaarey Shomayim in Lancaster, Pennsylvania, did so in 1933. The following year Mount Zion Temple in St. Paul, Minnesota, celebrated the first bar mitzvah in fifty years. Rabbi Joshua Liebman brought back bar mitzvah to Temple Israel in Boston. Hebrew content in prayer and in school was being expanded everywhere. As interest in Zionism grew, Hebrew was no longer seen as a dead language, and the Central Conference of American Rabbis began to encourage more Hebrew in the temples.[95] Where bar mitzvah was an option, confirmation often became primarily a ceremony for girls. At the Conservative Congregation Oheb Shalom in New Jersey, for example, every confirmation from 1926 through 1954 was exclusively female.[96]

In the twentieth century the old catechisms became briefer and then disappeared altogether. A confirmation manual published in New York in 1919 included just three questions, asking the confirmands if they were prepared to cling to the living God, choose the good, treasure the Jewish spiritual message, and "make sacrifice that its cause may prevail."[97] Another manual, published just three years later, contained no catechism at all.[98] Soon afterward, confirmation prayers were introduced instead. A surviving example from West London Synagogue from 1936 includes these words: "Creator and Ruler of all, we thank thee for our strength and our youth and for all the goodness and beauty and happiness that we enjoy. We thank thee for our parents and all our dear ones and for their love, of which we are especially conscious in this solemn hour. Help us to realize our blessings, and give us the will and the power to respond to them with generous hearts."[99] Gradually, confirmation disappeared from Conservative and Orthodox congregations, although the ceremony remains important to this day in Reform communities in the United States and Liberal communities in the United Kingdom. West London Synagogue (Reform) and Manchester Reform Synagogue kept group confirmations until the 1970s.

At West London the term *confirmation* came to be used also to signify bar mitzvah and bat mitzvah, which were often held on a Saturday morning for two children at age fifteen or sixteen. From time to time, particularly at Shavuot, larger ceremonies were held. The archives of the synagogue from the 1950s show a process of transition. In 1956 a member named Louis Garvin resigned his seat because the synagogue would not allow his son to have a bar mitzvah at age thirteen. He pointed out that the boy's grandparents were approaching the age of seventy and were "most upset at any suggestion that we should postpone."[100] In September 1957, in response to a request from another family, the executive committee "decided that in principle there is no objection to boys being barmitzvahed in the synagogue at the age of 13." In 1959 the question was raised about whether a thirteen-year-old boy could read his portion on the same day as older boys. There continued to be a wide variety of ages for the celebration, sometimes referred to as bar mitzvah (for boys) and sometimes as confirmation (for boys or for girls).

The celebrations for girls were consistently referred to as confirmation until the arrival of a new minister in 1959, Rev. Michael Leigh, who decided to use the term *bat mitzvah*. Tana Kudelka celebrated her bat mitzvah at West London at age fifteen, on May 28, 1960.[101] The change of terminology reflected a new reality that boys and girls could now celebrate both ceremonies if they wanted to. Julia Schwab shared her bat mitzvah at West London with her friend Victoria Neumark in December 1964 and continued to study for her group confirmation at the synagogue at age sixteen in May 1966. In 2011 she returned to West London as Rabbi Baroness Neuberger, senior rabbi of the congregation.[102]

Temple Emanu-El, New York, was one of the last congregations in the United States to reintroduce bar mitzvah. Having stopped boys reading their portions in 1848, it had taken 125 years for the congregation to come full circle, bringing back bar mitzvah in 1972 and introducing bat mitzvah at the same time.[103] An article about members of the temple in 1980 reported one as saying: "The trouble with Emanu-El is that it's gotten so Jewish. Now they even have bar mitzvahs there!"[104]

In Liberal synagogues in the United Kingdom there was strong parental pressure to reintroduce bar mitzvah beginning in the 1960s. Rabbi John Rayner, senior rabbi of the Liberal Jewish Synagogue, London, objected in terms that echo the criticisms of bar mitzvah made in the 1810s and 1830s:

It is disconcerting to find that Barmitzvah is coming back in many liberal synagogues . . . Why? . . . In nearly every case because they have surrendered to the pressure of Orthodox or pseudo- orthodox parents and especially grandparents: grandparents who, as often as not, have no real knowledge or understanding of Judaism, who have done nothing for its development and reconstruction, who probably never open a Hebrew Bible themselves from one year to another, but who have a sentimental obsession to hear the unsteady treble voice of their grandson chanting ill-understood Hebrew words from the Almemar to the admiration of a spell-bound congregation who would barely notice the difference if he chanted the words in Chinese instead of Hebrew.[105]

Rayner later changed his mind, and bar mitzvah and bat mitzvah were introduced to the synagogue in 1981, which thus became the last known Progressive congregation to bring back the old ceremony. The reintroduction was on the condition that the boys and girls would stay on and study for confirmation as well.[106]

During the years when bar mitzvah was offered only to boys, most confirmation classes attracted a majority of girls. After bat mitzvah became popular in the 1970s, it became increasingly difficult to persuade girls (as well as boys) to stay on for confirmation classes, even when this was a precondition of the temple agreeing to a bar or bat mitzvah. Rabbis found themselves resorting to ingenious methods of persuasion. This approach is well documented in Ferida Wolff's 1989 novel, *Pink Slippers, Bat Mitzvah Blues*. In the novel Rabbi Pearlman keeps phoning Alyssa after her bat mitzvah to remind her about confirmation classes, but she is far more interested in her daily ballet lessons and rehearsals. But when Alyssa's younger friend Ellen develops depression after a bout of pneumonia, Rabbi Pearlman notices Alyssa's concern and discusses with her how to cheer up her friend. Only when Alyssa plays her friend the practice tape for her bat mitzvah does she start taking an interest in the world again. Alyssa learns the true Jewish value of visiting the sick and how her understanding will be enhanced if she stays on for confirmation. Rabbi Pearlman and his classes receive a very positive portrayal in the novel, which may well have been written in an attempt to persuade girls to remain in class after bat mitzvah.

CONFIRMATION IS RENAMED

Where confirmation has survived as a group ceremony, it is often no longer called by that name, which is now seen as a Christianized term. Graduation and similar ceremonies for fifteen- and sixteen-year-olds are still widely celebrated and provide a means of honoring students' achievements. The most common Hebrew term for the ceremony today is *Kabbalat Torah*, which means "receiving Torah." It is a term that has a link to the long association of the celebration with the festival of Shavuot. Yet Shavuot is known traditionally as the "season of *giving* the Torah," and the notion of *receiving* it is a modern one. The phrase has been taken from the philosopher Abraham Joshua Heschel, who wrote in 1955: "Revelation does not happen when God is alone. The two classical terms for the moment at Sinai are *mattan torah* and *kabbalat torah*, 'the giving of the Torah' and 'the acceptance of the Torah.' It was both an event in the life of God and an event in the life of man . . . At Sinai God revealed His word, and Israel revealed the power to respond. Without that power to respond, without the fact that there was a people willing to accept, to hear, the divine command, Sinai would have been impossible. For Sinai consisted of both a divine proclamation and a human perception. It was a moment in which *God was not alone*."[107]

The term *Kabbalat Torah* thus implies that we have a choice, unlike the term *bar mitzvah*, which denotes responsibility for doing God's commands. For today's Jewish teenagers *Kabbalat Torah* is offered as the culmination of a course helping "the students clarify for themselves . . . their personal beliefs within the context of Judaism."[108]

Since the 1970s, in the new spirit of *Kabbalat Torah*, congregations have allowed their students to create and lead their own services for confirmation and to come up with their own ideas instead of repeating standard answers. This approach has proven to be a very positive experience for many Jewish teens, as a description from a young man, Chip Rosenthal, in 1975 shows:

> I found Confirmation to be an important and serious experience, with much more meaning to me than my Bar Mitzvah. At thirteen my Bar mitzvah had no impact on me, since I really didn't know what I believed or where I fit in Judaism. It felt more like a regular service in which the rabbi gave me a small part. The Confirmation, however,

felt like *my* service since I helped to create it . . . The most interesting part of the service . . . were the talks prepared by members of my class. They expressed our ideas about Judaism, Confirmation, life . . . I . . . even mentioned how and why I consider myself partially agnostic.[109]

This account illustrates the trend toward a creative ceremony encouraging self-expression. It is impossible to imagine the old catechisms having any appeal for an agnostic Jew.

Statistics from American supplementary Jewish schools in 2006–7 show that children's enrollment increased in seventh grade, the year of bar or bat mitzvah. The following year it drops by one third, but the decrease then slows until after *Kabbalat Torah*. Now that bat mitzvah is universal, the gender balance for *Kabbalat Torah* is also equal.[110]

Today, however, the ceremony no longer engages Jewish teens in the way it did in the past. A 2011 report on the Jewish involvement of teens in New York failed to mention confirmation / *Kabbalat Torah*, even though it indicated that 50 percent of these young people were receiving formal Jewish education, mainly in Jewish part-time schools.[111] Both survey and anecdotal evidence in the United States shows that enrollment in formal educational courses beyond bar/bat mitzvah has steadily declined. Now that bar and bat mitzvah are universal, the confirmation courses remain and are enjoyed, but a formal or informal ceremony is no longer the draw it once was.

William Weidenthal celebrated his confirmation at Congregation Tifereth Israel in Cleveland on the Sunday after Shavuot in 1904. Thirty-seven years later his son Bud and his daughter Margaret, fraternal twins, were confirmed there in a group of ninety-eight by Rabbi Abba Hillel Silver at Shavuot. Bud's daughter Susan was confirmed at the same synagogue by Rabbi Daniel Jeremy Silver at Shavuot in 1976 among a group of sixty-one confirmands, and her daughters Stephanie and Hayley along with twenty-seven others, were confirmed there by Rabbi Richard Block at Shavuot in 2006. Reflecting on the remarkable story of four generations of confirmands in the same community, Bud Weidenthal noted a dramatic decline in the numbers of young Jews being confirmed in the confirmation heartland of American Reform Jewry. His granddaughters' group of twenty-nine were all who had stayed on for confirmation out of a year group of eighty who had celebrated bar/bat mitzvah. His impression was that numbers had been in decline throughout American Reform for twenty years.[112]

In 2006 Rabbis Richard Chapin and Fred Guttman debated the future of confirmation. Chapin had tried to stem the decline by bringing confirmation forward to ninth grade, while Guttman's solution was to postpone it to twelfth grade. He claimed that moving the ceremony close to high school graduation and asking the students to talk about "What being Jewish means to me" had increased participation to 75 percent of the former bar/bat mitzvah students.[113] Guttman's way forward is imaginative. By placing the ceremony close to a new stage in a young adult's secular education, it fits with today's promotion of lifelong learning. And it is in keeping with those forgotten times, long ago in medieval France, when the new ceremony of bar mitzvah coincided with moving onto the next educational stage.

CHAPTER FIVE

Bat Mitzvah

> The first known synagogue coming-of-age ceremony for Jewish girls was held for a Miss Bevern and a Miss Bernsdorf at the Beer Temple in Berlin in 1817.

> In 1847, at a similar ceremony in Leipzig, Rabbi Adolf Jellinek used a German equivalent of the phrase *bat mitzvah* to describe the girls.

> Since 1901 annual ceremonies for girls were held in Alexandria, Egypt, and continued every year until the Jewish community left for Israel in the 1950s.

> In the United States some girls started to read the Ten Commandments from a Torah scroll during their confirmation ceremonies as long ago as the 1890s.

> Ida Blum (b. 1908), from Calumet, Michigan, claimed later in life to have had her own individual bat mitzvah. This would have been before Judith Kaplan's famous New York ceremony in 1922.

> Ceremonies for girls took place in Berlin when the Nazis were in power. Rabbi Manfred Swarsensky called Alice Redlich to the Torah at the New Synagogue on Prinzregentstrasse in 1936. Her certificate has been found to prove it.

> In the 1960s many American Reform rabbis wanted to halt the spread of bat mitzvah, claiming that it would double their workload to include girls along with the boys.

On March 28, 1922, Mordecai Kaplan, the rabbi of the new Society for the Advancement of Judaism in New York, wrote in his diary: "Last Sabbath a week ago (Mch.18) I inaugurated the ceremony of the bat mitzvah at the S.A.J. Meeting House (41 W. 86th St.) . . . My daughter Judith was the first one to have her bat mitzvah celebrated there."[1] Mordecai Kaplan had no doubt that he had done something really new. To this day the ceremony for Judith Kaplan on March 18, 1922, is celebrated as the very first bat mitzvah. The event became famous because she herself became a well-known Jewish theologian, composer, and lyricist, Judith Kaplan Eisenstein. She often talked about her bat mitzvah, and when she died in 1996, obituaries described her as "the mother of the bat mitzvah."

Judith's bat mitzvah took place when she was twelve and a half. Although invitations had been sent out in advance, the ceremony itself was devised in a hurry on Friday evening. The next day at the Shabbat morning ceremony, after the normal reading of the Torah and haftarah (reading from the Prophets) had been completed, Judith read part of the section *Kedoshim* (Lev. 19–20). She read from a printed book, not from a Torah scroll, but recited the traditional blessings before and after. The section was chosen by her father and was not the traditional reading for that week. It included the famous golden rule *"Love your fellow as yourself."*[2]

Judith remembered the doubts expressed by her two grandmothers before the ceremony, each of whom tried to persuade the other to speak to Judith's father about it.[3] But her feminist friends turned out in force and thoroughly enjoyed the occasion. "It must be remembered that in 1922 our country was in the first flush of active feminism," she explained later. "It was only two years after the adoption of the woman suffrage amendment."[4] Later in life she claimed that she had been encouraged by her father to question and challenge Orthodox views. "'When I was 11, I told my father that I didn't believe in God,' she recalled . . . 'There was a sense of freedom and freedom to change. There was a constant opening up of possibilities and enrichment' with his view of Judaism, she said. 'It made my being Jewish a great joy for me rather than a burden.'"[5]

When Mordecai Kaplan scribbled the note in his diary, he may well have meant that this was simply the first bat mitzvah in his new synagogue. But his words have been taken by many to mean that it was the first one in America or even the first one ever. Could this be correct? The answer depends on how you define a bat mitzvah.

If it means a ceremony precisely corresponding to the traditional boy's bar mitzvah, then Judith's ceremony was not a bat mitzvah because it took place after the main service and because she read the Torah from a printed book instead of a handwritten scroll. If the term *bat mitzvah* can be used more loosely to describe a Jewish coming-of-age ceremony for girls, then the first such synagogue ceremony was held for two girls in Berlin in 1817. If we are talking about a ceremony that at the time it happened, the girl was referred to as "bat mitzvah," then the first one was in Leipzig in 1847. If we define *bat mitzvah* as a ceremony for an individual girl (not a group) in which the Torah blessings are said, then Judith Kaplan's is certainly the first well-known one, though there probably had been others earlier.

Mordecai Kaplan, in his hastily constructed plan for the event, modeled his daughter's bat mitzvah on the boy's ceremony, though it was not exactly the same. Perhaps Judith would have read the weekly portion from the scroll had she had time to practice properly. It is rather strange that this event has become so celebrated as the very first bat mitzvah because the first edition of the *Encyclopedia Judaica* did not mention it at all, stating that bat mitzvah was first introduced in France and Italy.[6]

Rabbi Mordecai Kaplan was soon to find out how girls celebrated in Italy. He must have had doubts about whether his daughter was the first when only a few months later, in the summer of 1922, he went on holiday to Rome and witnessed a ceremony for girls in an Orthodox synagogue. He wrote about it in his diary:

> I was very much pleased to see that they had the custom of taking cognizance of a girl's becoming *bas mitzvah*. They call it entering *minyan* [a quorum for prayer] at the age of twelve. The ceremony consists of having the father called up to the Torah on the Sabbath that the girl becomes *bas mitzvah*. She accompanies him to the *bima* [platform] and when he is through with the part, she recites the benediction of *she-heheyanu* ["Who has preserved us in life," a benediction for happy occasions]. Before *Musaph* [an additional service, added at the end of the Sabbath morning service], the Rabbi addresses her on the significance of her entering *minyan*. On the Sabbath I was at the synagogue there were three girls and one boy who entered *minyan*. The assistant Rabbi who was supposed to address them, read something out of a book in a very mechanical fashion. The fathers of the girls acted as if they were very infrequent visitors at the synagogue.[7]

One puzzling aspect of Kaplan's account is his use of the phrase *entering minyan*, a term that describes becoming of an age when one could be counted in the quorum for prayer. In Venice the phrase *bar minian* had long been used as an alternative name for *bar mitzvah*.[8] What is puzzling here is the use of the term for a girl because a girl could not be counted in the quorum in an Orthodox synagogue, and so this use of the term makes no sense. However puzzling this use of the term may be, it is clear from Kaplan's account of the perfunctory style of the proceedings that this was quite a normal event in that community, even for families not particularly involved in synagogue life. A new ceremony would not have been performed mechanically, so this group ceremony clearly had a history behind it.

Why did Judith Kaplan's bat mitzvah take place at the age of twelve and a half? The ancient rabbinic rule book the Mishnah states that the vows of a boy are valid from the age of thirteen years and one day and the vows of a girl from the age of twelve and one day.[9] Out of this mishnah grew the tradition that a girl becomes subject to the commandments at the age of twelve, just as a boy does at thirteen. A girl, however, unlike a boy, was not considered mature on achieving the correct age and showing physical signs of maturity but had to wait for six months.[10] Rabbi Leon Modena of Venice, explaining Judaism for a non-Jewish readership in 1637, put it very simply: "A Girl, when she is come to the age of 12 years and a half, is called a *Woman*."[11]

This teaching has led to variations in the age at which bat mitzvah is now celebrated. Orthodox congregations celebrate at age twelve, while Reform congregations generally favour age thirteen for both boys and girls, in the interests of equality. This practice probably goes back to the early nineteenth century but was formalized at the Breslau conference of 1846.[12] The Orthodox view is based on a ruling that a girl is formally liable to punishment for her actions at age twelve,[13] and so this is the age to celebrate bat mitzvah, by analogy with the boys.[14] Many Conservative congregations used to celebrate at the age of twelve and a half (following Judith Kaplan), but this is now very unusual, mainly as a result of the influence of Israeli practice, in which celebrations at age twelve have become the norm.

Bat mitzvah gradually developed from the nineteenth-century Jewish confirmation ceremonies. When the first modern Jewish day schools were founded in Germany, designed to teach Jewish and secular subjects side by side, there were separate schools for boys and girls. The first such school for girls opened in Hamburg in 1798 to teach the "fundamentals of religion, math, reading and handicrafts." A second school for poor Jewish girls followed in the same town in 1810. Other German girls' schools were opened in Breslau (1801), Dessau (1806), Frankfurt (1809), and Berlin (1809), and in 1810 a girls' school was established in Copenhagen, Denmark.

The girls' school in Berlin was opened by Moshe Hirsch Bock (1781–1816), a teacher from Poland, and his published manifesto proclaimed that he was educating girls to be good wives, housewives, and mothers. The Jewish education in Bock's school appears to have been minimal; it concentrated on reading, writing, math, history, and home economics and attracted the daughters of Berlin's wealthy Jews.[15] In 1814 Bock published a second edition of his "catechism," the kind of book that was beginning to be used for boys' confirmation ceremonies. In the introduction he indicates that the book was used for services for the girls in his school on Shabbat and at other times.[16]

In 1806 David Frankel and Joseph Wolf founded the German-language journal *Sulamith* to promote Jewish religious Reform ideas and to gather and present news from around the country. The editors chose a woman's name for the title and pictured a woman on the cover of each issue. Clearly, one of their aims was to promote the education and the rights of Jewish women.[17] The very first surviving account of a synagogue confirmation, which describes a ceremony for a boy at the synagogue in Kassel, Westphalia, in 1810, makes it clear that the intention was to include girls in the ceremony at some point in the future.[18] But why were girls not included in the confirmation ceremony right from the start? Perhaps there was a fear of opposition. Confirmation was seen in some circles as replacing the traditional bar mitzvah with a Christian-type ceremony. Including girls would undoubtedly have provoked even greater objections.[19]

Israel Jacobson founded a Reform synagogue in his own home in Berlin in 1815, which soon came to the attention of the government. The Prussian king Frederick William III was very intolerant of new groups holding services outside the established synagogue and ordered the new synagogue to be closed. But in 1817 the main Berlin synagogue closed for repairs, and in August of that year services in German began in a converted room at the most glamorous house in Berlin, the palatial residence of Amalie and Jacob Herz Beer,[20] where the new style particularly appealed to the younger and wealthier sections of the Jewish community. Christian visitors also attended and participated in services.[21] The reception rooms in the Beers' house were decorated with gold columns and curtains embroidered with golden crowns. They were used as a salon for the Beers' non-Jewish friends during the week and as a synagogue for their Jewish friends on Shabbat. Amalie Beer made her way as a high-society hostess, pushing forward the boundaries of what was possible for an openly Jewish woman. When in 1816 she was awarded the Queen Louise award, the king himself made sure that it was in the shape of a medal rather than the traditional cross.[22]

THE FIRST CEREMONY FOR GIRLS

It was at the "Beer Temple," as it came to be known, that Eduard Kley led the very first synagogue coming-of-age ceremony for Jewish girls that September:

> Dr. Kley from Hamburg, the director of the new Jewish Free School there, blessed two daughters of Jewish parents (Demoiselle Bernsdorf and Demoiselle Bevern) in the splendid Beer Temple here in an extremely ceremonial manner. A gathering of 400 people, as many as the temple could accommodate, dissolved—so to speak—into tears. All of those present were uplifted by the excellent sermon of this good speaker and by this solemn Blessing. The lighted lamps, the two girls, the first in Israel who have been confirmed, having passed their examination with the greatest praise: in short, everything made this one of the most festive and most beautiful celebrations.[23]

Those familiar with Reform confirmation services today will be able to imagine the kind of ceremony that took place on that occasion. What is difficult for us today is to envisage the huge impact it had on the community at the time. Even allowing for some non-Jewish guests, this ceremony attracted around 10 percent of the total Jewish population of Berlin.[24] The new ceremony reflected the increasing importance now attached to a Jewish education for girls. Its popularity encouraged further changes in Jewish practice. Later in 1817, Eduard Kley published a German Jewish prayer book that left out the traditional blessing in which a man thanks God "who has not made me a woman."[25]

The new ceremony came to the attention of the king through an article in a St. Petersburg newspaper that claimed, quite erroneously, that he had approved the new ritual. The king's anger at this report only died down when he was assured that the Beer Temple was a temporary arrangement that would continue only until repairs to the real synagogue were complete. After that, he insisted, "the religious services of the Jews will be held nowhere else in Berlin but in the synagogue, and according to the traditional rite without the admixture of arbitrary innovations."[26] Eventually, the Beer Temple was allowed to continue until 1823, but the king became increasingly concerned about Christians attending its events.

The New Ceremony Spreads Quickly

Although it was not possible to hold further services for girls in Berlin, the concept spread rapidly to other towns and then to other countries. Confirmation ceremonies for girls were held in Hamburg (1818 by Eduard Kley), Dessau (1821), and Munich (1831).[27] Reporting the happy event in Hamburg, the journal *Sulamith* stated extravagantly: "The girl confirmands were on this day the most fortunate mortals on earth. This was one of the most beautiful festivals that mankind and Judaism could celebrate."[28] One recent study of the period notes that at that time in Germany women were thought to represent beauty and morality, progress and peace, purity and transcendence, all of them values that Reform Jews associated with their religion. It is therefore not surprising that a white-clad girl who proclaimed her faithfulness to Judaism in front of an enchanted congregation was viewed in such rapturous terms.[29]

But those who put on these ceremonies knew that this was just the beginning of a much longer struggle for women's equality. It became common for the male preachers to call for a more equal role of women in Judaism. These calls were taken up in a report presented by David Einhorn (1809–79) at the Rabbinical Conference in Breslau in 1846.[30] In the nineteenth century it was only such confirmation ceremonies that brought women out of the upstairs gallery or the women's section. But this situation was eventually to change. It came to be seen as illogical and unfair to allow girls to take part in a synagogue service only once in their lives.[31]

In France such events were known as *"initiation religieuse,"* and the first recorded ceremony for girls took place in Bordeaux in 1842. A contemporary Jewish journal devotes four pages to a description of the scene, written by the girls' teacher. A course of instruction for young Jewish girls had been established in 1841, with the ceremony taking place at noon on June 2 of the following year in the presence of local notables, leaders of other faith groups, and the consul from Hamburg. The group of thirty girls was addressed by the rabbi, one girl recited a prayer, and each one read a profession of faith in turn. In the synagogue hall afterward, certificates were given out, and further speeches were delivered. A separate ceremony for boys took place two days later.[32]

In Catholic France and in Italy girls wore white dresses for the ceremony, a tradition that has endured to the present time in Europe and the United States. A recent publication on bat mitzvah around the world is illustrated with photographs, many of which show girls wearing white dresses, occasionally with white hair bands, veils, or gloves and sometimes holding white flowers.[33]

It seems clear that the white costume was originally adopted in France and Italy because Christian girls wore white for their confirmation. But there is also another link, in the frequent association of confirmation with Shavuot. This Jewish festival celebrates the Revelation at Sinai and is parallel to the Christian feast of Revelation, known as Pentecost, often in English called "Whitsun," a name that means "White Sunday." The name was first given to the festival in England in 1549 and probably refers to the white and pure garments of candidates for baptism. In the Torah the people are told to wash their clothes before the Revelation at Sinai, which has been taken to mean they were in a state of purity.[34]

To this day processions and gatherings held for Shavuot across Israel often feature girls and women wearing white and sometimes boys as well. Around the world Jewish day schools often encourage students to wear white at this season. Occasionally, objections have been raised to the wearing of white, such as one offered by Rev. Michael Leigh, assistant minister at West London Synagogue from 1959: "I would not recommend the wearing of white by girls at this service in order to stress the simplicity of the service, the Jewish and non-Christian nature of the ceremony. Girls should wear rather a plain suit or dress."[35]

The first girls' ceremony in Italy was led by Rabbi Joseph Cameo in an Orthodox Synagogue at Verona on the first day of Passover 1844:

> Naturally, before being received at the temple the young girls must have studied Hebrew, and have a knowledge of history and sacred catechism, so that not everything is reduced to a single happy and moving day of celebration. For the record—the white dresses and white veils symbolising the purity of those souls still unaware of life, the temple festively lit and decorated with flowers, the passing of the crowds, their reception and accompaniment by the priests—all this is inextricably linked for the girls to their memory of the knowledge they have learned, and of the new and serious ideas, which their minds must hold. And since their imagination and their hearts are

so profoundly touched, it is so much more difficult for those ideas and knowledge to be lost. And not even time, which erases so many things, can wipe from their young minds the sweet impressions they experienced.[36]

Even allowing for the extravagant language and the fact that this vague description of what actually happened was published nearly sixty years later and may reflect the impressions of a non-Jewish visitor, it is quite clear that what is being described here is not, as it has been called, a bat mitzvah in the sense of an individual ceremony but, rather, a group confirmation ceremony for girls.[37]

It has been suggested that the modernizers of the day were instigating a feminist mini-revolution, motivated partly by a desire to imitate the popular Christian ceremonies of "first communion."[38] This suggestion provides an explanation for Mordecai Kaplan's 1922 account that the girls he saw in an Orthodox synagogue in Italy were described as "entering minyan." *Bar mitzvah* may have been considered parallel to Christian confirmation, and consequently *bat minian* for a girl could be regarded as parallel to first communion, marking the occasion when she is now able to participate fully.[39]

Elsewhere boys and girls shared the ceremony. A report from Paris (1852) describes the ceremony in an Orthodox synagogue.[40] In London, David Woolf Marks, the first rabbi of West London Synagogue (Reform), founded in 1840, announced at the opening of the new building in January 1842 that confirmation would be introduced for both boys and girls at the age of thirteen.[41] Women's participation in services was now a live issue everywhere. In the Reform congregation in Berlin in 1845, the women's gallery was made redundant, and men and women henceforth sat separately on the ground floor.[42]

Rabbi Adolf Jellinek introduced confirmation to Leipzig, Saxony, in the 1840s. He was a traditionally minded reformer, advocating a commitment to the 613 commandments as part of the ceremony. In a confirmation prayer in the Berliner Synagogue, Leipzig, on the second day of Shavuot, on Saturday, May 22, 1847, he used the phrase *Pflichtbare Tochter der Synagoge* (a dutiful daughter of the synagogue), which is currently the earliest known reference to a "bat mitzvah" girl using the modern terminology.[43] Parallel to the term *bar mitzvah*, the term *bat mitzvah* was used in the Talmud to mean a woman who had a responsibility to carry out a specific command. But not until this point had it been linked to a coming-of-age ceremony.

Jellinek moved on to Vienna, where he led annual confirmation ceremonies for boys and girls, but later he came to think that the ceremony was no longer improving educational opportunities for Jewish girls. At Shavuot 1864 he complained that the community and parents did not take it seriously enough. Instead of "ceremonies in which many girls marched past us in the synagogue," it would be better, he suggested, to educate Jewish girls at home.[44] The first preacher known to use the modern term *bat mitzvah* wanted something deeper than a display and processions.

At the first confirmation service held in Manchester, England, in 1852, also in an Orthodox synagogue, the Hungarian rabbi Solomon Schiller-Szinessy addressed himself to the eight girls and one boy taking part in the ceremony with these words:

> The Bar-Mitzwah ceremony, observed with respect to the male child, has dwindled to an empty form; and on the other hand, the female part of the Jewish community have demanded their full share in the employment of life, and have gained it. Now, with regard to the female part especially . . . how are they to be interested in the Jewish religion, and inspired with love for it, if not by a thorough religious instruction, at the close of which stands confirmation?[45]

The implication here is that if girls were receiving a secular education, they must be educated Jewishly too in order to be kept involved in the community. Such arguments are commonplace in our time and have led to a revolution in Torah learning among Orthodox women, but here we find similar sentiments from the mid-nineteenth century. Schiller-Szinessy was not the only British Orthodox minister to approve of Torah learning for girls; indeed, Chief Rabbi Nathan Marcus Adler is said to have given his approval to separate boys' and girls' ceremonies held at Bayswater Synagogue, London, beginning in 1864.[46]

THE BAT MITZVAH PARTY

There is no known evidence from this time of parties accompanying the celebrations, but it was certainly discussed. The earliest known mention is from Rabbi Avraham Musafiyah (Jerusalem 1760–Split 1837), who wrote that there was absolutely no difference between making a party for a boy at thirteen years old and a girl at twelve. Both can be considered a *se'udat mitzvah*, a "meal of obligation": "And this is a correct custom, and this is the way they make a *se'udat mitzvah* and a day of joy in the cities of France and other towns for a boy and also for a girl, and the practical implication is that if you are invited, you should go."[47]

Beyond this statement we have no evidence of girls celebrating in France during this time. Similar remarks were made by the Rabbi Yosef Hayyim of Baghdad (1834–1909), known as the Ben Ish Hai, after the title of his popular book of Jewish law. What he had to say is particularly important because he described having celebrated his own daughter's coming of age. His book was based on lectures he gave in the 1860s and is arranged in the form of commentaries on the week's Torah portion. In the first volume his lecture on *Re'eh* (a section of the Book of Deuteronomy) deals with blessings said on happy occasions, including bar mitzvah. After discussing the boy's ceremony, he noted:

> And also for a girl, on the day when she becomes obligated to per-
> form commandments, even though it is not the custom to make a
> special meal for her, even so it is a joyful day for her and she dresses
> in her Sabbath clothes, and if she is pious, she dresses in new clothes
> so she can say the blessing for happy occasions, and has in mind that
> she is at the gateway to the yoke of the commandments, and there
> are those who have the custom of making a party for her every year
> on the day of her birth, and this is a beautiful ritual and is the cus-
> tom in our house.[48]

Many commentators have mentioned this passage as an important precedent for an individual bat mitzvah,[49] but there is no mention of a synagogue ceremony of any kind here. It is partly about the permissibility of
birthday parties but adds that this particular birthday should be a special
one, a demarcation time for each individual girl. The Ben Ish Hai's remarks
are important because they are frequently cited as a precedent among
Orthodox Jews seeking to justify a social celebration for bat mitzvah.

Girls' ceremonies spread across Europe in the nineteenth century, moving to Serbia and Croatia, among other places, where they continued until
1941 at the festival of Shavuot. A recent study of the subject states: "There
are similar descriptions from different cities of girls wearing white dresses
and white gloves, holding white roses, which they laid in front of the Torah,

or baskets full of flowers, which they would scatter at the entrance to the synagogue. The languages in which the girls recited were Hebrew and Croatian, or other ones used locally, like Hungarian or Italian."[50]

Surprisingly, there is an isolated contemporary report of girls celebrating in Algeria in the 1850s,[51] but such a liberal attitude of traditional Sephardic communities did not continue. There have been no reports within living memory of bat mitzvah in Algeria, and Jewish girls' education has been much neglected there.[52] Only with the emigration of most Algerian Jews to France in the 1960s did opportunities once again develop for Algerian Jewish girls to celebrate their coming of age.

Oral history interviews have given us many reports of girls celebrating bat mitzvah across Eastern Europe, from Russian and Ukraine to Greece and the Balkans, in the 1920s and 1930s. Most of the interviews give few details and do not make clear if these were individual ceremonies or group ceremonies, but a few mention being part of a small group of girls. The transcribed interviews also do not make clear if the ceremonies were called "bat mitzvah" at the time. It is quite likely that the term was used because it was the way of describing such an event at the start of the twenty-first century, at the time when the interviews were made. Many reported that the girls were twelve years old; a few of the interviewees stated that they had bat mitzvah at thirteen or were part of a group of girls of different ages, especially during World War II, when the events were much more difficult to organize.[53]

One report sounds as if it was probably about an individual ceremony; there is certainly a surviving individual portrait photo. Vera Bluhm celebrated her bat mitzvah at the age of thirteen in Osijek (now part of Croatia) in 1930. The service was presided over by a rabbi named Dr. Ungar. Vera came from an Orthodox family and became an active Zionist as a teenager. She managed to survive the war in Belgrade, but her parents and grandparents perished in Auschwitz.[54]

The *initiation religieuse* in France formed the model for similar ceremonies held in Alexandria, Egypt, by Rabbi Eliahu Hazan (1846–1908). Like the first confirmation ceremonies held in Germany a century earlier, the ceremonies in Egypt were a form of school graduation. The *École des Filles* (girls' school) of the Alliance Israelite Universelle opened in 1900 for fifty-six Jewish girls aged from six to eleven, based entirely on a European model of Jewish education. The headmistress, Madame Rachel Danon, agreed with Hazan that the ceremony would attract students to the school. Hazan was motivated by the observation that the existing supplementary schools were not teaching Hebrew or Jewish studies properly to girls. Using the precise prayers from the ceremonies then held in Paris, the first *initiation* in Alexandria took place in 1901.[55] The girls were aged ten to eleven, and each one had to have a specially fitted white dress, veil, and pair of gloves. Despite the resulting publicity, the wealthier families whom Madame Danon and Rabbi Hazan wanted to attract preferred private tuition or the non-Jewish independent schools. Nevertheless, the annual ceremonies continued. Rabbi David Prato, speaking at the girls' *initiation* in 1929, complained that "a few laudable exceptions notwithstanding, the upper class Jewish families keep their distance and the ceremony is attended almost exclusively by the pupils of the communal school, *le figlie del popolo*."[56]

The ceremonies continued at least until the 1950s, when most Jews left for Israel. Racheline Barda celebrated her "communion," as it was called, with a group of forty girls at the Eliahou Navi synagogue in Alexandria in 1951. She recalled that the white dress and veil allowed rich and poor girls to take part without singling out those from disadvantaged backgrounds. Even then, fifty years after the first ceremony, most of the girls went to the communal school of the time, in those days L'École Aghion. After the Sunday morning ceremony there was a communal luncheon for family and guests.[57]

Toward the end of the nineteenth century, as more Jews became less observant, many middle-class Jewish women in both Europe and America retained an allegiance to religious observance, even when the men had abandoned it. Isaac Mayer Wise was the first to introduce mixed seating for men and women, in Albany, New York, in October 1851.[58] As the practice spread, it became more and more popular for women to attend services. A newspaper article in Chicago in 1897 asserted that "year in and year out, for many long years . . . efforts in sermons and lectures have been prepared for and delivered to congregational audiences composed almost exclusively of women."[59]

Against this background it is not surprising to note that at this time, although confirmation services were generally held for boys and girls together, often there were more girls taking part than boys. Wise made a particular effort to promote confirmation for girls, writing that the old "oriental notions," which confined women to the home, "have been extinguished by the onward march of western civilisation, and therefore that class of our people who progress with the time consider it the duty of the Synagogue to extend its benevolent influence over the daughters of Israel, as well as the sons. The act of confirmation is for the young of both sexes."[60]

There is no doubt that such sentiments had huge support across the Jewish world, as surviving press columns and letters show. At Hanukkah 1906 Francis Lyon Cohen, in his confirmation address to his congregation in Sydney, Australia, traced the prevalence of mixed marriages to the inadequate religious training of the young and argued that efforts should be concentrated especially on rearing a generation of pious and God-fearing women.[61]

In Europe, too, there were increased moves toward women's participation, although men and women still sat separately. Writing forty years after Isaac Mayer Wise, Meir Friedmann (Vienna, 1831–1908), known as Ish Shalom, was willing to go a step further than holding a group confirmation for girls. He wrote in 1893 of his distaste for that ceremony:

> Wouldn't it be better to call up our girls as *Bar Mitzvah* to the Torah exactly like the boys? The impression and the effect will definitely be greater . . . As far as I'm concerned, calling women to the Torah today will not offend. On the contrary, Jewish domestic and community life will gain extraordinarily if the women will be deemed worthy of this religious practice. It goes without saying that one must erect a covered staircase directly from the women's gallery to the *bimah*, so that those called up can ascend and descend without being seen.[62]

The suggestion of having a "covered staircase" either at the front or the center of a synagogue sounds anything but practical, and there is no evidence that this ever happened.

Against this background it is not surprising that a real bat mitzvah celebration was reported as having taken place in Lvov, Galicia, in 1902. Rabbi Yehezkel Caro held the celebration in his Reform community. It became notorious because Caro was an outspoken anti-Zionist, and the local Zionists gathered outside the synagogue to protest. Historians disagree about exactly what happened inside the hall, but it certainly caused a stir and started a debate about whether such a ceremony should be permitted.[63]

In 2010 a special exhibition was mounted at the orthodox Great Synagogue, Sydney, Australia, marking one hundred years of bat mitzvah in the synagogue. The ceremony in 1910 was a group celebration for six girls and followed earlier confirmation ceremonies that had been held for mixed groups. These earlier ceremonies were said to have been introduced to the congregation by the minister Alexander Barnard Davis (1828–1913), but the reports I have seen date from after his retirement.[64]

In the 1890s in America another important milestone was reached, when some girls began to read the Ten Commandments from a Torah scroll at their confirmation.[65] At this time in the United States confirmation was very widely practiced and marked an important stage in the lives of adolescent Jewish girls even for those from nonobservant families. Surviving diaries show how much the ceremony meant to many girls, including Irma Levy, who wrote: "My confirmation was the tremendous event of my youth. For a while I felt an acute regret that I was not a man, and therefore could not become a rabbi. I felt almost suffocated with wonder and joy at the moment when, before the open ark, my rabbi placed his hands on my head and blessed me. To myself I vowed that my life would be forever dedicated to my people."[66]

CRITICISMS OF THE GROUP CEREMONIES

Confirmation nevertheless began to be criticized by educators. New educational theories of adolescence stressed the importance of maintaining interest throughout the teenage years—which for religious education meant even beyond confirmation. There is evidence that around the start of the twentieth century confirmation began to be treated as a social occasion and became less successful in educational terms. In 1908, for example, the notices published in Philadelphia's *Jewish Exponent* consisted of invitations to open houses to celebrate socially, with no report of the synagogue service. By 1919 even the program produced by the synagogue itself included the addresses and "at home" times of the students.[67] Educators criticized the preparatory classes, which they saw as teaching for a test or ceremony rather than for a real religious commitment. The pioneer Zionist feminist Henrietta Szold wrote in 1903: "The confirmation service for girls . . . fell far short of fulfilling the hopes it had aroused . . . It failed to stimulate the Jewish development of women because it was an assertion of the principle of female education in theory only. In practice it put up with a minimum of superficial knowledge and an apology for Jewish training."[68]

The decline of these group ceremonies was to lead to renewed demands for a girl to have her own individual bat mitzvah. Henrietta Szold herself helped to found an egalitarian prayer group in the 1920s, after her move to

Palestine.[69] Ida Blum (b. 1908), who was brought up in Calumet, Michigan, recalled later in life that she had been tutored by her father and read a section from the scroll at her bat mitzvah. This may well have been before Judith Kaplan's celebration in March 1922.[70] Speaking to the 1921 convention of the United Synagogue of America, Rabbi Abraham Hershman argued for the introduction of equality for girls in the form of "a ceremony invested with dignity and beauty." Rabbi Louis Fineberg disagreed. Unless girls were going to take on wearing tallit and tefillin like the boys, it would be a hollow ceremony.[71]

In England at this time feminists were much more concerned about those girls growing up without any Jewish education at all. The Union of Jewish Women supported the creation of confirmation classes and ceremonies and expressed satisfaction as the practice gained in popularity.[72]

There is evidence that individual bat mitzvah ceremonies took place in Berlin before World War II. The moderate rabbi Dr. Max Weyl is said to have introduced bat mitzvah after his appointment to the Orthodox Rykestrasse Synagogue in 1917.[73] It has not yet been discovered whether or not such ceremonies antedated Judith Kaplan's 1922 ceremony in New York. But such ceremonies certainly did take place in Berlin in the 1930s, even after the Nazis came to power in 1933, when for many of the participants the moment provided one of the last vivid and happy memories in an otherwise very dark time.[74]

Charlotte Salomon (1917–43), the well-known Jewish artist, was born in Berlin. Lotte's aunt Charlotte Grunwald had committed suicide in 1913 at the age of eighteen. In the winter of 1925–26 the young Lotte's mother, Fränze Salomon, did the same, throwing herself out of the window. Over five thousand people died of suicide in Berlin between 1925 and 1927. Lotte's father remarried in 1930, to the singer Paula Lindberg, an experience that changed young Charlotte's life completely:

Fränze Salomon's holy day had been Christmas, when she sat at the piano leading "Silent Night." Her fantasies featured angels and the bearded God of folk Christianity. Fränze's parents were as German as could be, and practiced nothing Jewish, a relative recalled; they loyally chanted "Deutschland, Deutschland, über Alles" up through 1932.

But when Paula Salomon-Lindberg took over Lotte's home in 1930, things changed: To be Jewish meant to act it. She performed at the B'nai B'rith Lodge, a Jewish fraternal order which she and Albert supported for years. "Friday nights we lit Sabbath candles, Saturday morning and festival days we went to synagogue. Usually Albert had his work, but Lotte went along with me." As Paula told it, every year people asked Rabbi Leo Baeck, the leader of Progressive Judaism in Berlin, "Where do you have a seat for Yom Kippur?" "Wherever Paula's singing Kol Nidre, of course,"—the Jews' holiest prayer. Under Paula's influence Lotte even had a bat mitzvah, a modern ceremony in German, with her reading parts in Hebrew and writing her own speech.[75]

More details of ceremonies held for girls during the Nazi era in Berlin have been rediscovered by searches of the video archives of the Shoah Foundation Institute. Alice Fink (née Redlich), interviewed in Chicago in 1996, talked about her bat mitzvah in Berlin in 1936. In her interview in English she says she was able to study in "what you would call" a joint bar and bat mitzvah class with Rabbi Manfred Swarsensky at the New Synagogue on Prinzregentstrasse. In an unconnected interview Rabbi Swarsensky recalled that this was the last synagogue to be built in Germany before the Shoah and the only synagogue in Berlin where men and women sat together.

Alice later transferred to a group class at the Fasanenstrasse Synagogue, studying along with others for confirmation at Shavuot. But in the meantime her younger brother had his bar mitzvah, and it was decided that Alice would be allowed to come up to the *bimah* (the platform in the synagogue) as well. It was the first time that a woman had come up to the *bimah* in that synagogue. Her original certificate has been found in the Berlin archives, with the word *Knabe* (boy) crossed out by hand and replaced by *Mädchen* (girl). The certificate shows that she was called up to the reading of the Torah. She did not read from the scroll herself, but many of the boys also did not read from the scroll at that time. There is no reason to suppose it was not in all respects an equal ceremony.[76]

Henriette Bergman (née Wahls), interviewed in New York in 1996, talked about the group ceremony she had at the Johannisstrasse Synagogue in Berlin in 1935, led by Rabbi Dr. Benno Gottschalk. In the interview she called the service a bat mitzvah, but that was not the term used at the time—it would have been called an "*Einsegnung*" (a blessing).[77] Many German native speakers have used the term *bat mitzvah* when reminiscing in English or in Hebrew about their youth in Germany, but there is no documentary evidence that this term was the one originally used.

These stories told by survivors are a reminder that right up to the time of the final destruction by the Nazis, Jews were not afraid to celebrate and even to innovate. A poignant photo from Subotica in Serbia shows a group of ten girls celebrating as a group in May 1944, a month after the entire Jewish community had been moved to a ghetto. A few days later all of the girls were transported to Auschwitz.[78]

At the same time that a dark shadow was falling across Europe, the first regular ceremonies for individual girls were being held in the United States. The first individual bat mitzvah in an American Reform synagogue was at the Chicago Temple in 1931. A survey by the Rabbinical Assembly in 1932 discovered that 6 out of 110 Conservative rabbis in the United States had introduced bat mitzvah, and 2 others planned to incorporate it into Friday night services. Speaking to the Rabbinical Assembly convention that year, Rabbi Morris Silverman found it necessary to explain to the assembled rabbis precisely what a bat mitzvah was. He described the ceremony of his day: "The girl, upon reaching the age of 12 or 13, is called up to the pulpit after the *Haftara,* reads in Hebrew and English the prayer 'Make pleasant we therefore beseech Thee, etc.,' then reads a portion of the Bible in Hebrew and English, which is some congregations is followed by a brief original address which the *Bas Mitzvah* has written herself."[79] Like Judith Kaplan's bat mitzvah in 1922, this was a specially devised ceremony for girls, not the same as the boys' call to the Torah such as Alice Redlich had experienced in Berlin in 1936.

Although many girls continued to celebrate in small groups, by 1948 some form of individual bat mitzvah ceremony was held in about one-third of American Conservative congregations and by 1953 in roughly that number of Reform congregations. Unusually, the Orthodox rabbi Jerome Tov Feinstein allowed individual bat mitzvah ceremonies at Anshe Emes in Brooklyn in 1944. These services were held on a Friday night and included the lighting of Shabbat candles and the girl answering questions about what she had learned.[80]

WOMEN ARE CALLED TO THE TORAH

In 1955 the Rabbinical Assembly's Committee on Jewish Law decided to permit women to be called to the Torah. By the 1960s bat mitzvah had become a regular feature within the Conservative movement. Although the ceremony was often restricted to Friday evenings, some congregations allowed the bat mitzvah to recite the haftarah reading for the following morning.[81] Clearly, World War II increased women's emancipation and moves toward equality.

The arrival of a bat mitzvah into a congregation often raised more general issues of women's participation in the service. Sherry Rosen recalled the day she became the first girl to be bat mitzvah in Wheeling, West Virginia, in 1960: "Immediately after that occasion everything snapped back, and a woman would be invited up to the *bimah* only to light the candles, and maybe even say the blessings only in English."[82] Her experience illustrates the reluctance by community leaders to make the girls' ceremony equal to the boys: once women had enjoyed a taste of being full participants, they did not want to be forced back into a minor role. A particular dilemma was by now apparent in the American Conservative movement: whereas for a boy the bar mitzvah marked the beginning of his participation in the service, for a girl the bat mitzvah marked both the beginning and the end of hers.[83]

In the American Reform movement 25 percent of congregations had introduced bat mitzvah by 1950. Yet many Reform rabbis preferred to promote the group confirmations and were not keen to offer individual ceremonies for girls. Rabbi Israel Bettan, chair of the Rabbis' Responsa Committee, objected to *both* bar mitzvah and bat mitzvah in 1954, writing that "two figments do not make one fact."[84] Even in 1962 Rabbi Harold Silver was complaining about the new ceremony that "impels many of us, even against our wishes, to learn how to live self-respectingly and profitably with this new phenomenon in modern Jewish life . . . Of all the rabbis whom I contacted about Bas Mitzvah, only *one* openly and enthusiastically approved of the ritual."[85]

The generation of Reform rabbis who objected were equally opposed to bar mitzvah for boys, which they regarded as an empty ritual accompanied by unnecessarily lavish parties and followed by the boy's unwelcome absence from classes designed to prepare him for confirmation. In the early 1960s, however, many felt unable to resist parents' demands for boys' ceremonies as easily as they could those for the girls'. "Just when the rabbis believe that they have stemmed the tide somewhat in our movement today regarding the toning down of these wild Bar Mitzvah celebrations," wrote Silver, "the grim spectre of having to wage religious battle all over again with parents and their *daughters* is just more than the average rabbinical heart can take."[86]

Yet Silver and his colleagues were unable to stem the demand from parents, and bat mitzvah became common practice in American Reform beginning in the 1970s. The ordination of America's first woman rabbi, Sally Priesand, in 1972 was an inspiration to many Jewish women and gave a boost to the ceremony. Even in the 1970s, the ritual in Conservative congregations was often not a precise parallel of the bar mitzvah. It was often held at Friday night services, without a scroll being read, while boys' services were held on Saturday mornings. In the 1980s to see a woman read Torah in a Conservative synagogue was by no means an everyday occurrence.[87] By 1996, however, 80 percent of Conservative synagogues in the United States offered equal ceremonies and education for boys and girls.[88]

Orthodox communities had been among the pioneers for girls' ceremonies in the mid-nineteenth century. But gradually, Reform communities across Europe and elsewhere took up the idea. By the turn of the century the group ceremonies for girls were in decline in central Europe but were taking place elsewhere. From 1899 onward such services were often known as "girls' consecration," either because the term *confirmation was* at this time often used as an English translation of *bar mitzvah* or because *confirmation* had become firmly associated with Reform congregations.[89]

Rev. Dr. David Wasserzug held the first "consecration" for a group of girls (who had passed an examination in Jewish history and Hebrew) at the Johannesburg New Congregation in May 1899.[90] In England a conference of the Union of Jewish Women voted in February 1922 to promote the idea of classes leading to consecration ceremonies and began to lobby the (Orthodox) United Synagogue in London. Seven London congregations agreed to start classes, and by 1924 classes for girls were also being held at Cardiff, Hull, and Manchester; most classes were for girls between thirteen and sixteen years old. Chief Rabbi Joseph Hertz (1872–1946) became an enthusiastic advocate for such plans, which he saw as a means to boost educational standards for Jewish girls.[91]

In 1925 the Great Synagogue, London, began to hold consecration services annually at Hanukkah for groups of girls from the nearby Jews' Free School. The address and consecration prayer at the first service were given by Chief Rabbi Hertz.[92] The girls, aged twelve,[93] were dressed in white for the ceremony. The first time this celebration was reported in the school magazine, the editor was clearly not quite sure what to call it and referred to it as "Girls' Bar Mitzvah." "If *Bar Mitzvah*," he asked, "is such a great landmark in a boy's life, why should not his sister have an equal privilege?"[94] By the following year there was a set syllabus and a written examination for the consecration class, which was a voluntary class held after school every Monday. The girls seem to have had little to do in the service, other than to sit at the front and to recite (presumably in unison) a consecration prayer.[95]

These services were big events, with up to a thousand children from the school attending, while parents and relatives sat upstairs. They continued until the outbreak of World War II. A later date had to be chosen in January 1930 because Hanukkah had fallen during the school holidays. Dayan Dr. Feldman told the fourteen girls who took part to mold their future on "the Spirit of Justice, Friendship and Simplicity," excellent qualities that "could easily be remembered as their initials formed the name by which our famous school is known."[96]

These new ceremonies spread far beyond the British United Synagogue, as Orthodox synagogues across the English-speaking world came under pressure from parents to introduce group ceremonies for girls. Israel Levinthal, the first rabbi of the Brooklyn Jewish Center, introduced a girls' group consecration ceremony there in 1936.[97] Certificates were handed out on Shabbat to four girls who had completed a course of study at the Cape Town Hebrew Congregation in 1940.[98] Beginning in 1950, similar ceremonies were held on the Sunday before Shavuot at the Sephardic synagogue at Lauderdale Road in London.[99]

Starting in the 1970s, these ceremonies were often given the name *bat chayil* (daughter of worth). The name was based on the biblical phrase *eshet chayil* (woman of worth) from the Book of Proverbs, a well-known passage that emphasizes the woman's traditional role within the home.[100] Often at Orthodox ceremonies, the girls were asked to explain the duties of a Jewish wife and mother, and in this way such an obvious borrowing from Reform and Conservative Judaism was disguised. The *bat chayil* was normally held for a group of girls at the age of twelve on a Sunday afternoon, completely separate from the normal prayer services at which men and women sat separately. Following the model set in London in the 1920s, such services became more and more elaborate, perhaps including a cantor or a choir or a special theme. Reform communities also continued to hold group ceremonies for girls, sometimes using the term *benot mitzvah* for the group.[101]

Some Orthodox authorities adamantly opposed such innovations. Rabbi Moshe Feinstein (1895–1986) wrote first on the subject in 1956. When asked whether the hall in an American Orthodox synagogue could be hired for a bat mitzvah party, he responded that bat mitzvah was a Reform and Conservative innovation and was not permitted. Girls had no obligation to study Torah. If the girl's father wanted a small celebration in his house, that was fine, but it was not to be regarded as a *se'udat mitzvah*—a meal of obligation—but only as an ordinary birthday party. Orthodox premises could not be hired out for the purpose.

Feinstein went on, in the same reply, to talk about a new invention called a "dishwasher" and whether or not it was necessary to have two—one for milk and a separate one for meat. The impression was subtly given that Feinstein considered this question more important than the matter of a bat mitzvah.[102] Within a few years, however, Feinstein modified his view slightly. In 1959 he conceded that it was acceptable to give a kiddush—a reception after the service—in the synagogue, as for any other special birthday. Even a speech might be permitted.[103]

Writing in Israel, Rabbi Ovadiah Yosef (b. 1920) took a very different view, building his Sephardic practice on the view of the Ben Ish Hai. One of Yosef's earliest published books was a commentary on that work. Yosef took a much more positive view both on women's education and bat mitzvah. He wrote that "those who make a festive meal for a bat mitzvah in this generation are acting properly," and he even ruled that the father should say, "Blessed is He who has absolved me of halachic responsibility for this girl," parallel to the blessing given to a son. "Those who oppose celebrations upon girls' coming-of-age," Yosef asserted, "help transgressors to accuse the scholars of Israel of depriving the daughters of Israel and discriminating between boys and girls." Citing many precedents from previous Sephardic rabbis, Yosef wrote: "A girl that is obligated to perform all the mitzvot that women are obligated to perform, this is of great reward and merit, since she is obligated to perform them. Therefore, it is good and appropriate to make the bat mitzvah day like a holiday, and there is a great mitzvah here."[104]

The European halachic authority Rabbi Yehiel Yaakov Weinberg (1884–1996) went even further, arguing that a bat mitzvah is permitted to read from the Torah. Weinberg was a survivor of the Warsaw Ghetto and published his responsa under the title *Seridei Eish* (Remnants of the Fire). He argued that the intelligence of Jewish women must be harnessed to promote Jewish survival: "Those who take the permissive side with respect to a new custom of celebrating a bat mitsvah do so with hearts beating piously to strengthen the religious education of Jewish girls, for in the circumstances of contemporary life, they are in great need of spiritual fortifications and more encouragement as they reach the age of adulthood."[105]

Since 1970 Orthodox communities have gradually allowed individual bat mitzvah ceremonies to take place in synagogue, and these have largely replaced the group *bat chayil* celebrations, a system that lasted for a whole generation after World War II. The most common practice is for a girl to give a *devar Torah*, a brief speech on some aspect of Torah, in the synagogue after the Shabbat morning service has finished, and she is allowed to come down from the women's gallery for this purpose.

Some Orthodox synagogues have now gone further. In 2002 a feminist Orthodox community was founded in Jerusalem by Tova Hartman, becoming the first to allow women, including a bat mitzvah, to read the Torah on behalf of both men and women in the congregation. The congregation insists on both ten men and ten women being present. There are currently twenty-five other congregations in Israel, the United States, and Canada that follow similar practices.[106] More common are women's prayer groups, which allow a bat mitzvah to read from the scroll in the presence of women only and generally without reciting the blessings. There are at least one hundred such groups worldwide. Others, more numerous, follow the practice of the bat mitzvah giving her *devar Torah* at the festive meal. Allied projects include mother-daughter learning or charity programs. *Haredi* (ultraorthodox) communities mark the occasion with a party in the home at which the girl speaks, and Israeli *haredi* schools hold women-only parties.[107] Various Chabad groups run bat mitzvah clubs at venues around the world to allow the girls to prepare as a group. All these Orthodox celebrations take place when the girl is twelve years old.

Bat Mitzvah in Israel

Among secular Israelis a tradition of celebrating a bat mitzvah party without any religious ceremony has developed. It began in the kibbutz, with some following the custom of celebrating at age twelve and giving the girls twelve tasks as a bat mitzvah project. Elsewhere boys and girls would celebrate together at age thirteen. The tradition of having a bat mitzvah party is now firmly established in Israel, and many thousands of girls celebrate each year, nearly all of them today at the age of twelve.

A survey in 2009 showed that 83 percent of Israeli Jews think it is important to celebrate bat mitzvah (the figure for bar mitzvah is 91%).[108] Yet among those who think bar mitzvah is important, most (69%) say it is for religious reasons, but only half (49%) of those who think bat mitzvah is important responded that it is for religious reasons. This reflects the reality that bar mitzvah for boys is likely to be celebrated with a religious ceremony, whereas girls most often just have a party. Most synagogues in Israel do not allow girls to read from the Torah, although there are many that do allow it, and many well-publicized bat mitzvah ceremonies take place in this way, with the girl participating fully just as a boy would do. In 2010, however, one commentator wrote that "while secular Israelis may not view women reading from the Torah as forbidden, they tend to view it as utterly unnecessary."[109]

A 2007 press article reported that ultraorthodox communities discouraged private celebrations for girls and that many other religious girls were still celebrating quietly, without a party. Others might hold a lecture or see a movie or take a nature trek or invite their friends to join them in doing charitable activities.[110] Many Israelis have developed new approaches that combine traditions from their land of origin with those from Israel today. In 1997 Shira Melammed chanted Torah at her Jerusalem bat mitzvah using a Yemeni trope, while her seven-year-old brother chanted each line in the Aramaic translation after her. There was no known precedent for a woman chanting Torah publicly in Yemeni style.[111]

Bat Mitzvah Terror

On January 17, 2002, a terror attack took place at the bat mitzvah party of twelve-year-old Nina Kardashov, held on a Thursday evening in Hadera, Israel. Grenades were thrown into the Armon David wedding hall, and then a man opened fire in the hall. Six people were killed and over thirty injured. The al-Aqsa Martyrs Brigade, a group composed of members from various Palestinian organizations, claimed responsibility for the attack. Nina remembers someone pulling her down to the ground and saying, "I can't let you be killed at your own Bat Mitzvah celebration." The attack not only sent shock waves through the Jewish world, but in particular it caused sadness and reflection for other girls in Israel and around the world who were preparing for their celebrations at the time.[112]

Adult Bat Mitzvah

Judith Kaplan Eisenstein celebrated the seventieth anniversary of her bat mitzvah with a second ceremony at Flushing, New York, in 1992. On this occasion she wore a tallit for the very first time and shared memories about her original ceremony held seventy years earlier.[113] As we have seen, it is doubtful that the 1922 event really was the first bat mitzvah, but there can be little doubt that Judith was the first publicly to celebrate a "second bat mitzvah" on the seventieth anniversary. Just as her first ceremony became instrumental in promoting bat mitzvah for girls, so her second celebration helped to promote the very popular ceremony of adult bat mitzvah. Of course, few other women currently celebrating an adult bat mitzvah had a first ceremony when they were young, so they celebrate as an adult for the first time. Some ceremonies are for women who have converted to Judaism.

Adult bat mitzvah has older roots. At the first confirmation service held on the island of St. Thomas in 1843, there were five women and two boys who took part. In the list of names the report includes a "Mrs. Daniel Woolf" as well as "Misses Miriam and Rebecca Woolf" and "Alexander Woolf," suggesting that a mother took part along with her three children.[114] This is the first recorded instance of an adult Jewish woman celebrating her faith because she had been unable to do so as a child.

But it was really in the late 1960s and early 1970s in the United States that those who had missed out when they were younger began to be encouraged to celebrate. The Central Synagogue of Nassau County, like others, held its first bat mitzvah for a girl in 1949 and the first ceremony for adults in 1979.[115] But many ceremonies from that time took place outside of synagogues—at summer camps for young women and elsewhere. Many community leaders remained unaware in the 1970s of the huge potential for Jewish life of promoting adult bat mitzvah. The pioneer series of the Jewish Renewal movement, the *Second Jewish Catalog* (1976), for example, focused mainly on boys who had missed bar mitzvah when they were younger and failed to mention that most Jewish women had never celebrated. The 1990 American Jewish National Population Survey revealed that adult Jewish women were more than twice as likely as men not to have had any Jewish education.[116] Adult bat mitzvah has helped to remedy that void, with a steady growth in popularity over the last thirty years. Many special curricula and teaching materials have been developed. Soraya Nazarian, who grew up in Iran and now lives in Los Angeles, wrote:

As the education chair of Hadassah of Southern California, I got to together a group of thirty-two women from twenty to ninety years old. Together, we learned all the prayers and how to read the Torah, even though at first some of us didn't know aleph from Chinese. On Rosh Chodesh, the Sunday of Thanksgiving 1997, Southern California Hadassah had a most inspiring bat mitzvah event. The women conducted the full service. Since then, the program has continued, and groups of women conduct a service every year. Some of the women have continued their studies of Torah and Hebrew until this day.[117]

An estimated five hundred synagogues in the United States now offer courses leading to adult bat mitzvah. At the National Hadassah Convention in Miami Beach in 1996, a group of 122 women celebrated together. Adult bat mitzvah is part of a wider movement of adult Jewish study.[118] Interviews with women who have had adult bat mitzvah show it as a highly positive and deeply moving process, as this interview report shows:

> The adult bat mitzvah precipitated a series of decisions and actions that led to Louise developing a new sense of self, a new way of living, and new understanding of her past and her future. The most apparent changes took place in the realm of religious practice. However, a multidimensional complex of social, emotional, intellectual, and spiritual factors influenced these outward behavioral changes. Early in the interview, Louise said, "My level of observance has gone from cursory, I would say, to real serious."[119]

Today adult bat mitzvah ceremonies are held either for individuals or groups, most often on a Shabbat morning but in some Reform congregations on a Friday evening. Most of the women learn to chant the Torah or the haftarah, and many write a personal narrative about their Jewish journey that might become part of a booklet or an individually crafted blessing.[120] As adult bat mitzvah has grown, so has the age of the women participating in it. An article in 1988 describing adult bat mitzvah focused on a woman aged twenty-four.[121] But a report from 2009 describes a group of ten women, all in their nineties, preparing for the ceremony at the synagogue of the Menorah Park senior residence in Cleveland, Ohio. "A self-described 'feminist all my life,' Evelyn Bonder, 90, said she 'always thought girls should have the chance to participate' in something that Conservative, Orthodox and Reform congregations embraced in stages."[122]

The social aspects of adult bat mitzvah have become part of the occasion. One described in 1988 included a Friday night family meal, a buffet lunch in the synagogue after the Shabbat morning service, and a dinner party that evening.[123] Adult bat mitzvah has become a transformative experience, not just in the individual lives of those taking part but for American Reform Jewry as a whole, increasing involvement and supplying future congregation leaders.[124]

BAT MITZVAH AROUND THE WORLD TODAY

A recent study shows that bat mitzvah ceremonies are currently held around the world, including Jewish communities in mid-Africa and China. Today 80 percent of world Jewry lives in the United States or Israel, so inevitably it is their customs that are most influential worldwide. Because bat mitzvah has never had one set form, families, rabbis, and communities are creatively designing services and celebrations that not only reflect the customs and traditions of their families and their geographic roots but also the interests and skills of the individual girl or woman. Many reports from around the world show girls in white dresses and/or wearing a tallit for the ceremony. Havdalah ceremonies on Saturday evening are frequently held around the world at bat mitzvah and often celebrated with singing and dancing. In parts of the world where there is little Jewish education, it is common for a girl to be given a Hebrew name at her bat mitzvah and to talk about the choice of name. The age of twelve is common around the world but by no means universal.

Other customs are linked to specific places. In Kurdistan, before the emigration to Israel, the women sat on carpets, and the rabbi made a speech in Aramaic; at fourteen the girls were usually married. Indian Jews celebrate with the eating of different kinds of fruit and nuts and *melida*, a dessert made with rice flour and sugar. In Thailand local rituals for good weather are included in the ceremony. In Jamaica fresh roses are placed in the ark at the start of the service. In Brussels, Belgium, a collective bat mitzvah is held at the age of twelve at the Great Synagogue, followed by a communal party. In Madrid, Spain, girls gather under a flower-decorated *jupa* (canopy) for a collective ceremony.

A report from Cardiff, Wales, describes a bat mitzvah at age thirteen, followed by Shabbat lunch in a country hotel, accompanied by piano music. The girl went on to celebrate again at age sixteen in a ceremony called "Bat Torah." In Chile bat mitzvah celebrations are popular and are followed by lavish parties, with large orchestras, performers, and dancers. In Guatemala individual ceremonies ended when the Reform temple closed down and were replaced by group ceremonies on a Saturday evening. In Mexico big parties are held in parallel with the non-Jewish girls who celebrate quinceañera (fifteen years), while in Panama's capital city huge group celebrations are organized by a Jewish day school. In Montevideo, Uruguay, each year a group of girls takes part in a musical production with song, video, and dance. In Venezuela the ceremonies are organized by WIZO; as many as one hundred girls take part each year, and up to two thousand invitations are sent. The girls sing and pray together before a communal meal, at which each girl has a separate table for her family.[125]

The history of bat mitzvah is a rapidly advancing area of research, as more and more of the early accounts are being discovered. It is now recognized that Judith Kaplan's ceremony in 1922 did not come out of nowhere. The story of bat mitzvah needs to be set into the context of the whole question of women in the synagogue and the wider story of women's emancipation. It is now the norm, even in Orthodox communities, that a girl's coming of age is not allowed to pass without some kind of ceremony.[126] The old group ceremonies still exist but are in decline; life cycle celebrations have become the principal means by which many Jews identify with their culture and tradition, and it has become fully accepted that girls have a full right to celebrate. The issue of women's equality in the synagogue was important in the mid-nineteenth century, but it has become even more pressing in an era when parenting and education overwhelmingly emphasize the needs and best interests of the child.

In the United States and Canada bat mitzvah has been featured in dozens of novels, films, and TV episodes. In one episode of *Sex and the City* (2000) the character Samantha is hired by a wealthy thirteen-year-old to plan the bat mitzvah of the century. The girl calmly remarks, "We'll be lucky if we can swing this for under a mil." In the less well-known series *Joan of Arcadia*, the teen character Grace Polk is the only child of Sarah and Rabbi Polanski. She refused to be bat mitzvah at the normal age but decides to celebrate later, at age sixteen. To her surprise it means far more than the religious cynic was expecting: "It was a political thing and a daughter of the Rabbi thing . . . one last empty ritual and then I'm out of here. Then, when you handed me the Torah, it hit me. This is a genius way of attacking adulthood, this religion. There's no easy answers in here.

It's basically a book of questions . . . and I hope I'm up for it." Bat mitzvah became an opportunity to explore her own questions and beliefs in the search for her adult identity. As her father put it during the synagogue ceremony: "This Torah is being entrusted to you, Grace, with all it contains: the tradition, the history, the beauty, the pain, the struggle, and most of all . . . the mystery."[127]

CHAPTER SIX

Into the Modern Age

> Traditional Moroccan bar mitzvah celebrations could last nearly a whole week.
> In the midst of World War I Reuben Ginsberg wore a battle-stained tallit for his bar mitzvah.
> Stephen Bernstein celebrated his bar mitzvah in the ruins of Frankfurt, Germany, in 1947, the first bar mitzvah held in the city since before World War II.
> Candle lighting ceremonies and bar mitzvah cakes have been popular since the 1930s.
> The kibbutz movement developed thirteen tasks for the bar mitzvah year.
> Bar mitzvah was in sharp decline until synagogues introduced compulsory standards in the 1920s and 1930s.

In the nineteenth and twentieth centuries the ceremony for boys, like that for girls, developed many different forms and customs, both for geographical and ideological reasons. The principal division was between the Ashkenazic communities, in which the focus of the synagogue celebration was on Shabbat, and Sephardic bar mitzvah, with its focus on a weekday ceremony. The accounts that follow have been selected to give contrasting examples from different times and places, showing a variety of traditions from different corners of the Jewish world and different ideologies.

THE VARIETY OF BAR MITZVAH CELEBRATIONS

The Jews of Yemen had no tradition of bar mitzvah at all prior to their emigration to Israel. Boys were called to the Torah when they were able to say the blessings, sometimes as young as six or seven.[1] The Jews of North Africa (Algeria, Libya, Morocco, and Tunisia) are unlikely to have encountered bar mitzvah before the nineteenth century. An account of a typical ceremony, published in 1858 in a travel book written by Israel Joseph Benjamin II (1818–64), sheds light on the way it was conducted:

> On Monday morning the synagogue is festively decorated, and the Chacham with the teacher goes to the boy's house,[2] and adorns him in Taled and Tephilim, and then he is taken with his schoolfellows in procession with singing and bearing of lights to the synagogue. There, during divine service, as soon as the Pentateuch is brought out, the boy is called forward with his father and some near relation; the Chacham bestows on him his blessing, the boy then delivers his address, and the father and the relations bestow alms on the poor. When the ceremony is concluded, all present congratulate the boy, and accompany him home, where again an entertainment is prepared. The boy, still arrayed in his Taled and Tephilim, then proceeds, accompanied by his school fellows, to all his different female relations to make a visit and each of them undoes a fold of his Tephilim and makes him a present of a piece of money. When all the visits are paid, the boy returns home, lays aside the Tephilim, and in the afternoon takes a walk with his companions, on which occasion all the money he has received is expended. In the evening, all the relations and friends assemble again at the house of the parents of the boy to an entertainment, which lasts until the next morning, and concludes the ceremony.[3]

There are a number of distinctive features presented in this account: the ceremony occurs on a Monday; the blessing is performed by a rabbi; the boy walks with others through the streets in his tallit and tefillin; gifts are given directly to the poor; and the boy visits his female relatives, who do not attend the synagogue. The monetary gifts must have been modest indeed if the boy was really able to spend them all in one afternoon. The gift to the boy may have been a relatively new custom at this time, replacing the older European practice of the host sending small gifts to his guests.

Although some Moroccan Jews living in Israel claim not to have heard of it,[4] there is definite evidence for a Moroccan Jewish tradition of celebrating bar mitzvah at the age of twelve. There are a number of unusual customs, including a hair-cutting ceremony the night before and a ceremony in which henna is applied to the hand of the boy as well as his guests. Charity pledges are made in the synagogue, but some boys go further and pair their ceremony with one for a boy from a family who would otherwise be unable to afford it, meeting all expenses.[5] The main synagogue ceremony takes place on a Monday or Thursday morning and the principal banquet that evening. The father's blessing is said when his son puts on his tefillin for the first time.[6] Following the main Sephardic tradition, the boy delivers his speech, known as a "darush," in the synagogue, not at the party. Some more elaborate ceremonies would involve a gathering with a *darush* on the previous Saturday night and perhaps another one on the Sunday or Wednesday evening. This means in effect that the celebrations could extend for nearly a whole week.[7]

In some parts of the world bar mitzvah has been publicly celebrated in the streets. Western traditions are familiar with dancing at a bar mitzvah party, but in Kurdistan there was a custom of leading the boy through the streets to the synagogue, accompanied by dancing and the music of the local instruments, *zola* and *durna*. Non-Jewish musicians were hired to play these instruments on Shabbat.[8] The Kurdistani Jewish community took their customs with them to Israel but, like many other groups, found their traditions overtaken by the cultural norms of their new host society. The musical *Ana Kurdi* (1983) tells the story of an Israeli boy who asks his grandfather how bar mitzvah was celebrated in Kurdistan. To the dismay of his parents, he asks them for a Kurdish celebration instead of the modern Israeli-style party they were planning. The musical erupts into a colorful display of traditional Kurdish costumes, music, and food.[9]

A TRADITION WITH MANY VARIATIONS

There is a common Sephardic custom practiced around the world of having the main bar mitzvah celebration take place before the boy is thirteen. In Jerusalem a few families purchase tefillin for a boy of ten, but typically it happens a few months before the boy turns thirteen. This custom is called "Yom HaTefillin" (the day of tefillin), and parties are held then. The day after the thirteenth birthday is known as "Yom Hashlamat HaMinyan," the day when the boy can complete the quorum of ten in the synagogue. Wealthy families may hold a second party then.[10]

In Western Europe the boy's mother is occasionally described as having an important role. The Portuguese Synagogue in Amsterdam has preserved an unusual custom of the boy ascending the stairs to the women's gallery and receiving a blessing from his mother after he has read his haftarah. The origin of this custom is unknown.[11] *Alexander's Hebrew Ritual*, a sympathetic portrayal of Ashkenazic Jewish practice published in London in 1819, describes the bar mitzvah boy being "called up to the Law that is read on the altar on the Sabbath-day" and that "the boy's father or mother, or his nearest relation, gives a treat on the occasion." The mention of the mother as a possible host of the party is unusual.[12]

Ashkenazic bar mitzvah has a tradition focused around a celebration on Shabbat, but a weekday tefillin ceremony has also been an important part. It is the custom of Chabad that the boy begins to put on his tefillin two months beforehand. A meal with at least ten men present and a speech by the boy should take place on the evening at the end of the actual day of the bar mitzvah, even if the main celebrations are scheduled for a later date. The boy should give money to an educational charity. The first time the boy is called to the Torah should be on a Shabbat afternoon or a weekday morning, not a Shabbat morning.[13]

Some bar mitzvah boys began to put on tefillin even earlier than those who follow Chabad traditions. In the mid-eighteenth century a custom was noted in Lvov of a fatherless boy beginning to lay tefillin from the age of twelve. Like the regular reciting of *Kaddish*, this act was considered to be a praiseworthy act indicating the merit of the lost father. It was never a widespread custom.[14] Yet because the norm is to begin to lay tefillin at or shortly before the bar mitzvah, it has led some to suggest that an orphan should celebrate at the age of twelve.[15]

An account from Johannesburg, South Africa, from 1936 describes a traditional Eastern European bar mitzvah on Shabbat. Joshua Leib Radus published this account of his memories of the bar mitzvah of his brother at Slobodka in the Ukraine:

On Shabbat morning we all went, mother and father, my grandparents and all our relatives to the study house. My father had the honor of leading the prayers. After the morning service my father had the honor of taking the scroll out of the Ark and the reading of the Torah began. Almost all the gathering were called up to the reading of the Torah, and a blessing was said for each of them, and for the bar mitzvah and everyone in his family. And they pledged candles or oil for the study house on our behalf. My brother was called to read *maftir*, and he read the haftarah with a pleasant melody and my father said the blessing *barukh she-petarani*. . .[16] In our house, in the large spacious hall, they put up long tables covered with white tablecloths and with chairs around the tables. On the tables were many different wines, and also cakes, wafers and delicacies. All the guests sat around the tables, and joy and happiness filled the hall. My father took his place at the head of the table and said the blessing for Kiddush over the wine and all the guests answered Amen after him. After they had refreshed themselves a little, my brother stood on the chair on which he had been sitting and began to give his speech. His speech captured the heart of the audience and they were filled with awe, even though they knew and understood that its learning was produced by adults. After he finished his speech all the guests drank a blessing "To Life!" and to the life of the bar mitzvah and to the life of his parents and his family.[17]

Here we find a simple celebration taking place on a single day with one meal and one speech—not a large gathering but one with a deep spiritual content. For hundreds of thousands of strictly Orthodox Jews in the world today, the celebrations may be on a grander scale but follow a pattern very similar to the ceremony described here, with the boy reading *maftir* and haftarah in the synagogue and at the celebration meal speaking words of Torah that, as often as not, had been written for him.

The Effects of War

During the world wars, oppression, and Nazi destruction of the twentieth century, many boys missed their bar mitzvah, some celebrated later, and others held the ceremony under unusual circumstances. When Reuben Ginsberg had his bar mitzvah in Ramsgate Synagogue, England, in February 1916, he did so as a thirteen-year-old wounded war veteran. His father had joined the Canadian Expeditionary Force in Montreal, and when he was sent to England, young Reuben, who was twelve years old, stowed away on the ship. Discovered in the mid-Atlantic, he was allowed to join his father's company as mascot and trumpeter. He was wounded by shrapnel at the Battle of Ypres while riding his motorcycle and wore for his bar mitzvah the tallit he always wore under his tunic, with the traces of battle still visible upon it.[18]

Arno Herzberg has written about his bar mitzvah in the town of Wielún in Poland (formerly Filehne in East Germany). After the town was allocated to Poland in the Treaty of Versailles in 1919, Jews left for Germany, and Arno found himself in a quickly vanishing world:

There was nobody to teach me. My father showed me how to read the Torah and to say the *haftarah*. We planned every detail over and over again. Rabbi Nobel came. Some uncles and aunts showed up. They crossed into Poland on a two-day pass issued for those residing near the border. It was a small gathering. We could seat everyone comfortably in one room of our house. I was the last *Bar Mitzvah* boy in our Temple, the last in a long chain stretching back over the centuries. It was a day to remember, a fleeting moment in a life crowded with indelible impressions.[19]

The celebration of bar mitzvah was not possible in concentration camps, but several boys managed small celebrations in the ghetto of Terezin. Jerzy Bader, born 1930 in Kyjov, Czechoslovakia, had been preparing for his bar mitzvah when his family was deported to Theresienstadt in January 1943. He was able to have a small celebration in the youth club of the ghetto in April 1944. He subsequently perished in Auschwitz with his father.[20]

Since the end of World War II many survivors who were unable to celebrate under the Nazis have returned to hold their bar mitzvah in Europe, and many other younger people have done the same, in memory of members of their family. One of the first was Stephen Bernstein, son of a rabbi to the American military, who celebrated in the ruins of Frankfurt, Germany, in 1947. It was the first bar mitzvah held in the city since 1940. The hall where it was held had been used as a synagogue and served as a hospital for German war wounded. His father's speech, which was published, talked of Jewish survival even though the oppressor may triumph for a moment.[21]

In March 2011 Hollywood producer Branko Lustig returned to Auschwitz to hold a ceremony outside the barracks where he had been held in 1944. For younger generations the Remember Us Foundation offers facilities for children to commemorate the life and name of one specific child who perished in the Holocaust during their celebrations.[22]

A Secular Bar Mitzvah

In the 1930s an unusual bar mitzvah ceremony was held among a group of secular Yiddish speakers in the United States. The ceremony was completely secular but for readings and explanations from the Bible, especially about the return to Zion and future redemption:

We all gathered in a large hall. The tables were covered with pretty tablecloths, and on them were all kinds of cocktails. On the principal table, the place where the bar mitzvah boy and his parents sat, stood a gleaming candlestick, and its candles were alight and spread light. Next to the candlestick were pretty flowers. There was a cake on the table, and on it were inserted fourteen candles, like the American birthday custom. The tables were decorated with green leaves.

When the party began, the parents appeared with the bar mitzvah. All of us gave honor as they entered by standing up and singing in Yiddish, "Come let us greet the bar mitzvah." One of the guests opened the party with a short welcome and described the length of the celebration of bar mitzvah in the life of the Jews and how they, like other peoples, celebrated the firstborn. Also he emphasized the journey through life of the Hebrew child of our times and highlighted his duties to his people and to the workers' party. They sang songs of the pioneers and about the life of youth in Yiddish and English, accompanied on the piano.

The bar mitzvah read from Isaiah. His source was the beginning of the second chapter "In the days to come" [Isa. 2:2] and also the section of the prophet Ezekiel known as the "dry bones" [Ezek. 37] and then the section from Isaiah 66 that begins "Rejoice with Jerusalem and be glad for her, All you who love her!" This happened to be the haftarah for that week.[23] Then he read from a translation of Joshua. After the reading the boy spoke for about six minutes and promised joyfully to prolong his studies and not to abandon his Jewish learning.

After the reading and his declaration, his parents spoke and showered kisses on their son. They handed over to him these gifts: a Bible, a Hebrew book, one of the books of Abraham Mapu, and the *Folk Tales* of Peretz . . .

After that began the ceremony of lighting the candles in honor of the bar mitzvah, who was fourteen. Just as each one of the friends came up to light the candle, he blessed the boy. In general the blessings were that he would be deserving of prolonging the lives of the Jews and the Yiddish Jews. After the ceremony they read Peretz's story "Three Gifts." The participants stood up and sang in chorus the oath and "Strengthen."[24] And then they rejoiced over a hearty meal. This is how they celebrate bar mitzvah in the manner of real modern Jews.[25]

The ceremony described here, with its Bible readings, would have taken the place of a synagogue service. The milestone in the boy's life being celebrated was part of the revival of the Jewish people, of which secular socialist Zionism was the most important symbol.

Yiddish Speakers Celebrate

Some Yiddish educators worked hard to reconcile their secular culture with the tradition, particularly Leibush Lehrer (1887–1966), who introduced Shabbat services and sometimes celebrated a collective bar/bat mitzvah for boys and girls reaching the age of thirteen during residential stays at the Yiddish Camp Boiberik, near Rhinebeck, New York, which he directed from 1923 to 1964.[26] Reminiscing about these ceremonies, he wrote: "We make it clear that the celebration of bar mitzvah should normally be shared by three partners: the home, the synagogue, and the circle of friends. We wish to express our joy with the celebrants as the last of the three."[27]

The Nazi destruction led to the loss of Yiddish as a major vernacular language, with 85 percent of those Jews who died (around five million in total) being speakers of Yiddish. With the establishment of the State of Israel in 1948, Yiddish-speaking groups such as the ones described here gradually declined, many of them switching to English or Hebrew. What is fascinating to note is the way bar mitzvah had by the twentieth century become a common factor among radically different Jewish groups, laying a firm foundation for its renewed popularity after the war.

One interesting detail from the 1930s Yiddish account is the presence of a cake with candles. The modern custom of candles on a birthday cake comes from the German *kinderfest* and was mentioned by Goethe in 1799. Originally, large numbers of candles on the cake symbolized a hope for future years of life. It is thus not surprising that birthday candles appeared at bar mitzvah celebrations.

A photo survives from Georgia in the United States of Deana Baum Dreyer mixing the cake for the bar mitzvah of her son Baum in 1917.[28] After the consecration services for girls held by the Jews' Free School in London from 1925 to 1938, a so-called birthday cake was provided each year at the tea party held afterward by Mrs. S. Barling.[29] Ernest Weil recalled baking the cake for his own bar mitzvah in Germany in 1937.[30] The cake with candles became even more popular in the United States after World War II. Today there is a broad range of themes for the large iced cakes that form a centerpiece of the party, though the current fashion is to have cakes without candles, more in keeping with the tradition of a wedding than of a birthday.

Candles and Gifts

The candle lighting ceremony—claimed by some to have begun in the 1950s, though evidence shows it is older than that[31]—was to become a standard element of bar mitzvah celebrations. Often the boy himself would call the relatives and friends to light the thirteen candles on the cake—or perhaps fourteen, one for luck. The band might play different music for each person named. The cake was often in the shape of a scroll or a set of tefillin.[32] Such ceremonies remain popular, though they are no longer linked to the cake. Candle lighting ceremonies are popular in other cultures as well; they feature, for example, in the Hispanic American quinceañera ceremony for fifteen-year-old girls.

In the first half of the twentieth century most gifts given or recommended for children were very practical. In the magazine of a London school in 1925, the editor urged parents not to give jewelry to the boys and instead recommended "some good books . . . a microscope, telescope, mathematical instruments, field glasses, a box of chess or other games, a cricket bat, a football, a box of tools, umbrella, camera, hair brushes, box of paints, pocket-book, hand-bag, fountain pen."[33]

Mordecai Richler's comic novel *The Apprenticeship of Duddy Kravitz* (1959) gives an interesting fictional account of a bar mitzvah in a Reform Temple in Montreal in the 1950s: "Grandfather Cohen, wearing a prayer shawl, hands the Torah to Mr. Cohen who passes it to his son." The passing of the Torah through the generations, symbolizing the handing on of the tradition, is now commonplace in Reform ceremonies, and Richler's depiction is a very early example of the ritual. The father's blessing is replaced by one spoken by the rabbi, and a party is held with a live band. Animals modeled out of ice serve as decoration, and a table is laden with gifts:

Four Parker 51 sets, an electric razor, a portable record player, three toilet sets, two copies of *Tom Sawyer*, five subscriptions to the *National Geographic Magazine*, a movie projector, a fishing rod and other angling equipment, three cameras, a season's ticket to hockey games at the Forum, a set of phylacteries [tefillin] and a prayer shawl, a rubber dinghy, a savings account book open at a first deposit of five hundred dollars, six sport shirts, an elaborate chemistry set, a pile of fifty silver dollars in a velvet-lined box, at least ten credit slips (worth from twenty to a hundred dollars each) for Eaton's and Morgan's, two sets of H. G. Wells's *Outline of History*. . . numerous checks.[34]

In addition, Rabbi Goldstone presents an autographed copy of his book, *Why I'm Glad to Be a Jew*. This and the tefillin and prayer shawl are the only items of Jewish interest. Noticeable in the list is the large number of gifts of money and the considerable number of duplicate gifts, some of which (such as the subscriptions to *National Geographic*) seem to reflect more the tastes of the guests than of a thirteen-year-old boy. The ceremony was a religious one, but the party is completely secular. This is a good example of the compromise with the tradition still made by many families.

Israel

Celebrations among Israelis in the early years of the state took an entirely different form. Today's preparations have their historical roots in the early educational efforts of the kibbutzim, the collective socialist settlements. The kibbutz educators removed bar mitzvah from its place in the synagogue and placed it in their education system. The entire year's program was built around bar/bat mitzvah, commonly with thirteen tasks representing the thirteen years of the young people's lives. Some of the tasks would involve study or research, but others would be volunteer projects, either on the kibbutz or in a nearby town. This program was designed to instill a sense of civic duty because the age of criminal responsibility had been set at twelve.[35] Most often, the bar/bat mitzvah program in the kibbutz would begin at that age for both boys and girls, continue for around a year, and end with a communal party and a secular ceremony in the kibbutz dining hall, which often took place on a Friday night. Some even wanted to change the name to *bar mesimah*, indicating someone who has completed an assignment.[36]

These are the thirteen tasks that were given to bar/bat mitzvah students on Kibbutz Afikim, taken from its 1962 syllabus:

1. Knowledge of the Jewish tradition.
2. Knowledge of the history of the Jewish people.
3. Knowledge of the geography and economy of Israel and the local region.

4. The kibbutz movement—policies and current issues.
5. In the family (includes practical help).
6. In the peer group (includes practical projects helping others).
7. My kibbutz (probably including practical help).
8. Security duty.
9. One day survival alone plus acquaintance with someone of a different life style.
10. Getting to know neighbors (outside the kibbutz).
11. Saving items for reuse or recycling.
12. Cleaning tasks plus working at the kibbutz weather station.
13. Written research topic.[37]

One difficulty faced by the pioneer kibbutzim was that of relatives and friends from outside bringing in bar mitzvah presents, which conflicted with the ideology of communal ownership. Books and camping equipment were generally considered acceptable, as were small amounts of cash and day trips to appropriate outside events.[38]

"The Bar Mitzvah Party" is an evocative short story first published in 1961 by the Israeli poet Yehuda Amichai (1924–2000). The story uses biblical language and Jewish religious imagery in a secular context: "In the beginning was the rearrangement of furniture—in the big house, in the white stone house, across from the small café in which espresso steam rose day and night. The espresso machine was itself one of the many eternal lamps in the world."[39] The biblical account of creation has become the start of the preparations for the party, and the eternal lamp in the synagogue has become a coffee machine. In the story the guests are to arrive the following day, and the rearrangement of the house goes on as the boy practices his haftarah, his "voice a bird's voice." The narrator is taken to view the boy's presents—knapsack and blanket, canteen and walking stick, flashlights and binoculars, tefillin and (as always) fountain pens, books, paper and stationery, manicure kits, pocketknives, sports pants, a penknife, a watch, a clock, and a box of compasses. Every present is "either too late or too early" for him. The celebration dinner is a banquet held on the night before the synagogue service, in a "resplendent club in Jerusalem" on Friday evening.

The members of the host family, who (like the author) had come to Palestine from Prussia twenty-five years earlier, are described as spending more than they earned. The evening consists of alternate speechmaking and eating: "All the faces became false. From time to time God nudged my knee under the table, signalling me to pay attention to a defect or short-coming, signalling me to prophesy." Then there were photographs and dancing and the next day a service in a basement synagogue, followed by a party for the children and a film in the evening. Amichai offers the social criticism of an outsider; at no point does the narrator initiate any action. The list of gifts and the Friday night party reflect historical reali-ties, but the meaning and purpose of the whole celebration is questioned: "The boy's Haftorah wasn't long. He finished chanting it in a high voice, and his voice rose at the end as if in a question, the opposite of a rhe-torical question: one with no answer."[40] For Amichai the religious cere-mony in the basement synagogue has become a subculture that offers no answers to real issues.

Today the number of Jewish children who reach the age of bar/bat mitzvah annually in Israel is around eighty-five to ninety thousand. Most schools offer special programs in the seventh grade still based on the ones offered by the early kibbutz pioneers. In spite of the secular nature of much of their society, most Israelis today have returned to the tradition of reading from the Torah at the center of the boys' ceremony. When the celebration is held on Shabbat, the Ashkenazic custom of the boy read-ing the haftarah is common. Many celebrations are held on a Monday or Thursday morning, when the Torah is read, or on Rosh Hodesh, the new moon and start of the month. A survey of Israeli men in 2002 revealed that 86 percent of respondents stated it was "important" or "very important" to them for their son to be called to the Torah as a bar mitzvah. More-over, 42 percent said that they themselves had continued to wear tefillin on a regular or occasional basis after their own bar mitzvah ceremonies.[41]

As elsewhere in the Jewish world, parties in Israel are held after the synagogue service, and the boy makes a speech. One twenty-first-century trend, influenced by the TV show A Star Is Born, is the recording of the speech in a studio with background music, which allows scope for the rapper style speech. Presentations on family history or on the life of the bar/bat mitzvah are also common, and these may involve the use of com-puter technology. A candle lighting ceremony, at which thirteen candles are lit, is still popular, in the tradition of the 1930s American ceremony already described. Drum ensembles, popular singing groups, or a dee-jay are often a major part of the evening. Gift giving is an important part as well. Very commonly the parents hold their own party, with the child having a mini-event with friends in a separate part of the hall.

Around five thousand ceremonies take place annually at the Western Wall in Jerusalem, not only for Israelis but often for Jews from other parts of the world who have decided to celebrate in Israel. In the reverse direction, a bar mitzvah trip has been popular for Israelis since the 1980s. Sometimes, too, a nature hike or guided tour may form part of the celebration.[42]

In June 2011 Zehorit and Limor Sorek, a lesbian couple, celebrated the bar mitzvah of their son at Kehillat Yachad, an Orthodox congregation in Tel Aviv.[43] Such celebrations are not uncommon, but they are rare in Orthodox communities.

It has become the norm for both bar mitzvah and bat mitzvah to be celebrated in secular Israeli families. For a boy there is often a traditional religious ceremony in a synagogue or special outdoor setting; for a girl there is most often just a party. But a few young people choose a specifically secular humanistic celebration. Humanistic congregations in Jerusalem—as well as in New York, Washington, Boston, London, and elsewhere—offer full educational programs based on Jewish values and history and celebrations using poetry, songs, inspiring readings, and the presentation of projects written by the boy or girl. Such humanistic congregations employ rabbis, and ceremonies are likely to involve the wearing of a tallit and reading from a scroll of the Torah. They cater to large numbers of Jews ignored by many traditional communities, including lesbians, gays, mixed-faith and mixed-race families, and others with alternative lifestyles. Most such congregations are members of the Society for Humanistic Judaism founded by Rabbi Sherwin Wine in 1969.

EXPLORING IDENTITY

In *Mazal Tov: Celebrities' Bar and Bat Mitzvah Memories* (2007) a celebrity journalist gathered memoirs and photographs of nineteen people, mainly from the American show business world. The vast majority remember their celebrations as social and cultural, rather than religious, events, although their parties were not necessary large ones. A common theme, in fact, is the simplicity of celebrations remembered from the past, compared to today's parties. Larry King described his party in Brooklyn in 1946 as "a little brunch in the synagogue. After the little sandwiches were finished, I had no major reception, no dancing band."[44]

The learning of Hebrew in particular was an obstacle for many of the celebs featured in the book. Recalling his bar mitzvah in November 1958 at Congregation Habonim, Manhattan, Henry Winkler talked about his dyslexia: "I learned my haftarah phonetically because there was no way I was learning Hebrew. I was having enough trouble reading English from left to right . . . I was struggling. I had to memorize it like I was playing a part . . . My bar mitzvah was a real milestone for me because I was tackling the ultimate challenge . . . I was definitely not comfortable being in front of a crowd . . . all I thought was, Am I ever going to get through this?"[45]

Mazal Tov also introduced its readers to a new development, the "bark-mitzvah," celebrated by dog lovers for their pets, complete with head coverings and tallit and thank-you notes signed with their paw prints. Dog celebrations have become a fashionable American trend and have even spawned a children's story, *Alfie's Bark Mitzvah*, complete with a CD of specially written songs.[46]

Today a bar mitzvah may be celebrated almost anywhere. In December 2009 a convicted fraudster, Tuvia Stern, planned his son's bar mitzvah ceremony and party in a New York City jail, complete with kosher catering and a visiting singer. Chaplain Rabbi Leib Glanz, who arranged the bar mitzvah, was subsequently suspended for two weeks.[47]

The Search for a Deeper Meaning

"The Kerchief," a short story by the Israeli Nobel Prize winner Shmuel Yosef Agnon (1888–1970), describes a boy from a poor, pious family living in a village in Galicia at an unspecified date in the past. One Friday afternoon the boy's father brings home from the market in Lashkowitz a brown-and-white brocaded silk kerchief "adorned with flowers and blossoms," which his mother wears wound around her head as she lights the Shabbat candles. The kerchief is too fine an article to be used on an ordinary weekday, but when the boy reaches the age of thirteen, she ties it around his neck as he leaves for synagogue "dressed like a bridegroom." On his way home at midday, the boy meets a beggar who is unloved and rejected by the whole community. The boy gives the kerchief to the beggar, who "wound it around his sores." His mother forgives him, and he is filled with gladness.[48]

In the story no party and no guests are mentioned, and the only signs of celebration are the fine clothes and kerchief worn by the boy. Agnon's stories can be read at many levels; one clear message is that a true bar mitzvah consists of acts of kindness, not of dancing and feasting. Writing for a materialistic age, Agnon demonstrates a longing for the good deeds and even the poverty of the past. His story marks the start of a new phase in the history of bar mitzvah, one that focuses on the needs and feelings of the child.

Some accounts since this time portray children as rebellious or showing a lack of understanding of the deeper meanings of the ceremony, while in others the child finds his or her spiritual identity through it. Whatever the message, the novels, stories, and movies reflect cultures in which the needs and feelings of the child are at the center. They also provide a valuable historical record of changing attitudes, the feelings of the child and the family over the last fifty years. A child may be confused about being Jewish and have doubts about the whole experience. Bereavement or illness, redundancy or just bad timing, may make the celebration unusually stressful. Every child needs opportunities to explore his or her identity.

Bar Mitzvah Boy is a British television play, written by Jack Rosenthal and broadcast in 1976. An Off Broadway musical of 1987 changed the setting from 1970s Britain to 1946 Brooklyn, but the central story is the same. In the play young Elliot Green escapes from the synagogue on the day of his bar mitzvah, much to the consternation of his parents, who have invested in an expensive party to celebrate the occasion. As much as anything, he wants to escape from his squabbling parents: "Rita, for the first time in three months, may I eat without hearing seating plans and menus and caterers and 'Do we tip the Rabbi?' and 'Should we invite Miriam?' and 'What if it rains?' and 'Do I wear a long dress or a short dress, and nothing will spoil it, will it?'—In the morning he gets bar mitzvahed, in the evening we have the dinner dance, and by Sunday it's all a dream. Thank you, Amen." Elliot recites his *maftir*/haftarah portion in the park for the benefit of his sister Lesley, and the rabbi proclaims that the effort is good enough for him to be "barmitzvahed." His brief rebellion is designed to make the point that if the men in his family are examples of Jewish men, he does not really want to be one.

Other fictional accounts have the purpose of demonstrating a deeper meaning for bar mitzvah. Most notable are two movies made by Yehuda and Sara Wurtzel. In 1941 a young Russian boy, Nikolai Krohn, is seen off by his aunt Sonia at the Leningrad train station. He is embarking on a long journey to the state school in Vologda, where he will be taught to be a good Communist in the Soviet Union. By chance an American Jewish engineer, Joseph Levinson, is to be on the same train. Nikolai's aunt implores Levinson to tell him what being Jewish means because the boy will be thirteen the next day. Levinson, brought up in a secular family, knows little himself, but he did have a bar mitzvah.

This story was embellished and made into a dramatized video by Yehuda and Sara Wurtzel. Called *The Journey* (1989), it was frequently used as an educational tool for bar and bat mitzvah classes during the 1990s. In the film Sonia has two books that are heirlooms from her Jewish family. One of them she gives to Levinson, who finds he is only able to read the first two words of the *Shema*. After the overnight journey he tries to explain the significance of the book to Nikolai but is unable to do so. He then gives it to him as a birthday present. The other book is found when Sonia's apartment is raided by the Soviet authorities, who tell her suspiciously, "This is a guide book for a whole way of life, a blueprint for an entire social order." In spite of Levinson's inadequacy as a teacher, the realization dawns on Nikolai that the book Levinson has given him holds a key to a special tradition. The day of his bar mitzvah changed Nikolai's whole life.[49]

Yehuda and Sara Wurtzel also made a short cartoon, *The Mitzvah Machine* (1987), in which a boy is given a robot as a present and trains it to do his bar mitzvah instead of him. When the boy starts worrying that he has not had his bar mitzvah, the robot tells him "A bar mitzvah is not something you have: a bar mitzvah is something you become." The message is that unlike a machine, a bar mitzvah can say no to a command; becoming bar mitzvah is about having the freedom to choose.

The Australian movie *Hey Hey It's Esther Blueberger* (2008), written and directed by Cathy Randall, portrays Esther's ambivalence about her Jewish identity. Her bat mitzvah is a shared ceremony with her twin brother, Jacob. Although Jacob later moves to a Jewish school, the members of the Blueberger family are the only Jewish characters shown in the movie; they live in a non-Jewish environment in an Australian city. A contrast is drawn between their wealth and private education and the relative poverty of many of their non-Jewish neighbors. Esther feels an outsider both in her family and at school and finds herself drawn to the more accepting local public school community. At the ceremony, filmed at Adelaide Hebrew congregation, their father places a tallit around Jacob's neck after he has chanted his portion. He is supposed to put a necklace round Esther's neck but at the last moment changes his mind and puts his tie around her instead, as if indicating a wish that he had two boys. Although her brother becomes more religious after he changes schools, Esther's bat mitzvah is a step along the road to abandoning her Jewish heritage. Judaism makes her feel like an outsider, and she does not like it.

These fictional accounts illustrate a modern world in which bar and bat mitzvah have become child centered. Following modern educational theory, today's ceremonies are intended to be the outcome not just of learning Torah by rote but of a good educational experience that explains the deeper meanings of being Jewish. The movies show that this effort does not always work, but that has not dented the popularity of the celebration. Bar mitzvah declined in the nineteenth century, and it was by concentrating on the child's needs that an astonishing revival of bar mitzvah took place in the twentieth century. As bat mitzvah has also become universal, the ceremonies are now celebrated by a higher proportion of Jewish children than ever before.

The old texts rarely tell us how the boys felt. They concentrate more on what the fathers wanted to do, not the child. How did it feel to have your father say, "Blessed be the One who has freed me from punishment because of him?" How did it feel to be the subject of stringencies that perhaps you should not be bar mitzvah if you had not reached puberty? How did it feel to be told you had to give a long *derashah* on the Torah portion? The texts do not tell us.

Perhaps the first to look at bar mitzvah from the boy's point of view was Mordecai HaCohen of Safed, who in the sixteenth century suggested that after the age of thirteen a boy needs to say, "Blessed be the One who has freed me from punishment by Daddy!"[50] The first reminiscence from personal memory comes from Juspa the shammash of Worms in the seventeenth century. He was all ready with his preparation when the rabbi insisted that his bar mitzvah be postponed until the following week, in order that he should properly fulfill the requirement of being thirteen years old *plus one day* (see chap. 2). The incident presents an apparent clash of customs, with different rules being followed by teachers and rabbis. The very fact that he remembered the incident shows that it must have been distressing. It must be equally distressing today to have to relearn a bar mitzvah portion, and such incidents still happen.[51]

Juspa's account of how the community in Worms organized the parties gives a better impression. As the boy himself went from house to house on the Saturday afternoon to fetch his guests, each one would surely have greeted him and offered their congratulations as he arrived at their house.

A surviving census of the Worms ghetto community shows that members of the community were living in ninety-five households, so the boy would be walking around a small area to people he knew.[52] Juspa also records that not every boy was able to read from the Torah, so the community must have had to learn to adapt to the abilities of each child.

Giulio Morosini described how in Venice in 1683 the boy had to visit the community rabbi in advance. Doing so at least gave the child clear expectations of what he needed to know, and the test of knowledge ensured that he would not arrive unprepared on the day of the celebration. But one wonders what happened when boys failed the test. In 1769 in Metz clear rules were introduced stipulating that boys had to study for two years. The rabbi had to examine the candidates to make sure they were properly prepared.[53] In the following century it was common for synagogue rule books to insist that boys who had not passed the test could not have the ceremony. But as we will see, such tests often failed to raise standards of knowledge and Hebrew reading. Declining standards and the seeming irrelevance of bar mitzvah preparation lay behind the new idea of the ceremony of confirmation. Originally a graduation ceremony for a class in a Jewish day school, it provided a new opportunity for the boys to get up to an agreed-upon standard without undue pressure. And it brought girls in for the first time. Many descriptions of nineteenth-century confirmation mention how emotional an occasion it was. But perhaps it always appealed more to educators than to children or parents.

BAR MITZVAH IN DECLINE

As Reform and many Orthodox congregations promoted confirmation, bar mitzvah continued as a key rite of passage among the most Orthodox. But among many Western European communities during the nineteenth century, the amount of learning by the boys declined drastically.[54] Assimilation brought new difficulties in its wake. In 1886 the Orthodox rabbi Esriel Hildesheimer found himself grappling with the question of whether a Jewish boy could be called to the Torah on his bar mitzvah if he had not been circumcised. In Jewish legal terms there was no problem, for birth from a Jewish mother is sufficient to establish a child's Jewish status, but in terms of the religious politics of the time Hildesheimer thought it was not so easy to be lenient: "One who does not enter into the holy covenant [circumcision] is not like others who abandon the religion."[55]

The implication here is that while most nonreligious Jews would be tolerated within the context of an Orthodox religious service, one had to think long and hard before welcoming those who had abandoned something so fundamental as the covenant of circumcision. This debate has to be seen against the background of German Orthodox communities that had deliberately broken with the Reform majority in the country in order to preserve their traditions and way of life.[56] It shows a community with new priorities, one in which the popular custom of bar mitzvah could be viewed as more important by modernists than the ancient Torah covenant of circumcision.

By the end of the nineteenth century in France many Jews did not attend synagogue even on the High Holy Days. The five thousand synagogue seats in Paris were enough for only about an eighth of the total Jewish population. The five hundred strictly Orthodox Jews, mainly from Eastern Europe, accounted for at least a quarter of all the bar mitzvah ceremonies, which means that the vast majority of Jewish boys were not celebrating the occasion. The French Jewish periodical *L'Univers Israélite* published details of the numbers of ceremonies for each year from 1896 to 1908, showing a gradual decline from 263 in the first year to a mere 198 twelve years later. For those who did have a ceremony, the bar mitzvah tests had become a mere formality by the 1890s, with nobody being rejected. Typically, the boys prepared to read only five verses that they had learned by rote.[57]

In 1896 the same French journal published an anonymous lament about the uselessness of the current bar mitzvah tests. Because the exam took place only ten days before the celebration, after the invitations had already gone out, the examiners had no choice but to pass the candidate, and the parents imagined they had given their son a sufficient religious education. The article proposed that the test should be held three months in advance, so that if necessary the celebration could be postponed until an acceptable standard of Jewish education had been reached. Boys should be able not just to read their portion but to translate the principal prayers and know something of Jewish history, ceremonies, and beliefs. Too much time and effort went into learning to chant the Torah, and "the teachers sweat blood to get it down their reluctant throats." The author stated a preference for the German system, in which, he stated, the boys did not chant at all but simply recited the blessings. Time would be better spent on learning Jewish values. If they did want to chant, this should not be part of the test but should require a separate rehearsal.[58]

In London the principal Ashkenazic congregation in Dukes Place devised a unique method to try to ensure the continuity of bar mitzvah through the generations. The regulations from 1827 stipulate: "The parent who does not cause a boy to attend *la-alot laTorah* (to be called to the Law) when *bar mitzvah* (of age to be confirmed) shall pay a fine to be levied at the discretion of the Wardens . . . in any sum not less than two pounds and not exceeding five pounds."[59] This is an astonishing regulation because the celebration of bar mitzvah had up to this point never been considered compulsory, and it had grown in popularity because parents wanted to celebrate their sons' coming of age, not because rabbinic legislation insisted they do so. Perhaps in this large formal congregation, which was the seat of the chief rabbi, the work of the wardens was being made difficult if a bar mitzvah whom they were expecting failed to appear.

Yet despite its reappearance in the regulations of 1863,[60] the rule did nothing to halt the decline in standards. Speaking at the bar mitzvah of Desmond Tuck at North London Synagogue in April 1902,[61] chief rabbi Dr. Hermann Adler said, "If the preparations for this day are suffered to be perfunctory and mechanical, if they are limited to the parrot-like repetition of the words to be read out to the congregation, then this ceremonial is degraded to a so-called religious rite, with all the religion omitted."[62] There is an implied suggestion here that this is precisely what was often happening. For some families the ceremony marked the integration of a son into the full life of the community. For many others it marked the end of a son's Jewish education.

Jewish settlers in the United States in the first half of the nineteenth century often arranged for the boys to learn their portions as their only formal Jewish education. The supplementary schools ended at age thirteen and perhaps began only a year or two earlier. The Jews from Germany who arrived in the second half of the nineteenth century brought with them the new ceremony of confirmation and enthusiastically promoted it as a replacement for bar mitzvah in Reform and Conservative Judaism. But when large numbers of immigrants from Eastern Europe arrived, the situation changed.[63] There were frequent intergenerational clashes between the traditionally minded new arrivals and their more secular children. There were clashes, too, between Reform rabbis and their more traditionally minded congregants about the value of bar mitzvah.

In temples where nobody was called up to the Torah, bar mitzvah made little sense. Rabbi Kaufmann Kohler wrote in 1922: "Now I ask, is the calling up of the thirteen year old lad to become Bar Mitzvah by reading or listening to the reading of the Torah, which is still the practice in many Reform congregations, in harmony with the Reform service? . . . the whole Bar Mitzvah rite lost all meaning, and the calling up of the same is nothing less than a sham."[64] In apparent ignorance of the new ceremony of individual bat mitzvah, Kohler went on to argue that bar mitzvah was in any event an anachronism because girls were excluded.

With so little sympathy from leading rabbis, bar mitzvah standards continued to slip. It is of crucial importance to realize that low standards made the whole ceremony less popular. The boys themselves did not enjoy it. Morris N. Kimmel wrote in the memoir of his 1923 bar mitzvah: "I stood up at the front of the synagogue, kissed the Torah, and mumbled the blessing. My father hosted the congregation to a little wine and cake. Very little. And that was it. I was supposed to be a Jewish adult, but I knew absolutely nothing. It was a fraud. I have forgiven my father everything but not that. I was proud to be Jewish. I wanted to learn."[65]

Many parents also believed that bar mitzvah was of little value and did not enable their sons to achieve something worthwhile. In Cincinnati in 1927 and 1928, only 56 percent of Jewish thirteen-year-old boys celebrated bar mitzvah.[66] But the tide turned, and it did so because congregations began to introduce much stricter educational requirements. This was the most important event in the modern history of bar mitzvah and gradually led to the ceremony's popularity today among both boys and girls. Yet there was to be no return to the centuries of regulation of the size and menu of the party. In effect an unwritten and often unspoken agreement was made: synagogues, rabbis, and community officials were to control the educational standards, and families were now to have full control over their party. That arrangement did not of course stop rabbis from complaining about extravagant parties and families from objecting to what they saw as unnecessary educational requirements. But on the whole both sides learned to live with each other.

Stemming the Decline

One of the first congregations to insist on a high minimum standard was the Reconstructionist Temple Israel of Wilkes-Barre, Pennsylvania, which, not long after its founding in 1923, insisted that a bar mitzvah boy had to attend one of the local Hebrew schools for three sessions every week.[67] Typical of the new arrangements made in the 1930s was Chicago, where the Board of Jewish Education required all congregations to insist on three years of study before a bar mitzvah as well as appropriate standards of Hebrew reading. A similar standard was set for the whole United States by the Conservative movement in 1946.[68] These rules covered bar mitzvah, bat mitzvah, and confirmation, which was to be celebrated at age fifteen after two additional years' education. Gradually, the requirements were extended to include weekday classes.

A United Synagogue survey in the 1950s showed that 74 percent of responding Conservative congregations did not permit their students to attend school only on Sundays and that 50 percent required enrollment of children by the age of eight. Many members left for Reform communities, where requirements were less stringent.[69] Requirements imposed by the New York Federation of Reform Synagogues in 1945, for example, included two years' education and detailed specifications for the service. The boy or girl would be expected to lead part of the service, chant from the Torah, and read a haftarah in Hebrew or English. There had to be a suitable prayer or talk to "express the emotions or thoughts of the candidate himself." But a survey of 112 Reform communities in 1950 showed that nearly half (45%) still had no educational requirements for bar mitzvah; where requirements were in place, three years' Jewish education was the norm,[70] though attendance on Sunday mornings was deemed sufficient. A conservative rabbi in Youngstown, Ohio, reported that he had lost ninety families to the local Reform temple after three-day-a-week attendance was introduced in the 1940s. The local Reform rabbi declared, "Come one day a week to us and they will be just as good Jews."[71] Educational requirements in voluntary schools have never been easy to enforce, but they did raise standards and succeeded in reviving bar mitzvah and enabling the introduction of meaningful bat mitzvah ceremonies.

In England, on behalf of the Orthodox United Synagogue, the chief rabbi organized written tests for girls celebrating confirmation in the 1920s. One report suggested that girls who took the test were receiving a more adequate preparation for Jewish life than boys, who were simply learning to chant Hebrew.[72] These tests came to an end with the start of World War II. The London Sephardic community instituted a test for girls aged twelve in 1950, insisting that they reach the same standard as those for thirteen-year-old boys.[73]

In the United Synagogue in the 1950s the focus was on boys, who had to undertake a formal bar mitzvah test. At first it took the form of an oral test, centrally administered by a team of a few rabbis, but it was not particularly demanding and quite hard to fail. If you took the test, the bar mitzvah would go ahead anyway, though one rabbi insisted that those who failed would not be allowed to read the haftarah.[74] Reminiscing to his congregation in a sermon in March 2012, Rabbi Colin Eimer recalled the test he was given before his bar mitzvah in March 1958:

> My Barmitzvah test took place at Woburn House, the HQ of the United Synagogue. There I was—a rather chubby, shy, 12- and-something- year old boy, still in short trousers [pants], going with his father to Woburn House. The letter had told you to go to room number so- and-so. A doorman directed us to the room where there was a man with a very rabbinic looking beard, but also a very unrabbinic looking dog-collar . . .[75] The only question I remember him asking me was "what is your haphtarah about?" My Barmitzvah was on this Shabbat, Shabbat Parah, with its special haphtarah reading which spoke about menstruation, blood, women and their impurity and so on. What did a 12-year old know of such things? So when he asked me "what's your haphtarah about?" I hummed and hah-ed and stayed shtumm. At the end he told me that he had had to fail me because, while he was impressed with some of my answers, I hadn't been able to tell him about the content of my haphtarah. So I never did muff and huff.[76]

In the 1980s the United Synagogue oral test was replaced by a written bar mitzvah test with two levels, basic and advanced; those who passed the more advanced level had their names published in the Jewish press. But the advanced test did not last, and over the years more and more individual synagogues dropped out of the system altogether. In January 2007 a written test was introduced, held three times a year, for girls wishing to celebrate bat mitzvah.[77]

Unlike the original seventeenth-century tests, modern bar mitzvah tests have included questions on a wide range of topics, not just those necessary for the boy's entry into the ritual life of the community. Teaching syllabuses, gift books, coffee table books, and pamphlets all proclaimed the message that the boy is a living chain in the tradition and therefore needs to know as much as he can of those traditions. *The Bar Mitzvah Book* (1975) contains a variety of inspiring essays on episodes from Jewish history and proclaims on the dust jacket: "The book presents the outstanding aspects of the Jewish faith and the highlights of Jewish history in a manner that will appeal to the young Jewish adolescent of today, inspiring him with a sense of belonging to a community and to a living tradition."[78]

Helen Leneman's *Bar Bat Mitzvah Education* (1993) provides a wide range of programs suitable for American Jews. Leneman's own curriculum for the year was based around the topics of prayer, Torah, and Jewish festivals; other programs gave more emphasis to charity projects or Jewish history. One contributor to the book expressed the view that "Bar/Bat Mitzvah is the bane of Jewish education. It is the tail that wags the dog, the lens through which a youngster's entire Jewish schooling is viewed." Because the hope of a successful event brings parents to the doors of the synagogue or Jewish school, it is up to communities, it was argued, to set the ground rules and devise the most comprehensive program possible.[79]

The published syllabus of the United Synagogue London from 1994 was based around factual knowledge and included sections on Jewish values and Zionist history in the written test and on the Jewish year, the principal festivals, and prayers in the oral test.[80] And a law of the Chabad Hasidim published in a 1999 anthology asserts, "It is far better that the Bar Mitzvah boy should spend the months of preparation for his Bar Mitzvah learning Halachah (rules of behavior) that is needed on a day-to-day basis, than to spend a large amount of time learning to read his Sedrah."[81] The argument is that in previous generations, when boys were engaged most of the day in learning Torah, preparing to read from the Torah was done outside of their learning schedule in order not to take valuable time away from other studies. Nowadays, learning to read from the Torah has become the main part of the preparation, and that has to be changed.

Bar mitzvah and bat mitzvah are more popular today than they have ever been. In the English-speaking world the use of the word *bar mitzvah* in books has been rising steeply since the 1950s and *bat mitzvah* since the 1970s.[82] The popularity of the ceremony spans the entire Jewish community, from the most secular to the most religious. But it is a mistake to think that every Jewish child has one. A family education survey conducted in 1999 of almost two hundred people from thirty-eight congregations in Chicago revealed that 49 percent of respondents had no bar or bat mitzvah as a child. Three quarters of the survey respondents were women.[83]

The very popularity of the ceremony raises new issues because it creates social pressures within communities that every child is expected to perform and every parent is to look like a perfect parent. In 2012 the Union for Reform Judaism and Hebrew Union College–Jewish Institute of Religion launched a project called "B'nai Mitzvah Revolution." The aim was "to empower synagogues to improve the quality of Jewish education in their communities, reduce the staggering rates of post–b'nai mitzvah dropout, and return depth and meaning to Jewish learning. As a result, our mission is to address a root cause of all these challenges: the perception that b'nai mitzvah celebrations are like graduation ceremonies."[84] Recognizing that every child is different, and that the focus on performance has supplanted other aims of the religious school, the project was founded to work out ways of deepening the experience based on four key assumptions: the importance of community, the seeking of meaning, respecting differences between children and families, and developing deep and authentic Jewish learning. Some of the current issues and social trends that have led to the need for this and similar projects are explored in chapter 7.

CHAPTER SEVEN

Current Issues and Trends

➤ Valley Beth Shalom, a Conservative congregation in the Los Angeles area, has piloted a bar/bat mitzvah program for divorced families called "Celebration and Negotiation."

➤ The DVD *Praying with Lior* documented the story of a boy with Down syndrome working for and celebrating his bar mitzvah in 2004.

➤ In 1983 the CCAR declared that anyone who had one Jewish parent could become Jewish through appropriate acts of identification, including bar/bat mitzvah.

➤ In 2008 Dr. Eugene Gettelman celebrated his fourth bar mitzvah at the age of one hundred at Westwood Horizons, Los Angeles.

➤ In 1956 Rabbi Moses Feinstein proposed the abolition of bar mitzvah on the grounds that it did not bring the boys closer to Torah and led Jews to desecrate the Sabbath.

➤ In the comedy film *Keeping Up with the Steins* (2006), a Hollywood moviemaker tells his son, "I want you to have the biggest bar mitzvah in the history of bar mitzvahs."

➤ The Jewish Renewal movement suggests that instead of giving presents, guests support a meaningful cause. No Driving. No Shopping. No Wrapping.

➤ Today the celebration of bar or bat mitzvah is more popular than at any time in the past.

THE POSTMODERN FAMILY

Not every Jewish family has two happy parents and their loving children. Bar and bat mitzvah are popular family celebrations taking place in a world in which family life has become increasingly stressful and more difficult and the definition of what constitutes a family have changed dramatically. David Grossman's Hebrew novel *The Zigzag Kid* (1994) tells the story of Nonny Feuerberg, who takes a surreal journey across Israel in the week before his bar mitzvah. In the course of the journey he uncovers the story of his dead mother and other secrets that have helped to shape his own identity.

The bar mitzvah celebration itself is not part of the story, but it is crucial to the plot because it denotes a time of discovery. The novel reflects the reality of postmodern family life, when bar mitzvah can be a time when long-buried family secrets are revealed: "Your mother, Zohara. Before she died. She told me to find you and tell you the whole story before your bar mitzvah. She said you must know everything about her."[1]

Nonny uncovers the past, including his mother's identity, her crimes, her gift, and the people she loved. The novel suggests a new meaning for bar/bat mitzvah as a time that looks to the past rather than to the future, when a child needs to know the real truth about his or her roots and family influences and the way they have shaped his personality.

On one hand, the increasing prosperity of the twentieth century has led to the gradual growth of bar/bat mitzvah as a social occasion and the seemingly unstoppable trend toward more and more lavish parties. Some have rejected extravagance and explored alternatives, such as bar mitzvah in Israel and eco- and DIY celebrations. On the other hand, family life has become more stressful and more difficult. Bar/bat mitzvah takes place in mixed-faith families or those in which the parents are divorced or in which the child has special educational or health needs. These issues require new solutions, specialist help, and caring professionals.

Bar/Bat Mitzvah and Divorce

An important social change that has affected bar/bat mitzvah for the most recent generation is the growth of the number of children with divorced or separated parents. Historically, orphans were recognized as lacking a parent, and Jewish communities set up funds to arrange a bar mitzvah for them. Today the problems—and their solutions—are very different. An impending bar/bat mitzvah can risk exposure to a decaying relationship; after separation or divorce, one parent may be absent during the preparation; some divorced parents may want two separate parties to be held; and battles played out during the divorce may be reenacted publicly or privately as the event takes shape. Although divorce occurs between the parents, some absent parents have also divorced themselves from the children.

An early attempt to write about this issue in 1982 made the assumption (which would be unacceptable today) that in remarried families old or new schisms are bound to eradicate good feelings completely. The answer suggested was described as "treatment" and included advice such as: "Parents must be guided in asserting their needs and rights in appropriate ways, without using their children as pawns in the divorce game."[2] It soon became apparent that, well intentioned though it was, such advice was insufficient. The 1990 American Jewish population survey showed that half of all Jewish marriages were ending in divorce, and only 17 percent of children were brought up in a family with two first-marriage parents and their two children.[3] That year a paper was presented to the annual convention of the American Psychological Association offering two contrasting case studies.

In the first case the bat mitzvah's father, who had moved to another town and was returning for the celebration, was told by the rabbi that his new wife would not be allowed to sit on the *bimah*, as a matter of synagogue policy. The father decided to sit with her in the congregation, but during his public words of encouragement to his daughter during the service, he broke down and sobbed. His daughter was deeply affected and found it all but impossible to continue. In the second case the absent father had been out of touch with his son for eleven years. Skillful work done by the rabbi before the ceremony made it into a healing occasion, with the possibility of a renewed relationship between father and son.[4]

Realizing the importance of putting the child first and of working with families, Valley Beth Shalom, a Conservative congregation in the Los Angeles area, piloted a program for families called "Celebration and Negotiation." It looked at not only the traditional preparations for the ceremony but also the implications of studies on the changing Jewish family, the importance of individual family counseling in some situations, and even practical guidance, such as appropriate ways to word the invitation.

Since then, celebrations for children of divorced parents have become normal in congregations. Not every parent requires professional help, and most expect to plan it properly as they would any other event in their children's lives. But regarding divorce as normal can lead to complacency. Every child experiences loss, and if the event is to be a process of growth, that loss has to be managed and absorbed with sensitivity. The issue of divorce and bar/bat mitzvah requires continued time and attention, and the congregation, the rabbi, and other professionals can make a huge difference when a family is in crisis. So far, the growing incidence of divorce has not undermined the popularity of the celebration in Jewish communities.[5]

Helen Leneman's guide book *Bar/Bat Mitzvah Basics*, first published 1996, includes a chapter on "Celebrating and Negotiating: Avoiding a Post-Divorce Battle on the *Bimah*." It offers simple advice such as "You divorced each other, not your child" and suggestions for workarounds for sensitive issues, for example, when parents publicly present a tallit to their child during the ceremony. It also gives suggestions on the wording of invitations, whom to invite, and where to seat them. "For every family, there is a 'right' solution," wrote Leneman. "The task lies in carefully and sensitively discussing and negotiating these solutions . . . you will find a growing sense of strength and empowerment as you discover solutions which seemed impossible are, indeed, within your grasp."[6]

Having a bar mitzvah when your parents are going through a divorce is one of the themes of the Coen brothers' satirical 2009 movie, *A Serious Man*. Set in an unnamed Minnesota town in 1967 but reflecting contemporary concerns, the characters inhabit a world in which unexpected events keep happening to them and all attempts to explain them flounder. The message of Rabbi Marshak, the emeritus rabbi of the Conservative congregation, to the bar mitzvah, Danny Gopnik, sounds profound until you realize he is quoting the Jefferson Airplane song "Somebody to Love":

"When the truth is found to be lies,
    And all the hope within you dies,"
Then what?

Here the bar mitzvah ceremony simply adds to the confusion of a boy growing up in a dysfunctional family. And when his father seeks advice from the temple rabbis, they fail to help or confuse him more, speaking cryptically or telling irrelevant stories. The message is that family life can have multiple stresses and that communities and rabbis are not always good at dealing with them.

Facilitating Those with Special Needs

Another area in which congregations have sometimes been less than helpful is when the child has special needs. There are, however, many examples of good practice. The key text for the history of bar mitzvah, by Rabbi

Solomon Luria (1510–74), tells the Talmudic story of the blind Rav Yosef, who wanted to keep the commands even though the general rabbinic view was that a blind person was exempt.[7] Although this classic text was available to support special needs children who might want to celebrate the occasion, it does not mean that in practice such events happened. It was only in the nineteenth century that the majority of Jewish children started to celebrate, and then a need was felt from time to time to make an appropriate celebration for a child with a disability.

A memorable bar mitzvah occurred in 1869 at the Portland Street Synagogue London, as the *Jewish Chronicle* reported: "An inmate of Jews' Deaf and Dumb Home, having attained the age of *bar mitzvah*, was called to the *Sefer*, and pronounced the Blessings in a distinctly audible voice. The boy was what is conventionally called a deaf-mute . . . We need scarcely say the incident evinced considerable emotion among those present. After the service, many persons crowded round the Bar Mitzvah boy and congratulated him."[8]

A short story by the American writer Hugh Nissenson, "The Law" (1965), describes the bar mitzvah of a boy with a stammer. Even though his father had never had a bar mitzvah and even though Danny is worried about speaking in public, his father, a concentration camp survivor, is determined that Danny should go through with the ceremony because he wants the boy to learn Hebrew: "It was something out of our past, the really distant past. It somehow seemed to me to be the only part of our consciousness that was left uncontaminated."[9] It is as if the father is handing on his own burden of survival to his son. Danny accepts the burden, and the story ends as he stammers through the blessing for his haftarah.

Today preparing a bar/bat mitzvah for a child with special needs has become commonplace. Or Hadash, the Lyons Centre for Progressive Judaism in Haifa, Israel, holds about thirty-five such celebrations each year, with the education team headed by Rabbi Dr. Edgar Nof. He claims that physically or mentally disabled children are often turned away by Orthodox synagogues because of lack of wheelchair access or because of halachic restrictions. In many cases Or Hadash represents the only opportunity for these children to have a meaningful Jewish ceremony. As is common in Israel, the ceremonies are held on a Monday or a Thursday morning.

Yet many still find themselves in congregations that are seemingly unable to recognize such children's needs. Rabbi Elyse Goldstein of Holy Blossom Temple, Toronto, wrote in 1986: "I have stopped counting the number of deaf Jews I have met who never had a bar/bat mitzvah because 'the Rabbi didn't know what to do with me.' Or the deaf Jew was handed an English translation and told, 'Just read this for your bar mitzvah' . . . This is the 'good enough for them' syndrome. This is the bane of a disabled Jew's existence."[10]

The documentary *Praying with Lior* presents the story of a boy with Down syndrome working for and celebrating his bar mitzvah in 2004. Lior had enjoyed daily prayer from a young age,[11] and his deep religious belief and obvious delight and happiness proved an inspiration to other parents to take up the challenge of celebrating with a child who has special needs. Lior's father, Reconstructionist rabbi Mordecai Leibling, allowed the film to be made in order to encourage synagogues to be more inclusive: "Because of his passion for prayer, we thought he would be a wonderful example for synagogues all over the country for inclusion. Most synagogues do not include children with disabilities and do not have a bar or bar mitzvah for a child with disabilities. The main message of the film is that inclusion benefits the entire community . . . all of us are enriched."[12]

Interfaith Families Celebrate

Many websites and books facilitate the celebration for children of mixed parentage. The online publication "Bar/Bat Mitzvah Ideas and Primer for Interfaith Families" (2006) highlights how non-Jewish parents and family can be involved. In the past the celebrations would have involved the Jewish parent and wider family only. As a general rule, says the guide, the more liberal the movement to which the synagogue belongs, the more flexibility the congregation will allow in offering roles in the service to family members and friends. The guide makes suggestions about how the synagogue service can be explained to a non-Jewish "audience." There are also suggestions such as creating a child's study project that looks at the family history and the interactions between the parents' different cultures. In 2000 the *Half Jewish Book* asserted that in the United States there were more children under the age of eleven with one Jewish parent than with two.[13] The non-Jewish family heritage will therefore play an increasing part in future celebrations.

An early teen novel that explores issues around having parents of different faiths and cultural backgrounds is Judy Blume's popular *Are You There God? It's Me, Margaret* (1970). Margaret explores her personal relationship to God in spite of her Jewish father and Christian mother, who have decided to bring her up with no religion at all. Margaret develops a relationship with both sets of grandparents, each of them keen that their granddaughter should adopt their own faith. At school and to her friends Margaret says that she has no faith, and she ends up feeling, as her parents repeatedly tell her, that she is "nothing." In spite of the existence of bat mitzvah, it does not become a theme in the book, showing that in 1970 there was still not a general expectation that a Jewish girl might celebrate like the boys. Instead, Margaret's rite of passage is when she has her first period.[14]

The high percentage of families with a non-Jewish partner has also set synagogue movements thinking about the Jewish identity of the children. Since early rabbinic times the tradition has been that being Jewish by birth depends on having a Jewish mother.[15] But today coming-of-age ceremonies have become a marker of Jewish identity for patrilineal Jews or even (in the interests of equality) for Jews with a non-Jewish father. The celebration of coming-of-age ceremonies by such children was discussed by the Central Conference of American Rabbis (CCAR) after World War II. In 1947 it resolved that the parents in mixed marriages could make a declaration to a rabbi that it was their intention to raise their children in the Jewish faith and that the children could then be considered converted and enrolled in the religious school. This change enabled such children to celebrate bar or bat mitzvah, and eventually "the ceremony of Confirmation at the end of the school course shall be considered in lieu of a conversion ceremony."[16]

Confirmation had throughout its history been an occasion marking the completion of a formal course of study, so using this ceremony as a marker of Jewish status made sense. One difficulty, however, remained unresolved. The resolution made no mention of what the status of a child would be if the parents failed to keep their commitment to a Jewish upbringing. This issue was clarified in 1961, when the conference first ruled about a child of a mixed marriage: "Reform Judaism . . . accepts such a child as Jewish without a formal conversion, if he attends a Jewish school and follows a course of studies leading to Confirmation." This move gave the confirmation an even more important status, no longer simply marking a conversion that had taken place earlier but now actually conferring Jewish status on the child. A similar resolution of the Federation of Reconstructionist Congregations and Havurot (1968), among which not every community offered confirmation, used the wording "if the children fulfill the requirements of bar/bat mitzvah *or* confirmation."[17] I have added the italics here to note that this is an important distinction. A lot had changed since 1922, when a well-known confirmation manual stated: "The purpose of Confirmation is not to lead us into the ranks of the Jewish people. Even if we are not confirmed we are Jews."[18]

Finally, in 1983 bar and bat mitzvah were used in the same way by the much larger CCAR. Since the 1961 resolution bar/bat mitzvah has generally been celebrated by the vast majority of boys and girls in American Reform synagogues, and confirmation's popularity has declined. There has also been a major change in the numbers of mixed-faith families in the United States: studies suggested that in 1964 the intermarriage figure was thought to be between 7 percent and 18 percent of marriages involving Jews, but by 1970, only six years later, the figure had risen to an alarming 31 percent.[19]

This huge change was met head on by CCAR with its radical 1983 resolution. Over many centuries the age thirteen for boys had become an important demarcation date, marking the status of the boy as an adult for the purposes of participation in the prayer and ritual life of the community. But celebrating the occasion had never been considered compulsory. In 1983 the CCAR declared that anyone who had one Jewish parent, the offspring of a mixed marriage, could be presumed to be of Jewish descent and that the child could continue to full Jewish status "through appropriate and timely public and formal acts of identification with the Jewish faith and people . . . Depending on circumstances, mitzvot leading toward a positive and exclusive Jewish identity will include entry into the covenant, acquisition of a Hebrew name, Torah study, Bar/Bat Mitzvah, and *Kabbalat Torah* (Confirmation). For those beyond childhood claiming Jewish identity, other public acts or declarations may be added or substituted after consultation with their rabbi."[20]

This declaration gave a completely new status to bar/bat mitzvah within the American Reform movement. The history presented here shows that bar mitzvah grew and developed primarily as a folk custom, not a compulsory demand by synagogues and rabbis. Back in Poland, recalled Joseph Hen in 2004, "nobody checked if you had a bar mitzvah or not."[21] But for children from mixed-faith households in the United States, it was a different story. The twentieth-century synagogue rules laying down years of study as a condition of bar mitzvah paved the way for this new and startling innovation.[22]

In the twenty-first century the daughter of a mixed-faith family cannot avoid the issue of whether or not she is to have a bat mitzvah. This is the theme of Nora Baskin's *The Truth about My Bat Mitzvah* (2008). The story begins as Caroline prepares for the funeral of her Jewish grandmother, who leaves her a Star of David. Caroline's father is not Jewish, and although she is very involved in the preparations for her best friend Rachel's bat mitzvah, her family has not planned one for her. In the end she discovers the "truth," that she does not need a bat mitzvah in order to be Jewish. There is an implied criticism here of American Reform Jews making bat mitzvah a marker of Jewish status.

Group Ceremonies

Group ceremonies for bar mitzvah are not new, even in Orthodox communities. The Jews' Free School London was holding them as long ago as 1929.[23] Today they are popular for both boys and girls who live or have lived in areas without an organized community life. This is another instance of the thinking that a Jewish child has really missed out on something important if he or she has not celebrated bar or bat mitzvah.

Many mass ceremonies around the world are organized by Chabad and other organizations, particularly in Russia and in Israel for Russian immigrants and others. Chabad began holding such ceremonies in Israel in 1991. A report from March 2001 describes a thousand children celebrating together at the Western Wall in Jerusalem.[24] In 2005 a group of sixty children celebrated together in a five-day event at Khabarovsk in Siberia, with twenty of them having traveled overnight from the Pacific port city of Vladivostok. This event was organized by the American Joint Distribution Committee, and more such events were held in subsequent years.[25]

Adult and Second and Third Bar Mitzvah

Adult bar mitzvah is becoming just as popular as adult bat mitzvah ceremonies. There are men of all ages celebrating for the first time as well as those celebrating anniversaries of their original bar mitzvah. In 1951 a bar mitzvah ceremony was held for eight adult men at Temple Beth-El in Great Neck, New York.[26] Group adult celebrations have since become popular and are celebrated all over the world.

In 1979 Bill Sackter celebrated his bar mitzvah at the age of sixty-six at Agudas Achim Synagogue in Iowa. Diagnosed as "subnormal" and "feeble-minded" as a child, he had lived in institutions for forty-four years, and it was only after his release in 1964 that his Jewish identity was confirmed. Bill found work as a special developmental disabilities coordinator and celebrated his bar mitzvah at a Saturday afternoon service and havdalah ceremony with over a hundred people present. The ceremony ended with Bill playing his harmonica.[27]

An episode of *The Simpsons* about the adult bar mitzvah of Krusty the Clown aired in 2003. Krusty celebrated twice, first in a Hollywood extravaganza and then in a simple ceremony that enabled him to reconnect with his estranged father, Rabbi Hyman Krustofski. Krusty pursues the idea about celebrating his bar mitzvah when he realizes he has no star in the sidewalk of the Jewish Walk of Fame in Springfield. When he inquires why, he is told he cannot be a Jewish man because he did not have a bar mitzvah. This entirely erroneous information fits with the modern and previously unheard-of idea that bar mitzvah can help create a Jewish identity; indeed, the whole concept of adult bar mitzvah and bat mitzvah is built around the idea that there is something missing if a Jew has never had one. Because of this idea, some have promoted alternative names for the adult ceremony, such as *Ben Torah* (Son of the Torah) and *Chaver Le'Toruh* (Friend to the Torah).

"The span of our life is seventy years, or, given the strength, eighty years," wrote the Psalmist.[28] This text is the basis for the modern tradition of celebrating a second bar mitzvah at the age of eighty-three, which is seventy years plus thirteen.[29] Drawing on the newly established custom of having a "second bar mitzvah" at that age, Lionel Cowan celebrated his first bar mitzvah in Manchester, England, in 1988, at the age of eighty-three; like many, he had missed the original celebration because of World War I. A lifetime pacifist, printer, and educator, he knew, like all good educators, that it is never too late to learn.[30]

The actor Kirk Douglas, after surviving a helicopter crash and a stroke, celebrated his second bar mitzvah in December 1999 amid a crowd of two hundred guests. "If my mother is in heaven," he said, "she will look down and she will smile. That's why I had my second bar mitzvah, for my mother. And, just exactly like I ended my first bar mitzvah, I promise to be a good boy."[31]

Increased longevity has brought with it more new additions to the repertoire of bar mitzvah celebrations. In 2003 Abe Immerman, famous as South Africa's "blind hazzan," celebrated his third bar mitzvah at Highlands Home in Cape Town at the age of ninety-six. He passed away two days later.[32] And in 2008 Dr. Eugene Gettelman celebrated his fourth bar mitzvah at the age of one hundred at Westwood Horizons, Los Angeles. His second and third celebrations had been group ceremonies.[33]

THE GROWTH OF BAR/BAT MITZVAH
AS A SOCIAL OCCASION

The United States has led the way in the twentieth-century development of bar mitzvah as a social occasion. Immigrants from Eastern Europe had celebrated with a light snack or meal for close family only, but as they moved up the social scale, parties became more lavish. Before World War I it was customary to host a luncheon at home after the ceremony or on the Sunday following it. In the United States in the 1920s portrait photos were taken in studios, and parties began to be held in halls and hotels, accompanied by music and dancing. Dinners could consist of up to five or six courses.[34]

In Europe at that time most families still had small family parties at home. But the more Orthodox in the United States continued to celebrate just as their families had in Europe, as Is Crystal recalled: "Sunday my mother had twenty friends and relatives to the house for a chicken dinner. I stood up on a chair and gave a little talk in Yiddish . . . Then I went outside and played with the kids and let the adults do whatever they wanted."[35]

A valuable insight into British celebrations comes from the archive of Rabbi Moses Gaster (1856–1939), whose personal papers, consisting of 170,000 items, were given to University College London in 1974.[36] In the archive are many bar mitzvah invitations he had received. They came from the wealthier Jewish families of London and Manchester and were printed on a card with the name of the invitees written in by hand. Invitations were to both the ceremony and the party. The synagogue ceremonies were invariably held in synagogue on a Shabbat morning. From the 1880s until World War I, the bar mitzvah party would be held at home and was referred to as a "reception," a "breakfast," or simply "at home." Invitations might be for a Saturday or Sunday afternoon or evening, and sometimes a choice of times was offered. Parties began to be held in reception rooms and hotels after the war.

In 1919 Gaster received an invitation to a bar mitzvah shortly after Passover, to be held at the Spanish and Portuguese Synagogue, Withington, Manchester, on a Shabbat morning, with the reception being held at the Midland Hotel in central Manchester, from 8:30 p.m. to midnight on the following Tuesday.[37] This timing would have enabled guests from London or elsewhere to come by train for the midweek party without attending the ceremony itself.

Clearly, the social aspects of the event were upgraded once the war was over, a development that might have been commercially driven. Kosher caterers, unable to cater for weddings during the Omer period, may well have encouraged this new market for their services because, unlike weddings, bar mitzvah meals could still be held at this time of the Jewish year. Invitations from then on were for parties held in hotels or reception rooms, with one from January 1920 stating intriguingly, "Fancy and Evening Dress Optional."[38]

A most remarkable feature of the British archived invitations, from 1892 through 1925, is the constant use of the English term *confirmation*, either in addition to but more commonly instead of the term *bar mitzvah*. Was this simply an alternative name, or did it indicate that the ceremony itself was being viewed in a different way? All the archived invitations are to Orthodox synagogues, but these were the days of clean-shaven rabbis who wore clerical collars and used the title "Reverend" rather than "Rabbi," following regulations laid down by Nathan Adler, chief rabbi of the British Empire, in 1847. One historian wrote, "Well into the twentieth century, a Jewish minister staring benignly out of the photograph of a Bar Mitzvah class would be indistinguishable from an Anglican priest with his confirmation class."[39]

But substituting the term *confirmation* for *bar mitzvah* meant more than just using an English term instead of a Hebrew one; it was a usage that viewed the ceremony as something done to or for the boy, which eventually morphed into the mid-twentieth-century usage of *bar mitzvah* as a transitive verb, in sentences such as "The Rabbi barmitzvahed our son."

Robert Leiter remembered his bar mitzvah in Philadelphia: "I was inconsequential to the whole thing. My bar mitzvah was not for me and my friends. It was for my father and his friends . . . It had nothing to do with education. It was a ticket that enabled my father to stage a massive party that would prove to his peers that he had arrived."[40]

By the 1930s in the United States some celebrations had become much more extravagant. A lavish bar mitzvah was portrayed by Herman Wouk in his novel *Marjorie Morningstar*, published in 1955 but set in New York in 1933. Seth Morgenstern's bar mitzvah is seen through the eyes of his older sister Marjorie. Although celebrated primarily as a social occasion, the service, held in a Conservative temple, is described as having an unexpected spiritual impact as Seth chants his haftarah: "Despite herself, the girl found awe creeping over her as her brother's voice filled the vault of the temple, chanting words thousands of years old, in an eerie melody from a dim lost time."[41]

The description focuses on huge amounts of food served at a buffet lunch after the Shabbat morning service and at a banquet that night. The celebrations are both extravagant and tasteful: "The flower-decked ballroom, the spacious dance floor, the waiters in the blue mess jackets, the murmuring orchestra behind potted palms, the fine linen and silver on the tables, the camellias by each lady's plate, left nothing even for the Goldstones to desire."[42] Here the bar mitzvah is the fulfillment of both a spiritual and a materialist dream. Rabbi Mordecai Kaplan, the father of the celebrated 1922 bat mitzvah girl, denounced such catered affairs as showing "the disintegration of Jewish life."[43] They were not the norm in Eastern Europe even for wealthy Jewish families.

It is interesting to compare the bar mitzvah in *Marjorie Morningstar* with an Eastern European account of a party for a boy from a wealthy family. Juraj Adler's bar mitzvah was held at the Orthodox synagogue at Pesinok in Slovakia in 1936. The family had a large house, and the children had a governess. The bar mitzvah party was held in the children's living room at home on the evening before the synagogue ceremony. "The culmination of the evening was a swan made of parfait, that's what today's ice cream was called. They brought it in a box packed with ice all the way from Bratislava, from some fancy restaurant."[44] This item was extravagant for them but much more modest than the American equivalent at the time. But by the mid-1930s the vast majority in the United States were far less fortunate, as the years of the Great Depression took their toll. Many a family had to be content with feasting on the cookies known as "kichels" served with herring and a bottle of schnapps.[45]

After World War II increasing affluence saw the start of themed parties, with lavish decorations and expensive entertainers. The "bar mitzvah cake" with thirteen candles became a popular feature. Lavish parties in the United States provoked a good deal of criticism from 1950 onward, especially from Reform rabbis. Some critics were concerned with the disastrous effect on poorer Jews, who might feel they had to get into debt to host a bar mitzvah; others were concerned that the social aspects had eclipsed the religious significance or spoke out against irreverent behavior they had witnessed as guests at such parties. Although Reform Jews had traditionally promoted confirmation as an alternative to bar mitzvah, the older ceremony had gradually come back, with boys being given the opportunity to have a bar mitzvah at thirteen as well as a confirmation at fifteen or sixteen. In 1952, 92 percent of American Reform temples offered bar mitzvah, and by 1960 the figure was 96 percent.[46]

At the 1951 convention of the Central Conference of American Rabbis, Rabbi Max Maccoby pointed out that parties held for girls were much more restrained and tasteful than those for boys and suggested that the boys' celebrations should be reduced to the more modest size of bat mitzvah parties.[47] But although both Conservative and Reform movements urged restraint, the days had gone when they could bring back the kind of restrictions that had been the norm in the seventeenth and eighteenth centuries; indeed, the old communal regulations were no longer even remembered.

In 1964 the Central Conference of American Rabbis criticized "the steady and alarming deterioration in the character of the Bar Mitzvah affair" and warned against "extravagant consumption, conspicuous waste, and the crudity" of parties, which were "rapidly becoming a public scandal."[48] The "public scandal" was publicity in magazines, novels, and films, such as *Marjorie Morningstar*. There was undoubtedly a feeling, as there had been in Europe two hundred years earlier, that indulgent displays could and would encourage anti-Jewish sentiments among the wider population and help to perpetuate the myth that all Jews were wealthy.

More Bar than Mitzvah

In 1956 Rabbi Moses Feinstein proposed the abolition of bar mitzvah on the grounds that it did not bring the boys closer to Torah and led Jews to desecrate the Sabbath.[49] Another notable critic of the way things were going was Rabbi Harold Saperstein of Temple Emanu-El, Lynbrook, New York, who in various sermons from 1957 to 1962 popularized the phrase "more bar than mitzvah" to describe celebrations in which the religious commitment took second place to the party. Saperstein practiced what he preached and decided to hold modest celebrations within his own family, as his son Professor Marc Saperstein, also a rabbi, recalls:

Especially meaningful to me was the sermon dated 31 May, 1957, as my own Bar Mitzvah was at the end of June that year, and I remember discussing with my parents months earlier the kind of reception we would have, and their explaining that it would not be a Saturday night dinner with dancing (as most of my friends had both from our Reform Congregation and the neighboring Conservative congregation), because my parents simply did not believe in that kind of event; it would be a much more modest luncheon following the service. I confess that I was a bit disappointed at first, but did not protest.[50]

The look and feel of parties from the late 1970s to the early 1990s has been well documented in the book *Bar Mitzvah Disco*, a collection of photos and reminiscences. The book's introduction, written in 2005, quips that the authors are looking back from the materialist age of the twenty-first century to an age of innocence twenty years earlier. In its proclamation that the child is becoming an adult overnight, bar/bat mitzvah is described as "a ritualized act of self-deception." The 1980s were remembered as the days of the long children's table, the disco, the sign-in board, the chair dance, the velvet *kippot*, and the kiss photo, featuring two girls kissing the boy from either side. But none of the boys' and girls' memoirs suggest that the celebrations had cost too much; that, it seems, was only the parents' perspective.

One alternative strategy that worked (at first only for a few committed Zionist families) was that of encouraging families to spend the money they would have used for the celebration on taking their son to Israel. The *Reconstructionist* magazine urged in 1963: "Instead of being exposed to the eating, drinking and dancing, which has nothing whatever to do with his entrance into the household of Israel, he would find himself upon the soil where the words he chants echoed millennia ago."[51]

Bar and bat mitzvah in Israel for American Jews grew slowly but surely during the last four decades of the twentieth century. Israel Discovery Tour Company (ITAS) of Millburn, New Jersey, began to offer holiday bar/bat mitzvah packages in 1970. In 1998 a guidebook was published for the independent traveler, listing useful contacts—rabbis, synagogues, hotels, guesthouses, tour guides, adventure holidays, and even themed holidays linked to the book of the Torah the boy or girl might be studying. The book grew out of the authors' own experiences and contacts, aiming to list "creative responsible people who are excited about the Bar and Bat Mitzvah facilities and events they can offer."[52]

By 2010 bar and bat mitzvah in Israel had become a thriving business, with two to three hundred children celebrating daily at the Western Wall at the height of the summer season. In that year the Israeli website

Ynetnews.com reported a sharp rise in celebrations by visitors to the country. The idea of Israel being a cheaper alternative to a celebration at home had failed, as hosts flew out more and more guests at their own expense. The website reported that American families were spending five to ten thousand dollars per person on their Israel celebrations and identified three main groups of visitors:

1. American Reform and Conservative Jews who take a tour of the country with expert tour guides and regard the celebration as recharging their Jewish identity.
2. Larger Orthodox groups from the United States and Europe who prefer to celebrate in Jerusalem, using the Western Wall and hotel facilities.
3. Groups ranging from one to two hundred from the Syrian Jewish communities in New York and the wealthier Sephardic communities in Latin America. They tend to use Israeli event planning services, and the celebrations include performances by popular Israeli singers.[53]

Before the economic downturn that began in 2008, the most wealthy had been spending even more, with the largest groups bringing up to four hundred guests.

Bar Mitzvah Lessons, a young adult novel by Martin Elsant (1993), tells the story of a child in an Orthodox community too scared to "perform" in public or even to admit to his teachers that he has a problem. He simply refuses to learn his portion, and one by one everyone refuses to teach him. Eventually, his father sends him to Reuven Weiss, a garage mechanic, who discovers the problem and deals with it successfully. In an interesting subplot Reuven turns out to be a skilled teacher who had been dismissed from his job for criticizing an overly expensive celebration and calling it a "meal of sin." He recalls: "The students would come home from school and hear their parents express passionate longings for . . . a mink coat, a fancy sports car, a more expensive house, an exotic vacation, or a party to end all parties to celebrate an upcoming Bar Mitzvah, and this effectively cancels out so much of what the students have learned."[54] This fictionalized account revealed a growing problem of very large celebrations in some American Orthodox communities and of the courage necessary to speak out against them.

The Ultimate Bar/Bat Mitzvah Celebration Book (2004) is about how to plan the perfect party. Written by two caterers and party planners, the book states that many parents are looking for a way to avoid falling into the peer pressure trap. Nevertheless, the outlook promoted by the book is unashamedly commercial, with whole chapters devoted to budgeting, guest lists, location, lighting as a decor tool, music, and flowers. Celebrating in Israel is described as a device used by families "who have side-stepped the issue."[55]

The party themes, menus, and recipes presented in the book provide a fine historical record of celebrations among Reform and Conservative Jews in North America in the first decade of the twenty-first century. Buffet stations enabled international menus, each station serving food from a different part of the world. Pomegranate martinis, heirloom tomato salad, seared tuna loin, double chocolate decadence, benei mitzvah cake, and mini–buffet desserts—these offerings reflect the decade's contradictory trends of healthy and unhealthy eating side by side.

Extravagant parties still bring protests in their wake. Rabbi Shmuley Boteach combined criticism of both wedding and bar mitzvah parties on his blog in 2010:

> American Jews often exhibit the worst tendencies of immigrant communities, endeavoring their best to show how they not just landed but arrived . . . And what's the point of having it if your friends are ignorant of your success? . . . you can utterly vulgarize the spirituality of the occasion by transforming it into a showcase of material consumption and excess.
>
> I remember growing up in Miami Beach and the over-the-top, utterly ridiculous Bar Mitzvahs that were de rigueur. One in the late '70s featured Darth Vader and R2D2 greetings guests as they arrived at the reception . . . One wondered, apart from its celestial setting, Star Wars had with the spirituality of the moment. On another occasion I arrived to see a full ice sculpture of the Bar Mitzvah boy, which perfectly suited the freezing cold religious aspect . . .
>
> A remedy is needed. Rabbis should be thundering from the pulpit that extravagant weddings are not only a betrayal of a sense of personal inadequacy, but are an abrogation of Jewish values. You're so rich? Then impress your friends by giving the money to charity.[56]

Extravagant expenditure can take the form of spending more per person or of greatly increasing the number of guests. The old sumptuary laws from 1595 onward had sought to control expenditure principally by restricting numbers. In many Hasidic communities the bar mitzvah tradition has included a modest celebration, but today's affluence and ease of travel has led to greatly increased numbers attending celebrations for sons or grandsons of important rabbis. In 2008 and 2010 thousands attended celebrations in Jerusalem for the two oldest grandsons of the Grand Belzer Rebbe, Rabbi Yissahar Dov Rokeah. Separate parties were held for men and women, and the men's celebration took the form of a traditional *tish* but was held in a sports stadium. As the rabbi has seven grandsons, the Belzer Hasidim can look forward to being invited to many other large bar mitzvah celebrations.[57]

In 2012 complaints began to be voiced in the United States that bat mitzvah parties had also become too glitzy and just as extravagant as the boys' celebrations, though in a different way. In a March 2012 magazine article Marjorie Ingall expressed real outrage at the way girls' parties are conducted today:

These days, I'm often gobsmacked by girls' outfits at their parties— and sometimes in shul, as well: gynecologically short skirts, bustier tops cantilevered over barely developed curves, nosebleed-inducing stratospheric heels. The bat mitzvah girl's friends teeter into the party like a herd of newborn foals. Some hostesses provide baskets of ankle socks so that the girls can dance more comfortably after they take off their foot-bindings . . . What's the point of having a bat mitzvah—a symbolic ceremony marking the time when a girl becomes a Jewish adult, fully responsible for her own actions and choices—if she's going to focus more on the clothes and the party than the ritual? . . . The ungapatchka same-sameness seems particularly sad when you consider how hard individual girls and women worked to win the right to celebrate this milestone at all.[58]

But extravagance is not universal. Online comments about Ingall's article show a wide measure of agreement with the writer. Many of her readers indicated their determination to spend less, even as they pointed out that others were willing to spend fifty thousand dollars on a party. And of course not every child wants the bar/bat mitzvah to be viewed in entirely material terms. That is the message of the comedy movie *Keeping Up with the Steins* (2006). Adam Fiedler, Hollywood filmmaker, tells his son Benjamin: "I will always be there for you, you know that. I just want you to have the biggest bar mitzvah in the history of bar mitzvahs."

Yet that is not what Benjamin wants, and his father is persuaded to change his plans. Although the Steins held the party on a cruise ship and their son was pulled in on a lifelike model of the *Titanic*, Benjamin opts for a party in his garden at home, with traditional Jewish foods, a klezmer band, and a candle lighting ceremony like the one described earlier from the 1930s. It becomes an American bar mitzvah party from two generations back, in line with contemporary popularity of retro style but also emphasizing the importance of Benjamin's grandfather for his Jewish journey, this being the second theme of the movie's plot.

A problem related to overly extravagant parties is the misbehavior of children. Many find themselves invited to large numbers of parties throughout the year. Caught up in a new and luxurious lifestyle, their unruly behavior is the inevitable result. Yet in fact there is nothing new about this potential for bad behavior—it was an issue at bar mitzvah parties in Hamburg-Altona in 1712—but it is a recurring problem that occasionally makes headlines or reaches the community gossip columns, such as one case from 2005:

> Our sages taught that a parent is responsible for the actions of a child until that child reaches the age of 13 years and a day. At that point he's ready to assume full responsibility for observing the commandments and for all his deeds. Perhaps our sages should have specified that all deeds include downing the remains of alcoholic beverages, stuffing toilets with rolls of paper, running wild in hotel parking lots, having elevator races, destroying someone else's furniture and (gasp) sexually precocious acts in bathrooms with other newly pubescent Jewish "adults."[59]

Misbehavior at bar mitzvah parties is often talked about but rarely written about. It does not feature as an issue in any of the published guides. Not surprisingly, reminiscences from the child's point of view give a very different perspective on such events.[60]

Worship of the Child

The bar mitzvah service in *Keeping Up with the Steins,* held in a California Reform Temple, shows the family sitting on the *bimah* throughout the ceremony and the rabbi introducing the haftarah like an impresario introducing an act. The scene provides background for a related contemporary issue. On December 15, 2007, Rabbi Eric Yoffie, preaching to nearly five thousand delegates at the Biennial Conference of the U.S. Union for Reform Judaism, lamented that the Shabbat morning services in Reform congregations across the United States were failing because they had become private celebrations for the families of those celebrating bar/bat mitzvah:

> With the morning worship appropriated by the Bar and Bat Mitzvah families, our members who come to pray with the community often sit in the back of the sanctuary and feel like interlopers in their own congregation . . . These are serious matters. If we allow our services to be privatized; if we give up ownership of Shabbat and of our own sanctuaries; if communal celebration gives way to a bar mitzvah performance—if all these things happen, how can we remain the dynamic Movement that we have become? . . . Absent a knowledgeable congregation, worship of God gives way to worship of the child—and self-serving worship is a contradiction in terms. Rabbis, cantors, educators and presidents all told me how painful it is to sit in a service where the child is the star . . . Inevitably, this leads to speeches in which every boy or girl is smarter than Einstein, a better soccer play than Mia Hamm, more of a computer whiz than Bill Gates and more of an activist than Bono.
>
> Let's be honest. There is something profoundly wrong here. On every Shabbat of the year, there are hundreds and hundreds of bar and bat mitzvahs in Reform congregations. But rarely does anyone walk out of those worship services saying: "That was so spiritually fulfilling that I can't wait to come back next week."[61]

Such criticisms were not new; similar sentiments had been voiced in articles and letters in the *Journal of Reform Judaism* since 1974. Many of them suggested that the emphasis on bar/bat mitzvah was weakening efforts at fostering a religious community.[62] Rabbi Yoffie's focus was on how to improve the Shabbat morning service for ordinary members of the community, but the problem he highlights is a serious one for the bar/bat mitzvah as well. You cannot welcome a child into the community as an adult member of the Jewish people if the community is not there. It sounds hollow to emphasize to a child the importance of Jewish spiritual identity if it seems to the child that the rest of the community does not apparently identify with the spiritual life of the Jewish people. The emphasis within the synagogue on one family ends up inevitably with their being seen as modeling the tradition, whatever their personal feelings. Rabbi Yoffie insists that the Reform temple services are meaningful for the child, but the problem, he argues, is that the rest of the community does not want to attend.[63]

Reform communities have tried to tackle the problem by providing a choice of services on a Shabbat morning. This effort has been successful in bringing back the congregation, but the problem of welcoming the bar/bat mitzvah into a community that is not there remains. And raising the child to celebrity status is an issue not just in the temple but also in the social aspects of contemporary celebrations.

In an important article published in 2010 the educator Isa Aron argued that the successful introduction of bar/bat mitzvah programs since the 1930s has had unintended consequences. The concentration on the ceremony as the main motivator for Jewish education has led to an undue focus on a one-time performance, rather than enculturation to a unique way of life. This has led to an unacceptably high dropout rate after the ceremony, a degradation of Hebrew language learning, and too many celebrations taking place outside the traditional congregational framework, as part of a vacation or on a cruise. Jewish educators need to review their programs and goals in an age when commitment to Jewish life comes primarily through education.[64]

BRINGING BACK THE CORE VALUES

These separate issues—very extravagant parties, teen misbehavior, a community absent from the synagogue, and too much focus on a one-time performance—are all connected. They reflect celebrations that sometimes lose their way and can be devoid of spiritual meaning. It is therefore not surprising that other contemporary trends have highlighted ways of getting back to the core values of the ceremony.

The *havurah* movement, which became popular in the 1970s, promoted small-scale autonomous alternatives to large Jewish institutions. Its members were the first to take up the challenge of how to celebrate bar/bat mitzvah in a simpler, more meaningful way. *The Second Jewish Catalog* (1976) gives a comprehensive guide to the background of the ceremony and even mentions the little-known sumptuary laws once used by communities to limit expenditures. This information is in keeping with the whole ethos of the *Jewish Catalog* series, which is about doing as much as possible oneself. In it we find families encouraged to assemble their own congregation, borrow their own scroll, compose their own service booklet, design their own invitations, and cook their own food. Not only is the rabbi unnecessary, but the caterer is too:

> *Some things you might think you need but don't*
> 1. a rabbi (you're reading Torah, not seeking spiritual advice)
> 2. a bar (keep things simple)
> 3. professional musicians (any of the kids have a guitar? an accordion? a zither?)
> 4. vast flower arrangements (they wither anyway).[65]

Other suggestions included making one's own Kiddush wine and an embroidered tallit for one's son or daughter. Few have gone as far as to dispense with temple, rabbi, and caterer altogether, but the book undoubtedly started a voluntary trend back to limiting spending.

Putting God on the Guest List: How to Reclaim the Spiritual Meaning of Your Child's Bar or Bat Mitzvah was written by Rabbi Jeffrey K. Salkin in 1992 to try to put the mitzvah back into the occasion. It was a bold attempt to divert parents from party planning and guest lists into finding meaning in the ceremony, perhaps through their own family history ("the tears of passing years" and "the river of sacred time"), the sacred drama of the worship service, and a new prayer for non-Jewish parents:

> O God of all humanity:
> We lift our voices in gratitude that the Torah has come into the world through the Jewish people.
> We lift our voices in gratitude for the ideals it teaches: justice; compassion; devotion; the partnership of mind, heart, and deed.

We lift our voices in gratitude that our son/daughter today takes
his/her place among the people of Israel. We pray that he/she will
do so with pride and joy. As You called Israel to be a light to the
nations, so too, we pray that our son/daughter will be his/her own
ray of light to the world.[66]

There is an assumption here that the non-Jewish parents believe in God,
and as the title of the book indicates, there is no attempt to address the
needs of secular or nonbelieving families.

The choice of tallit has become another example of the search for a
deeper meaning and the focus on the spirituality of the individual child.
The tallit has a special place in the history of bar mitzvah because it was
the obligation to wear fringes on the corners of the garment by a boy aged
thirteen and one day that was taken as the key command on which the
whole notion of becoming bar mitzvah was based: "Just as a man has to
perform this command, so when he reaches the age of thirteen years and
one day he becomes obligated for all the commandments of the Torah."[67]
It became traditional to buy a new tallit for the bar mitzvah, to enable the
special blessing for happy occasions to be said.[68]

The general custom is that the tallit is worn by Jewish men for morning
prayer, except in Eastern Europe, where the custom was applied to married men only, and this is still the practice in congregations that follow
the Eastern Ashkenazic tradition.[69] But in all traditions it was worn for
the occasion by someone who had a special duty (known as a "mitzvah")
in the service, such as a bar mitzvah called up to the Torah.

Those Reform congregations that abolished bar mitzvah in the nineteenth century also abandoned the covering of the head for worship and
the wearing of the tallit, except by the minister or service leader. With
the return to tradition, the wearing of the special garments for prayer
returned as well and, like so many aspects of bar/bat mitzvah, has sometimes become commercialized. *Kippot* to cover the head are often supplied
by hosts for guests, in colors favored by the child and sometimes with a
motif or logo to match a favorite sports team or the theme of the party.
A tallit is often worn by a girl celebrating her bat mitzvah in those synagogues where men and women have an equal role. An adult bat mitzvah
might well acquire her first tallit for the occasion.

Although traditionally a white garment with blue or black stripes, tallitot with colored stripes have been marketed since the 1950s, the most

popular being the "B'nai Or" tallit with a kabbalistic design by Rabbi Zalman Schachter-Shalomi (1961).[70] Sometimes the tallit is presented publicly to the bar/bat mitzvah and placed on his or her shoulders at the start of the service. Because a tallit can also be used as a wedding canopy, the donning of the new tallit looks forward to that time as well as marking the entry into responsibility for the *mitzvot*.

The tallit worn for the ceremony is sometimes not new but a family heirloom. The short teen story "Noah's Choice" (2002) tells how wearing the tallit of his dead grandfather inspired Noah to carry on and study for his bar mitzvah in memory of the grandfather who had planned to teach him.[71] This is a story with many parallels in real family events; Matan Goldman, for example, wore his great-grandfather's brightly colored tallit for his bar mitzvah in Philadelphia in 2010. His mother, and the traditional community of which they were part, generally favored a simple white woolen tallit with black stripes, but the significance of the heirloom won the day.[72]

Heirlooms also feature in Judith Davis's *Whose Bar/Bat Mitzvah Is This, Anyway?* (1998), a book about the stress of the occasion and how to avoid it. It suggests that bar/bat mitzvah is a major transitional event in the life of the entire family, a time not only of great joy but of great turmoil as well. So, helping the child through the doubts and fears, choosing a tutor who can be a role model, discovering the family heirlooms and making them meaningful, turning the guest list from a minefield to a gold mine—the book argues that all these can pave the way to a calm and happy celebration in a stressful age.

Rabbi Arthur Waskow of the Jewish Renewal movement has suggested an eco-celebration as an alternative to a consumerist approach. Many of his ideas bring us full circle back to the self-help approach of the *Second Jewish Catalog* but with the use of modern technology: "Instead of bringing wrapped and packaged presents, guests simply RSVP and make secure online contributions that are pooled for the purchase of ONE memorable gift and to support ONE meaningful cause. Select an eco-friendly birthday party invitation, choose a cause and invite your friends. No Driving. No Shopping. No Wrapping."[73]

This is another example of the way in which many teachers, rabbis, and families are seeking to put meaning into the preparation and the ceremony and how to individualize the ceremony so that it does not just reflect but enhances the good qualities and interests of the child as well as putting something back into the community. It brings us to a very important trend that is part of most celebrations today, the mitzvah project.

The Mitzvah Project

The traditional blessing recited for a Jewish baby boy at his circumcision includes the words "Just as he has entered the covenant, so may he enter to Torah, the wedding chamber, and good deeds." Doing good deeds is a central part of the tradition of Torah that the boy undertakes at bar mitzvah.

An unusual story in the Zohar describes Satan arriving uninvited at the weaning feast that Abraham and Sarah gave for their son, Isaac. Satan is disguised as a poor man, but Abraham and Sarah will not invite him in. Satan complains to God. Because of his lack of hospitality, Abraham is punished by having to offer up his son on Mount Moriah. Sarah dies in sorrow, and this is because they did not give to the poor.[74]

The story becomes important because the party hosted by Abraham and Sarah was regarded as a biblical model for the bar mitzvah party. The Zohar story warned of the consequences of failing to think of others while celebrating in one's own family. It is therefore not surprising that when communal regulations began for bar mitzvah, gifts to the community charity funds were included, such as in this one from Krakow in 1638: "We have established as a binding rule that every householder from here, whose son begins to learn Torah, shall give a donation to this Society of 18 tefalim [small coins], and also that anyone who makes a bar mitzvah meal for his son must also give a donation of 18 tefalim to this Society."[75] The open soliciting of funds for the community has a long and fascinating history that continues to the present time. John Adler, celebrating his bar mitzvah in London in 1947, remembered the rabbi giving him a quiet few words during the synagogue ceremony, including the important reminder, "Don't forget to ask your father to make a donation."[76]

In the twentieth century the onus of giving was not just for the parents but for the child as well. A confirmation manual from 1922 insisted: "Unless the celebration makes you more unselfish and more considerate . . . it is not sacred but a show and a sacrilege. It ought especially to make you more charitable and to this end you should on Confirmation Day connect yourself as contributor for the rest of your life with some charitable institution."[77] Today it is normal for community bar/bat mitzvah programs to include a project of some kind. Many of these projects began during the years of campaigning for Soviet Jewry (1970–93), when it became customary to twin the celebration with that of a Jewish child in the Soviet Union who was unable to celebrate or unable to emigrate. The bar/bat mitzvah wrote to the "twin," and often a tallit and prayer book would be placed in an empty chair on the *bimah* to symbolize the twin's participation in the ceremony. In the late 1980s and since then, as more Jews have been allowed to emigrate from the Soviet Union, some of the former twins were able to meet for the first time.[78]

Some of the ideas that arose at that time still continue. The New Jersey organization Areyvut, for example, offers a wide choice of projects, such as twinning a bar/bat mitzvah with a child in the Ukraine, supporting elderly Jews in the former Soviet Union, sending care packages to Israeli soldiers, sponsoring English literacy in Jerusalem, assisting asylum seekers in Israel, raising funds for Israeli hospitals, supporting orphans in Rwanda, and helping children affected by cancer or AIDS.[79] In Britain the charity My Israel encourages direct involvement with small Israeli charities. In 2009 Barney Burns collected five hundred toothbrushes for his mitzvah project, which were distributed by the Dental Volunteers Clinic in Jerusalem.

In 2004 the British charity UJIA began to twin Ethiopian children in Safed (Tzefat), Israel, who were celebrating bar/bat mitzvah, with children from Britain. As well as paying for their visit, the British families contribute toward the bar/bat mitzvah education for the Ethiopian children. The program grew; in 2010 twenty-two families flew out to Israel to celebrate with their twins. The British children keep in touch throughout the year, with project work, letters, and gifts, and then fly to Israel for a week in July to celebrate together: "Despite their differences, the teenagers find common ground. Translated letters about their family, football, music and studies in school, as well as their Bar/Bat Mitzvah, provide plenty of opportunity to forge friendships. For the British twins and their parents who travel to Jerusalem for the communal ceremony, there is tremendous excitement when they meet their Ethiopian twin for the first time. There are no barriers, just an instant bonding between the children that deepens as the celebrations and ceremony take place."[80]

Doing a Mitzvah for Your Bar/Bat Mitzvah

In the English-speaking world a considerable impetus was given to the bar/bat mitzvah *tzedakah* project by the publication of *Danny Siegel's Bar and Bat Mitzvah Mitzvah Book* in 2004, a follow-up to his many other publications promoting giving to charity. Siegel simply explains the Jewish

concepts of *tikkun olam* ("repairing the world") and charity ("the obligation of each of us to be righteous") and then takes the reader through "24
Questions Parents May Wish to Ask Themselves," which include "Have I
ever asked myself, 'Is my child gifted in Tikkun Olam–type Mitzvahs?'"
"What do I mean when I say, 'I want my child to be successful'?" and
"What is the relationship between my child's Jewish education and what
kind of person he or she is and will possibly become?" Following these
questions are numerous inspiring stories and practical examples of how to
put the mitzvah into the bar/bat mitzvah by helping others and undertaking charity projects. These efforts were supported by an online fund, the
ZivTzedakah fund. The fund closed in 2008, but in its thirty-three years
of operation, it distributed fourteen million dollars to small charities in
the United States and Israel. Upon its closure followers and supporters
opened a "Mitzvah Heroes" online fund.

Among Israelis, too, mitzvah projects flourish. In Beit Shemesh bat mitzvah girls, working for the charity Melabev, have run a Bat Mitzvah Meals
on Wheels program, while boys cooked food, packed it, and distributed
it to needy families and memory-impaired seniors to kick off their 2012
Bar/Bat Mitzvah Hesed programs.[81]

As with many other aspects of modern life, there are contradictory
trends in the celebration of bar/bat mitzvah. Increasing affluence is a spur
to greater expenditures for parties but also provides an incentive for spending more on items of spiritual significance as well as for increased charitable
giving. Recession can quickly reverse these trends. Whatever the future
holds, the tension between the *bar* and the *mitzvah* is likely to remain.

WHY IS BAR MITZVAH SO POPULAR?

Bar mitzvah and bat mitzvah have always been family celebrations that
normally begin in a synagogue. Therefore, the success and popularity of the
ceremonies depend on agreement between family and institution, between
child and teachers. From the time bar mitzvah became an established custom in the sixteenth century, communities started to make rules, which
at first covered the size of the celebration, the kinds of food to be served,
the fees to the community, and gifts to charitable funds. A boy would be
taught by his father or by a private teacher. In the mid-twentieth century
the balance changed. Instead of the community regulating the party and
the parents arranging the tuition, it became the other way around. Communities made rules about minimum standards and class attendance, and

the family could do as they wished with their party, their guests, their menus and entertainment.

The ongoing setting of a balance that works is the key to the future popularity of bar and bat mitzvah. Without involvement of family, on the one hand, and teachers and community, on the other, the ceremony would be impossible. And for every family and every child the terms of the deal must be negotiated individually. There are plenty of instances of families leaving a community because they did not like what was offered, and there are also instances, probably fewer, of congregations refusing bar or bat mitzvah because of a child's lack of attendance, participation, or learning. But both situations are rare. In general families go along with what is demanded of them because doing so is seen as a way of creating successful celebrations, and communities work with the fact that for many the desire for a bar or bat mitzvah is the main motivation for the family's participation. Sometimes a family or a child can successfully negotiate reduced demands and expectations, and often communities enjoy the continued involvement of a family for many years beyond the celebration itself.

Bar/bat mitzvah in our time supports many aspirations parents and grandparents have for the children. It marks an educational achievement and a chance to rejoice at what a child has learned and adds to the broad range of activities the child takes part in; it also appeals to the pull of ethnicity, roots, and family history and offers, for those interested, a spiritual dimension to family life and an opportunity for charitable giving and projects. The celebration can also give a reason for those living elsewhere to travel to Israel or for Israelis to tour other countries. It strongly appeals to societies where positive thinking is encouraged and demanded, and for the wealthy and successful it offers a good spending opportunity, which can either be well used or misused.

Citizens of developed societies are often out of touch with the Sabbaths and festivals that have punctuated Jewish life for centuries past. The months and years are marked by time on a calendar rather than by the phases of the moon and the changing seasons, and the weekends are marked by leisure activities rather than by study and prayer. Perhaps for this reason events that mark various stages in life have grown in popularity. Families and individuals search out their own ancestry and ethnicities, and modern technology both enables their research and gives them the ability to trace distant relatives. Among families the most common celebration in the world today is probably a birthday. Bar/bat mitzvah appeals here as well, giving young people a very special way of marking a particular birthday. It is therefore not surprising that these celebrations are more popular today than at any time in the past.

There are many points in history when bar mitzvah could have become less popular and even faded away. The communal regulations from many Jewish communities from 1595 onward, which sought to place restrictions on the numbers, the menu, or the entertainment to be offered at a bar mitzvah party, show how bar mitzvah had begun to fulfill a social as well as a religious need. It was this social aspect that led bar mitzvah to persist throughout Ashkenazic Europe. After the first printing of *Zohar Hadash* in 1597, scholars and then ordinary Jews were able to attach mystical significance to the ceremony. The Zohar was thought to be an ancient work and was frequently mentioned as an authority for the bar mitzvah party.

A ceremony had been created that was able to appeal to all groups within Jewish society. The more observant appreciated the marking of the age of majority, while scholars appreciated the display of learning of the bar mitzvah speech. The account of the party in the Zohar helped to ensure that even the eighteenth-century Hasidim continued to celebrate bar mitzvah, while the fulfillment of social needs meant that during and after the Enlightenment bar mitzvah never totally lost its appeal, even among the less observant. But the repeated regulations over several centuries and across many different communities also show how community attempts to curb extravagance often ended in failure. There was an underlying difference of approach between community officials, who were determined to regulate the celebrations, and wealthy families, who were equally determined to show off their sons to their friends.

Such tensions have been openly discussed since the mid-nineteenth century. At that time German Reform rabbis proposed the abolition of bar mitzvah, dismissing it as an empty ceremony.[82] In 1956 Rabbi Moshe Feinstein also proposed it be abolished on the grounds that it did not bring the boys closer to Torah and led Jews to desecrate the Sabbath.[83] In 2007 Rabbi Eric Yoffie lamented that the Sabbath morning services in Reform congregations across the United States had become "privatized," in effect only attended by the families of those celebrating bar mitzvah or bat mitzvah.[84]

By 1800 the main tensions and issues still felt today had already been documented. From the earliest days of the bar mitzvah speech, teachers were writing speeches for the boys.[85] In Worms in the seventeenth century Juspa the shammash lamented that not every boy who came for bar mitzvah could read from the Torah;[86] in Metz in 1769 community leaders felt it was necessary to issue a regulation that a boy had to study regularly with a teacher for at least two years if he was to be allowed to celebrate a bar mitzvah in the synagogue, such was the concern felt about ignorance, truancy, and delinquency among the boys.[87]

By the end of the eighteenth century bar mitzvah had become a vital mechanism through which boys asserted their Jewish identity. The ceremony had become popular in an unplanned way and embodied both religious and social elements. Thus, it was able to appeal to all sections of the community, but its popularity also created problems within the Jewish community that persist today. For many families the ceremony marked the integration of a son into the full life of the community. For plenty of others, however, it marked the end of a son's Jewish education. By 1800 bar mitzvah had become both a force for integration and a force for assimilation.

The nineteenth century in Western Europe saw the decline of ceremonies for boys and the beginning of ceremonies for girls. Boys and girls often celebrated confirmation together. This ceremony, devised by teachers and modernist rabbis, emphasized belief rather than practice and becoming a good citizen rather than a traditional Jew. There was no need to learn Hebrew to have a confirmation, and therefore girls who had little or no Hebrew education could fully participate. But a heavy price was paid by the acceleration of the decline of Hebrew learning and Jewish knowledge. The history of bat mitzvah can only be understood in conjunction with the history of confirmation, a story that has been well studied but largely forgotten. Few today realize that confirmation was once common in Orthodox synagogues. Today's bat mitzvah grew so gradually out of the group confirmation ceremonies that no single date can easily be assigned to the change.

A NEW LEASE ON LIFE
FOR A CEREMONY IN DECLINE

The twentieth century witnessed the most remarkable changes in the history of bar mitzvah, with the tradition in steep decline up to the 1920s. At that time it could easily have disappeared altogether from non-Orthodox synagogues; indeed, it really had been dropped by most Reform congregations. Yet new educational requirements and the return of Hebrew as an educational priority eventually helped to bring back bar mitzvah into all the communities that had abandoned it. The rise of Zionism in American Reform Judaism, with its concern for the security and well-being of the State of Israel, raised the question of dual allegiances and even divided loyalties. Confirmation had been designed to nurture within young Jews devotion to both their faith and the society and country in which they lived. Although this purpose remained important, and continues to, over time the ceremony became increasingly insufficient as a way to bolster young people's sense of commitment. Parental pressure to bring back bar mitzvah came not only from families that felt an allegiance to tradition but also from families whose commitment to the Jewish community emphasized the importance of learning Hebrew.

The pressure on American Reform to introduce bat mitzvah in the 1960s and 1970s was undoubtedly bolstered because the feminist movement of the time had so many Jewish leaders and Jewish involvement. Some of them were clearly motivated by memories of having been excluded from aspects of Jewish ritual.[88]

The decision by many Orthodox communities to introduce a form of bat mitzvah also has a very clear background. Women are now studying Torah in Orthodox institutions worldwide, although for many centuries the practice was prohibited. The tradition accepts that there are times when established rules have to be changed to ensure the preservation of Torah observance and learning. It is not possible to have a world in which women can extend their secular education to any level and yet not learn Torah. Although many Orthodox bat mitzvah ceremonies emphasize a traditional women's domestic role, it is always seen as a step along the path of Jewish learning. Extending the study of Torah to women is bound to lead to pressure from them to participate further, as it has in Conservative congregations.[89] The last generation has seen an explosion of new ceremonies, with the arrival on the scene of adult bar mitzvah, adult bat mitzvah, second (and even third) bar mitzvah, and bar/bat mitzvah for children of divorced parents, those with special needs, and those from interfaith families. There have even been bar/bat mitzvah celebrations by non-Jews, including African Americans. As bat mitzvah did not become really popular until the 1970s, it will be the 2040s before "second bat mitzvah," to be held at the age of eighty-three, takes its place among the list of ceremonies regularly offered by congregations.[90]

In the twenty-first century we have witnessed a decline in the confirmation ceremony, and its two hundredth anniversary was hardly noticed.

It continues as a low-key event, but as a rite of passage, it has been completely overtaken and overshadowed by the return of bar mitzvah and the new popularity of bat mitzvah. The historical importance of confirmation now rests primarily on its role in having provided a means for girls to celebrate for the first time.

Today bar and bat mitzvah have such a powerful hold on Jewish life that it is difficult to imagine the ceremonies being replaced with new alternatives. In a materialist age emphasis on the party is likely to continue, but because this way of life has its share of critics, simple celebrations are also likely to become more frequent in the future. Group ceremonies for those who were unable to celebrate at the ordinary time will be less frequent, but later celebrations by those who have converted to Judaism as adults are likely to grow in number. As bar/bat mitzvah has now become both a legal and popular marker of Jewish identity, celebrations by and for those with special needs are likely to grow in number as well.

Many who have celebrated have found the occasion deeply meaningful and an inspirational experience; others have treated it as an obligation or even an unpleasant chore. Bar and bat mitzvah are so popular today that boys and girls who are unlikely to get much out of the ceremony are as likely to celebrate as those for whom it is a deeply spiritual experience. The nature of much of the learning, based on memorizing Hebrew that non-Hebrew speakers are unlikely to understand, can turn the whole experience into a strange ordeal for many children. Yet it is the unchanging nature of the core of the ceremony, the reading of Torah, that is at the heart of its popularity, as people search for values and ideas that have stood the test of time. Young people may seek novel themes for their parties, but they want the synagogue ceremony to remain unchanged. Other ideas, other texts, other ways of celebrating, come and go, but this tradition has endured and is valued.

CHAPTER EIGHT

The Evidence Assessed

> The first attempts to document the history of bar mitzvah and confirmation appeared in 1875.
> Isaac Rivkind collected all the sources for the history of bar mitzvah then available, in New York in 1942, and published them in Hebrew.
> Bar mitzvah is a rite of passage that can be compared to those in other cultures; the Jewish rite was very unusual in having at first no alternative for girls.
> My approach registers the early evidence by the date we know it to have been recorded, and this narrows down the origin of bar mitzvah to northern France in the second half of the thirteenth century. Many Jewish boys married at the age of thirteen, and others left home for further study, so the age marked a real transition in their lives.
> Of the many possible cultural influences that could have led to the popularity of bar mitzvah in Germany in the sixteenth century, the only likely parallel is the new Protestant approach to Christian confirmation, which linked it to tests of knowledge.
> Bar mitzvah was in decline in the late nineteenth and early twentieth centuries, but this trend was halted by synagogues and communities insisting on compulsory educational standards.
> Oral testimony, novels, and movies provide invaluable evidence to supplement written records from modern times.
> Ethnicity of ritual exists because families need to demonstrate or invent roots and a shared history to give themselves meaning and purpose.

THE HISTORIOGRAPHY OF BAR MITZVAH

Assessing evidence from history can never be totally objective: it depends on who you are and the era and culture in which you happen to live. This concluding chapter gives an academic assessment of the evidence so far presented and the reasoning behind my conclusions. Like every researcher, I have built on the work of those who have studied the subject before. Previous studies of the history of bar/bat mitzvah and confirmation have reached very different conclusions, even when they were looking at the same evidence. In some cases it is possible to see how and why a particular bias has come into the work. A little information on the background of previous researchers can help in understanding not only why they became interested in the subject but also why they reached the conclusions they did and in some cases why they got it wrong.

Leopold Löw

The first academic study of the history of bar mitzvah and confirmation was made by Leopold Löw (1811–75), a Hungarian congregational rabbi. Löw attended the Leipzig synod of Reform rabbis and leaders in 1868 and the Augsburg synod of 1871. At the Pest congress of Hungarian Jewry of 1868, a Reform majority emerged, and Löw became the leading rabbi of the moderately Reform "Neolog" movement.[1]

Early Reformers had introduced the new rite of "confirmation" into their day schools in the first decade of the nineteenth century. By the middle of the century more radical Reform communities argued that confirmation should completely replace bar mitzvah everywhere.[2] Löw's own ideas of religious reform were based on his understanding of history and *halakhah*; from a detailed historical study, for example, he argued that it should be acceptable for men to pray in synagogue bareheaded.[3] Löw approved of bar mitzvah, and in writing the history of bar mitzvah, he set out to defend it against its more radical critics. Not that he was against confirmation; his eight pages on "Die Bar-Mizwah Institution" are followed by a further five pages in praise of confirmation as a Jewish rite.[4]

Löw discovered many of the crucial references that are part of the history of bar mitzvah, including the key text, Maharshal's reference to the bar mitzvah meal as an established Ashkenazic custom. He argues that it was the inclusion of Pirkei Avot in the prayer book that helped to popularize the custom, with its well-known saying "at thirteen for the commandments." The concluding part of his study is a polemic against the *pilpul* often then used in the *derashah* delivered by the boy at the celebration meal, which Löw thought nonsensical. But what is most striking is his opening paragraph, in which he describes bar mitzvah as "an anti-Talmudic Reform." By this Löw meant, first, that the new celebration allowed the marking of the age of thirteen regardless of whether or not the boy showed any physical signs of puberty and, second, that with the advent of bar mitzvah, the laying of tefillin by younger boys and the calling up of younger boys to the Torah were now prohibited. Löw argued that all this was contrary to the Talmud.

Löw's brief history was highly influential; it was extensively quoted by later writers and encyclopedia articles, and no scholar really reconsidered the primary sources in detail for another sixty-five years. Although Kaufmann Kohler, in *The Jewish Encyclopedia* (1901–6), argued that bar mitzvah was an ancient rite, most accepted Löw's opinion that the ceremony was a medieval invention. Löw correctly dated the common usage of the term *bar mitzvah* to the fourteenth century. No earlier evidence has since been found to change that date.

Although Löw's account long remained the standard history of bar mitzvah, it did not go unchallenged. Israel Lebendiger wrote an essay for the Alumni Association Prize of the Jewish Theological Seminary in the 1913–14 academic year. Lebendiger argued that Löw was erroneous in promulgating bar mitzvah as a fourteenth-century reform. He suggested that already in the Talmud there was an assumption that a thirteen-year-old boy could be considered to be physically mature and that the arrival of bar mitzvah simply followed the same assumption.[5]

Isaac Rivkind

Isaac Rivkind (1895–1968), a bibliographer, was librarian of the Jewish Theological Seminary from 1923 to 1959. He became fascinated by rare Hebrew books and particularly by finding variants in copies of the same book.[6] He wrote his Hebrew volume *Le-Ot u-le-Zikkaron: Bar Mitzvah. A Study in Jewish Cultural History* for the bar mitzvah of his son, Baruch Daniel Rivkind, to whom the book is dedicated and whose photograph forms the frontispiece. Rivkind published the book himself in 1942 and had a thousand copies printed. His comprehensive collection of sources on the history of bar mitzvah and on its contemporary significance is unlikely ever to be surpassed. The bibliography lists 468 items, and others are referred to in footnotes. Rivkind's book remains an essential resource for this topic, and all subsequent histories are built on his foundations. It is unlikely that any father of a bar mitzvah has ever undertaken such extensive preparation for his son's celebration. The only significant texts Rivkind did not uncover were those not known in his time—though the more recently discovered texts are absolutely crucial for the origin of bar mitzvah in the synagogue.

Rivkind was clearly irritated by Löw's Reform approach and by the fact that his short essay remained the standard work on the subject. He poured scorn on confirmation and contemporary secular celebrations, which he saw as uprooting the tradition. It was very apparent from Rivkind's multiplicity of sources that the ceremony had grown in popularity in medieval Europe, but to Rivkind's uncritical eye it was no unjustified innovation but thoroughly in the spirit of ancient tradition. In his chapter on the bar mitzvah meal, Rivkind was the first to point to the importance of a passage in the Zohar, which he describes as the "most influential" source. Rivkind's own comments on the sources were brief; his interest was in collecting them. He did not analyze his texts in detail, and he did not make any attempt to set them in the historical and cultural context of their time and place. Perhaps because Rivkind's work was privately published in Hebrew in New York during World War II, it is remarkably little known and has never been reprinted.

Hayyim Schauss

Hayyim Schauss's book *The Lifetime of a Jew* (1950) was the first to introduce the history of "bar mitzvo," as he called it, to an English readership. Schauss was also a teacher in New York, one more sympathetic to Löw's approach than to Rivkind's. The eight pages he devoted to the subject follow the general outline of Löw's work. But Schauss was unsympathetic to the ceremony: "The bar mizvo celebration never succeeded in deeply rooting itself in Jewish life as a synagogue observance or as a home ritual. The institution was of too recent origin and was not surrounded by an atmosphere of religious reverence."[7] Bar mitzvah was for Schauss part of a Jewish folk tradition and therefore not to be taken seriously. For a more objective account English readers had to wait until 1972 and the publication of the *Encyclopedia Judaica*, in which there is a well-documented article by Zvi Kaplan.

Unpublished Dissertations

Important scholarly contributions have been made by writers of unpublished theses and dissertations, which have remained largely unread until recently, when online catalogs have publicized their availability. David Herschel Wice wrote his rabbinic thesis for Hebrew Union College in 1933 on "Bar Mitzvah and Confirmation in the Light of History and Religious Practice." It is an accurate and very useful summary of the knowledge then available, drawing information not only from Löw but from Leopold Zunz, who had himself been confirmed in 1807 and who compiled a list of early instances of the ceremony.

A very important scholarly contribution was made in 1971 by Meir Maynard Sered in a master's thesis for Northwestern University, entitled "The Bar Mitzvah Speech: History and Decline 1575–1970." Sered's studies were in the field of speech education, and this background gave him an unusually fascinating perspective on his subject, leading him to look at surviving examples of the bar mitzvah *derashah* from the point of view of their effectiveness as texts for public speaking. Sered traced the simplification of the speeches through the centuries as they gradually became shorter, easier to follow, with fewer learned allusions.

Ivan Marcus

Byron Sherwin devoted a chapter of his book *In Partnership with God* (1990) to bar mitzvah and bat mitzvah. The chapter offers no new primary sources for the history of the ceremony but is valuable because of its detailed discussion of how thirteen became the age of majority and precisely what this meant. But it was Schauss's book that remained the standard English work on the subject until the publication of Ivan G. Marcus's *Jewish Life Cycle* in 2004.

Marcus, a specialist in medieval Jewish history, received his doctorate from, and then became a professor at, the Jewish Theological Seminary in New York, the same college where Rivkind had been librarian. After becoming professor of Jewish history at Yale in 1994, Marcus began his work on bar mitzvah in the concluding part of an earlier book, *Rituals of Childhood* (1996). This work is about the medieval Ashkenazic school initiation ceremony, which rewarded young children with eggs, cake, and honey on the occasion of their first Hebrew lesson. Marcus has suggested that bar mitzvah replaced the ritual for young children, at a time when it became dangerous to perform that ritual, which looked like a mock communion. Bar mitzvah mirrored the Cistercian rite of "oblation," or initiation into a monastery, which took place at age twelve or fourteen.[8]

Israel Ta-Shma

Marcus's views have been vigorously challenged by the Israeli scholar Israel Ta-Shma (1936–2004) of the Hebrew University, Jerusalem, and their debate is discussed in detail here. Ta-Shma has clearly shown a greater knowledge of the Hebrew sources, while Marcus has demonstrated a deeper knowledge of the general cultural influences from the Christian European environment. It is no coincidence that Marcus is an American scholar and Ta-Shma an Israeli. As a result of the debate, the medieval sources have come sharply into focus, and of late less attention has been paid to more recent sources. In his later book *The Jewish Life Cycle* (2004) Marcus concentrated on the medieval evidence, but his account of the subsequent history of the celebration is much more sketchy. He dated the spread of the ceremony to the eighteenth century and linked it to "the newly fashioned notion of childhood."[9]

Scholarly Studies of Confirmation

Löw was also the first historian of Jewish confirmation, which he saw as a direct borrowing from the Protestant Church, which had already discarded the Catholic sacramental ideas of the laying on of hands and holy unction. Löw gave a brief list of the first Jewish communities in Germany to celebrate confirmation.[10] For the nineteenth and early twentieth centuries Jewish confirmation has received more official documentation than bar mitzvah. Many synagogues published and preserved service booklets, many of them giving the names of the confirmands. The Jewish press reported annual confirmation services, but an individual bar mitzvah was not newsworthy. Until recent decades it was not customary for communities to keep records of the names and dates of bar mitzvah or bat mitzvah ceremonies. This practice reflects the fact that these occasions continued to be observed at the request of parents, whereas confirmation was an official group celebration following the end of a specific educational course established and promoted by the rabbi and community. Bar mitzvah was undoubtedly far more common during this period than the surviving official records suggest.

For confirmation, too, unpublished theses and dissertations provide an important resource. David Herschel Wice's 1933 thesis covered confirmation as well as bar mitzvah. Carol Matzkin Orsborn's 2002 thesis on the origin of confirmation was inspired by her own confirmation ceremony. She discovered that the man who developed the ceremony originally in Germany, Israel Jacobson, had been strongly criticized by his biographers, and she mounted a strong defense of his reputation. In an unusual psychosocial analysis she explained Jacobson's immersion in communal life as a way of coping with the grief caused by the death of his father.

Stuart Schoenfeld

For the modern period Stuart Schoenfeld's many published articles on both bar mitzvah and confirmation have made a crucial contribution. Schoenfeld is a sociologist and educationalist who is interested in historical background. His work draws on a distinction made by Charles Leibman in 1973 between "elite religion" and "folk religion." Applied to bar mitzvah, its growth and history are part of folk religion, promoted and developed by individuals and ordinary people. But the attempts to regulate it show the influence of elite religion, in which community leaders and rabbis make the rules.

Scholarly Confusion about Bat Mitzvah

Research on the origin of bat mitzvah has given wildly differing accounts. Judith Kaplan's 1922 ceremony is called the "first bat mitzvah" in hundreds of online and published articles and reports; some of them state, more precisely, that this was the "first American bat mitzvah." The *Encyclopedia Judaica*, however, concentrates more on the European precedents. This applies both to the first and the greatly expanded second edition article on this topic. Both these articles and other writers on the subject are hampered by the lack of a clear definition of what constitutes a "bat mitzvah." Bar mitzvah is easy to define, but girls' ceremonies have had many different forms, and all of them are part of the history. It is only by placing the group ceremony of confirmation and the individual ceremony of bat mitzvah together, as is done in the present study, that the development of the ceremony can clearly be seen.

More information on the development of bat mitzvah is appearing all the time, including an important article by David Golinkin from 2011 and a fascinating account from the same year by Dario Miccoli of the annual *initiation* ceremonies for Jewish girls held in Alexandria, Egypt, from 1901 onward.[11] But much more remains to be done, particularly on the all-important question of equal treatment of boys and girls. No history of bat mitzvah really makes clear when and where girls were first allowed to take precisely the same ceremonial role as the boys, and further extensive archival work needs to be undertaken in the United States and Canada on this point.

THEORETICAL CONCERNS

When was the first birthday party? Who first lit candles on a birthday cake? We do not know. In general people do not realize when they are starting a new custom. Mordecai Kaplan was an exception when he wrote in his diary that he had inaugurated bat mitzvah. Perhaps he meant only that his daughter's ceremony was the first in his new synagogue, but that is not how people have have read it. For bar mitzvah and confirmation the evidence is also very difficult to assess. Confirmation began in schools, not in synagogues, so precisely what happened in Germany in the first decade of the nineteenth century cannot easily be established. For bar mitzvah the medieval sources are still being brought to light, so it is quite likely that as more is discovered and published, the story of the first synagogue ceremony may change.

The New Jewish Cultural Studies

This new history has only been possible because of a new approach to Jewish cultural studies. In the introduction to their book *Jews and Other Differences: The New Jewish Cultural Studies* (1997) Jonathan and Daniel Boyarin suggested that the work of establishing a "Jewish place" within the shifting field of cultural studies had barely begun: "The conception according to which the Holocaust and the establishment of the State of Israel constitute a Jewish return to history reinforces a conception of premodern, post-Exilic Jewish experience as being primarily of antiquarian or philological interest, rather than critical resources for the necessary refashioning of Jewishness in the present."[12]

In universities, suggested the Boyarins, Jewish studies had in the past been carried out predominantly by Jews, leading few outside the Jewish community to imagine that anything they said was worth listening to. At the same time, a disproportionate number of academics in the social sciences had come from Jewish backgrounds but had little or nothing to say about Jews as an ethnographic specialty.

The Boyarins wrote from a North American context and from within the academic discipline broadly known as "New Historicism." Within the field of European studies, the tensions they describe have been even more keenly felt. Many of the founders of European social theory came from a Jewish background—Karl Marx, Sigmund Freud, Lucien Lévy-Bruhl, Émile Durkheim, Walter Benjamin, Max Horkheimer, Emmanuel Levinas, Claude Lévi-Strauss, and Jacques Derrida. Of these only Levinas applied his theories to the study of specifically Jewish sources. As European universities were stripped of Jews by the Nazis, a whole generation of scholars was forced to flee. A thousand years of Jewish life in central Europe tragically came to an end. Over time the study of Jewish life in Europe became a search into a lost past of antiquarian interest, carried out mainly by non-Jewish academics. But in recent years a younger generation, especially in Germany, aware of what had been lost, has created a more popular interest in the history of Jews in Europe. The Jewish Museum in Berlin today attracts two million visitors a year to its exhibition on the history of Jewish life in Germany; very few of them are Jewish.

Sadly, some of this new interest reinforces the incorrect notion that the Jewish people have uniquely preserved an unchanged, ancient way of life in exile. The extent to which European Jewry created new forms of cultural expression across history has hardly been recognized, except by specialists in the field. Both Jews and non-Jews attending a bar mitzvah ceremony or party imagine they are witnessing an ancient ritual. Putting the record straight is not just a matter of uncovering the facts; it requires a complete rethinking of what the proper boundaries of Jewish history are, so that popular cultural developments can take their place as a vital area of study, as aspects of Jewish history that profoundly influence Jewish life today and contemporary Jewish identities.

My own account of the history brings together the traditional work of academic Jewish study and a newer approach to Jewish cultural studies. An accurate knowledge of the origin and spread of bar mitzvah and bat mitzvah requires attention to dusty manuscripts and obscure local periodicals in many languages. But these sources often reveal more than dates and places where ceremonies took place in Europe. They show that some of the tensions and issues that surround bar/bat mitzvah today—tensions between religion and culture, between synagogue officials and families, between faith and practice—are not new. Reflecting on descriptions from the past illuminates contemporary policy issues.

Bar Mitzvah and Bat Mitzvah as "Rites of Passage"

The much used term *rite of passage* was invented by the French anthropologist Arnold Van Gennep as the title of his book *Les Rites de passage* in 1908. Van Gennep distinguished three phases of "life crises" which he termed "separation," "transition," and "reincorporation."[13] Rites of adolescence formed a core part of Van Gennep's studies, and he considered such rites to have a surprisingly uniform pattern across different societies. A child is rarely considered a full member of a religion from birth but must be incorporated into it through a special ceremony.[14] Van Gennep's genius lay in his demonstration of how a particular function across cultures results in the same form of activity.[15] Applied to bar mitzvah and bat mitzvah, he might have regarded the rite of separation as the period of individual training and education; the transition, or "liminal" stage, as the synagogue ceremony; and the reincorporation celebrated by the bar mitzvah party.

Van Gennep's work was rediscovered by the British anthropologist Victor Turner in the 1960s. In his many writings, particularly *The Ritual Process: Structure and Anti-Structure* (1969), Turner refined and developed Van Gennep's ideas, describing ritual as a "socially subversive, ritually inversive" act. Turner was fascinated by liminality; in the transition stage of a ritual, the entrants are passive, obeying instructions and showing intense comradeship as their secular status disappears in the ritual moment, as each one becomes a blank slate shaped by more than human powers. Turner drew up a table of opposites, contrasting the liminal state with normal status: liminality is a total state, status is a partial state; liminality is equal, status is unequal; and so on. Judaism and Christianity, he suggested, have institutionalized these states, but vestiges remain.[16]

Some of these descriptions, which were based on his work in Zambia with the Ndembu tribe, fit well with bar mitzvah and bat mitzvah, while others are very different. Turner described liminality, for example, as a condition of anonymity in which sex distinctions and personal appearance are irrelevant. Of particular interest are his vivid descriptions of Ndembu ritual; the material element of ritual, he says, is shaped by life experience and includes the bringing of personal objects into a ring of consecrated space, thus bringing along the power that such objects possess.[17] The ritual of reading the Torah in a synagogue, whether at a bar mitzvah or at other times, could be described in precisely such terms.

The Role of Performance

Unlike Van Gennep, Turner recognized the limitations of applying theories based on the observation of rural tribal societies to Western religions. In *From Ritual to Theatre* (1982), without departing from theories of liminality, he added an important notion of *performance* to his conception of ritual, arguing that drama and theatrical performance are secular replacements for rituals enacted by religion. The notion of bar mitzvah as a well-rehearsed performance is one that frequently occurs in modern descriptions of the synagogue ceremony. Among Jewish educators it has become a term of criticism, a "mere performance."[18] Turner suggested that religious rituals, combining both performance and liminality, have the power to transform lives.[19] Expanding on this theory, Tom Driver has suggested that "rituals partly substitute for society's codes of behavior special codes of their own . . . and partly they foster spontaneous performance and 'inspired' words and actions."[20]

Driver's thesis is that rituals help to foster the transformation of society. They do not simply represent a cultural norm, but rituals themselves actually contribute to and help create a culture. Applied to bar mitzvah and bat mitzvah, this theory would indicate that the ceremony does not simply mark a transition but indeed helps to create the sense of having entered an age of responsibility. This powerful function can help to explain the enduring popularity and enduring nature of the ceremony among both religious and secular groups in Jewish societies.

Anthropologists have traditionally based their studies on their own field observations of rituals. Such studies are necessarily restricted to the anthropologist's own era. Mary Douglas (1921–2007) was a pioneer of historical anthropology, a discipline that attempts to supply the same level of understanding to rituals practiced in ancient times. This undertaking is much more difficult because direct observation has to be replaced by reports from others, who may have applied their own biases to what they observed.[21] Can these insights nevertheless be applied to the history of bar mitzvah?

An anthropological understanding of the story of bar mitzvah has to begin with the assertion that a concept of childhood existed in medieval Europe. This point would not need stating at all, had it not been for the work of Philippe Ariès, whose influential *L'Enfant et la vie familiale sous l'ancien régime* stated that "there was no place for childhood in the medieval world."[22] Regarding medieval Europe generally, his ideas have been fully and comprehensively refuted by Shulamith Shahar.[23] Likewise, Israel Ta-Shma has shown that the Jewish pietists of medieval Germany played games with their children and undertook many of the same challenges and tasks as today's parents.[24] But although Ariès's general theory has been challenged, the detailed information he provides is of great value, and his work has focused attention on changes in attitudes toward children and education that are of great importance for our story.

Bar Mitzvah's Liminal Moment

The history of the celebration of bar mitzvah shows that the ceremony began with a simple five-word Hebrew blessing said by the father, here translated as "Blessed be the One who has freed me from punishment because of him." These words, which could be described as marking a ritual rejection of the son by the father, show precisely a moment of dangerous inversion, the liminal moment when the son accepts responsibility, when the boy becomes a man. The fifth-century midrash *Bereshit Rabbah*, from which the words of the blessing are taken, does not specify where they are to be said or even that the son has to be present.[25] When in thirteenth-century France a few fathers recited these words, they chose the day and the place for their sons to approach the sacred symbol of their faith, the Torah, and to read from it.[26]

As later recorded in Ashkenazic prayer books, the blessing most often immediately follows the son's blessing after reading the Torah, words that affirm the truth of Torah and his belief in eternal life—two beliefs that bring safety at the time of danger. The first time a father uttered the five simple words as his son was called to the public reading of the Torah was the moment the synagogue ceremony of bar mitzvah was created. This was the liminal moment, and it may have been accompanied by a party; much later a specific preparation beforehand was added, completing the formation of the ritual as a rite of passage.

Bar Mitzvah and Puberty

The link between the age of bar/bat mitzvah and puberty is, as we have seen, completely deliberate. Arthur Waskow and Phyllis Berman have suggested that growing sexual awareness was seen as fraught with danger, and bar mitzvah was an attempt to control it.[27] We have seen that in thirteenth-century France and nineteenth-century Poland it was customary among some communities to seek even further control by arranging marriages for boys as young as thirteen, sometimes to coincide with their bar mitzvah.

Among the strictly Orthodox, it is the first call to the Torah in the synagogue or the first laying of tefillin that marks the liminal moment, the rite of passage. In the rest of the Jewish world, and especially for the boys and girls themselves, it is now the party that marks the real rite of passage to the adult world to larger Jewish communities; the child's own party is but one of a whole year of parties, as each child attends the celebrations of their year group and meets the same friends over and over again. The book *Bar Mitzvah Disco* (2005) is a collection of memories from the party scene of the 1970s and 1980s, and many of those memories are of children flirting or attempting to flirt when they thought their parents were not looking. The book makes clear that many of them regarded the real passage to adult life as taking place not in the synagogue but on the dance floor or afterward: "The parallels between my experience with Debbie and my Bar Mitzvah are striking to me now. Both events took place in the spring of 1977 at Sinai Temple. Both felt like a line of demarcation between childhood and not-childhood. One was a religious coming-of-age. The other was a sexual coming-of-age. One was the greatest thing that can happen to a Jewish boy and the crowning achievement of the first thirteen years of my life. The other was my Bar Mitzvah."[28] Most accounts are less cynical than this one, but the real test of such memories comes when the child grows up and has to decide what to offer his or her own children. In different ways both parents and children are keen to acknowledge the process of growing up at the time of puberty.

THE MEDIEVAL EVIDENCE

"Medieval society fostered intimacy and distance at the same time. Princes and beggars stumbled over one another in the same street, masters and servants lived in the same household ... suffocatingly close ... yet experienced a different world. So it was with Jews and Christians."[29] With these words John Van Engen began his introduction to *Jews and Christians in Twelfth Century Europe* (2001). The intimacy of Jews and Christians was disrupted by the massacres of the first Crusade. The period that followed was a highly inventive one for both, a period in which new educational methods and rituals "selectively recaptured earlier Jewish elements and themes and appropriated Christian theological motifs and rites to fashion a Jewish anti-Christian social polemic." Ivan Marcus contributed an essay to the book that explains that Jews and Christians shared a similar enthusiasm for retrieving ancient sources and adapting them to contemporary life; individuals could make new choices.

This was precisely the process at work in the origins of the bar mitzvah ceremony. Fathers retrieved the ancient text of the father's blessing from *Bereshit Rabbah* and created a new ceremony by reciting it in synagogue: the words were ancient, but the ritual of a father reciting it in public with his hand on his son's head was completely new. Whoever created this synagogue ritual created a paradox. The *words* of the father's blessing express his delight in being freed from responsibility for his son, but in the early days of the ceremony, before it became a popular custom, the recital of the blessing in public marked a moment of transition to the next educational stage, which the father was expected to support. The legal responsibility for the son had ended, but the financial responsibility was likely to continue. Indeed, the whole of the educational system in early Ashkenaz was one designed to produce scholars; even basic education emphasized the study of scholarly texts.[30] The simple ceremony of bar mitzvah marked the transition not to adult life but to the next stage of scholarly achievement. Among Christians in medieval Europe general education for boys was from around the ages of seven to fourteen.[31]

As for the choice of age, Jews and Christians reached similar conclusions. Many churchmen argued that the duty of confession should not be imposed on boys before the age of fourteen, which was the most common age of criminal responsibility in medieval Europe.[32] Even in places where confirmation took place at a younger age, there was a recognition of transition in the early teenage years that must have been influential. A fourteen-year-old was allowed to make a formal vow and become an acolyte in church, carrying a candle and serving water and wine.[33]

The early practitioners of bar mitzvah had intellectual links to the Hasidei Ashkenaz of twelfth- and thirteenth-century Germany.[34] Christian influence on the Hasidei Ashkenaz was first proposed by Yizhaq Baer in 1937 and features also in studies by Asher Rubin (1965) and Joseph Dan (1971).[35] Even Gershom Scholem, who was much more cautious than most in accepting notions of Christian influence, admitted that the pietists' doctrines of penitence were "undoubtedly" affected by Christian penitential tracts and practices.[36]

Honoring Antiquity

Because Jewish tradition valued antiquity, the rabbinic tradition often tended to push back the date of the start of new customs. This practice goes back to the ancient "pseudepigraphic" literature, books that were written as if they had been composed by a biblical character. Among the rabbis sayings were frequently attributed to older sources. The only safe way of assessing the early evidence for the synagogue ceremony is therefore to ignore the statements that this was begun by "Judah the son of Barukh" or by "the Gaon Rabbi Yehudai" and to date the evidence by when it was recorded.[37] The first two medieval sources come from Barcelona and Marseilles but do not mention any synagogue ceremony, only the father saying the blessing. So, it is the two sources from northern France that are crucial. Unfortunately, neither is easy to date. *Horaot meiRabbanei Tzarfat* is a tiny collection of brief rulings discovered in a manuscript appended to works by Rabbi Yehiel of Paris. Yehiel was appointed head of the yeshiva in Paris in 1225 and resided there until he set off on a long journey to live in the Holy Land, where he arrived in 1260. But we do not know whether or not he wrote the *Horaot*, so this does not get us very far.

Who Was Avigdor?

The other source, published in 1996 under the name of Avigdor Tzarfati ("Avigdor the Frenchman"), is the only medieval source to mention both a blessing in the synagogue and a party. But precisely who Avigdor was, and whether he really was French, is unclear. The work survives in two manuscripts, an incomplete one in London and a full one in Hamburg. The London manuscript gives the author's name as Bekhor Shor, a reference to Joseph son of Isaac Bekhor Shor of Orléans, who lived in the second half of the twelfth century. As the manuscript mentions thirteenth-century scholars, however, the attribution must be incorrect.

Arthur Marmorstein examined the British Library manuscript in the early 1920s and published a report under the title "On an Unknown French Author of the Thirteenth Century". Marmorstein discovered the names of many teachers and relatives of the author and was able to demonstrate that the unknown author repeatedly approved of French customs and disapproved of German ones.[38] He also noted that the author's grandfather was Rabbi Yomtov of Joigny, who is known to have moved to England and died at York in the massacre of 1190. A number of French Jewish scholars took refuge in England when Jews were expelled from the Île-de-France from 1182 to 1198.

The Hamburg manuscript identifies the author's name as "Avigdor," and another work in the same manuscript is attributed to "Avigdor Cohen." Most modern scholars assume these two references are to the same Avigdor and identify him with Avigdor the son of Elijah HaKohen (c. 1200-75), who is known to have grown up in Verona and lived in Vienna. He also taught in Ferrara and Speyer.[39] When the book was published in 1996, however, the editor, Efraim Fishel Herskovitz, decided it was by a different Avigdor, Avigdor son of Isaac from Falaise in Normandy, whom he called "one of the last tosafists." Herskovitz gave a great deal of information about Avigdor, most of which comes from internal evidence within the manuscripts. He identified Avigdor as French from a story told by Rabbi Yosef the son of Natan Official, in his book *Sefer Yosef Hammakane*, another thirteenth-century text, which was first published in 1970. Rabbi Yosef the son of Natan Official tells of the disputation of Rabbi Yehiel of Paris in 1240 and says this was witnessed by our author's teacher Samuel of Falaise, Judah of Metz, Rabbi Isaac, and Avigdor his son. Avigdor was an unusual name, "hardly used" among French-speaking Jews at the time.[40]

Avigdor from Falaise?

As for where he lived, at one point in our manuscript, the author states that he was a teacher in a town called פלייש. Herskovitz proposed that this was in fact Avigdor's hometown and identified it with Falaise in Normandy.[41] This would fit well with the author's very frequent references to "French" authorities, indicating that he knew all the French customs but perhaps did not consider himself to be French. In the twelfth century Normandy was ruled by the English monarchy, and in the thirteenth century it still had a separate cultural identity from France, even though it was part of the same kingdom.[42]

But in the London manuscript the reading of the name of the town is unclear.[43] Marmorstein suggested it was טלייש מלייש, טלייש (Italians?) or סלייש. From my own examination of the London manuscript, the word appears to be סולייש. But the initial *samech* is very squashed, and we have four different opinions about what the letter is. If you regard the start of the word as a smudge, we are left with לייש, the second part of "Orléans" (which appears in the same manuscript as אורלייש), one of the oldest centers of

Jewish scholarship in France, to which scholars from all parts of France, from Germany, and from England made their way. Avigdor mentions Joseph Bekhor Shor of Orléans and other French rabbis who flourished after 1170.[44] Therefore, it seems much more likely from the manuscript evidence that he lived there rather than at Falaise. How Herskovitz could read פלײנש as *Falaise* is not clear.

The manuscript does make it clear, however, that Avigdor was a student of Samuel of Falaise in Normandy and of Rabbi Judah of Metz. It also gives the names of some of the author's family, from which we discover he was related to many of the important rabbis of the day. As Avigdor of Vienna spent his life in central Europe and Italy, it does indeed seem likely that our work is by a different Avigdor. Precisely who he was and where he lived is still being researched;[45] for our purposes what is important is that he calls bar mitzvah a "French custom" and that he lived in the mid-thirteenth century.

Both of the important French sources are linked with each other and with the leading rabbis of their day. The first source is found appended to teachings of Rabbi Yehiel of Paris: Avigdor was a student of Samuel of Falaise, a participant in the Paris disputation in 1240 and an assistant to Rabbi Yehiel there. This was the first of the three well-known public medieval disputations and led to the public burning of the Talmud and other Jewish books in Paris in 1242. It was the beginning of the end for medieval French Jewry. Yet in the final decades the community in northern France continued to flourish, and Samuel of Falaise was one of its wealthiest as well as one of the most learned members. This information gives us an accurate date and place for the start of bar mitzvah—after 1240 in northern France. Samuel of Falaise and Yehiel of Paris were teachers of Rabbi Meir of Rothenburg (1215–93), whose student Shimshon the son of Tzadok also mentions the father's blessing.[46] There is thus a clear train of tradition connecting many of the early sources.

Whoever he was, Avigdor mentioned a large number of his contemporaries and clearly had a good view of the current French Jewish customs. The possible links with England are intriguing. In his classic study *The Jews of Angevin England* (1893) Joseph Jacobs maintained that large numbers of French Jewish scholars at the end of the twelfth century had links with England, particularly those from Orléans. He also maintained that the name "Sir Morel" (who has also been identified with Avigdor's teacher Samuel of Falaise) meant that he had lived in England. Jacobs identified him with Rabbi Morel of Norwich, who is mentioned in the *Hagahot Maimoniot*, a commentary on Maimonides' *Mishneh Torah*.[47] Yet much of Jacobs's evidence has been discredited, and we know that Rabbi Morel of Norwich lived fifty years before Samuel of Falaise. Jacobs also listed "Isaac of Joigny" as having lived in London in 1186.[48] This means he is very unlikely to be the man who accompanied his son Avigdor to Paris in 1240. The dates do not match up, and this question needs further research. Normandy had been taken by the French king at the start of the thirteenth century, and Anglo-Jewry was in terminal decline by the time of the evidence for bar mitzvah; Jews were expelled in 1290. The whole issue of Norman and French Jewish scholars in medieval England needs revisiting, as Jacobs's work was completed more than a century ago and has never been properly updated.

Both crucial sources are linked to northern France. In suggesting that bar mitzvah may have developed among parents sending their sons to the high school in Rouen, the medieval capital of Normandy, I have built on the pioneering research of Norman Golb, who identified the Hebrew *Rodom* with the town and the word *darom*, meaning "South," as a frequent misspelling of the town's name. Golb has claimed that the knowledge of Rouen as an important center of medieval learning was lost, and this explains why scribes frequently misspelled the name of the town; modern scholars then proceeded to make incorrect identifications. When in 1976 a medieval building was found in the old Jewish quarter of Rouen, Golb was quick to identify it as the school, though this identification is still disputed. In the preface to his detailed study *The Jews in Medieval Normandy* (1998) Golb expressed the hope that the book would serve as a stimulus for historians to reconsider their prolonged silence on the subject of the cultural achievements of the medieval western European Jewry: "If during a span of only three decades discoveries in the number, and of the quality, described in the chapters below, all pertaining to the Jews of this one region, have occurred with such notable regularity, one may hardly rule out the eventuality that new surprises may follow."[49]

One such surprise has indeed resulted from the publication of Avigdor's work, a book unknown to Golb when he published his history in 1998, with its mention of bar mitzvah and with Herskovitz's introduction suggesting Avigdor was from Normandy. That suggestion may not be correct, but his links with the wider area of northern France seem clear. It was Golb who identified the strange anonymous education guide *Sefer*

Huqqei HaTorah with the Rouen school. Others think the rule book came from Provence or Germany or England.[50] The identification with Rouen fits best with our other evidence. The ceremony there described, as the father leaves his son to be educated at boarding school, links with the bar mitzvah ceremony described by Avigdor, which could have developed for boys leaving home. In addition, both texts mention a party, and both mention placing the hands on the boy's head as a moment of transition. So, here is an occasion that could be the origin of the custom of bar mitzvah, even though there is a contradiction in the text about whether the school ceremony took place at the age of thirteen or sixteen. Kanarfogel attempts to reconcile the conflict: "The formal initiation took place when the student was thirteen, although it could be postponed (or perhaps renounced) until age sixteen."[51]

COMPARATIVE STUDIES OF
THE ORIGIN OF BAR MITZVAH

Apart from the work of Ivan Marcus, most previous studies of the history of bar mitzvah have confined their attention to Jewish sources. Leopold Löw (1875) followed his brief history of bar mitzvah with a similar history of Jewish confirmation, which was becoming popular in his time. Only in considering this modern aspect did he mention Catholic and Protestant antecedents to the ceremony. Isaac Rivkind, keen to emphasize the antiquity of bar mitzvah, confined his attention to Jewish sources, and in more recent years Israel Ta-Shma has done the same. Debra Reed Blank's study "Jewish Rites of Adolescence" was published in a volume devoted to both Christian and Jewish life cycle events, but although she mentioned Van Gennep, no wider cultural background was mentioned for bar mitzvah. Joseph Gutmann provided a brief unsourced comment: "Bar Mitzvah was probably modelled on or influenced by the Christian rite called the *sacrament of adolescence* or *spiritual progress*, which confirmed the baptismal vows of grace."[52]

Only Ivan Marcus had made a more extensive study of Christian parallels. His book *Rituals of Childhood* takes as its main topic a medieval European initiation rite for young children starting school. Descriptions of the rite survive in seven accounts: three from Germany discussing the laws and customs of the festival of Shavuot and four others from northern France and Provence. The earliest French account is from the well-known prayer book the *Machzor Vitry* (c. 1100), and the earliest German account is from the *Sefer HaRokeah* by Rabbi Elazar the son of Judah of Worms (c. 1160–1230). All of them describe the day on which a Jewish boy is taught his first Hebrew letters at the age of five or six. The teacher smears honey over the letters on a tablet and encourages the child to lick the honey off. Cakes and eggs on which biblical verse have been written are eaten, and in some versions magical incantations are recited, urging the "prince of forgetfulness" to go away.

Marcus argued that the rites of circumcision and school initiation were parallel to the Christian rites of baptism and confirmation, confirmation being followed by the first administration of communion. Baptism and first communion had originally been part of a single ceremony for adults.[53] Child baptism became the norm from around the seventh century,[54] which made it necessary to delay communion until the child could understand its meaning. The ceremony of confirmation in Western Europe from around the thirteenth century generally took place when a child was about seven years old and was followed by first communion, with its administration of bread and wine. Such ceremonies often took place at Easter or Pentecost. In part the Jewish ceremony reflects a social polemic or defensive reaction—Torah, not Christ, is the true food of faith.[55]

Marcus suggested that the childhood initiation rite gradually disappeared and that bar mitzvah replaced it, marking a later educational stage. The childhood rite was discouraged by rabbinic opinions that raised objections both to the writing of names of God on a cake and to the eating of the Hebrew letters.[56] The influential Rabbi Meir of Rothenburg (d. 1293) objected both to the writing and to the magical aspects of the ceremony. By the sixteenth century the older ceremony had disappeared from Germany.

The newer ceremony of bar mitzvah, according to Marcus, was parallel to oblation, the dedication of a Christian child to a monastery. For centuries it was the practice to donate very young boys to monasteries. In 670 Bede was oblated at the age of seven; Thomas Aquinas (1225–74) was oblated at the age of six, but Aquinas himself argued that an older age, an age of reasoned consent, would have been better. Gradually, oblation was delayed to twelve for girls and fourteen for boys. Marcus pointed out that prior to the thirteenth century, younger Jewish boys were permitted to perform ritual obligations of adult Jews, such as putting on tefillin and reading Torah.[57] Objections to this practice were raised from the thirteenth century and summarized by Isserles in his comments on the *Tur*: "The custom is as the author of *Ittur* states, that minors should

not put on tefillin until bar mitzvah, that is, thirteen years and a day."[58]
A boundary, suggests Marcus, had been created at age thirteen between
childhood and adulthood, and it was to bridge that gap that bar mitzvah gradually developed, a ritual of the voluntary acceptance of the age
of religious majority.

Marcus versus Ta-Shma

Oblation is a strange parallel to bring to bar mitzvah because entry into
a monastery was not accompanied by a family ceremony. Marcus's discussion was far too vague not only about the details but also about the
times and places he was comparing. It is not surprising that Marcus's
suggestion that Jews were copying monks was vigorously challenged.
He was taken to task by Professor Israel Ta-Shma. Ta-Shma was able to
write fluently and swiftly on a broad range of subjects, drawing on his
vast knowledge of medieval Hebrew sources. In a wide-ranging review,
published in English, Ta-Shma praised the scholarship of the first part
of Marcus's book but took issue with his view of the origin of bar mitzvah, arguing that the ceremony was older than Marcus realized and that
Marcus had missed key sources from Rabbeinu Gershom (960–1040)
and from the time of Rashi (1040–1105). Ta-Shma did not comment
on Marcus's use of Christian parallels, but he was able to demonstrate
that Marcus's understanding of the sources for bar mitzvah was highly
inadequate.[59]

Marcus took Ta-Shma's criticism seriously and included some of the
suggested sources in the Hebrew edition of the book, published in 1998.
This effort, however, provoked an even more scathing review from Ta-
Shma, this time in Hebrew, who described Marcus's understanding of
the primary sources on bar mitzvah as full of mistakes and a complete
muddle.[60] The polemical tone of the article is not uncommon in rabbinic
Hebrew but would not be found in an English scholarly journal. Marcus
did not reply directly but made further corrections in his later book *The
Jewish Life Cycle*, which gives a thorough explanation of the sources cited
by Ta-Shma.

In light of my own research, it is worth revisiting the theory proposed
by Ivan Marcus, namely that the origin of bar mitzvah was copying oblation, when young Christians entered a monastery. Ta-Shma's early dating
of the sources on bar mitzvah was swayed by his traditional approach,
which dated each text by the names mentioned therein, not by the date the
saying was recorded. Marcus had proposed his own theory before look-

ing in detail at the history of bar mitzvah, and even when he did publish his account of bar mitzvah history, he did not discover the Avigdor text. So, it is remarkable that here I have reached a parallel conclusion, that bar mitzvah may have its origin in a leaving ceremony for boys going off to school. The "laying on of hands" was copying a twelfth-century Christian model, and the schools themselves reflect the culture of what has become known as the "twelfth-century Renaissance," in which the new schools for Christians in France promoted the principle of reason, the liberal arts, grammar, dialectic, and neo-Platonism.[61]

This was a period of great cultural exchange between Jew and Christian, when Rashi's grandson Rashbam (Rabbi Samuel son of Meir [1085–1174]) and his exact contemporary Hugh of St. Victor both promoted the study of the literal meaning of Scripture. Hugh referred to his teachers as "Hebraei," and Rashbam at one point shows an awareness of Latin. Bar mitzvah during this period, consisting as it did only of the father's blessing, does not require us to presuppose a precise cultural model, but we can say that it arose among small communities living in a completely Christian environment and that there were real and important intellectual exchanges between the two faiths.[62] Marcus was the first to identify not a parallel ceremony but a parallel occasion.

BAR MITZVAH AND THE REFORMATION

We have only isolated reports from the medieval period of bar mitzvah, which was then a practice of a few pious individuals. Early reports that appear to describe a bar mitzvah party might be about a wedding feast. The social and cultural background for the growth and popularity of both the ceremony and the party has to be sought in the sixteenth century.

During the sixteenth century bar mitzvah developed from a ceremony observed by a few pious individuals into a popular custom, with a party and speech by the boy. There are many possible cultural influences, both religious and secular, that might have helped shape this development. At this time Jewish society underwent a process that has been described as a "ritualisation of life." The invention of printing helped to spread new rituals and ideas and itself made the learning of reading by every child a vital part of education.[63] Drawing on a model used in the history of literature, Avriel Bar-Levav has pointed to the usefulness of distinguishing "beginnings" and "thresholds" in the history of ritual.[64] Bar mitzvah had its beginning as first recorded in thirteenth-century France and reached its threshold of becoming popular in sixteenth-century central Europe. The threshold stage of a ritual is brought about by social criteria that make it popular.

Ta-Shma suggested that Jews prohibited even the ordinary celebration of birthdays as an idolatrous custom.[65] He did not offer any reason why bar mitzvah became an exception. The fact is that before the keeping of clear records, most people would have been aware of the season but not the precise date of their birthday. Although *Mishnah Niddah* 5 specifies various ages as the minimum for betrothal and for the validity of vows, the formulation of such rules does not mean that everyone would have been aware of the exact date.

Among those living in peasant societies in Europe, many were unaware of their precise birthdays until the early twentieth century.[66] Among the middle classes in England precise dates of birth are known only from the 1560s. At Winchester School before then, the date of birth was given approximately, by the nearest saint's day or religious festival.[67] The date of Shakespeare's birth in 1564 was not recorded. From France and Spain, Philippe Ariès quoted examples of vagueness about the age of a child from Mathurin Cordier's *Colloques* (1586) and Miguel de Cervantes' *Don Quixote* (1605).[68] According to Marcus, Jews as well as Christians began to enter birth dates in family Bibles, starting in the fifteenth century.[69] The celebration of annual birthdays among Jews did not become popular until modern times,[70] but once birth records existed, it facilitated and helped to popularize the celebration of bar mitzvah. Changes in general education from the sixteenth century show an increased awareness of the age of the child. Among non-Jews it was now considered desirable for schools to be organized in year groups according to age. For those who were better off, the new humanist education led to the founding of new schools. The period of education lengthened, and as it did so, the medieval system of apprenticeship declined.[71] All these changes facilitated and encouraged the marking of the passing of the years of a child's life.

The Exclusion of Women from the Ritual

In the Ashkenazic liturgy for the ritual of circumcision, all present respond to the father's blessing with the words "Just as he has entered into the covenant, so he may enter into Torah, marriage and good deeds."[72] As bar mitzvah became popular, it would be natural to imagine that the traditional words "enter into Torah" denote the time of bar mitzvah for the boy. "The father has performed his first obligation: the men charge him with the others."[73] The duty of teaching Torah is laid firmly on the father; no role is envisaged for the mother in the education of a male child.

Bar mitzvah was invented and popularized as a ritual for boys only. This practice is different from most coming-of-age ceremonies in other cultures, which generally have had different but parallel rituals for boys and girls.[74] In early Ashkenazic culture it was not uncommon for women to take a role in certain Jewish religious rituals. The new popularity of bar mitzvah in the sixteenth century coincides with the exclusion of women from other religious rituals, and this helped to create a climate in which a ritual only for boys was acceptable throughout the community. In early Ashkenaz, for example, some deemed it acceptable for a woman to wear tallit and tefillin. Avigdor, whose evidence for bar mitzvah is crucial, also indicated that a woman may sound the shofar, wear fringes or tefillin, and eat in the sukkah, and for each one she is permitted to recite the blessing. He added: "A few pious women have the custom of donning tefillin and of reciting the blessing, and wrap themselves with fringed garments."[75]

Howard Tzvi Adelman has documented how, over the following centuries, women were gradually excluded from this and other synagogue rites in Italy.[76] Similarly, Lawrence Hoffman has documented how women in medieval Europe gradually came to be excluded from the circumcision ceremony.[77] At the end of the thirteenth century Rabbi Shimshon the son of Tzadok objected to the common custom of the boy sitting on his mother's lap throughout the operation. In sixteenth-century Poland, Moses Isserles ruled that the mother could accompany her husband to the synagogue, but it was better for a man to do everything without a woman.[78] Her role was to be subordinate and supporting. Women were excluded from public ceremonies and began to create their own prayers.[79] It was precisely at that moment in Ashkenazic history when women had the least involvement in public worship that bar mitzvah became popular. Women's spirituality had now become a private matter; only the spiritual and educational development of a boy could be celebrated publicly.

Many of the community decrees that regulated bar mitzvah parties from 1595 onward excluded women other than close relatives from the party. The arrangements for both synagogue ceremony and party were made by the father, and the mother played a purely supporting role. According to Juspa the shammash of Worms in the mid-seventeenth century:

> The father clothes his son for bar mitzvah in new and pretty clothes, and he wears them when Shabbat comes in. And at the time of the afternoon prayers on Shabbat, they make a meal for him, but the community servant does not announce this meal; but one hour before the afternoon prayer the bar mitzvah boy himself summons the guests to his meal. And he goes dressed in his new clothes and goes right into the guests' houses and says to each one that he should eat with him the third Sabbath meal, which will include the bar mitzvah meal. And they come and they eat and they drink, and they rejoice with the boy and his father and his mother and their friends. And the boy gives a speech at that meal based on the customs of bar mitzvah, and the custom is that the bar mitzvah boy leads grace after meals with a quorum of three.[80]

The bar mitzvah boy in Worms learned the duties of an adult not just through his learning of Torah but also by his first prominent role in the social life of the community. His father provides the model, and his mother is simply there to lend support. Only through the nineteenth-century ritual of confirmation were women brought into the ceremony.

Christian Confirmation at the Time of the Reformation

Maharshal (Solomon Luria) has provided the key evidence of the spread of bar mitzvah in the sixteenth century. He included his remarks about the bar mitzvah meal to follow his discussion of the festivities held for *brit milah*, a circumcision feast, and *hanukkat habayit*, the dedication of a house.[81] Similarly, many of the seventeenth- and eighteenth-century decrees that laid down regulations for the bar mitzvah meal included it immediately after their discussion of the circumcision feast. No doubt it was one way of stressing that bar mitzvah, like circumcision, was for boys only. But it was also a way of denoting the size of the party. Repeatedly, it was stressed that the parties should be of the same size. In a similar way Christian writers have defined confirmation as the second part of the initiatory rite begun with baptism.[82] This view comes from the medieval Scholastics who were the contemporaries of the Jewish scholars known as tosafists. Thomas Aquinas declared that confirmation was a completion of baptism and should be conferred by one who has the highest power (*summam potestatem*) in the Church.[83]

Aspects of the development of Christian confirmation among both Catholics and Protestants during the Reformation period present striking and important parallels to the rise of bar mitzvah. The sixteenth century, during which bar mitzvah developed into a widely practiced custom, was a time of great religious ferment in Germany and Poland. Among Catholics the age of Christian confirmation was now older than it had been when the synagogue ceremony of bar mitzvah began. The Lateran Council of 1215 had linked it to the "years of discretion," generally taken to mean seven to ten, but the Council of Trent (1545) suggested ten to twelve and prohibited the distribution of communion to younger children.[84] The rising age of confirmation was one factor that may have influenced the new popularity of bar mitzvah.

Gerard Austin has suggested that confirmation was a "neglected sacrament" in the Catholic Church at this time and that repeated legislation about its importance suggests that it was not being taken seriously. But in the second half of the sixteenth century confirmation was revived among Catholics as part of the strategy of the Counter-Reformation. The Council of Trent, which laid down the program for revival, marked the beginning of a process leading to organized parishes across Europe and primary education for all children.[85]

Influence of New Protestant Ideas and Practices

Although Jews would not have been interested in theological debates about confirmation, they might well have known the common Catholic practice that the confirmation was closely followed by the first communion. Both Leon Modena (in 1637) and his apostate student Giulio Morosini (1683) reported that in Venice a bar mitzvah was also known as "bar minian," marking the stage at which a man was able to be counted among the quorum for community prayer.[86] If bar mitzvah was parallel to confirmation, then *bar minian* could be regarded as parallel to first communion, with one now able to participate fully in society.

But by this time Catholic practice was not the only factor. Martin Luther's "Ninety-Five Theses," affixed to the door of the church in Wittenberg in 1517, objected to confession and indulgences being administered by priests because, he claimed, repentance comes from within. To proponents of the Reformation "the word of God no longer assumed flesh: it assumed meaning."[87] Rituals involving sacraments and ceremonies were replaced by rituals involving words, such as preaching. Violent crowds destroyed models and images in churches in Augsburg in 1522 and Ulm in 1530.[88] Few German Jews would have had much interest in the finer points of the theological debate, but they could understand the general issues and could see what was happening around them. Many of the new Protestants called on the secular authorities to expel Jews from their territories; at the instigation of Luther and his clergy, Jews were driven out of Hanover, Saxony, and other areas.

For many Jews the Reformation was seen as increasing the threat of Christianity. Although there were very few Jews who left Judaism and became Christians, many adopted a more public profile, conveying mixed images of Jews to the Christian world. Martin Luther had great hopes of converting Jews, which he saw as a central plank of his Protestant program.[89] By the end of the century, however, Jewish life was more secure and relatively free from persecution, largely because neither Protestants nor Catholics were able to break the power of the rival Church, and as a result, "all three of the major churches in Germany were permanently weakened."[90]

Among Protestants the more radical thinkers such as John Calvin and Huldrych Zwingli did not approve of the confirmation ceremony, but the main groups retained it and promoted more strictly than Catholics the link to adolescence.[91] Protestant ritual favored simplicity rather than excess and uniformity of practice throughout the Church.[92] Luther objected to the "sacramental" nature of confirmation and the bishop's role but did not want to abolish the ceremony: "Confirmation should not be observed as the bishops desire it. Nevertheless we do not find fault if every pastor examines the faith of the children to see whether it is good and sincere, lays hands on them, and confirms them."[93]

The Lutheran Church developed a program for confirmation following the views of the humanist Erasmus of Rotterdam, who proposed in 1522 that baptized boys at puberty should attend lectures explaining the meaning of the faith:

> Then they should be carefully examined in private by approved men whether they sufficiently retain and remember the things which the priest has taught. If they be found to retain them sufficiently, they should be asked whether they ratify what the godparents promised

in their name in baptism. If they answer that they ratify them, then let that profession be renewed in public at a gathering of their equals, and that with solemn ceremonies, fitting, pure, serious, and magnificent, and such things as become that profession, than which there is none more sacred.[94]

This text presents a remarkable parallel to bar mitzvah as it developed in the sixteenth and seventeenth centuries—for boys at puberty, with a formal ceremony following a period of instruction and examination. For the first time it was a ceremony that began to appeal to Jews not simply as a pious practice but as constituting part of mainstream Jewish life. What developed was clearly parallel to Reformation ideas. Bar mitzvah was no longer simply reciting a blessing. From the seventeenth century onward come reports of boys having to be examined about their knowledge and abilities before being allowed to celebrate bar mitzvah. We can now see that this development, too, had Christian precedents.

In Poland, too, Protestantism became an important factor. There was close intellectual contact between Poland and the West, and Polish students who had studied in Germany brought back Reformation ideas.[95] Magda Teter's *Jews and Heretics in Catholic Poland* (2006) describes the Polish Catholic Church of the day as "beleaguered." The Counter-Reformation was eventually to lead to the exclusion of Jews from Polish society. But in the sixteenth century Calvinism was strong in Poland. Many Jews worked for Polish nobles on their large estates and appreciated the settled conditions under which they lived. Many of the Polish nobility adopted Calvinist beliefs. The 1573 constitution guaranteed religious toleration. "In the Jews' own opinion," according to Zenon Guldon and Waldemar Kowalski, "it was a country of considerable freedom."[96]

The writings of Ronnie Hsia are invaluable for an understanding of Jewish social attitudes to the Reformation. His book *The Myth of Ritual Murder* (1988) details the blood libels and ritual murder accusations that repeatedly surfaced in medieval Europe. Although the language of many Reformers, especially Martin Luther, was strongly anti-Semitic, their condemnation of Catholicism was just as forthright. Hsia has suggested that the removal of blood symbolism from Christian worship by Protestants helped to undermine the psychological and intellectual foundations of the ritual murder discourse. As the "magic and superstition" of the Roman Church was condemned, charges of magic and murder against Jews began to diminish.[97]

It is not surprising that, against this background, Jews were able to construct a more public affirmation of what it meant to be Jewish. A contemporary innovation was the outdoor portable canopy used for a wedding service and described by Isserles: "The custom today is widespread to call *chuppah* a place where one places a sheet over poles and bring the groom and the bride under it in public."[98]

The proliferation of bar mitzvah as a general custom is a second example of this more public confidence. The spread of rules and restrictions on the party in itself suggests that non-Jews could see what was going on and that therefore appropriate care had to be taken not to create envy by spending too much. Sometimes this motive is explicitly stated. Beginning in the early seventeenth century, Christians began to visit synagogues and write reports on what they had seen. The general approval they gave to bar mitzvah may in turn have helped to increase its popularity. To this day the celebration is an assertion of public confidence by the family and by the community—confidence in the performance of the child and in the value of the ceremony, and for many it is a rare opportunity to show off Jewish culture to non-Jewish friends and family.

Just as Protestants emphasized the importance of preaching as a central aspect of religious ritual, so Jews added their own "ritual of the word" to the traditional synagogue bar mitzvah ceremony, in the form of the bar mitzvah speech to be given by the boy at the family celebration meal. The earliest report of a bar mitzvah speech comes from Poland;[99] the argumentative method known as *pilpul*, accompanied by interruptions, mirrored in a more boisterous form the question-and-answer method of the Christian catechism. The first Polish catechism was published in 1543,[100] not long before the earliest report of the bar mitzvah speech. In the synagogue the ceremony was no longer simply an act performed by the father. The detailed accounts from seventeenth-century Worms indicate that the boy himself took the initiative, both in preparing to read from the Torah and in inviting the guests to the party. The term *bar mitzvah* itself indicates that this was a ceremony with the boy and his performance at its center.

ASSESSING THE MODERN EVIDENCE

The history of Jewish coming-of-age ceremonies in the nineteenth and twentieth centuries presents very different issues from those related strictly to bar mitzvah. No longer is this the story of one ceremony but three— bar mitzvah, confirmation, and bat mitzvah. Many readers of this book may not have heard of Jewish confirmation, and yet it provides the vital evidence for the background to bat mitzvah and explains why girls often still celebrate as a group.

Like bar mitzvah, confirmation began in Christian Europe. Here the Christian influence is much more obvious, as the name of the ceremony indicates. Jacobson and the early Reformers were quite open about copying Protestant models. Deborah Hertz, in *How Jews Became Germans* (2007), has provided a vivid account of life among assimilated Jews in Berlin at the time confirmation began, demonstrating how the worries about Jews being baptized as Christians were real ones and, using statistics eerily gathered from Nazi records, showing how the early Reform services helped to slow the rate of baptism.

The dilemma faced by German Jews was explained by the young historian Marcus Jost in 1822:

> The Jews stand today in the midst of a dilemma. University students simply can not find employment and only baptism saves them for mankind. If we don't push the crafts, our entire next generation will turn Christian. And rightly so, for what should tie them to the religion of their fathers? Only childhood memories still hold us together, no more. Our children live in another world, and they have no reason to give up their entire life just to be called Jews, when they no longer are.[101]

For Jost attempts to reform and modernize Judaism were futile, but many wanted to try. Confirmation and bat mitzvah came about as a result of their deliberate and sustained efforts. The historical background to the rise of confirmation and bat mitzvah is thus clear. The emergence of Jews into the modern world, new educational ideas, the need for modern Jewish schools to have graduation ceremonies, extensive Christian influences, the gradual rise in women's consciousness, and the struggle for women to be accepted as equals in religious rituals—all these are very well documented and provide sufficient explanation for our history.

But these trends that were part of the formation of today's society do not explain why a particular event happened at a certain time in a certain place. Carol Matzkin Orsborn, in an unusual study from 2002, has linked the promotion of confirmation to the personal psychological needs of Israel Jacobson. For bat mitzvah there was no inevitability about Mordecai Kaplan holding a ceremony for his daughter in 1922; it seems to have been decided on a whim, in line with his ideals and the kind of Judaism he wanted to promote.

A clear turning point in the history of bar mitzvah came when many American communities in the 1930s decided to introduce formal educational requirements. This move was by no means inevitable; they could have allowed bar mitzvah to continue to decline and promoted confirmation as a modern alternative. But this was a time when Conservative and then Reform Jews began a long slow return to more traditional practices, which was boosted and reinforced by Zionism, the founding of the State of Israel, and the new usefulness of Hebrew as a living language. Bar mitzvah had a large Hebrew learning component that confirmation rarely provided. In his history of Reform, Michael Meyer entitled his chapter on this period, between the world wars, with the single word *Reorientation*. The Columbus platform of 1937 represented a sharp departure from its Pittsburgh predecessor of 1885. It used the traditional categories of God, Torah, and Israel and promoted Reform religious observance.[102] Although it was to take several decades before all American communities brought back bar mitzvah and introduced individual bat mitzvah, it was the thinking of the 1930s and the resulting educational reforms that paved the way.

Collecting Balanced Evidence

The principal difficulty encountered in researching the modern period is not in understanding the evidence but in collecting properly balanced evidence. For the nineteenth century confirmation and girls' ceremonies are better documented than bar mitzvah. Records from Western Europe and North America exist, while those from Eastern Europe were largely destroyed. The record of the old community rule books (*pinkasim*) ends before 1800, and the old sumptuary laws fell into disuse. We know from family histories and surviving anecdotes that arrivals in England, France, and North America from the 1880s brought a tradition of bar mitzvah with them. But the documentary evidence from Eastern Europe, if it existed at all, has not survived. What we have are stories such as "The Kerchief" and statistics from Paris from the 1890s showing that families from Eastern Europe brought with them a strong tradition of bar mitzvah that had been largely abandoned by most Jews in France.[103] Yet many authors of biographies and autobiographies did not consider the bar mitzvah to be of sufficient note to be worth mentioning. While rabbis and teachers were debating confirmation and women's rights, bar mitzvah continued unchanged in millions of European Orthodox families, primarily as an undocumented custom of the people. Historians can only use the evidence available, and it is simply not possible to tell the undocumented stories. But it is necessary to add a caveat that this history is inevitably a skewed picture.

Biases related to the evidence continue to the present time. Academic articles and studies now concentrate primarily on North America. Guidebooks for parents are predominantly about the American Reform tradition. So much is now published that it is easier to document the decline in confirmation from its current absence from research studies than from statistics. The secular bat mitzvah in Israel—a party without a synagogue ceremony—is an important innovation in historical terms that deserves its own sociological study.

Every historian of times within living memory has to judge carefully the value of oral testimony. Where it fits well with other available evidence, particularly if the interviewee has no knowledge of that evidence, it can be deemed to be trustworthy. Such convergence of evidence has been given the name "triangulation" by academic historians.[104] So, in 2012, when Walter Hart, at the age of ninety, told me that he remembered girls dressing in white for confirmation at the Jews' Free School London before World War II, this made sense to me because it fits well with the other available evidence, even though it is not mentioned in the school's official history. An archival search of contemporary newspapers and old magazines from the school confirmed and expanded his personal testimony. But sometimes judging the value of an unsupported personal anecdote is much more difficult. When Ida Blum (b. 1908) from Calumet, Michigan, claimed in a phone call in 1985 that she had had a bat mitzvah as a child, it can neither be proved nor disproved without independent evidence. It can only be reported for what it is—a personal anecdote or memory.

In writing the history of bar/bat mitzvah in the modern period, I have made extensive use of evidence from novels, TV programs, and movies. Judging these materials, too, requires careful interpretation because they are intended to be fictional. Where the authors or directors have deliberately tried to make a particular point about bar mitzvah or to describe a specific issue, the material is certainly of interest. But other information can emerge in passing, such as the 1950s gift list in Mordecai Richler's 1959 novel, *The Apprenticeship of Duddy Kravitz*. Descriptions of settings for ceremonies and parties often look as if they are based in reality. Movies have generally filmed bar mitzvah ceremonies on location and have often used a thirteen-year-old reciting his or her real portion for the occasion. Nearly all the fictional accounts provide strong evidence of presumed interest by readers or spectators in the feelings of the child. Yet the evidence provided by fictional accounts has to be carefully sifted. The *Simpsons* episode about Krusty's bar mitzvah, for example, is good evidence that adult bar mitzvah was popular at the time, but the suggestion that it somehow makes a person Jewish is included as part of the humor.

There is a huge amount of documentation and online information about bar/bat mitzvah in the period since World War II until the present time. But even academic studies and educational theories tend to consider it in isolation, without comparing similar rituals from other cultures. One notable exception is Elizabeth Pleck, who in her 2000 study, *Celebrating the Family*, compared the social aspects of American bar/bat mitzvah with the Hispanic American quinceañera for fifteen-year-old girls. She argued that both ceremonies at an unconscious level celebrate sexual maturation and that they have played an important part in the creation of modern Jewish and Hispanic identity in the United States. Both have religious elements, and both have retained and built on their popularity by embracing consumer culture. Just as rabbis have criticized excessive spending on bar mitzvah parties, priests have complained about the size and expense of quinceañera celebrations. In both cases pressure has come from families for the event to be celebrated at their place of worship. Just as Reform rabbis in the 1960s had to allow bar and bat mitzvah because they were losing members to Conservative congregations, in the same way Catholic churches permitted quinceañera to prevent families from leaving for the local Protestant church.[105]

Such comparisons are invaluable not because they suggest that Jews and Hispanics have been copying each other but because they help us clearly define those moments of joy and pressures for change that come from common societal expectations. They show a common desire by families to celebrate key dates in their children's lives.

An Invented Tradition

It is striking to discover that bar mitzvah is not as old as people imagine it to be; the evolution of such a misperception is interesting in itself. Partly it comes from a thought process that says that because it is Jewish, it must be ancient, and partly from a related idea that festivals and popular Jewish celebrations have survived unchanged through the centuries. Bar mitzvah has a history stretching back 750 years, not 2,000 years. And even though its basic form has remained the same, it has taken on different meanings as times have changed and has multiple layers of meaning today. A lawyer wearing a wig meant nothing in an age when all gentlemen wore wigs; as soon as the practice changed, it became recognized as an invented tradition.[106]

For those who participate in Jewish worship throughout their lives, bar/bat mitzvah is likely to be the first of many opportunities to read from a Torah scroll. But it has a different meaning for those Jews who read the Torah only once in their lives; it has become an invented tradition from a world outside normal existence. Elizabeth Pleck used the word *postsentimental* to describe rituals that take place in postmodern families. Such rituals show that family life is not in irrevocable decline; in fact, the performance of the ritual reinforces the family by forcing it to show itself to the wider community. Even the divorced and those rarely seen with their families come together to celebrate. This behavior is not simply market driven; the ethnicity of ritual exists because families need to demonstrate or invent roots, a shared history, a shared culture, to give themselves meaning and purpose. The work of blending the traditional and the new continues and will endure through such rituals.[107]

When called up for the reading of the Torah, it is customary to grasp the wooden rollers of the Torah scroll while saying the blessing. In Hebrew they are known as "eitzei-hayim," or "trees of life." As the reader recites the blessing after reading Torah, he or she thanks God for planting eternal life within us. Many no longer believe that eternal life is granted to us individually but, rather, that we can glimpse it in the continuity of the tradition through the generations, both through the people as a whole and through individual families. As the child grasps the wooden rollers for the first time, he or she becomes part of a tradition that celebrates and proclaims the wisdom of Torah as a tree of life to those who grasp it, so that those who hold fast to it have the potential for happiness. Its ways are ways of pleasantness, and all its paths are peace.[108]

NOTES

INTRODUCTION

1. Magida, *Opening the Doors of Wonder*, 91–92.
2. Magida, *Opening the Doors of Wonder*, 91.
3. Mitchell and Reid-Walsh, *Girl Culture*, 168; and www.youtube.com/
   watch?v=N8Yk_EPlgWE (accessed May 12, 2012).
4. The word *bar* is Aramaic, corresponding to the Hebrew *ben*. The word
   mitzvah is Hebrew. Mixed phrases of Aramaic and Hebrew are very common in rabbinic literature, and the phrase *bar mitzvah* is used several
   times in the Talmud, though not with the meaning it has today.
5. The *maftir* who is to read from the Prophets is called up first to the Torah
   in order to demonstrate that the teachings of the Prophets are not considered equal to those of the Torah (Rashi on B. *Megillah* 23a).
6. *Midrash Bereshit Rabbah* 63.10.
7. The blessing has died out in many Orthodox synagogues, though it
   remains in Ashkenazic prayer books. Gaguine, *Sefer Keter Shem Tov*,
   318, writes that he has never seen or heard of the blessing being used by
   Sephardim at all on the occasion of a bar mitzvah. It has not been the general practice of non-Orthodox synagogues to use the blessing. In modern
   Hebrew the traditional words associated with the blessing have come to
   be a popular phrase meaning "good riddance." This has probably discouraged its use for bar/bat mitzvah, even though, as we shall see, the original
   meaning of the phrase was quite different.
8. For further information on my own Jewish upbringing, see Michael Hilton, "How Did the Jewish Community Come to Be Where It Is Today?" in
   Bayfield, Race, and Siddiqui, *Beyond the Dysfunctional Family*, 13–29.
9. Magida, *Opening the Doors of Wonder*, 4–6.
10. Grimes, *Deeply into the Bone*, 336.
11. Turner, *From Ritual to Theatre*.

1. HOW BAR MITZVAH BEGAN

1. *Bereshit Rabbah* 38:11; *Pirkei de Rabbi Eliezer* gives the age of thirteen (26). This is probably from the eighth century, suggesting that by this time thirteen was considered an important demarcation age.

2. Genesis 40:20. For modern birthday parties, see Pleck, *Celebrating the Family*, 141–61

3. 2 Maccabees 6:7.

4. Mark 6:21; Matthew 14:6. Salome's name is not mentioned in the stories but is given by Josephus in *Antiquities*, 18.5.4.

5. Genesis 24:67.

6. Esther 2:18.

7. Rashi on Genesis 21:8.

8. Deuteronomy 6:7 (the *Shema*); Exodus 12:26,13:8,13:14; Deuteronomy 6:20.

9. Hezser, *Jewish Literacy in Roman Palestine*. Hezser discounts later Talmudic reports suggesting a widespread elementary school network. The Mishnah only mentions parents and individual teachers instructing children, never schools.

10. Genesis 17:25.

11. Josephus, *Antiquities*, 1.12.2.

12. Rashi on Genesis 17:26.

13. Numbers 1:1–3.

14. Rashi on Numbers 1:3; Ramban on Numbers 1:3.

15. Gilat, "Ben Shelosh-Esrei LaMitzvot."

16. Exodus 23:14

17. M. *Hagigah* 1.1.

18. Luke 2:41–51.

19. Numbers 30:3.

20. M. *Niddah* 5.6.

21. B. *Niddah* 48b.

22. M. *Arot* 5:21. Some manuscripts give the saying in the name of a different rabbi of that time, Shemuel HaKatan.

23. Gilat, "Ben Shelosh-Esrei LaMitzvot."

24. Following M. *Avot* 4.19, in the name of Shemuel HaKatan. Amram Tropper also leaves it out of his edition, following the Budapest ms Kauffman. See Gilat, "Ben Shelosh-Esrei LaMitzvot," 39; Tropper, *Wisdom, Politics, and Historiography*.

25. M. *Avot* 5.20.

26. From the *Tosafot* on *Bava Batra* 21a and *Ketubot* 50a, where it is quoted. See Marcus, *Rituals of Childhood*, 43–44.

27. Verbal usages such as this have been taken to support a later date for the whole of *Avot*, as was argued by Guttmann, "Tractate Abot."

28. Kaufmann Kohler erroneously took the text as evidence for a bar mitzvah ceremony at the beginning of the Christian era, and this was printed in the *Jewish Encyclopedia* of 1901–6. He was mistaken about both the date and the meaning of the text. The Babylonian Talmud seems to be unaware of the ages for learning given in our Mishnah; age six is given for the start of learning Bible (see B. *Ketubot* 50a).

29. *Avot de Rabbi Natan* 16.2.

30. Genesis 34:25.

31. *Bereshit Rabbah* 80.10. Rabbi Shimon lived in the second half of the second century CE.

32. Pseudo-Rashi on *Avot* 5.21, מכניסים אותו לקיים מצות. The same verb was used by Maharshal in the sixteenth century when discussing bar mitzvah. Its use for bar mitzvah is based on the use of the word in the naming blessing said at a circumcision (כשם שנכנס לברית כן יכנס לתורה).

33. This is mentioned and satirized by Sandra Satten in her novel for young readers, *In the Thirteenth Year*, 6 and 72. In Britain the words "Today I am bar mitzvah" have been more common as the opening of the speech. See Levy, *Becoming and Remaining Barmitzvah*, 9.

34. Oppenheimer, *Thirteen and a Day*, 250; Appel, "Today I Am a Fountain Pen, Again."

35. *The Simpsons*, season 15, episode 6.

36. M. *Megillah* 4.6.

37. J. Berakhot 7.2,11b; *Shulchan Arukh Orach Chayyim* 282.3.

38. *Machzor Vitry*, 133.

39. Hagahot Maimoniot on Rambam *Hilkhot Tefilah* 12.17.

40. *Mishnah Berurah* on *Shulchan Arukh Orach Chayyim* 282.3.

41. Blank, "Jewish Rites of Adolescence," 83–86.

42. J. *Sukkah* 3.2.

43. Gilat, "Ben Shelosh-Esrei LaMitzvot."

44. *Seder Rav Amram, Seder Tefillah* (ד"ה והשיב כך).

45. *Soferim* 16.12.

46. The last part of *Tractate Soferim* is now thought to be later than the year 1000, which is roughly when European Jewish scholarship began. The whole book was revised and updated in Ashkenazic Europe to reflect the practices of European Jews. This makes it very hard to work out exactly which demarcation ages were used at which time (see Blank, "It's Time to Take Another Look at 'Our Little Sister,'" 5).

47. *Machzor Vitry*, 133.

48. Wieseltier, *Kaddish*, 45–48, 74.

49. Yosef Caro, *Beit Yosef Orach Chayyim* 53.6.

50. *Shulchan Arukh Orach Chayyim* 199.10 (concerning grace after meals).

51. Commentary Darkhei Moshe on *Tur Orach Chayyim* 37; see also *Shulchan Arukh Orach Chayyim* 37.3.

52. From the commentary attributed to Rabbeinu Gershom on B. *Menachot* 43b.

53. Ta-Shma, "Ivan Marcus, Rituals of Childhood," 237.

54. Waskow and Berman, *Time for Every Purpose under Heaven*, 63.

55. Pleck, *Celebrating the Family*, 162–83.

56. *Soferim* 18.7 (Higger) *Minhag tov berushalayim*. This is numbered 18.5 in the Soncino edition.

57. In B. *Ketubot* 50a, thirteen is given as the age when boys are able to fast for a full night and day, but there are textual difficulties with this source as well.

58. Isaac Rivkind considered this text important evidence for the antiquity of bar mitzvah. See Rivkind, *Le-Ot u-le-Zikkaron*, 16.

59. Gilat, "Ben Shelosh-Esrei LaMitzvot," 45. Gilat uses the evidence of six manuscripts, some of which were not available to Michael Higger (see his edition of *Massekhet Soferim*, 319, para. 18.7).

60. Kanarfogel, *Peering through the Lattices*, 42–43.

61. *Bereshit Rabbah* 63.10.

62. *Bereshit Rabbah* 63.10, in the name of Elazar son of Pedat (third century) or Elazar son of Shimon (second century). Literally, the text means "from punishment because of this one."

63. *Sefer HaIttur*, gate 3, *Hilkhot Milah* 53a.

64. Judah the son of Yakar's commentary on the prayer book was published in 1968 (*Peirush ha-tefilot veha-berakhot* [Jerusalem: Meore Yisrael]). I have used the text as quoted by the editor in Avigdor Tzarfati, *Sefer Perushim*, ח (sedra Toledot).

65. *Horaot miRabbanei Tzarfat* 23, published in *Piskei Rabbeinu Yehiel MiParis*, ed. Pines, 1973. This was the first printing of the text. Pines found it appended to two of the medieval manuscripts of the *Piskei R. Yehiel* and included it in his edition of that work.

66. He was a teacher of Rashi, who refers to him in a comment on B. *Hullin* 47a. See Gilat, "Barukh She-Petarani," 176–77.

67. Gilat, "Barukh She-Petarani," 176–77.

68. The blessings said are discussed in B. *Pesahim* 121b. For other sources, see Rubin, "Coping with the Value of the pidyon ha'ben Payment."

69. Kanarfogel, *Peering through the Lattices*, 38–39, 43–44.

70. According to Kanarfogel, *Medieval Ashkenaz*, 329, Yehiel was forced to return to France because of failing health and died there sometime before 1265.

71. Avigdor Tzarfati, *Sefer Perushim*, ח (sedra Toledot). The various views about who Avigdor was and when and where he lived are discussed in chapter 8.

72. Leviticus 16:21; M. *Menahot* 9.8.

73. Genesis 48:14.

74. Deuteronomy 34:9.

75. Austin, *Anointing with the Spirit*, 21–22.

76. Carried out by Peter and John in Acts 8:17.

77. Banting, "Imposition of Hands in Confirmation."

78. Hilton, *Christian Effect on Jewish Life*, 120–22.

79. Herskovits in Avigdor Tzarfati, *Sefer Perushim*, 13. .

80. *Sefer Huqqei HaTorah*, published in Kanarfogel, *Jewish Education and Society*, 106–15. English translation in Kanarfogel, "A Monastic-like Setting for the Study of Torah," in Fine, *Judaism in Practice*, 191–202. The Oxford manuscript was written by another Avigdor, a scribe called Avigdor, the son of Jacob Israel. Further research is needed to identify his family; it is not impossible that the scribe Avigdor was a grandson of Avigdor Tzarfati. See Golb, *Jews in Medieval Normandy*, 455.

81. Fine, *Judaism in Practice*, 201–2.

82. Golb, *Jews in Medieval Normandy*, 137–67.

83. Golb, *Jews in Medieval Normandy*, 176–95.

84. Line 68.

85. Fine, *Judaism in Practice*, 201–2; Golb, *Jews in Medieval Normandy*, 183.

86. The link here suggested between early bar mitzvah and the school in Rouen is discussed in more detail in chapter 8.

87. Hilton, *Christian Effect on Jewish Life*, 118–22, 161–65.

88. Wieseltier, *Kaddish*, 52.

89. Ta-Shma, *Creativity and Tradition*, 85.

90. Rabbi Yomtov of Joigny, said by Marmorstein to be Avigdor's grandfather, visited England and died at York in 1190. Jacobs, in *The Jews of Angevin England*, wrote that Samuel of Falaise (teacher of Avigdor) had lived in England, but this account has not been generally accepted. These conundrums are considered in more detail in chapter 8. See Marmorstein, "Sur un auteur français inconnu du treizième siècle."

91. Translated from the Hebrew text cited in Gilat, "Barukh She-Petarani," 177, corrected against the text in Rivkind, *Le-Ot u-le-Zikkaron*, 16. Aaron was once thought to come from Lunel and is cited as such in many sources.

92. Roth, "Bar Mitzvah," 18; Rivkind, *Le-Ot u-le-Zikkaron*, 16; Sherwin, *In Partnership with God*, 153.

93. Mann, "Responsa of the Babylonian Geonim," 461.

94. E.g., by Roth, "Bar Mitzvah," 18; Rivkind, *Le-Ot u-le-Zikkaron*, 16; Sherwin, *In Partnership with God*, 153. In preferring the reading "Yehudah" to "Yehudai," I follow Marcus, *Jewish Life Cycle*, 88–90.

95. Ta-Shma, *Creativity and Tradition*, 123.

96. Rashi, the Tosafot on the Talmud, the *Sefer Hasidim*, Rabbi Moses of Coucy, the Rosh and the Tur.

97. *Tashbetz Katan* 390. Shimson was a student of Rabbi Meir, the son of Baruch of Rothenburg (Maharam, 1215–93), whose rulings he collects in his book. Maharam himself had studied with French teachers, including Yehiel of Paris.

98. *Sefer Maharil*, 453.

99. Mordecai was also a student of Rabbi Meir of Rothenburg, so there is a clear chain of tradition in the accounts of bar mitzvah.

100. Levy, *Becoming and Remaining Barmitzvah*, 3–4.

101. Wieseltier, *Kaddish*, 504.

102. Gilat, "Barukh She-Petarani." Marcus, *Jewish Life Cycle*, states erroneously, "There is no proof of the continuity of this new practice" (91).

103. Tyrnau, *Sefer Minhagim, Minhag shel Shabbat*, 41.

104. *Shulchan Arukh Orach Chayyim* 225.2.

105. See *Siddur Tefilat Yaakov*, 205; Zalman, *Siddur Rabbeinu HaZakein*, 302.

106. Shabtai Sofer, *Tefilah*, 110; also in Solomon, *Daily Prayers*, 110. Henry Solomon was headmaster from 1817 to 1822, and the first edition of the book was in 1819. Although the title page gives the author as Shabtai Sofer, there is no mention of bar mitzvah in Shabtai's original prayer book, first published in 1617; see Shabtai Sofer, *Siddur*.

107. Genesis 21:8; *Bereshit Rabbah* 53.10.

108. From the first two letters of the word הגמל, which add up to the number 8, indicating the eighth day. The other two letters, taken alone, mean "circumcised."

109. The *Midrash Aggadah* was first published by Solomon Buber in 1894 from a single manuscript found in Aleppo. It is said to date from the twelfth century.

110. The text referred to is discussed later in this chapter. It is *Zohar Hadash Parashat Bereshit*, 10c (Margoliot), 18b (Bar Ilan).

111. Z. 1.10b–11a.

112. Sarah suckled children (see Gen. 21:7); Abraham offered up his son (see Gen. 22).

113. *Pesikta Rabbati* 42.4 also describes miracles that occurred when Isaac was born and on the occasion of Abraham's party.

114. Genesis 18.

115. Hermannus Quondam Judaeus, *Opusculum De Conversione Sua*. There is a published English version in Morrison, *Conversion and Text*.

116. Hermannus Quondam Judaeus, *Opusculum De Conversione Sua*, 71. The translation here is my own.

117. This was Arnoldo Momigliano (1908–87), professor of history at University College London. See Momiligiano, "Medieval Jewish Autobiography."

118. Morrison, *Conversion and Text*, 60–70.

119. Skinner, *Jews in Medieval Britain*, 93.

120. "Religious responsibility depends on intelligence, whereas legal liability depends on age." Ta-Shma, *Creativity and Tradition*, 140.

121. Avigdor Tzarfati, *Sefer Perushim*, ז.

122. See, e.g., Ta-Shma, "Earliest Literary Sources for the Bar-Mitzva Ritual and Festivity," 594.

123. M. *Avodah Zarah* 1.3.

124. B. *Shabbat* 67b (= T. *Shabbat* 7.9).

125. *Mishneh Torah, Hilkhot Avodah Zarah* 9.15.

126. Avigdor Tzarfati, *Sefer Perushim*, ח (sedra Toledot).

127. "Sefer Huqqei HaTorah," lines 128–29. Hebrew text, Kanarfogel, *Jewish Education and Society in the High Middle Ages*, 106–15. English translation in Kanarfogel, "A Monastic-like Setting for the Study of Torah," in Fine, *Judaism in Practice*, 191–202.

128. Z. 1.118b (Ishmael), Z. 1.119b (Isaac).

129. *Zohar Hadash Parashat Bereshit*, 10c (Margoliot), 18b (Bar Ilan).

130. B. *Menahot* 43b.

131. From the commentary attributed to Rabbeinu Gershom on B. *Menahot* 43b.

132. Israel Ta-Shma has traced many of the Ashkenazic customs in the Zohar and written about them in Ta-Shma, *Ha-Nigle She-BaNistar*. He explains further how Ashkenazic scholars went to Spain in *Creativity and Tradition*, 184–93.

133. *Zohar Hadash Parashat Bereshit* 15d Margoliot (27a Bar Ilan).

134. Biale, "Eros and Enlightenment," 64.

135. Z. 2.97b–98a.

136. Leviticus 19:23.

137. It is not possible here to explain the concept of the *sefirot* in detail. The interested reader is referred to Green, *Guide to the Zohar*.

138. Marcus, *Jewish Life Cycle*, 162–66.

139. Alluding to Joel 2:16, "let the bridegroom come out of his chamber (*heder*), and the bride from her chamber (*chuppah*)."

140. Marcus, *Jewish Life Cycle*, 84–105, suggests parties were a later invention. Ta-Shma, however, finds the Avigdor Tzarfati text particularly significant

("Earliest Literary Sources for the Bar-Mitzva Ritual and Festivity," 587–98). But neither scholar considers the other possible reason for such parties suggested here.

141. On childhood marriage during this period, see Agus, *Heroic Age*, 278–83; Suzanne Bartlet, "Women in the Medieval Anglo-Jewish Community," in Skinner, *Jews in Medieval Britain*, 113–27; Grossman, "Historical Background to the Ordinances on Family Affairs"; and Grossman, *Pious and Rebellious*, 37–44. Mishnah *Avot* 5.21, the same paragraph that gives the age of thirteen for the commandments, states that eighteen is the age of marriage, but the Talmud gives examples of those who married younger. See, e.g., Rav Hisda (B. *Kiddushin* 29b). See Gilat, "Ben Shelosh-Esrei Lamitzvot," 41.

142. Tosafot on B. *Kiddushin* 41a; *Mishneh Torah, Hilkhot Issurei Biah* 21.24.

143. Hermannus Quondam Judaeus, *Opusculum De Conversione Sua*, chap. 10.

2. HOW BAR MITZVAH BECAME POPULAR

1. Ta-Shma, *Creativity and Tradition*, 184–93.

2. Ta-Shma, *Creativity and Tradition*, 134; Hilton, *Christian Effect on Jewish Life*, 161–99.

3. M. *Avodah Zarah* 1:3; Ta-Shma, "On Birthdays in Judaism."

4. Pärdi, "Crumbling of the Peasant Time Concept in Estonia."

5. Ariès, *Centuries of Childhood*, 16.

6. Marcus, *Jewish Life Cycle*, 40.

7. Marcus, *Jewish Life Cycle*, 41; Schapiro, "Birthdays in Halacha."

8. Ariès, *Centuries of Childhood*, 150–54, 189–230.

9. Luria, *Sefer Yam Shel Shelomoh Bava Kamma* 7.37.

10. The phrase is first found in Gaonic writings.

11. Wertheim, *Law and Custom in Hasidism*, 108.

12. Luria, *Sefer Yam Shel Shelomoh Bava Kamma* 7.37.

13. As pointed out first by Freehof, "Ceremonial Creativity among the Ashkenazim."

14. B. *Kiddushin* 31a; and B. *Bava Kamma* 87a.

15. This interpretation follow that of Abrams, *Judaism and Disability*, 195–96.

16. Luria, *Sefer Yam Shel Shelomoh Bava Kamma* 7.37. The strange punctuation of the Hebrew printed there has not been followed in my translation.

17. B. *Niddah* 48b: "Rava said: a girl who has reached the required number of years need not undergo a physical examination since we can make a presumption that she has produced the marks of puberty."

18. *Shulchan Arukh Orach Chayyim* 199.10.

19. Sherwin, "Bar Mitzvah, Bat Mitzvah," *In Partnership with God*, 150–68. But Chabad Chasidim to this day rarely allow a bar mitzvah to read from the Torah because of the doubt about physical maturity (Naftali Loewenthal, pers. comm.).

20. Commentary *Darkhei Moshe* on *Tur Orach Chayyim* 37; see also *Shulchan Arukh Orach Chayyim* 37.3.

21. Those parts of the *Zohar* published earlier were used as a mine of evidence and proof texts from the sixteenth century onward. See Jacob Katz, "Post-Zoharic Relations between Halakhah and Kabbalah," in Cooperman, *Jewish Thought*, 283–307.

22. Yisrael the son of Binyamin of Belzec. *Yalkut Hadash*, 183a, Likutim 29.

23. *Magen Avraham* to *Shulchan Arukh Orach Chayyim* 225.4, citing Maharshal and *Yalkut Hadash.*

24. Juspa, *Minhagim di-K.K. Vermaisa.* English translation from Eidelberg, *R. Yuzpa Shamash*, 25.

25. Juspa, *Minhagim di-K.K. Vermaisa.* English trans. from Eidelberg, *R. Yuzpa Shamash*, 25 (trans. simplified).

26. Juspa, *Minhagim di-K.K. Vermaisa.* English trans. from Eidelberg, *R. Yuzpa Shamash*, 25.

27. The "Four Lands" were Greater Poland, Little Poland, Ruthenia, and Volhynia.

28. London, *Takkanot*, (1791 and 1827); London, *Laws of the Congregation of the Great Synagogue*, 1863.

29. Rivkind, *Le Ot u le Zikkaron*, 20–22.

30. Rivkind, *Le-Ot u-le-Zikkaron*, 23. The Krakow regulations of 1595 are the earliest community regulations to mention bar mitzvah.

31. Graupe, *Die Statuen der drei Gemeinden*, 2:4–5 (text): 1.72–73 (German trans.).

32. London, *Takkanot* (1827), 57, rule 226; Rivkind, *Le-Ot u-le-Zikkaron*, 30–31.

33. Jakimyszyn, *Di Takkana Kuf Kuf Krake*, para. 68, p. XLI, fol. 43b–44a.

34. Rivkind, *Le-Ot u-le-Zikkaron*, 33–35.

35. In the regulations from London a change can be traced. The rules from 1810 and 1827 specifically state that a bar mitzvah can be held on the middle Shabbat of a festival. This was no longer permitted in the 1863 rule book. See London, *Takkanot* (1810), rule 28, and (1827), 64, rule 255; London, *Laws of the Congregation of the Great Synagogue* (1863), 54, rule 230.

36. *Bye-Laws of the Constituent Synagogues* (1881), 53, rule 179; Levy, *Becoming and Remaining Barmitzvah* (1971), 4. Today the bar mitzvah takes second place to a bridegroom in these synagogues ("Bye-Laws for Member Synagogues" (2010), 30, schedule 1, rule 4.

37. E.g., *Magen Avraham*, 282, *Kitzur Shulchan Arukh* 78.11.

38. Rivkind, *Le-Ot u-le-Zikkaron*, 37; Hilton, *Christian Effect on Jewish Life*, 168, 263.

39. Rivkind, *Le-Ot u-le-Zikkaron*, 37–38.

40. Rivkind, *Le-Ot u-le-Zikkaron*, 39.

41. E.g., *Shulchan Arukh Orach Chayyim* 284.4; and more recently, *Mishnah Berurah* 282.12.

42. Strictly speaking, the "presumption of Rava," which permits this practice, only applies to rabbinic commands such as reading from the Torah on Shabbat. See Balsam, "Can a Bar Mitzvah Boy Read Parshas Zachor."

43. *Sefer Maharil*, 453.

44. Amsterdam, *Seder Hanhagot*, 23; Rivkind, *Le-Ot u-le-Zikkaron*, 36–37.

45. "Seder Chazzanut Amsterdam."

46. A lenient view was given by Mendelson in 1925 (*Mishnat Yaavetz*, no. 11), but more recent views prohibit dividing the haftarah between two readers; for an article in English, see Bleich, *Contemporary Halakhic Problems*, 1:74–77. He writes that "it has now become *de rigueur* for the Bar Mitzvah to chant the *haftarah*." The London United Synagogue gives priority for the *maftir* to a member who reserved the date first for his or her son, but a later reservation can take priority if it is for the first Shabbat after the boy's thirteenth birthday. See "Bye-Laws for Member Synagogues," 34–35, schedule 4.

47. For a full study of this subject, see Sered, "Bar Mitzvah Speech."

48. Luria, *Sefer Yam Shel Shelomoh Bava Kamma* 7.37.

49. Sered, "Bar Mitzvah Speech," 12; Neusner, *Understanding Rabbinic Judaism*, 93–94.

50. Löw, *Die Lebensalter in der Jüdischen Literatur*, 214–15. The formal procedure of interrupting the speech is still practiced in some circles. See Dubov, *Yalkut Bar Mitzvah*, chap. 3.

51. Sered, "Bar Mitzvah Speech," 26.

52. Łęczyca, Poland (1550–1619). It was published in his *Olelot Efrayim* (Lublin, 1590). See Rivkind, *Le-Ot u-le-Zikkaron*, 40.

53. Löw, *Die Lebensalter in der Jüdischen Literatur*, 217.

54. Saperstein, *Jewish Preaching*, 402.

55. Modena, *Letters*, ed. Boksenboim, 60, letter 19.

56. Adelman, "Success and Failure in the Seventeenth Century Ghetto of Venice," 323–27.

57. Leon Modena, *Midbar Yehudah* (Venice, 1736), 94b–96a and 96b–98b.

58. Saperstein, *Jewish Preaching*, 407. Bar mitzvah speeches from Venice from the same period were also composed by Rabbi Naftali Ashkenazi of Tzefat (d. Venice, 1602) and published in his sermon collection, *Imrei Shefer*.

59. Sered, "Bar Mitzvah Speech," 27.

60. Rivkind, *Le-Ot u-le-Zikkaron*, 41.

61. Sered, "Bar Mitzvah Speech," 32–57.

62. Selikovitch, *Jewish-American Orator*, 5–6 (English section).

63. Gryn, *Chasing Shadows*, 113–14.

64. "Jewish Witness to a European Century," interview with Daniel Bertram.
65. From Allan Gould and Danny Siegel, *The Unorthodox Book of Jewish Records and Lists*, as quoted in Swartz, *Bar Mitzvah*, 95.
66. Speech by Isaiah Kuperstein from Congregation Beth-El Zedeck in Indianapolis. Quoted from Rabbi Sandy Eisenberg Sasso, "What to Say to Your Child on the Bimah," in Leneman, Bar/Bat Mitzvah Basics, 109–15.

3. THE SPREAD AND REGULATION OF BAR MITZVAH

1. More rules were added in 1610 and 1638.
2. Rivkind, *Le-Ot u-le-Zikkaron*, 49 n. 9.
3. Jakimyszyn, *Di Takkana Kuf Kuf Krake*, para. 68, p. XLI, fol. 43b–44a; text checked against Balaban, "Die Krakauer Judengemeinde-Ordnung," 348. The rules are not available in English; Jakimyszyn's publication is in Yiddish and Polish.
4. Jewish Legal Heritage Society, "Takkanot neged Motarot," lita1623.doc, 327. Translation adapted from Strassfeld and Strassfeld, *Second Jewish Catalog*, 65.
5. Jewish Legal Heritage Society, "Takkanot neged Motarot."
6. Bell, *Jewish Identity in Early Modern Germany*, 45–48.
7. Fichman, "Sumptuary Laws of the Jews," 5–9.
8. Rubens, *History of Jewish Costume*, 188.
9. Rubens, *History of Jewish Costume*, 189.
10. Jewish Legal Heritage Society, "Takkanot neged Motarot," shneitoch.doc.
11. Roth, "Sumptuary Laws of the Community of Carpentras," 363.
12. Cooper, *Child in Jewish History*, 187.
13. Brann, *Die Alten Statuen der Glogauer Judenschaft*, 89, para. 8.
14. Jewish Legal Heritage Society, "Takkanot neged Motarot," berlin1730.doc, תקנות חדשות שנעשו כסליו ת"צ בית לפ"ק.
15. Jewish Legal Heritage Society, "Takkanot neged Motarot," runkel.doc, para. 29, mentioning Hillel's *prozbul*.
16. Ellinson, *Women and the Mitzvot*, 2.22.
17. Juspa Schammes, *Minhagim*, 2:165–67.
18. Schudt, "Neue Franckfurter Jüdische Kleider-Ordnung," 2726.
19. Schudt, "Neue Franckfurter Jüdische Kleider-Ordnung," 2726; Rubens, *History of Jewish Costume*, 102.
20. Max Grunwald in *Mitteilungen zur jüdischen Volkskunde*, page reproduced by Macdowell, "18th Century Chanukah Pastime."
21. Jewish Legal Heritage Society, "Takkanot neged Motarot," prague.doc.
22. Cooper, *Child in Jewish History*, 188.
23. Adelman, "Success and Failure," 237.
24. Modena, *Letters*, ed. Boksenboim, 60, letter 19.

25. Rivkind, *Le-Ot u-le-Zikkaron*, 56.

26. Jewish Legal Heritage Society, "Takkanot neged Motarot," ancona1793.doc, para. 25.

27. Rivkind, *Le-Ot u-le-Zikkaron*, 23.

28. Morgan, "Judaism in Eighteenth-Century Georgia," 45. There is a biography of Mordecai Sheftall by B. H. Levy entitled *Mordecai Sheftall; Jewish Revolutionary Patriot*.

29. Jewish Legal Heritage Society, "Takkanot neged Motarot," altona.doc.

30. Sephardic regulations from Hamburg, original Portuguese text; Jewish Legal Heritage Society, "Takkanot neged Motarot," hamburg.doc, German trans.; Cassuto, "Aus dem ältesten Protokollbuch."

31. Rabbi Abraham Levy, pers. comm.; and reminiscences of the Sephardic community in Gibraltar.

32. Roth, "Bar Mitzvah," 16.

33. Roth, *Venice*, 63–71; name of Joseph Pardo from Jewish Virtual Library entry.

34. Modena, *Letters*, ed. Boksenboim, 60, letter 19.

35. David Cassuto, "New Notes on the Venetian Synagogues in the Time of Leon Modena" (Hebrew), in Malkiel, *Lion Shall Roar*, קמג--קסב.

36. Italian text: Jewish Legal Heritage Society, "Takkanot neged Motarot," livorno1655.doc and livorno1664.doc.

37. Pool and Pool, *Old Faith in a New World*, 39–40, 159–60; and Rabbi Marc D. Angel, pers. comm., June 2012. The archives of congregation Shearith Israel are in storage and not available for consultation.

38. Matt Goldish, "The Amsterdam Portuguese Rabbinate in the Seventeenth Century: A Unique Institution Viewed from Within and Without," in Brasz and Kaplan, *Dutch Jews*, 13.

39. Roth, "Bar Mitzvah: Its History and Its Associations," 21–22.

40. "Seder Chazannut Amsterdam."

41. Mussafia, *Hayyim veHesed*, 3.

42. Gaster, *History of the Ancient Synagogue*, 44. *Kadish* here perhaps refers to mourner's *Kaddish*, if the boy was an orphan, or perhaps to his leading *Kaddish* during the service, a prayer that required a musical rendition in that congregation.

43. De Sola, *Blessings*; Gaguine, *Sefer Keter Shem Tov*, 318, states that Sephardim do not use the father's blessing.

44. Hyamson, *Sephardim of England*, 345.

45. Monypenny, *Life of Benjamin Disraeli*, 1.19; Weintraub, *Disraeli*, 28–32; Richmond, "Disraeli's Education," 16–17.

46. Weintraub, *Disraeli*, 31 offers a quotation from "the book of Jewish ritual in use in London since 1780" as evidence that Disraeli was preparing for his

bar mitzvah. An account in almost the same words is given in Alexander, *Alexander's Hebrew Ritual*. Levy Alexander was a prominent member of the Ashkenazic Great Synagogue, and his book therefore gives no indication of bar mitzvah among the London Sephardic community.

47. Weintraub, *Disraeli*, 28–32; Richmond, "Disraeli's Education," 16–17.

48. Roth, "Bar Mitzvah," 21; Gaguine, *Sefer Keter Shem Tov*, 16, 318.

49. Carlebach, *Divided Souls*, chap. 10.

50. R. Po-Chia Hsia, "Christian Ethnographies of Jews in Early Modern Germany," in Waddington and Williamson, *Expulsion of the Jews*, 223–33. Yaacov Deutsch recognized the polemical and anti-Jewish nature of many of these writings by calling them "polemical ethnographies." See Deutsch, "Polemical Ethnographies," in Coudert and Shoulson, *Hebraica Veritas*, 202–33.

51. Carlebach, *Divided Souls*, 201.

52. Buxtorf, *Synagoga Judaica*.

53. Schroeder, *Canons and Decrees of the Council of Trent*, 197; Meyers, "Christian Rites of Adolescence," 60.

54. Malkiel, *Lion Shall Roar*, 8.

55. Morosini, *Derekh Emunah*, 1.165; Weinstein, "Rites of Passage," 83.

56. Hsia, "Christian Ethnographies of Jews in Early Modern Germany," 223–33.

57. Shlomo Berger, "Isaac de Pinto's Testaments: A Case of Multiple Images," in Brasz and Kaplan, *Dutch Jews*, 86.

58. Facchini, "City, the Ghetto and Two Books."

59. Modena, *History of the Rites*, 212–13, 214.

60. Juspa Schammes, *Minhagim*, 2:166.

61. Robert Leiberles, "On the Threshold of Modernity: 1618–1780," in Kaplan, *Jewish Daily Life in Germany*, 46.

62. Marx, *Studies in Jewish History and Booklore*, 192–93.

63. Abrahams, *Life of Glückel of Hameln*.

64. Emden, *Megillat Sefer*, ed. David Kahana, 57; English trans., Schacter, "Rabbi Jacob Emden," 30. The last sentence in my extract is added from Emden, *Megilat Sefer* (trans. Leperer and Wise), 124.

65. Bacharach Responsa, "Havvot Yair," 124, Bar-Ilan text.

66. On this incident, see also Pollack, *Jewish Folkways in Germanic Lands*, 61–62. Pollack states that the bar mitzvah took place in Wandsbeck, but the text uses the abbreviation ק״ק וו, which is Bacharach's normal way of referring to Worms, where he lived.

67. Graupe, *Die Statuen der drei Gemeinden*, 2:5.

68. Hoffman, "Organisation and Administration of Schools," 421.

69. Kerner, "Le règlement de la communauté juive de Metz," 209. The manuscript, which was discovered in New York, is in Hebrew, but this section

has been published only in French translation. The translation from the
French is mine.

70. Biale, "Eros and Enlightenment," 64.

4. JEWISH CONFIRMATION

1. Heinemann, *Religions-Bekenntniss für Israeliten*, 5.
2. Jagel, *Catechismus Judaeorum*, 4–5; Faierstein, "Abraham Jagel's Leqah
   Tov."
3. E. Schreiber, "Catechisms," *Jewish Encyclopedia*, 3.621–24; Faierstein,
   "Abraham Jagel's Leqah Tov." Faierstein argues that the German catechisms
   were not influenced by Jagel, but his work was the only Jewish precedent.
4. A review appeared in *Allgemeine Literatur-Zeitung* 4 (1807): 146–48. See
   Eliav, *Jüdische Erziehung*, 334.
5. Eliav, *Jüdische Erziehung*, 336. Bock brought out a second revised edition of
   his own catechism in the same year.
6. Philipson, *Confirmation in the Synagogue*, 16, numbering of items omitted.
7. Marcus, *Rituals of Childhood.*
8. For the development of Shavuot from a harvest festival to a celebration of
   Torah and the parallels between the Jewish and Christian festivals of Pentecost and Shavuot, see Hilton, *Christian Effect on Jewish Life*, 47–60.
9. Löw, *Die Lebensalter in der Jüdischen Literatur*, 218–19; Wice, "Bar Mitzvah
   and Confirmation," 47–48; Herrmann, "Jewish Confirmation Sermons in
   19th-Century Germany," 97–101, 103.
10. Alexander, *Textual Sources for the Study of Judaism*, 40.
11. Michael Meyer, "The Freischule as a Mirror of Attitudes," in Lohmann,
    Hevrat Hinukh Nearim, 1–5.
12. Meyer, "Freischule as a Mirror of Attitudes," 1–5; and also the article by
    Samuel Feiner, "The Freischule on the Crossroads of the Secularization
    Crisis in Jewish Society," in Lohmann, *Hevrat Hinukh Nearim*, 6–12.
13. Meyer, *Origins of the Modern Jew*, 146–48. On the small size of the old
    school, see Kober, "Emancipation's Impact," 169.
14. Zunz, "Mein erster Unterricht in Wolfenbüttel," translation adapted from
    Herrmann, "Jewish Confirmation Sermons," 91.
15. Laura Janner-Klausner, "Leopold Zunz (1794–1866)," in Romain, *Great
    Reform Lives*, 19.
16. Meyer, *Origins of the Modern Jew*, 148.
17. Zunz, *Gessammelte Schriften*, 2.215.
18. Zunz, *Gessammelte Schriften*, 2.215.
19. I have written a fuller of account of Jacobson's life in Romain, *Great
    Reform Lives*, 12–18, and have drawn upon that account here.
20. Meyer, *Origins of the Modern Jew*, 148.

21. Meyer, *Response to Modernity*, 32–33.
22. Marcus, *Israel Jacobson*, 55.
23. Philipson, *Confirmation in the Synagogue*, 4: for the original, see "Pflichten der Rabbiner," 302.
24. "Westphalen," *Sulamith* 3.1 (1810): 6–15.
25. Marcus, *Israel Jacobson*, 95–96. But Meyer, *Response to Modernity*, 40 dates this episode to 1810, when the ceremony was held in the school, as the temple had not yet been opened.
26. Hertz, *How Jews Became Germans*, 146.
27. Endleman, "Emergence of Disraeli's Jewishness," 111.
28. Hertz, *How Jews Became Germans*, 135, 136.
29. Kley, *Predigten in dem Neuen Israelitischen Tempel zu Hamburg*, xvii, xviii, 47–65, 128–50.
30. Weil, "Copenhagen Report concerning 'Reform,'" 93.
31. Meyer, *Response to Modernity*, 145. On this ceremony, see also Rose, *Jewish Women in Fin de Siècle Vienna*, 30; Weil, "Copenhagen Report concerning 'Reform,'" 94.
32. Meyer, *Response to Modernity*, 146–52. Because confirmation *replaced* bar mitzvah in places where it became the practice, many nineteenth- and early early-twentieth-century sources refer to bar mitzvah itself by the term *confirmation*.
33. Maimon Fränkel, "Über die Konfirmation," extract translated in Plaut, *Rise of Reform Judaism*, 172–73. Fränkel appealed for the introduction of confirmation into all the Jewish day schools.
34. Herrmann, "Jewish Confirmation Sermons," 93.
35. Hertz, *How Jews Became Germans*, 136.
36. Hertz, *How Jews Became Germans*, 149.
37. Hertz, *How Jews Became Germans*, 192.
38. Lowenstein, *Mechanics of Change*, 90–91.
39. Plaut, *Rise of Reform Judaism*, 174.
40. Liberles, "Leopold Stein."
41. Philipson, *Reform Movement*, 77–78.
42. Quoted from Gesundheit, "Bat HaMitzvah Behalakhah," 12.
43. Herrmann, "Jewish Confirmation Sermons," 108.
44. Löw, *Die Lebensalter in der Jüdischen Literatur*, 210–22.
45. Conigliani, "Iniziazione religiosa delle fanciulle."
46. "Confirmation in Paris, 1852," in Plaut, *Rise of Reform Judaism*, 177.
47. Philipson, *Reform Movement*, 39–74.
48. Wice, "Bar Mitzvah and Confirmation," 60; see also Ruben, *Max Lilienthal*, 257. The background to the formation of the congregation is described in Dash Moore, "Freedom's Fruits."

49. Philipson, *Reform Movement in Judaism*, 332.

50. Dash Moore, "Freedom's Fruits," 13–17.

51. Leeser, *Catechism for Jewish Children*, vii.

52. Leeser, *Catechism for Jewish Children*, 132–34.

53. *The Occident* 1.10 (January 1844). The service took place on October 14, 1843.

54. *The Occident* 4.5 (August 1846).

55. *The Occident* 5.4 (July 1847).

56. Ruben, *Max Lilienthal*, 34–35.

57. Ruben, *Max Lilienthal*, 85–86.

58. Stephan F. Brumberg, "Education of Jewish Girls in the United States," in Hyman and Ofer, *Jewish Women*, jwa.org/encyclopedia/article/education-of-jewish-girls-in-united-states (accessed February 6, 2012).

59. Ruben, *Max Lilienthal*, 85–86.

60. *The Occident* 6.4 (July 1848). Five girls and three boys took part.

61. Wise, *Selected Writings*, 106–7.

62. *Israelite* 4 (1857–58): 364, as quoted by Rubinstein, "Isaac Mayer Wise," 66.

63. Rubinstein, "Isaac Mayer Wise," 66.

64. *The Occident* 9.4 (July 1851).

65. *The Occident* 10.3 (June 1852).

66. Wice, "Bar Mitzvah and Confirmation," 51–52.

67. *Plain Dealer*, June 13, 1864, 3.

68. Wice, "Bar Mitzvah and Confirmation," 63.

69. Silverstein, *Alternatives to Assimilation*, 19, 54, 85.

70. Philipson, *Confirmation in the Synagogue*, 3; K. Kohler and M. Landsberg, "Confirmation," *Jewish Encyclopedia*, 4.219–20.

71. Abraham J. Karp "Overview: The Synagogue in America—A Historical Typology," in Wertheimer, *American Synagogue*, 11; and "New York Architecture," Temple Emanu-El.

72. Silverstein, *Alternatives to Assimilation*, 95.

73. Silverstein, *Alternatives to Assimilation*, 95.

74. Marks, *Sermons*, 21.

75. Meyer, *Response to Modernity*, 175.

76. "Confirmation at the West London Synagogue, Burton St., on ר״ה (New Year)," *Jewish Chronicle*, October 2, 1846, 222–23.

77. Ascher, *Hinukh Nearim: Initiation of Youth*, 11.

78. A form of service survives from the confirmation Mendes held at Sukkot, 1853. Printed in Mendes, *Sermons*, 185–200.

79. Schiller-Szinessy, *Confirmation*. This booklet from the 1852 ceremony gives the complete order of service and the text of his sermon.

80. *Hebrew Observer* 2.79, July 7, 5614 (1854), p. 1 (425).

81. Loewe, "Solomon Marcus Schiller-Szinessy," 154–57.

82. Loewe, "Solomon Marcus Schiller-Szinessy," 165.

83. "Bayswater Synagogue, 1863–1938"; for Hampstead, see www.hampstead shul.org.uk (accessed February 7, 2012).

84. Endelman, *Jews of Britain*, 167–68.

85. *Jewish Standard*, June 8, 1888.

86. "Pflichten der Rabbiner"; "Phlichten der Israelitischen Syndiken."

87. Philipson, *Confirmation in the Synagogue*, 10–11.

88. K. Kohler and M. Landsberg, "Confirmation," *Jewish Encyclopedia*, 4. 219–20; see also Enelow, Faith of Israel, 10, in which he writes that confirmation takes place at "fourteen, or fifteen, or even later" (1917).

89. Resnick, "Confirmation Education," 220.

90. Stein, "Road to Bat Mitzvah in America," 223–24.

91. Philipson, *Confirmation in the Synagogue*, 17–18.

92. Schoenfeld, "Changing Patterns of North American Bar Mitzvah," 13.

93. Resnick "Confirmation Education," 224.

94. Silverstein, *Alternatives to Assimilation*, 157.

95. Leon A. Jick, "The Reform Synagogue," in Wertheimer, *American Synagogue*, 100.

96. Raphael, *Synagogue in America*, 83.

97. Harris, *Story of the Jew*, 74–75.

98. Lyons, *At Sinai.*

99. *Order of Service, The West London Synagogue*, June 7, 1936, West London Synagogue Archives, ms140/a2049/433/6.

100. West London Synagogue Archives, ms140/a2–49/1/9.

101. West London Synagogue Archives, ms140/a2–49/1/9.

102. Julia Neuberger, pers. comm., August 2, 2012.

103. Baer, *Self-Chosen*, 324.

104. Birmingham, "Temple That 'Our Crowd' Built," 46.

105. Rayner, "From Barmitzvah to Confirmation." The word *almemar* in the quotation is another term for bimah, the platform from which the Torah is read.

106. Rigal and Rosenberg, *Liberal Judaism*, 256.

107. Heschel, *God in Search of Man*, 260.

108. Resnick, "Confirmation Education," 221–22.

109. Chip Rosenthal, in Strassfeld and Strassfeld, *Second Jewish Catalog*, 82–83.

110. Resnick, "Confirmation Education," 221–22.

111. Sales, Samuel, and Zablotsky, *Engaging Jewish Teens.*

112. Weidenthal, "Confirmations in Cleveland."

113. *Eilu V'Eilu* 4.1, May 22, 2006; 4.2, May 29, 2006; and 4.3, June 5, 2006.

5. BAT MITZVAH

1. Entry from the diary of Rabbi Mordecai Kaplan, March 28, 1922, quoted from Marcus, *Jewish Life Cycle*, 108.
2. Leviticus 19:18. This was the section which Judith remembered reading.
3. Kessner, "Kaplan and the Role of Women," 350.
4. Quoted in Vinick and Reinharz, *Today I Am a Woman*, 256.
5. Quoted in Cohen, "First Bat Mitzvah."
6. "Bar Mitzvah, Bat Mitzvah," *Encyclopedia Judaica* (1972), 4:243–47.
7. Quoted in part from Vinick and Reinharz, *Today I Am a Woman*, 258; and in part from Kessner, "Kaplan and the Role of Women," 351.
8. The phrase can be found in the *Riti Hebraici* of Leon Modena (1637) and also in the account of the ceremony given by Modena's apostate student Guilio Morosini in *Derekh Emunah Via delle Fede* (1683).
9. M. *Niddah* 5:6.
10. Maimonides, *Mishneh Torah Hilkhot Ishut* 2:2; Bamberger, "Qetana, Na'arah, Bogereth."
11. Modena, *History of the Rites*, 215.
12. Rose, *Jewish Women in Fin de Siècle Vienna*, 29.
13. Maharil, *Sefer She'elot uTeshuvot*, 51.
14. This argument works by linking the institution of bar mitzvah with the traditional blessing said by the father, which passes the responsibility for punishment for his actions to his son.
15. Eliav, "Pioneers."
16. Bock, *Emunat Yisrael*, v–x. This book is cited by Eliav, *Jüdische Erziehung*, 341 and 344, as the source for his view that the first confirmation for girls was in 1814. Although the book was no doubt used in his school, there is no mention of confirmation, which was always a significant life event and involved more than the recital of the daily catechisms described in the book. Nevertheless, Eliav's date of 1814 for the first Jewish girls' coming-of-age ceremony has found its way into many publications.
17. Hertz, *How Jews Became Germans*, 139. The entire collection of *Sulamith* journals is available online at www.compactmemory.de.
18. "Westphalen," *Sulamith* 3.1 (1810): 6–15.
19. Eliav, *Jüdische Erziehung*, 331.
20. Meyer, "Religious Reform Controversy"; Hertz, *How Jews Became Germans*, 136.
21. Meyer, "Religious Reform Controversy."
22. Hertz, *How Jews Became Germans*, 136, 119. Amalie and Jacob's son, Giacomo Meyerbeer, grew up to become the most celebrated opera composer of his day.
23. "Aus einem Briefe aus Berlin," *Sulamith* 5.1 (1817): 279. The translation is adapted from Herrmann, "Jewish Confirmation Sermons," 103–4.

24. The Jewish population of Berlin in 1817 was 3,699; Seeliger, "Origin and Growth," 162.
25. Herrmann, "Jewish Confirmation Sermons," 104.
26. Meyer, "Religious Reform Controversy."
27. Zunz, *Die gottesdienstlichen Vorträge der Juden*, 472. The sermon given by Eduard Kley in Hamburg survives.
28. *Sulamith* 5.1 (1817): 402.
29. Baader, *Gender, Judaism, and Bourgeois Culture*, 40.
30. Philipson, "Reform Movement in Judaism," 219–20; Herrmann, "Jewish Confirmation Sermons," 105.
31. See Meyer, "Women in the Thought and Practice of the European Jewish Reform Movement."
32. Fonséca, "Instruction religieuse."
33. Vinick and Reinharz, *Today I Am a Woman*.
34. Exodus 19.10; Hilton, *Christian Effect on Jewish Life*, 59.
35. Leigh, "Women in the Synagogue," 105.
36. Conigliani, "Iniziazione religiosa delle fanciulle."
37. The early Italian ceremonies were documented at the turn to the twentieth century in a journal, *Il Vessillo Israelitico*, made available online in 2000 (see Di Segni, *Il Bat Mitzva in Italia*). This 1844 ceremony is erroneously described as the very first bat mitzvah in the widely available article by Norma Baumel Joseph, "Bar Mitzvah, Bat Mitzvah," *Encyclopedia Judaica*, 2nd ed., 3:164–66.
38. Di Segni, *Il Bat Mitzva in Italia*.
39. Subsequent issues of the journal describe similar ceremonies held at Bologna and Ancona at the festival of Shavuot.
40. Anon., "Confirmation in Paris, 1852"; From Plaut, *Rise of Reform Judaism*, 177.
41. Meyer, *Response to Modernity*, 175.
42. Golinkin, "Participation of Jewish Women in Public Rituals," 46–47.
43. Jellinek, *Die erste Confirmations-Feier*, 24; "as a dutiful daughter of the synagogue, as an adult member of the larger community of Israel"; Herrmann. "Jewish Confirmation Sermons," 106.
44. Rose, *Jewish Women in Fin de Siècle Vienna*, 30–31.
45. Schiller-Szinessy, *Confirmation—A Genuine Jewish Institution*, 6. This booklet from the 1852 ceremony gives the complete order of service and the text of his sermon.
46. *Bayswater Synagogue, 1863–1938*; Apple, *Let's Ask the Rabbi*, 18.
47. Golinkin, "Participation of Jewish Women in Public Rituals," 48.
48. Hayyim, *Ben Ish Hai*, vol. 1, *Re'eh* 17.
49. Joseph, "Bar Mitzvah, Bat Mitzvah." Many websites also cite this as a precedent for today's Orthodox bat mitzvah ceremonies.

50. Vinick and Reinharz, *Today I Am a Woman*, 162.

51. Benjamin, *Eight Years in Asia and Africa*, 286.

52. Vinick and Reinharz, *Today I Am a Woman*, additional material not in book.

53. "Jewish Witness to a European Century."

54. Interview with Vera Tomanic, in "Jewish Witness to a European Century."

55. Miccoli, *Moving Histories*. His detailed account shows that the date 1907 cited by Joseph and many others is incorrect.

56. Miccoli, *Moving Histories*. The last phrase means 'the daughters of the people.'

57. Vinick and Reinharz, *Today I Am a Woman*, 236–37.

58. Golinkin, "Participation of Jewish Women in Public Rituals," 47.

59. *Reform Advocate*, March 27, 1897, 90, as quoted in Hyman, *Gender and Assimilation*, 24–25.

60. W., "The Confirmation and the Bar Mitzvah," *Asmonean*, New York, 1854, reprinted in Marcus, *American Jewish Woman*, 186–89.

61. "From the Colonies. Australia," *Jewish Chronicle*, January 25, 1907, 14.

62. Golinkin, "Participation of Jewish Women in Public Rituals," 49.

63. Golinkin, "Participation of Jewish Women in Public Rituals," 49–50. This event is now often cited as an early bat mitzvah, but Marcus, in *Jewish Life Cycle*, maintains that it was only a party, not a religious ceremony (280). Gilad Gevaryahu maintains it was a confirmation, not a bat mitzvah with an aliyah to the Torah (e-mail recorded on h-net.msu.edu, December 12, 2001).

64. Benjamin, "Surprise Bat Mitzvah." For the origin of the Sydney ceremonies, see "From the Colonies. Australia," *Jewish Chronicle*, January 25, 1907, 14. This piece describes the confirmation ceremony held at Hanukkah 1906 as an "innovation." Eleven boys and girls aged —fourteen to seventeen took part.

65. Meyer, *Response to Modernity*, 285.

66. Irma Levy (1886–1978), pioneer Zionist; from Marcus, *American Jewish Woman*, 332.

67. Klapper, *Jewish Girls Coming of Age in America*, 170–76.

68. Klapper, *Jewish Girls Coming of Age in America*, 174.

69. Golinkin, "Participation of Jewish Women in Public Rituals," 50.

70. Ida Blum, telephone interview with Rochelle Berger Elstein in 1985. See e-mail from Elstein, h-net.msu.edu, 7 July 2005.

71. Stein, "Road to Bat Mitzvah in America," 225–26.

72. Tananbaum, "Jewish Feminist Organisations," 384.

73. According to Klapheck, *Fräulein Rabbiner Jonas*, 24.

74. Herrmann, "Jewish Confirmation Sermons," 112.

75. Felstiner, *To Paint Her Life*, 30–31.

76. Herrmann, *History and Oral History*, 68, 84–85, and dvd; and Swarsensky, "Oral Histories," tape 5, side 2 (1980 interview).

77. Herrmann, *History and Oral History*, 86–87 and dvd. The term *Einsegnung* was used in the journal report of the very first ceremony for girls in Berlin in 1817. From the root *to sign* it originally denoted "to make the sign of a cross over" but developed into a more general term for "a blessing."

78. Vinick and Reinharz, *Today I Am a Woman*, 164. Beneath the photo is a list of the countries the women moved to after liberation.

79. Golinkin, "Participation of Jewish Women," 51.

80. Meyer, *Response to Modernity*, 472; Feinstein, "Bas Mitzah Comes to Our Synagogue"; Stein, "Road to Bat Mitzvah in America," 227–28.

81. Hyman, "Introduction of Bat Mitzvah"; Stein, "Road to Bat Mitzvah in America," 226. From the United States individual benot mitzvah spread to Conservative and Masorti congregations in other countries, including Argentina in 1968 (see Vinick and Reinharz, *Today I Am a Woman*, 176–78).

82. Sherry Rosen, video interview for the exhibition *Bat Mitzvah Comes of Age*.

83. Stein, "Road to Bat Mitzvah in America," 232.

84. Stein, "Road to Bat Mitzvah in America," 228–29.

85. Silver, "Rabbi and His Congregation," 39–40.

86. Silver, "Rabbi and His Congregation," 42.

87. Klagsbrun, "How the Bat Mitzvah Has Changed."

88. Shuly Rubin Schwartz, "Conservative Judaism in the United States," in Hyman and Ofer, *Jewish Women*.

89. "In the Communal Armchair. Here and There. By Mentor." *Jewish Chronicle*, January 13, 1928, 9. The commentator thought the term *girl's consecration* absurd and praised Dayan Lazarus for using *confirmation* instead.

90. "Jottings from South Africa," *Jewish Chronicle*, June 2, 1899, 24.

91. Eichholz, "Confirmation for Girls." The seven London congregations that originally agreed to adopt the proposal were Borough, Brixton, Central, East London, Hampstead, New West End, and St. John's Wood. Yet not all of them carried through their plans. By 1924 East London and Hampstead had held consecration ceremonies; Bayswater, Brixton, and Brondesbury had started classes; and Golders Green and North London planned to do so. They were all Orthodox communities.

92. Jews' Free School, "Girl's Consecration Service," *Jewish Chronicle*, December 18, 1925, 18.

93. Walter Hart, personal recollections, 2012. I have seen no contemporary account of the age of the girls.

94. "Bar Mitzvah Girls," *Jews' Free School Magazine* 5.48 (December 1925): 618.

95. "Girls' Consecration Service," *Jews' Free School Magazine* 6.51, December 1926, 59.

96. "Girls' Consecration Service," *Jews' Free School Magazine* 7.61, April 1930, 176.

97. Wertheimer, *American Synagogue*, 313–14.

98. Vinick and Reinharz, *Today I Am a Woman*, 15.

99. Hyamson, *Sephardim of England*, 415; also information from the congregation's archives supplied by Miriam Rodrigues-Pereira.

100. Proverbs 31:10–31.

101. E.g., in Blackpool, England, in 1963 (*Synagogue Review* [July–August 1963]: 279).

102. Feinstein, *Igrot Moshe* Orach Chayyim 1.104 (1956), vol. 1 (1959), 170.

103. Feinstein, *Igrot Moshe* Orach Chayyim, 4. 36 (1959), vol. 4. (1982), 47–48; Norma Baumel Joseph, "Rabbi Moses Feinstein," in Hyman and Ofer, *Jewish Women*.

104. Zohar, "Oriental Jewry Confronts Modernity," 134–35; and Ariel Picard, "Rabbi Ovadiah Yosef b. 1920," in Hyman and Ofer, *Jewish Women*.

105. Weinberg, *Seridei Eish*, 3.94, p. 298, as quoted in Sperber, "Congregational Dignity and Human Dignity," 13.

106. "Minyanim Worldwide."

107. Paula E. Hyman, "Bat Mitzvah: American Jewish Women," in Hyman and Ofer, *Jewish Women*.

108. Arian and Keissar-Sugarmen, *Portrait of Israeli Jews*, 42–43.

109. Sommer, "In Israel, Bat Mitzvahs Where Torah Is Read Remain Rare."

110. Amsel-Arieli, "Bat Mitzvahs in Israel Run Gamut from Fancy to Frum."

111. Vinick and Reinharz, *Today I Am a Woman*, 233–35.

112. Levine, "Understanding the Bat Mitzvah Attack"; also see press reports from the time.

113. Vinick and Reinharz, *Today I Am a Woman*, 256.

114. *The Occident* 1.10 (January 1844). The service took place on October 14, 1843.

115. Vinick and Reinharz, *Today I Am a Woman*, 269.

116. Cousens, *Adult Bat Mitzvah*, 2.

117. Vinick and Reinharz, *Today I Am a Woman*, 220.

118. Grant, "Finding Her Right Place in the Synagogue," 279–81.

119. Grant, "Restorying Jewish Lives Post Adult Bat Mitzvah," 39.

120. Grant, "Finding Her Right Place in the Synagogue," 288.

121. Schoenfeld, "Integration into the Group."

122. Maag, "Having a Bat Mitzvah in Their 90s."

123. Schoenfeld, "Integration into the Group," 127.

124. Cousens, *Adult Bat Mitzvah*, 4.

125. Vinick and Reinharz, *Today I Am a Woman*.
126. Lipstadt, "Feminism and American Judaism," 301.
127. *Sex and the City*, season 3, 2000, episode 15: "Hot Child in the City"; *Joan of Arcadia*, season 2, 2004, episode 10: "The Book of Questions"; Mitchell and Reid-Walsh, *Girl Culture*, 168.

6. INTO THE MODERN AGE

1. Rivkind, *Le-Ot u-le-Zikkaron*, 60–61.
2. *Chacham*, the term used for a Sephardic principal rabbi, means "wise man."
3. Benjamin, *Eight Years in Asia and Africa from 1846–1855*, 285–86.
4. Gindi, "Tefilin."
5. Also recorded from Tunisia and Libya. See Reilly and Metter, *Bar Mitzvah, Bat Mitzvah*, 56.
6. Gilat, "Barukh She-Petarani," 181. Gaguine, *Sefer Keter Shem Tov*, 318, insisted, however, that he had never heard of Sephardim using the father's blessing (1934).
7. This account is from Eliany, "Bar Mitzvah and Education," in "Jews of Morocco." The tradition of bar mitzvah at age twelve was mentioned in an 1839 article in a German newspaper. See Rivkind, *Le-Ot u-le-Zikkaron*, 65–66.
8. Ingber, *Seeing Israeli and Jewish Dance*, 175–76.
9. Ingber, *Seeing Israeli and Jewish Dance*, 178–80.
10. Gindi, "Tefilin," using his own reminiscences from the United States, oral testimony in Israel, and Gaguine's *Sefer Keter Shem Tov*.
11. "Seder Chazzanut Amsterdam."
12. Alexander, *Alexander's Hebrew Ritual*, 212–13.
13. These and many other distinctive Chabad traditions are explored in Dubov, *Yalkut Bar Mitzvah*, esp. chaps. 2–3.
14. Michaelson, *Sefer Pinot HaBayit*, no. 85; Schneerson, *I Will Write It in Their Hearts*, letter 503.
15. Swartz, *Bar Mitzvah*, 64.
16. Gilat, "Barukh She-Petarani," 181–82, mentions another Eastern European custom of the father saying this blessing at the party after his son has finished his speech.
17. Rivkind, *Le-Ot u-le-Zikkaron*, 70–71.
18. *Jewish Chronicle*, March 3, 1916; Macdowell, "Bar Mitzvah of the Child Soldier Grandson of Rabbi Shmuel Salant."
19. Herzberg, "Town in Eastern Germany," 335.
20. "Bar Mitzva in Teresienstadt," In YadVaShem, "To Live with Honor and to Die with Honor."
21. Swartz, *Bar Mitzvah*, 32–33.

22. "Remember Us: The Holocaust Bnai Mitzvah Project" website, www
.remember-us.org (accessed February 18, 2014).

23. Isaiah 66:10. This is from the haftarah for Shabbat Rosh Hodesh ("new
moon").

24. The name of a song by Haim Nahman Bialik (1873–1934), later adopted as
a labor anthem in Israel.

25. From the *Yiddisher Derziung*, 1939, as reported by Rivkind, *Le-Ot u-le-
Zikkaron*, 72–73.

26. Pilch, "Leading Jewish Educators," 16.

27. Lehrer, *Camp Boiberik*, 33.

28. Block, "When Friends Become Family." On the history of domestic cake
baking, see Pleck, *Celebrating the Family*, 144–45.

29. *Jews' Free School Magazine*, 7.61 (April 1930): 176; 9.75 (December 1934):
154; 10.64, (December 1937): 71.

30. Weil, "About the Author."

31. Cohen and Weinrott, *The Ultimate Bar/Bat Mitzvah Celebration Book*, 154.

32. Pleck, *Celebrating the Family*, 174.

33. *Jews' Free School Magazine*, 5.48 (December 1925): 618.

34. Richler, *Apprenticeship of Duddy Kravitz*, 176–84.

35. Paz, Almog, and Rudin, "Bar Mitzvah Celebrations in the Secular Sabra
Community."

36. Lilker, *Kibbutz Judaism*, 207–10.

37. Lilker, *Kibbutz Judaism*, 212–13 (paraphrased and summarized).

38. Lilker, *Kibbutz Judaism*, 215.

39. Amichai, *World Is a Room*, 51. The Hebrew title of the story is "Hagigat Bar
Mitzvah," and it was first published in *Baruah Hanora'ah Hazot* (1961).

40. Amichai, *World Is a Room*, 63, 67.

41. Paz, Almog, and Rudin, "Bar Mitzvah Celebrations in the Secular Sabra
Community."

42. Paz, Almog, and Rudin, "Bar Mitzvah Celebrations in the Secular Sabra
Community."

43. Jeffay, "Rainbow Flags Aflutter."

44. Rappaport, *Mazal Tov*, 37.

45. Rappaport, *Mazal Tov*, 113.

46. Rappaport, *Mazal Tov*, 123–28; Cohen, *Alfie's Bark Mitzvah*.

47. Matthews, "Convict Stages Son's Bar Mitzvah in NYC Jail."

48. "The Kerchief," in Agnon, *Book That Was Lost*, 55–66.

49. *Jewish Life Cycle* (DVD).

50. Mordecai HaCohen, *Sefer Siftei Cohen*, 13a; Rivkind, *Le-Ot u-le-Zikkaron*,
37–38.

51. Cantor Marshall Portnoy, in Leneman, *Bar/Bat Mitzvah Basics*, 30.

52. Friedrichs, "Jewish Household Structure in an Early Modern Town."
53. Kerner, "Le Règlement de la communauté juive de Metz," 209.
54. Schoenfeld, "Changing Patterns of North American Bar Mitzvah," 9–10.
55. Ferziger, *Exclusion and Hierarchy*, 160–61, 166–68.
56. Ferziger, *Exclusion and Hierarchy*, 90–186.
57. "Un Peu de statistique," *L'Univers Israélite*, February 5, 1909, 657–58; Marrus, *Politics of Assimilation*, 56–59.
58. "L'Examen de la Bar-Mitzwa," *L'Univers Israélite*, November 20, 1896, 267–70.
59. London, *Takkanot* (1827), 63–64, rule 254.
60. London, *Laws of the Congregation of the Great Synagogue* (1863), 54, rule 229.
61. The Tuck family ran a successful postcard business in London, founded by Desmond's grandfather Raphael Tuck in 1866.
62. Adler, *Rite of Bar-Mitzvah*, 5.
63. Schoenfeld, "Changing Patterns of North American Bar Mitzvah."
64. Wice, "Bar Mitzvah and Confirmation," 45–46.
65. Kimmel, *Bar Mitzvah*, 45.
66. Pleck, *Celebrating the Family*, 300.
67. Jack Wertheimer, "The Conservative Synagogue," in Wertheimer, *American Synagogue*, 144.
68. Stuart Schoenfeld, "Folk Judaism, Elite Judaism and the Role of Bar Mitzvah in the Development of the Synagogue and Jewish School in America," in Leneman, *Bar/Bat Mitzvah Education*, 81.
69. Wertheimer, "Conservative Synagogue," 129.
70. Schoenfeld, "Folk Judaism," 82.
71. Wertheimer, "Conservative Synagogue," 129.
72. "Girls' Consecration Service," *Jews' Free School Magazine* 6.51 (December 1926): 60.
73. Information reported from the congregational bulletin by the archivist, Miriam Rodrigues-Pereira.
74. Michael Binstock, pers. comm., January 30, 2009.
75. See also the reminiscences of Raymond Apple, rabbi of Hampstead Synagogue, London: "Being young and clean-shaven, I also ordered a clerical collar (we called them dog collars) in order to visit hospitals without having to prove my credentials every time. Many senior rabbis including the Chief used such collars; it was said that one or two wore them to bed, maybe because these collars were so hard to do up and undo" ("When Rabbis Wore Dog Collars," *Jewish Chronicle*, January 10, 2011).
76. Eimer, "Vayakhel-Pikudei." ("Muff and huff" means "*maftir* and haftarah.")
77. "Your Bat Mitzvah / Bat Chayil."
78. Paterson, *Bar Mitzvah Book*.

79. Carol K. Ingall, "Bar/Bat Mitzvah: Policies and Programs," in Leneman, *Bar/Bat Mitzvah Education*, 39–57.
80. *Becoming Bar Mitzvah.*
81. Dubov, *Yalkut Bar Mitzvah*, chap. 2.
82. Google Books Ngram Viewer, http://books.google.com/ngrams.
83. Grant, "Finding Her Right Place in the Synagogue," 281.
84. Aron et al., "B'nai Mitzvah Revolution: About Us."

7. CURRENT ISSUES AND TRENDS

1. Grossman, *Zigzag Kid*, 226.
2. Perlmutter, "Coming of Age in Remarried Families."
3. Sally Weber, "Celebration and Negotiation: How to Keep the Divorce Battle Off the Bimah," in Leneman, *Bar/Bat Mitzvah Education*, 318–24.
4. Geffen and Kaplan, "Divorce and Bar Mitzvah."
5. I am grateful to Yoav Landau-Pope for his help with discussing this issue.
6. Leneman, *Bar/Bat Mitzvah Basics*, 129–37.
7. Luria, *Sefer Yam Shel Shelomoh, Bava Kamma* 7.37; B. *Kiddushin* 31a; and B. *Bava Kamma* 87a.
8. *Jewish Chronicle*, January 22, 1869, 5.
9. Quoted from Swartz, *Bar Mitzvah*, 18, in which the whole story is reprinted. "The Law" was originally published in *A Pile of Stones* (1965).
10. Goldstein, "Deaf, Jews Who Live in Silence."
11. From an article by Devora Bartnoff, Lior's mother: "Praying with Lior," *Philadelphia Jewish Exponent*, February 20, 1997. Devora died when Lior was six years old, and the title of the DVD was taken from this article.
12. Interview with Rabbi Mordecai Liebling, *Barry Z Show*, www.youtube.com/watch?feature=endscreen&NR=1&v=0F_mykl7vew (accessed March 8, 2012).
13. Klein and Vuijst, *Half-Jewish Book*.
14. Krasner and Zollman, "Are You There, God?"
15. The matrilineal principle can be deduced from M. *Kiddushin* 3:12, M. Yevamot 2:5 and 7:5, and T. *Kiddushin* 4.16. These texts are not easy to interpret. There is a helpful discussion in Cohen, *Beginnings of Jewishness*, 263–307.
16. "Reform Movement's Resolution on Patrilineal Descent."
17. Staub, "Reconstructionist View on Patrilineal Descent," 97, my emphasis.
18. Lyons, *At Sinai*, 8.
19. Krasner and Zollman, "Are You There, God," 28.
20. "Reform Movement's Resolution on Patrilineal Descent."
21. "Jewish Witness to a European Century," interview with Joseph Hen (b. 1923), 2004.

22. The Rabbinic Conference of the British Liberal movement has followed the same path, though the precise dates of the various resolutions are different. See Rigal and Rosenberg, *Liberal Judaism*.

23. "Barmitzvah Class," *Jews' Free School Magazine* 7.58 (March 1929): 93.

24. Keyser, "Mass Bar Mitzvah."

25. "Group Bar/Bat Mitzvah Ceremony"; and various reports from the American Jewish Joint Distribution Committee, www.jdc.org.

26. Olitzky and Raphael, *American Synagogue*, 234.

27. Report by Linda Kerber in *Moment* magazine, reprinted in Swartz, *Bar Mitzvah*, 38–39.

28. Psalm 90:10.

29. Union for Reform Judaism, "Adult B'nei Mitzvah."

30. Michael Hilton, personal archives.

31. Dean, "Aish.com Interview with Kirk Douglas"; and Rappaport, *Mazal Tov*, 55–59.

32. Schneider, "South Africa's 'Blind Chazzan.'"

33. Kahn, "Centenarian Celebrates Fourth Bar Mitzvah."

34. Pleck, *Celebrating the Family*, 174.

35. Frommer and Frommer, *Growing Up Jewish in America*, 185.

36. Freedman, "Anglo-Jewish Society."

37. Gaster Papers, Personal Papers/Ephemera: Gaster/1/A/Coh/8; invitation to the confirmation of Moise Claude Cohen, April 26 and 29, 1919.

38. Gaster Papers, Personal Papers/Ephemera: Gaster/1/A/Sou/1; invitation to the confirmation of Elie Souhami, January 10, 1920.

39. Black, "Anglicization of Orthodoxy," 306.

40. Frommer and Frommer, *Growing Up Jewish in America*, 195.

41. Wouk, *Marjorie Morningstar*, 84.

42. Wouk, *Marjorie Morningstar*, 87–88. The book was later made into a film that features Seth's synagogue service but not the bar mitzvah party.

43. Pleck, *Celebrating the Family*, 175.

44. "Jewish Witness to a European Century," interview with Alica Gazikova.

45. Appel, "Today I Am a Fountain Pen, Again."

46. Kranson, "More Bar than Mitzvah," 9–10, 12.

47. Stein, "Road to Bat Mitzvah in America," 228.

48. Kranson, "More Bar than Mitzvah," 13.

49. Feinstein, *Igrot Moshe Orach Chayyim*, 1:104.

50. Marc Saperstein, pers. comm., April 2012.

51. Kranson, "More Bar than Mitzvah," 19–20.

52. Isaacson and Rosenbloom, *Bar and Bat Mitzvah in Israel*, 5.

53. Chen, "Incoming Bar Mitzvah Tourism."

54. Elsant, *Bar Mitzvah Lessons*, 49.

55. Cohen and Weinrott, *Ultimate Bar/Bat Mitzvah Celebration Book*, 16.
56. Boteach, "Extravagant Weddings and Bar Mitzvahs."
57. Fendel, "Thousands at Belzer Bar Mitzvah in Jerusalem."
58. Ingall, "Bat Mitzvahs Get Too Glitzy."
59. Estroff, "Policing Bar Mitzvah Crowd."
60. For example, those recorded in Bennett, Shell, and Kroll, *Bar Mitzvah Disco*.
61. Yoffie, "Sermon by Rabbi Eric H. Yoffie at the San Diego Biennial."
62. Schoenfeld, "Changing Patterns of North American Bar Mitzvah," 22.
63. Rabbi Eric Yoffie, pers. comm., January 24, 2012.
64. Aron, "Supplementary Schooling and the Law of Unanticipated Consequences"; Woocher, O'Brien, and Isaacs, "Driving Congregational School Change," 335–36.
65. Strassfeld and Strassfeld, *Second Jewish Catalog*, 73.
66. Salkin, *Putting God on the Guest List*, 116.
67. From the commentary attributed to Rabbeinu Gershom on B. *Menachot*, 43b.
68. *Shulchan Arukh Orach Chayyim* 22.1. The rule generally followed is that the special blessing for happy occasions is not said the first time one performs a particular mitzvah, so at a bar mitzvah it is said for a new item of clothing, not for the occasion itself.
69. This tradition follows earlier Ashkenazic sources, such as *Tashbetz Katan* 462. It may perhaps date from a time of early marriage, when a wedding and bar mitzvah could coincide.
70. Gershom, "Story of Reb Zalman's B'nai Or Tallit."
71. Michele Order Litant, "Noah's Choice," in Cohen et al., *Jewish Love Stories for Kids*, 139–70.
72. Goldman, "My Zaydie's Tallit." The tallit worn by Matan had Reb Zalman's "B'nei Or" design.
73. Shalom Center, "Guide to an Eco-Bar/Bat Mitzvah Observance."
74. Z. 1.10b–11a.
75. Rivkind, *Le-Ot u-le-Zikkaron*, 76.
76. John Adler recalling his bar mitzvah at Finchley United Synagogue, Kinloss Gardens, London.
77. Lyons, *At Sinai*, 62.
78. Kadden and Kadden, *Teaching Jewish Life Cycle*, 29.
79. "Areyvut: Bnai Mitzvah."
80. Helena Miller, United Jewish Israel Appeal (UJIA) London, pers. comm., 2012.
81. Melabev, "Melabev Bat-Mitzvah Outreach"; and "Intergenerational Bar-Mitzvah Project in Beit Shemesh."

82. Marcus, *Jewish Life Cycle*, 113–14.
83. Feinstein, *Igrot Moshe Orach Chayyim*, 1:104.
84. Yoffie, "Sermon by Rabbi Eric H. Yoffie at the San Diego Biennial, December 15, 2007."
85. Two were published in Venice in 1602; see Modena, *Midbar Yehudah*, fol. 95–98.
86. Juspa Schammes, *Minhagim di-K.K. Vermaisa*, 2.166.
87. Kerner, "Le Règlement de la communauté juive de Metz," 209.
88. Rosenbaum, "Jewish Feminist Leaders."
89. Ross, "Modern Orthodoxy and the Challenge of Feminism"; Schacter, "Changing Status of Orthodox Jewish Women."
90. The age of eighty-three represents a recognized life span of seventy years (Ps. 90:10), plus an extra thirteen years.

8. THE EVIDENCE ASSESSED

1. Meyer, *Response to Modernity*, 188–96.
2. Marcus, *Jewish Life Cycle*, 113–14.
3. Plaut, *Rise of Reform Judaism*, 178–80.
4. Löw, *Die Lebensalter in der Jüdischen Literatur*, 210–1/ (bar mitzvah), 218–22 (confirmation).
5. Lebendiger, "Minor in Jewish Law."
6. For the life of Isaac Rivkind, see Preschel, "Isaac Rivkind"; and Kabakoff, "Some Notable Bibliographers I Have Known."
7. Schauss, *Lifetime of a Jew*, 117.
8. Marcus, *Jewish Life Cycle*, 114, 125.
9. Marcus, *Jewish Life Cycle*, 102–3.
10. Löw, *Die Lebensalter in der Jüdischen Literatur*, 218–22.
11. Golinkin, "Participation of Jewish Women in Public Rituals"; Miccoli, "Moving Histories."
12. Boyarin and Boyarin, *Jews and Other Differences*, viii.
13. Van Gennep, *Rites of Passage*, vii.
14. Van Gennep, *Rites of Passage*, 101.
15. Van Gennep, *Rites of Passage*, 189.
16. Turner, *Ritual Process*, ix, 97–107.
17. Turner, *Ritual Process*, 106–7, 42–43.
18. See, e.g., Stuart Schoenfeld, "Folk Judaism, Elite Judaism, and the Role of Bar Mitzvah in the Development of the Synagogue and Jewish School in America," in Leneman, *Bar/Bat Mitzvah Education*, 78–90, esp. 82.
19. Turner, *From Ritual to Theatre*, 80.
20. Driver, *Liberating Rites*, 164.
21. Muir, *Ritual in Early Modern Europe*, 5.

22. English version: Ariès, *Centuries of Childhood*, 31.
23. Shahar, *Childhood in the Middle Ages*.
24. Ta-Shma, "Children in Medieval Germanic Jewry: A Perspective on Aries from Jewish Sources," in *Creativity and Tradition*, 127–41.
25. *Bereshit Rabbah* 63.10, commenting on Genesis 25:27.
26. *Horaot meiRabbanei Tzarfat*, 23; and Avigdor Tzarfati, *Sefer Perushim*, ח (sedra Toledot).
27. Waskow and Berman, *Time for Every Purpose under Heaven*, 63.
28. David Kohan, "The Ultimate Aphrodisiac," in Bennett, Shell, and Kroll, *Bar Mitzvah Disco*, 239–40.
29. Signer and Van Engen, *Jews and Christians in Twelfth Century Europe*, 1.
30. Kanarfogel, *Jewish Education and Society*, 63.
31. Shahar, *Childhood in the Middle Ages*.
32. Shahar, *Childhood in the Middle Ages*, 176–77.
33. P. H. Cullum, "Boy/Man into Clerk/Priest," in McDonald and Ormrod, *Rites of Passage*, 55.
34. For links between the Hasidei Ashkenaz and the tosafists, see Kanarfogel, *Peering through the Lattices*.
35. See Marcus, *Piety and Society*, chap. 1.
36. Scholem, *Major Trends in Jewish Mysticism*, 104.
37. This is the method adopted by, among others, Daniel Boyarin in *Border Lines*. In assessing the evidence of the Yavneh legend from classical rabbinic texts, Boyarin writes, "Rather than attempting to reconstruct an obscure period out of the centuries-later legends that attest to it, I attempt to historicize the texts of a well attested period, namely the periods in which those legends about Yavneh and its consequences were produced" (76–77). The same rabbinic method, by which rulings were established founded on legends from past teachers, was at work in early Ashkenaz, and therefore the same principles should be applied.
38. Marmorstein, "Sur un auteur français inconnu du treizième siècle."
39. Ta-Shma, "Earliest Literary Sources," 594, and *Ha-Nigle She-BaNistar*, 123; Kanarfogel, *Peering through the Lattices*, 94, 97, and 107–9, and *Medieval Ashkenaz*, 25, 360, 473.
40. Golb, *Jews in Medieval Normandy*, 455.
41. Avigdor Tzarfati, *Sefer Perushim*, 14.
42. Golb, *Jews in Medieval Normandy*, 188.
43. British Library Manuscript Or. 2853, "Commentary on Pentateuch Hebrew," fol. 7b.
44. Marmorstein, "Sur un auteur français inconnu du treizième siècle," 113.
45. Kanarfogel, *Medieval Ashkenaz*, 360.
46. *Tashbetz Katan*, 390.

47. Jacobs, *Jews of Angevin England*, 406–16.

48. Jacobs, *Jews of Angevin England*, 88; "Ysaac de Jueignj."

49. Golb, *Jews in Medieval Normandy*, xx.

50. Gershom Scholem and Isadore Twersky; Kanarfogel, *Jewish Education and Society*, 101–5; Jacobs, *Jews of Angevin England*, 342–44.

51. Kanarfogel, *Jewish Education and Society*, 191.

52. Löw, *Die Lebensalter in der Jüdischen Literatur*, 210–17 (bar mitzvah), 218–22 (confirmation); Rivkind, *Le-Ot u-le-Zikkaron*; Ta-Shma, "Ivan Marcus, Rituals of Childhood," and "Earliest Literary Sources"; Blank, "Jewish Rites of Adolescence"; Gutmann, *Jewish Life Cycle*, 10.

53. Marcus, *Rituals of Childhood*, 106–7.

54. Jeffrey A. Trustcott, "Initiation," in Bowden, *Christianity*, 624.

55. Marcus, *Rituals of Childhood*, 107–11.

56. Marcus, *Rituals of Childhood*, 117–28.

57. Marcus, *Rituals of Childhood*, 117.

58. Moses Isserles, *Darkhei Moshe, Orach Chayyim*, 37.

59. Ta-Shma, "Ivan Marcus, Rituals of Childhood."

60. Ta-Shma, "Ivan Marcus, Rituals of Childhood"; Ta-Shma, "Earliest Literary Sources for the Bar-Mitzva Ritual and Festivity."

61. Abulafia, *Christians and Jews in the Twelfth Century Renaissance*, 11–33.

62. "Rashbam and Hugh of St. Victor," in Hilton, *Christian Effect on Jewish Life*, 120–22.

63. Bar-Levav, "Ritualisation of Jewish Life and Death," 69.

64. Bar-Levav, "Ritualisation of Jewish Life and Death," 73.

65. *M. Avodah Zarah*, 1:3; Ta-Shma, "On Birthdays in Judaism."

66. Pärdi, "Crumbling of the Peasant Time Concept in Estonia."

67. Orme, *Medieval Children*, 46.

68. Ariès, *Centuries of Childhood*, 16.

69. Marcus, *Jewish Life Cycle*, 40.

70. Marcus, *Jewish Life Cycle*, 41; Schapiro, "Birthdays in Halacha."

71. Ariès, *Centuries of Childhood*, 151–230.

72. This text is first attested (with slight variations) in T. *Berukhot*, 6.12.

73. Hoffman, *Covenant of Blood*, 83; Lawrence A. Hoffman, "The Role of Women at Rituals of Their Infant Children," in Fine, *Judaism in Practice*, 99–114.

74. Turner, *Ritual Process*, 106–7.

75. Avigdor Tzarfati, *Sefer Perushim*, קעצ (*Sedra Emor*). Grossman, *Pious and Rebellious*, 194, gives the correct reference but attributes the text to "the thirteenth century French sage Avigdor Kara," instead of Avigdor Tzarfati. Avigdor Kara lived in Prague in the *fifteenth* century and died in 1439. Grossman's mistake has been widely reproduced in online discussions about women wearing tallit and tefillin.

76. Howard Tzvi Adelman, "Italian Jewish Women at Prayer," in Fine, *Judaism in Practice*, 52–60.

77. Hoffman, *Covenant of Blood*, 205.

78. The texts (in English) are conveniently collected in Lawrence Hoffman, "Role of Women at Rituals of Their Infant Children," in Fine, *Judaism in Practice*, 99–114.

79. Chava Weissler, "Measuring Graves and Laying Wicks," in Fine, *Judaism in Practice*, 61–73.

80. Juspa Schammes, *Minhagim*, 2:166–67, my emphasis.

81. Luria, *Yam Shel Shelomoh Bava Kamma*, 7.37.

82. Lowther Clarke and Harris, *Liturgy and Worship*, 443.

83. Aquinas, *Summa Theologica*, 3:72:11.

84. Lowther Clarke and Harris, *Liturgy and Worship*, 456; Austin, *Anointing with the Spirit*, 19.

85. Austin, *Anointing with the Spirit*, 20; Benedict, "Catholic Response to Protestantism," 113; Bossy, "Counter-Reformation and the People of Catholic Europe."

86. Modena, *History of the Rites*, 214; Morosini, Derekh Emunah, 1:165.

87. Muir, *Ritual in Early Modern Europe*, 182.

88. Muir, *Ritual in Early Modern Europe*, 204.

89. Carlebach, *Divided Souls*, 47–66.

90. Jonathan Israel, "Germany and Its Jews (1300–1800)," in Hsia and Lehmann, *In and Out of the Ghetto*, 299.

91. Williams, *Radical Reformation*, 94–95, 235–36; Lowther Clarke and Harris, *Liturgy and Worship*, 454–57; Fisher, *Christian Initiation*, 254–60.

92. Burke, "The Repudiation of Ritual in Early Modern Europe," in *Historical Anthropology of Early Modern Italy*, 223–38.

93. From a sermon of 1523; Fisher, *Christian Initiation*, 173.

94. Fisher, *Christian Initiation*, 169. From Erasmus, *Paraphrase on St. Matthew's Gospel*, translated by W. Lockton.

95. Fox, *Reformation in Poland*, 73–78.

96. Teter, *Jews and Heretics*, 33, 46; Guldon and Kowalski, "Between Tolerance and Abomination," 169.

97. Hsia, *Myth of Ritual Murder*, 136–43.

98. *Even Ha-Ezer*, 55.1, my emphasis. The translation is from Marcus, *Jewish Life Cycle*, 164.

99. Luria, *Yam Shel Shelomoh Bava Kamma*, 7.37.

100. Fox, *Reformation in Poland*, 37.

101. Schorsch, "From Wolfenbüttel to Wissenschaft," 116.

102. Meyer, *Response to Modernity*, 319.

103. "Un Peu de statistique," *L'Univers Israélite*, February 5, 1909, 657–58; Marrus, *Politics of Assimilation*, 56–59.
104. Leavy, *Oral History*, 149–50.
105. Pleck, *Celebrating the Family*, 172–83.
106. Hobsbawm and Ranger, *Invention of Tradition*, 1–14.
107. Pleck, *Celebrating the Family*, 247.
108. Adapted from Proverbs 3:18, 17.

GLOSSARY

aggadah. The parts of rabbinic literature that can be described as homily, story, or narrative rather than legal discussions, or in Hebrew *halakhah.*

Almemar. Alternative name for the bimah.

ascamot. The formal rules of a Sephardic synagogue following the Spanish and Portuguese tradition.

Ashkenaz. Term used during the Middle Ages and beyond to designate northern France, Germany, and Austria.

Ashkenazic. Up to about the year 1600 this term was used specifically to denote the Jews of *Ashkenaz,* more recently, it has been extended to include all those carrying the traditions of Jews living in Christian Europe.

aufruf. Yiddish term meaning "call up," used especially for the calling of a bridegroom to the reading of the Torah on the Shabbat before his wedding.

Bemidbar. A *sedra* from the Book of Numbers (1:1–4:19).

bimah. Platform in the center or at the front of a synagogue, with a desk for the reading of the Torah.

brit milah. Circumcision.

Chabad (or **Chabad-Lubavitch**). *Hasidic* group that has adopted a worldwide outreach mission. Today they form the world's largest single Jewish organization.

chuppah. Term used in the Bible and rabbinic literature to denote the bridal chamber. Since the sixteenth century the term has been used to denote a portable canopy under which a wedding ceremony takes place.

derashah (also **darush, droshe**). A speech based on *midrash.*

Gaon (pride). Rabbinic title first used for the head of the two important academies in Babylon and later for a few other rabbis of distinction.

gematria. Every Hebrew letter can be used as a number; in *gematria* the numerical equivalent of the letters in a word are added up in order to find a hidden meaning.

haftarah. Hebrew for "conclusion." Term used for a reading from one of the Hebrew prophets from the Bible, read after the Torah reading on Sabbaths and on fasts and festivals.

haham. Chief rabbi of a Sephardic community, especially of the Spanish and Portuguese Jews' Congregation, London.

halakhah. The law or the rules of behavior on a particular subject, as agreed to by the rabbis. From this word is derived an English adjective, *halachic*.

Hanukkah. Winter eight-day festival. Candles are lit each night in the home to celebrate the rededication of the Temple by the Maccabees in 164 BCE.

hanukkat habayit. Celebration for the dedication of a new home.

Hasidei Ashkenaz. Pietistic group in twelfth- and thirteenth-century Germany.

Hasidim (adj., **hasidic**). Ultraorthodox pietistic groups with distinctive clothing for men, originally based in Eastern Europe but now found all over the world.

havdalah. Ceremony for the end of Shabbat, with candle, wine, and spices.

hazzan. Term originally denoting an overseer, with the same meaning as the Christian term *bishop*. Since the sixteenth century it is the term used for a cantor who sings or chants the prayers and scriptural readings.

Kabbalah (adj., **kabbalistic**). A body of literature that uses (sometimes openly but often in a concealed fashion) the imagery of the *sefirot* to describe aspects of God.

Kaddish. A prayer in praise of God, written in Aramaic, which from the time of *Rashi* has been recited regularly by mourners.

Ki Tissa. A *sedra* from the Book of Exodus (30:11–34:35).

Kiddush (sanctification). (1) Blessing said over a cup of wine on Shabbat and festivals, declaring the day holy. (2) Provision of food and drink in a synagogue after the service, to accompany the blessing.

kippah, pl. *kippot.* Disc-shaped cap worn on the head.

maftir. The person who reads the *haftarah*, traditionally after being called up for the repetition of the last few sentences of the week's Torah portion.

machzor. Prayer book for festival or High Holy Day worship.

Marranos. Term used in Spain and Portugal for Christians of Jewish ancestry suspected of living Jewish lives secretly. Also known as "Conversos"; certain groups were also called "New Christians."

midrash, pl. **midrashim** (inquiry). (1) A homiletic comment or story that quotes a biblical text or texts to make its point. (2) A compilation of such comments on a particular theme or biblical book. (3) The whole body of such rabbinic literature.

Mishnah (M). The earliest and most important compendium of rabbinic teaching, thought to have been compiled by Rabbi Judah Ha-Nasi about

200 CE. Conflicting opinions are frequently cited in it. The English translation is about eight hundred pages long. The Mishnah is divided into six separate sections (orders) and sixty-three smaller divisions (tractates).

mitzvah, pl. *mitzvot* (commandment). The word is used for a religious duty, whether an obligation or a meritorious deed.

Nahamu (comfort ye). *Shabbat* on which the *haftarah* is Isaiah 40:1–26.

Omer (sheaf). The seven weeks from Pesach to Shavuot, kept as a period of mourning, during which weddings are not permitted.

Parah. A special *maftir* and *haftarah* reading (Num. 19:1–22 and Ezek. 36:16–38).

Passover. Spring festival celebrating the Exodus from Egypt.

Pesach. Hebrew term for *Passover.*

pilpul (sharp analysis). From the Hebrew word for *pepper.* A method of study or speaking using hair-splitting argumentation particularly to reconcile seemingly contradictory texts.

pinkas, pl. *pinkasim.* Community record books.

Pirkei Avot. A section of the Mishnah, known in English as "Ethics of the Fathers."

Purim. Term described in Esther 3:7 as meaning "lots." The annual festival in the last month of winter, Adar, of which the origin and celebration are described in the Book of Esther.

Purim-Spiel. A comic play performed at Purim.

Rabbi, Rav, Rebbe. Titles used for Jewish scholars. The words are polite forms of address meaning "master" or "my master." The form *Rav* was the norm in Babylonia in Talmudic times; it has been revived by some Orthodox rabbis in modern times because the title Rabbi is used by Reform leaders. The form *Rebbe* is used by *hasidic* groups for their leaders.

Rashi. Rabbi Shlomo son of Yitzhak (1040–1105, northern France), commentator on the Bible and Babylonian *Talmud.*

Re'eh. A *sedra* from the Book of Deuteronomy (11:26–16:17).

Rosh Hashanah (head of the year). The Autumn New Year festival, which falls on 1 Tishri, developed by the rabbis into a day of solemnity and reflection on God's kingship and judgment of the world. See also *shofar.*

Sedra. Section of the Torah for a particular week.

sefirah, pl. *sefirot.* Technical term used in *kabbalistic* literature to denote any one of ten aspects of God.

Sephardic (Spanish). Term used (1) for the Jews of Spain and Portugal and (2) more recently for all those Jews carrying the traditions of Jews living in Muslim lands.

Shabbat (Sabbath). The weekly day of rest lasting from sunset on Friday evening to nightfall on Saturday evening.

Shavuot (weeks). Festival fifty days after the first day of *Passover*, described in Leviticus 23:16–21, later considered by the rabbis to be the anniversary of the giving of the Torah at Sinai.

Shekhinah. God's indwelling presence in the world.

Shema (hear). This word denotes the three paragraphs beginning with this word, which are recited twice daily in prayer. The paragraphs are Deuteronomy 6:4–9 and 11:13–20 and Numbers 15:37–41.

shofar. Horn from a ram or other animal sounded on *Rosh Hashanah*.

Shulchan Arukh. A summary of practical Jewish law and regulations that Rabbi Joseph Caro first published in 1565. It became an authoritative guide for Jews throughout the world.

siddur. Prayer book for daily and/or Sabbath worship.

Simchat Torah. The festival of Rejoicing of the Law, a medieval innovation following the conclusion of the festival of Tabernacles. The annual cycle of Torah readings is completed and the new cycle begun.

Sukkot. The festival of Tabernacles, also marking the autumn harvest (Lev. 23:39–43).

takkanot. Rabbinic or community decrees.

tallit, pl. **tallitot.** Fringed shawl worn during prayer.

Talmud. There are two completely separate Talmuds: the Jerusalem Talmud (J, known as the "Yerushalmi"), written in Palestine; and the longer Babylonian Talmud (B, known as the "Bavli"). Because of the ascendancy of Babylonian Jewry, it was the Bavli that became authoritative for medieval and modern Jewry. When the term *Talmud* is used alone, it refers to the Babylonian Talmud. Both Talmuds contain the *Mishnah* and voluminous discussions and comments on the Mishnaic material, known as the "Gemara" (commentary). The older material is generally written in Hebrew, with the later discussions in Aramaic. The English translation of the Babylonian Talmud runs to eighteen large volumes.

TANAKH. The correct term for the Jewish Bible, known to Christians as the "Old Testament." The word is an acronym of *Torah*, *Nevi'im* (prophets), and *Kethuvim* (writings), the three sections of the Hebrew Bible.

tefillin. Leather boxes containing biblical verses attached to the forehead and arm, especially for weekday morning prayers.

Tetzaveh. A *sedra* from the Book of Exodus (27:20–30:10).

tikkun olam (repairing the world). Popular term for *mitzvot* that help to improve society.

tish (table). A joyful gathering of *Hasidim*, with Torah speeches interspersed with singing. The principal guests sit around a table and are served refreshments.

Torah (teaching). Used in various senses: (1) the Pentateuch (the written Torah); (2) the traditions embodied in the *Mishnah* and *midrash* and *Talmud* (the oral Torah); and (3) the whole body of Jewish religious literature.

tosafists. A group of scholars in northern France and Germany who lived in the generations following Rashi.

Tosafot. (1) Well-known digest of commentaries on the Babylonian *Talmud* by *tosafists*. (2) Other works by *tosafists*, mainly biblical commentaries.

Tosefta (T). A parallel work to the *Mishnah*, arranged in the same sections but containing longer and fuller discussions. It is frequently quoted in the *Talmud*.

tzedakah. Giving to charity.

UAHC. Union of American Hebrew Congregations (Reform).

Vayera. A *sedra* from the book of Genesis (18:1–22:24).

yahrzeit. German and Yiddish word meaning "year-time," "anniversary." The term was borrowed from the Catholic Church to denote the anniversary of the death of a relative.

yeshiva (sitting). A school or college for male students devoted to the study of rabbinic literature.

Yom Kippur (day of atonement). A day described in the Bible as a day for "afflicting the soul" and "cleansing from sin." It takes place in autumn on 10 Tishri. It was developed by the rabbis as a day of fasting and prayer, asking for God's forgiveness.

złoty. Polish currency unit.

Zohar (Z). A *kabbalistic* commentary on sections of the Bible in the Aramaic language; it appeared in Castille in northern Spain in the 1280s.

BIBLIOGRAPHY

Hebrew texts mentioned in the notes but not found here have been taken from the Bar-Ilan Responsa CD.

Abrahams, Beth-Zion, ed and trans. *The Life of Glückel of Hameln, 1646–1724, Written by Herself.* Philadelphia: Jewish Publication Society, 2012.

Abrams, Judith Z. *Judaism and Disability: Portrayals in Ancient Texts from the Tanach through the Bavli.* Washington DC: Gallaudet University Press, 1998.

Abulafia, Anna Sapir. *Christians and Jews in the Twelfth Century Renaissance.* London: Routledge, 1995.

Adelman, Howard E. "Success and Failure in the Seventeenth Century Ghetto of Venice: The Life and Thought of Leon Modena, 1571–1648." PhD diss., Brandeis University, 1985.

Adler, Hermann. *The Rite of Bar-Mitzvah: A Sermon Preached at the North London Synagogue on Sabbath, April 5th, 5662–1902.* The North London Pulpit: A Special Series of Sermons Delivered at the North London Synagogue, No. 17. London: Alfred T. Isaacs and Sons, 1902.

Agnon, S. Y. *A Book That Was Lost and Other Stories.* New York: Schocken Books, 1995.

Agus, Irving A. *The Heroic Age of Franco-German Jewry: the Jews of Germany and France of the Tenth and Eleventh Centuries, the Pioneers and Builders of Town-Life, Town-Government and Institutions.* New York: Yeshiva University Press, 1969.

Aharon HaCohen of Lunel. *Orhot Hayim.* Florence: Isaac of Fez, 1751.

Alexander, L. *Alexander's Hebrew Ritual, and Doctrinal Explanation of the Whole Ceremonial Law, Oral and Traditional, of the Jewish Community in England and Foreign Parts; Being a Necessary Companion to the Holy Scriptures. Together with Several Remarkable Events Relating to the People of the Jews, from the Most Ancient Records.* London: Printed by and for the author, 1819.

Alexander, Philip, ed. *Textual Sources for the Study of Judaism.* Manchester: Manchester University Press, 1984.

Allgemeine Literatur-Zeitung. Newspaper, Jena. 1785–1849.

Amichai, Yehuda. *The World Is a Room and Other Stories.* Philadelphia: Jewish Publication Society of America, 1984.

Amsel-Arieli, Melody. "Bat Mitzvahs in Israel Run Gamut from Fancy to Frum." *JewishJournal.com.* Online publication. Tribe Media, Los Angeles, 2007. www.jewishjournal.com/bar_and_bat_mitzvahs/article/bat_mitzvahs_in_israel_run_gamut_from_fancy_to_frum_20070111 (accessed May 14, 2012).

Amsterdam. *Seder Hanhagot Beit HaKnesset MiKol HaShanah De-Kahal Kadosh Amsterdam.* 1759. Reprint. Amsterdam: Yaakov Proops, 1776.

———. *Takkanot miHaHevrah Kadishah MiGadlei Yetomim.* Amsterdam: Proops, 1789.

Appel, Allan. "Today I Am a Fountain Pen, Again." *New Haven Independent,* May 23, 2011. Online version. www.newhavenindependent.org/index.php/archives/entry/retro_bar_mitzvahs_enliv (accessed May 21, 2012).

Apple, Raymond. *Let's Ask the Rabbi: Replies, Responses and Reflections.* Milton Keynes: Authorhouse UK, 2011.

Aquinas, Thomas. *The Summa Theologica of St. Thomas Aquinas.* Translated by Fathers of the English Dominican Province. 22 vols. 2nd rev. ed. London, 1920–29. Online edition, 2006, by Kevin Knight. www.newadvent.org/summa (accessed February 15, 2008).

"Areyvut: Bnai Mitzvah." Online publication. Areyvut, Bergenfeld NJ, 2009. www.areyvut.org/bnai_mitzvah (accessed January 14, 2012).

Arian, Asher, and Ayala Keissar-Sugarmen, eds. *A Portrait of Israeli Jews: Beliefs, Observance, and Values of Israeli Jews, 2009.* Jerusalem: Guttman Center for Surveys of the Israeli Democracy Institute for The AVI CHAI–Israel Foundation, 2012.

Ariès, Philippe. *Centuries of Childhood: A Social History of Family Life.* Translated by Robert Baldick. New York: Vintage Books, 1962.

Aron, Isa. "Supplementary Schooling and the Law of Unanticipated Consequences: A Review Essay of Stuart Schoenfeld's 'Folk Judaism, Elite Judaism and the Role of Bar Mitzvah in the Development of the Synagogue and Jewish School in America.'" *Journal of Jewish Education* 76.4 (2010): 315–33.

Aron, Isa, Bradley Solmsen, Lisa Langer, Diane Tickton Schuster, Anna Marx, Josh Mason-Barkin, Nachama Sholnik Moskowitz, Sharon Feimer-Nemser, and Rob Weinberg. "B'nai Mitzvah Revolution: About Us." Online publication. www.bnaimitzvahrevolution.org (accessed November 4, 2012.)

Asaf, Simhah, ed. *Mekorot leToldot HaHinukh Beyisrael.* Tel Aviv: Devir, 1925.

Ascher, B. H. *Hinukh Nearim: Initiation of Youth: Containing the Principles of Judaism, Adapted for the Period of Confirmation, Arranged in a Catechetical Form.* London: Samuel Solomon, 1850.

Austin, Gerard. *Anointing with the Spirit: The Rite of Confirmation: The Use of Oil and Chrism.* New York: Pueblo Publishing, 1985.

Avigdor Tzarfati. *Sefer Perushim U-Fesakim Al HaTorah.* Edited by Efraim Fishel Herskovitz. Jerusalem: Makhon Harerei Kedem, 1996.

Baader, Benjamin Maria. *Gender, Judaism, and Bourgeois Culture in Germany, 1800–1870.* Bloomington: Indiana University Press, 2006.

Bacher, W. "The Jews of England in the Twelfth Century." *Jewish Quarterly Review* 6.2 (1894): 355–74.

Baer, Jean L. *The Self-Chosen: "Our Crowd" Is Dead, Long Live Our Crowd.* New York: Arbor House, 1982.

Balaban, Majer. "Die Krakauer Judengemeinde-ordnung von 1595 und ihre Nachträge." *Jahrbuch der Jüdisch-Literarishen Gesellschaft* 10 (1912 [published 1913]): 296–360; and 11 (1916): 88–114.

Balsam, Yehuda. "Can a Bar Mitzvah Boy Read Parshas Zachor?" Online publication. Beit HaKnesset of North Woodmere, New York, 2012. www.bknw .org/uploads/5/9/9/5/5995719/can_a_bar_mitzvah_boy_read_parshas_zachor.pdf (accessed June 21 , 2013).

Bamberger, Bernard. "Qetana, Na'arah, Bogereth." *Hebrew Union College Annual* 32 (1961): 281–94.

Banting, H. M. J. "Imposition of Hands in Confirmation: A Medieval Problem." *Journal of Ecclesiastical History* 7 (1956): 147–59.

"Bar/Bat Mitzvah Ideas and Primer for Interfaith Families." Online publication. InterfaithFamily.com, 2006 (accessed February 20, 2012).

Bar-Ilan University Responsa Project. "Judaic Library Plus Responsa." CD. Version 12. New York: Torah Educational Software, 2004.

Bar-Levav, Avriel. "Ritualisation of Jewish Life and Death in the Early Modern Period." *Leo Baeck Institute Year Book* 47 (2002): 69–82.

Baskin, Nora Raleigh. *The Truth about My Bat Mitzvah.* New York: Simon and Schuster, 2008.

Bat Mitzvah Comes of Age. Exhibition. Philadelphia: National Museum of American Jewish History and Moving Traditions, 2012. http://bat mitzvahcomesofage.com (accessed April 2, 2012).

Bayfield, Tony, Alan Race, and Ataullah Siddiqui, eds. *Beyond the Dysfunctional Family: Jews, Christians and Muslims in Dialogue with Each Other and with Britain.* Charleston SC: CreateSpace Independent Publishing Platform, 2012.

Bayswater Synagogue, 1863–1938 Origin and History Issued in Commemoration of the 75th Anniversary. London: United Synagogue, 1938.

Becoming Bar Mitzvah. London: United Synagogue Publications, 1994.

Bell, Catherine. *Ritual Theory, Ritual Practice.* New York: Oxford University Press, 1992.

Bell, Dean Phillip. *Jewish Identity in Early Modern Germany: Memory, Power and Community*. Aldershot UK: Ashgate, 2007.

Benedict, Philip. "The Catholic Response to Protestantism: Church Activity and Popular Piety in Rouen, 1560–1600." In *The Reformation: Critical Concepts in Historical Studies*, edited by Andrew Pettegree, 4:107–34. London: Routledge, 2004.

Benjamin, Henry. "A Surprise Bat Mitzvah . . . from 1910." *JWire*, December 15, 2009. Online publication. www.jwire.com.au/news/a-surprise-batmitzvah-from-1910/5884 (accessed May 2, 2012).

Benjamin, J. J., II. *Eight Years in Asia and Africa from 1846–1855*. Hanover: Published by the author, 1859.

Bennett, Roger, Jules Shell, and Nick Kroll. *Bar Mitzvah Disco: The Music May Have Stopped, but the Party's Never Over*. New York: Crown Publishers, 2005.

Ben-Yakov, Haim. "The Bar Mitzvah in Central and Eastern Europe in the 18th–20th Centuries." In *Central and East European Jews at the Crossroads of Tradition and Modernity*, edited by Jurgita Šiaučiunaitė-Verbickienė and Larisa Lempertienė, 266–73. Vilnius: Centre for Studies of the Culture of East European Jews, 2006.

Berger, Doreen. *The Jewish Victorian: Genealogical Information from the Jewish Newspapers, 1861–1870*. Witney, Oxfordshire UK: Robert Boyd Publications, 2004.

Berkovitz, Jay R. "Social and Religious Controls in Pre-Revolutionary France: Rethinking the Beginnings of Modernity." *Jewish History* 15 (2001): 1–40.

Biale, David. "Eros and Enlightenment: Love against Marriage in the East European Jewish Enlightenment." *Polin* 1 (1986): 49–67.

Birmingham, Stephen. "The Temple That 'Our Crowd' Built." *New York Magazine*, April 21, 1980, 45–48.

Black, Eugene C. "The Anglicization of Orthodoxy: The Adlers, Father and Son." In *Profiles in Diversity: Jews in a Changing Europe, 1750–1870*, edited by Frances Malino and David Jan Sorkin, 295–325. Detroit MI: Wayne State University Press, 1997.

Blank, Debra Reed. "It's Time to Take Another Look at 'Our Little Sister': Soferim: A Bibliographical Essay." *Jewish Quarterly Review* NS 90.1–2 (July–October 1999): 1–26.

———. "Jewish Rites of Adolescence." In *Life Cycles in Jewish and Christian Worship*, edited by Paul F. Bradshaw and Lawrence A. Hoffman, 81–110. Vol. 4 of *Two Liturgical Traditions*. Notre Dame: University of Notre Dame Press, 1996.

Bleich, J. David. *Contemporary Halakhic Problems*. Vol. 1 of the Library of Jewish Law and Ethics series, vol. 4. New York: Ktav and Yeshiva University Press, 1977.

Block, Susan Taylor. "When Friends Became 'Family': Mcgrath, Part II." *Susan's Blogue*, August 26, 2010. Online publication. http://susantaylorblock .com/2010/08/26/friends-become-family (accessed February 29, 2012).

Bloom, Emily Haft, and Sheri Giblin. *The Bar/Bat Mitzvah Planner*. San Francisco: Chronicle Books, 2007.

Bock, M. H. *Emunat Yisrael oder Katechismus der Israelitischen Religion: sowohl nach den dogmatischen und moralischen Grundsätzen, als auch nach den Ceremonial-Verordnungen der heiligen Schrift alten Bundes*. Berlin: Nicolatschen Buchhandlung, 1814.

Bodleian Library. Manuscript. Opp Add 4° 127.

Bossy, John. "The Counter-Reformation and the People of Catholic Europe." *Past and Present* 47.1 (1970): 51–70.

Boteach, Shmuley. "Extravagant Weddings and Bar Mitzvahs Humiliate the Jewish Community." *Beliefnet.com*, 2010. Online publication. http://www .beliefnet.com/search/site.aspx?q=Extravagant+Weddings+and+Bar+Mitzv ahs+Humiliate+the+Jewish+Community (accessed February 24, 2012).

Bowden, John, ed. *Christianity: The Complete Guide*. London: Continuum, 2005.

Boyarin, Daniel. *Border Lines: The Partition of Judaeo-Christianity*. Philadelphia: University of Pennsylvania Press, 2004.

Boyarin, Jonathan, and Daniel Boyarin, eds. *Jews and Other Differences: The New Jewish Cultural Studies*. Minneapolis: University of Minnesota Press, 1997.

Brann, M. *Geschichte der Juden in Schlesien*. Vol. 7 of *Die Alten Statuen der Glogauer Judenschaft*. Breslau: Schatzky, 1917.

Brasz, Chaya, and Yosef Kaplan, eds. *Dutch Jews as Perceived by Themselves and by Others: Proceedings of the Eighth International Symposium on the History of the Jews in the Netherlands*. Leiden: Brill, 2001.

British Library. Manuscript. Or. 2853. "Commentary on Pentateuch Hebrew."

Burke, Peter. *The Historical Anthropology of Early Modern Italy: Essays on Perception and Communication*. Cambridge: Cambridge University Press, 1987.

Buxtorf, Johannes. *Synagoga Judaica (Juden-schül)*. Translated by Alan Corré. www.uwm.edu/People/corre/buxdorf/chp3.html (accessed March 3, 2008).

"Bye-Laws for Member Synagogues. Adopted by Resolution of the US Council on 12th July 2010." London: United Synagogue Publications, 2010. www .theus.org.uk/the_united_synagogue/about_the_us/us_jigsaw/byelaws (accessed July 14, 2012).

Bye-Laws of the Constituent Synagogues. London: United Synagogue, 1881.

Cahen, Abraham. "Règlements somptuaires de la communauté juive de Metz à la fin du XVIIe siècle, 1690–1967." *Annuaire de la Société des Études Juives* 1 (1881): 77–121.

Carlebach, Elisheva. *Divided Souls: Converts from Judaism in Germany, 1500–1750*. New Haven: Yale University Press, 2001.

Cassuto, J. "Aus dem ältesten Protokollbuch der Portugiesisch-Jüdischen Gemeinde in Hamburg." *Jahrbuch der Jüdisch-Literarishen Gesellschaft* 6 (1909): 1–54; 8 (1911): 227–90; 9 (1912): 318–66; 10 (1913): 225–95; 11 (1916): 1–76; 13 (1920): 55–118.

Catholic Encyclopedia, The. Edited by C. G. Herbermann et al. 16 vols. New York: McGraw-Hill, 1967.

Chen, Shoshana. "Incoming Bar Mitzvah Tourism: Jewish Identity, and Local Businesses, Benefit from Sharp Rise in Trend of Diaspora Jews Celebrating Children's Coming of Age in Israel." Online publication. Yedioth Internet, Tel Aviv, 2010. www.ynetnews.com/articles/0,7340,L-3917999,00.html (accessed May 14, 2012).

Cohen, Boaz. "Ledinei haKatan baMishpat ha-Ivri veHaroma-i." In *Jewish and Roman Law: A Comparative Study*. Vol. 2. New York: Jewish Theological Seminary, 1966, Hebrew section, 1–9.

Cohen, David. *The Circle of Life: Rituals from the Human Family Album*. London: Aquarian Press, 1991.

Cohen, Debra Nussbaum. "First Bat Mitzvah, Judith Kaplan Eisenstein, Dies at 86." *Jweekly.com*, February 23, 1996. Online publication. www.jweekly.com/article/full/2631 (accessed February 7, 2012).

Cohen, Jayne, and Lori Weinrott. *The Ultimate Bar/Bat Mitzvah Celebration Book: A Guide to Inspiring Ceremonies and Joyous Festivities*. New York: Clarkson Potter, 2004.

Cohen, Leslie, Devorah Grossman, Tovah S. Yavin, Michele Order Litant, and Tiferet Peterseil. *Jewish Love Stories for Kids*. New York: Pitspopany Press, 2002.

Cohen, Shari. *Alfie's Bark Mitzvah*. Chandler AZ: Five Star Publications, 2007.

Cohen, Shaye J. D. *The Beginnings of Jewishness: Boundaries, Varieties, Uncertainties*. Berkeley: University of California Press, 1999.

Conigliani, Emma Boghen. "Iniziazione religiosa delle fanciulle." *Vessillo Israelitico* (1899): 185ff. http://digilander.libero.it/parasha/varie/batmizva/11.htm (accessed July 31, 2010).

Cooper, John. *The Child in Jewish History*. Northvale NJ: J. Aronson, 1996.

Cooperman, Bernard Dov, ed. *Jewish Thought in the Sixteenth Century*. Cambridge MA: Harvard University Press, 1983.

Coudert, Allison P., and Jeffrey S. Shoulson, eds. *Hebraica Veritas? Christian Hebraists and the Study of Judaism in Early Modern Europe*. Philadelphia: University of Pennsylvania Press, 2004.

Cousens, B. *Adult Bat Mitzvah as Entree into Jewish Life for North American Jewish Women*. Waltham MA: Hadassah International Research Institute on Jewish Women, 2002.

Dash Moore, Deborah. "Freedom's Fruits: The Americanization of an Old-Time Religion." In *A Portion of the People: Three Hundred Years of Southern Jewish Life*, edited by Theodore Rosengarten and Dale Rosengarten, 10–21. Columbia: University of South Carolina Press, 2003.

Davis, Judith. *Whose Bar/Bat Mitzvah Is This, Anyway? A Guide for Parents through a Family Rite of Passage*. New York: St. Martin's Griffin, 1998.

Dean, Ayala. "Aish.com Interview with Kirk Douglas." Online publication. Aish HaTorah, Jerusalem, 2000. www.aish.com/sp/so/48892702.html (accessed May 10, 2012).

De Sola, D. A. *The Blessings, or, Expressions of Praise and Thanksgiving: Said by All Israelites on Various Occasions*. London: J. Wertheimer, 1829.

Di Segni, Riccardo. *Il Bat Mitzvà in Italia: una riforma discussa*. Online publication. Rome, 1990. http://digilander.libero.it/parasha/varie/batmizva/indice.html (accessed July 31, 2010).

Driver, Tom F. *Liberating Rites: Understanding the Transformative Power of Ritual*. Boulder CO: Westview Press, 1998.

Druckerman, S. *Bar Mitzvah Derashot: Ai Zamlung Fon Konfirmatsions Redes. Bar Mitzvah: A Selection of Confirmation Speeches in Hebrew, Yiddish and English and Condensed Code of Laws Concerning the T'fillin*. 3rd ed. 1907. Reprint. New York: Druckerman, 1921.

Dubov, Nissan Dovid. *Yalkut Bar Mitzvah: An Anthology of Laws and Customs of a Bar Mitzvah in the Chabad Tradition*. Brooklyn NY: Merkos Linyonei Hinukh, 1999.

Eichholz, Ruth. "Confirmation for Girls." *Jewish Chronicle*, November 7, 1924, 16.

Eidelberg, Shlomo. *R. Yuzpa Shamash di-Kehilat Vermaisa R. Juspa, Shammash of Warmaisa (Worms): Jewish Life in 17th Century Worms*. Jerusalem: Hebrew University, Magnes Press, 1991.

Eilu V'Eilu. Online publication. Union for Reform Judaism, New York. Weekly since 2006. urj.org/learning/torah/ten/eilu (accessed April 15, 2012).

Eimer, Colin. "Vayakhel-Pikudei." Sermon. Sha'arei Tsedek North London Reform Synagogue, March 17, 2012.

Eliany, Marc (El Hi Ani). "The Jews of Morocco: Traditions and Customs." Art Engine Virtual Publications. http://artengine.ca/eliany/html/traditionsof moroccanjews/01tableofcontents.html (accessed February 27, 2012).

Eliav, Mordechai. *Jüdische Erziehung in Deutschland im Zeitalter der Aufklärung und der Emanzipation*. Münster: Waxmann, 2001.

——— . "Pioneers of the Modern Jewish and Religious Education for Girls: The First Schools in Germany in the 19th Century." In *Abiding Challenges: Research Perspectives on Jewish Education: Studies in Memory of Mordechai Bar–Lev*, edited by Yisrael Rich and Michael Rosenak, 145–59. London: Freund, 1999.

Ellinson, Getsel. *Woman and the Mitzvot*. Vol. 2: *The Modest Way*. Translated by Raphael Blumberg. [Jerusalem]: Department for Torah Education and Culture in the Diaspora, World Zionist Organization, 1992.

Elsant, Martin. *Bar Mitzvah Lessons*. Los Angeles: Alef Design Group, 1993.

Emden, Jacob. *Megillat Sefer*. Edited by David Kahana. Warsaw: Izdanīe Akhīasaf, 1896.

———. *Megilat Sefer: The Autobiography of Rabbi Jacob Emden (1696–1776)*. Translated by S. B. Leperer and M. H. Wise. Baltimore MD: PublishYour Sefer, 2011.

Encyclopedia Judaica. 16 vols. Jerusalem: Keter, 1972.

———. 2nd ed. 22 vols. Detroit MI: Thomson Gale, 2007.

Endelman, Todd M. "'A Hebrew to the End': The Emergence of Disraeli's Jewishness." In *The Self-Fashioning of Disraeli, 1818–1851*, edited by Charles Richmond and Paul Smith, 106–30. Cambridge: Cambridge University Press, 1998.

———. *The Jews of Britain: 1656 to 2000*. Berkeley: University of California Press, 2002.

Enelow, H. G. *The Faith of Israel: A Guide for Confirmation*. Cincinnati: Union of American Hebrew Congregations, 1917.

Epstein, Steven. A. *Wage Labor and Guilds in Medieval Europe*. Chapel Hill: University of North Carolina Press, 1991.

Estroff, Sharon. "Policing Bar Mitzvah Crowd: Parents Must Model Good Behavior for Young Adults." *JWeekly.com*, April 29, 2005. Online publication. www.jweekly.com/article/full/25881/policing-bar-mitzvah-crowd (accessed March 16, 2012).

Faccini, Christiana. "The City, the Ghetto and Two Books: Venice and Jewish Early Modernity." *Quest: Issues in Contemporary Jewish History* 2 (October 2011). Online journal. www.quest-cdecjournal.it (accessed February 27, 2012).

Faierstein, Morris M. "Abraham Jagel's 'Leqah Tov' and Its History." *Jewish Quarterly Review* NS 89.3–4 (January–April 1999): 319–50.

Feinstein, Jerome Tov. "The Bas Mitzvah Comes to Our Synagogue." *JOFA Journal* 9.1 (Fall 2010): 42–43. Reprinted from *Orthodox Union*, October 1944.

Feinstein, Moshe. *Sefer Igrot Moshe*. 7 vols. New York: Moriah, 1959–85.

Felstiner, Mary Lowenthal. *To Paint Her Life: Charlotte Salomon in the Nazi Era*. New York: HarperCollins, 1994.

Fendel, Hillel. "Thousands at Belzer Bar Mitzvah in Jerusalem." *Arutz Sheva* 16 (March 2010). Online publication. www.israelnationalnews.com/News /News.aspx/136545#.Ua_JeuBZA0y (accessed June 2, 2012).

Ferziger, Adam S. *Exclusion and Hierarchy: Orthodoxy, Nonobservance, and the Emergence of Modern Jewish Identity*. Philadelphia: University of Pennsylvania Press, 2005.

Fichman, David. "Sumptuary Laws of the Jews from the Fifteenth to the Eighteenth Centuries." Rabbinic thesis, Hebrew Union College, New York, 1913.

"Fiducia" (pseud.). "La maggiorità religiosa delle fanciulle." *Vessillo Israelitico* (1900): 197ff. http://digilander.libero.it/parasha/varie/batmizva/indice.html (accessed February 27, 2012).

Fine, Lawrence, ed. *Judaism in Practice: From the Middle Ages through the Early Modern Period*. Princeton: Princeton University Press, 2001.

Fisher, J.D.C. *Christian Initiation: The Reformation Period: Some Early Reformed Rites of Baptism and Confirmation and Other Contemporary Documents*. London: SPCK, 1970.

Fishman, Talya. *Shaking the Pillars of Exile: 'Voice of a Fool,' an Early Modern Jewish Critique of Rabbinic Culture*. Stanford CA: Stanford University Press, 1997.

Fonséca, Cécile. "Instruction religieuse." *Archives Israélites de France* 3 (1842): 312–16.

Fox, Paul. *The Reformation in Poland: Some Social and Economic Aspects*. Baltimore MD: Johns Hopkins Press, 1924.

Fränkel, Maimon. "Über die Konfirmation bei den Israeliten." *Sulamith* 3.1 (1810): 110–24.

Freedman, Vanessa. "Anglo-Jewish Society in the Late 19th / Early 20th Century: A Window on the Social and Cultural World of Rabbi Dr. Moses Gaster." *JHSE Newsletter* 25 (April 2012): 3.

Freehof, Solomon B. "Ceremonial Creativity among the Ashkenazim." *Jewish Quarterly Review*, 75th anniversary vol. (1967): 210–24.

Freidrichs, Christopher R. "Jewish Household Structure in an Early Modern Town: The Worms Ghetto Census of 1610." *History of the Family* 8.4 (2003): 481–93.

Frommer, Myrna, and Harvey Frommer. *Growing Up Jewish in America: An Oral History*. Lincoln: University of Nebraska Press, 1999.

Gaguine, Shem Tov. *Sefer Keter Shem Tov*. Pts. 1–2. Jerusalem, 1934.

Gamaliel ben Pedahzur. *The Book of Religion, Ceremonies, and Prayers of the Jews*. Translated by Abraham Mears. London: J. Wilcox, 1738.

Gaster, Moses. *History of the Ancient Synagogue of the Spanish and Portuguese Jews, the Cathedral Synagogue of the Jews in England, Situate in Bevis Marks. A Memorial Volume Written Specially to Celebrate the Two-Hundredth Anniversary of Its Inauguration, 1701–1901. With Illustrations and Facsimiles of Deeds and Documents*. London: Harrison and Sons, 1901.

———. Gaster Papers. University College London Archive. Paper and Digital Collection. http://digitool-b.lib.ucl.ac.uk (accessed April 15, 2012).

Geffen, Michael, and Earl Kaplan. "Divorce and Bar Mitzvah: A First Look." Paper presented at the 98th Annual Convention of the American Psychological Association. Boston MA, August 10–14, 1990. Online publication. www.eric.ed.gov (accessed February 29, 2012).

Gershom, Yonassan. "Story of Reb Zalman's B'nai Or Tallit: Interview with Rabbi Zalman Schachter-Shalomi." Online publication. Havurah Shir Hadash, Ashland OR, 2005. www.havurahshirhadash.org/story-of-reb-zalmans-bnai-or-tallit (accessed July 23, 2012).

Gesundheit, Beni. "Bat HaMitzvah Behalakhah. Celebrating a Bat Mitzvah: What Does Halakha Say? Sources and Guided Study." Online publication. Alon Shevut, 2004. www.tefilah.org/שונות/בת-מצוה-בהלכה (accessed May 23, 2012).

Gilat, Yitshak D. "Barukh She-Petarani Me-Onsho Shel Zeh." *Sinai* 118 (1996): 176–86.

———. "Ben Shelosh-Esrei LaMitzvot?" In *Mehkerei Talmud: Talmudic Studies*, edited by Yaakov Sussman and David Rosenthal, 1:39–53. Jerusalem: Hebrew University, Magnes Press, 1990.

Gindi, Steve bar Yakov. "Tefilin." Online publication. Milknhoney Publications, Bet Shemesh, 1998. www.milknhoney.co.il/torah/barmit_history.html (accessed May 9, 2012).

Goitein, S. D. *The Individual: Portrait of a Mediterranean Personality of the High Middle Ages as Reflected in the Cairo Geniza.* Vol. 3 of *A Mediterranean Society: The Jewish Communities of the Arab World as Portrayed in the Documents of the Cairo Geniza.* Berkeley: University of California Press, 1988.

Golb, Norman. *The Jews in Medieval Normandy: A Social and Intellectual History.* Cambridge: Cambridge University Press, 1998.

Goldin, Barbara Diamond. *Bat Mitzvah: A Jewish Girl's Coming of Age.* New York: Puffin Books, 1997.

Goldman, Stacey. "My Zaydie's Tallit: A Lesson in Respect." *Jewish Woman.* Online journal. Chabad-Lubavitch Media Center, 2010. www.chabad .org/theJewishWoman/article_cdo/aid/1185865/jewish/My-Zaydies-Tallit. htm#comments (accessed June 15, 2012).

Goldstein, Elyse. "The Deaf, Jews Who Live in Silence." *Sh'ma* 16.307 (1986): 52–53.

Golinkin, David. "The Participation of Jewish Women in Public Rituals and Torah Study 1845–2010." *Nashim: A Journal of Jewish Women's Studies and Gender Issues* 21 (2011): 46–66.

Google Ngram Viewer. books.google.com/ngrams.

Grant, Lisa D. "Finding Her Right Place in the Synagogue: The Rite of Adult Bat Mitzvah." In *Women Remaking American Judaism*, edited by Riv-Ellen Prell, 279–301. Detroit MI: Wayne State University Press, 2007.

———. "Restorying Jewish Lives Post Adult Bat Mitzvah." *Journal of Jewish Education* 69.2 (2003): 34–51.

Graupe, Heinz Mosche, ed. and trans. *Die Statuten der drei Gemeinden Altona, Hamburg and Wandsbek: Quellen zur Jüdischen Gemeindeorganisation im 17. und 18. Jahrhundert.* (Teil I Einleitung und Übersetzungen, Teil II Texte.) Hamburg: Hans Christians Verlag, 1973.

Green, Arthur. *A Guide to the Zohar.* Stanford CA: Stanford University Press, 2004.

Greenspoon, Leonard J., ed. *Rites of Passage: How Today's Jews Celebrate, Commemorate and Commiserate.* Studies in Jewish Civilization, vol. 21. West Lafayette IN: Purdue University Press, 2010.

Greenwood, E. B. "Poetry and Paradise: A Study in Thematics." *Essays in Criticism* 17.1 (1967): 6–25.

Grimes Ronald L. *Deeply into the Bone: Re-Inventing Rites of Passage.* Berkeley: University of California Press, 2000.

Grossman, Avraham. *Hakmei Ashkenaz ha-rishonim.* Jerusalem: Hebrew University, Magnes Press, 1981.

———. "The Historical Background to the Ordinances on Family Affairs Attributed to Rabbeinu Gershom Me'or ha-Golah ('The Light of the Exile')." In *Jewish History: Essays in Honour of Chimen Abramsky,* edited by Ada Rapaport-Albert and Steven J. Zipperstein, 3–23. London: P. Halban, 1988.

———. *Pious and Rebellious: Jewish Women in Medieval Europe.* Waltham MA: Brandeis University Press; Hanover NH: University Press of New England, 2004.

Grossman, David. *The Zigzag Kid.* Translated by Betsy Rosenberg. London: Bloomsbury, 1997.

"Group Bar/Bat Mitzvah Ceremony Is First for Youth in Russian Far East." Online publication. Jewish Federations of North America, 2005. http://central.ujcfedweb.org/page.aspx?id=75905 (accessed May 14, 2012).

Gryn, Hugo, with Naomi Gryn. *Chasing Shadows.* London: Viking, 2000.

Guldon, Zenon, and Waldemar Kowalski. "Between Tolerance and Abomination: Jews in Sixteenth Century Poland." In *The Expulsion of the Jews: 1492 and After,* edited by Raymond B. Waddington and Arthur H. Williamson, 161–76. New York: Garland, 1994.

Gutmann, Joseph. *The Jewish Life Cycle.* Leiden: Brill, 1987.

Guttmann, Alexander. "Tractate Abot: Its Place in Rabbinic Literature." *Jewish Quarterly Review* NS 41.2 (October 1950): 181–93.

Harris, Maurice H. *The Story of the Jew: Briefly Told from the Patriarchal Era to the Present Day, Together with a Confirmation Manual.* New York: Bloch, 1919.

Harris, Monford. "The Concept of Love in *Sepher Hassidim.*" *Jewish Quarterly Review* NS 50 (1959–60): 13–44.

Hayyim, Yosef, of Baghad. *Ben Ish Hai.* Baghdad: Yehoshua Shelomo, 1912. http://he.wikisource.org/wiki/בן איש חי (accessed February 2, 2012).

Hebrew Observer. Newspaper. London, 1854–69.

Heinemann, Jeremiah. *Religions-Bekenntniss für Israeliten in Fragen und Antworten: zum Gebrauche derer welche die Konfirmation verrichten*. Vienna: G. Ueberreuter, 1813.

Hermannus Quondam Judaeus Opusculum De Conversione Sua. Edited by Gerlinde Niemeyer. Monumenta Germaniae Historica, vol. 4. Weimar: Hermann Böhlaus Nachfolger, 1963.

Herrmann, Klaus. "Jewish Confirmation Sermons in 19th-Century Germany." In *Preaching in Judaism and Christianity: Encounters and Developments from Biblical Times to Modernity*, edited by Alexander Deeg, Walter Homolka, and Heinz-Günther Schöttler, 91–112. Berlin: De Gruyter, 2008.

Herrmann, Klaus, Verena Lucia Nägel, and Hans Joachim Teichler, eds. *History und Oral History—Jüdisches Leben in Berlin*. Booklet and DVD. Berlin: Freie Universität Berlin, Institut für Judaistik, und CeDiS, 2010.

Hertz, Deborah. *How Jews Became Germans: The History of Conversion and Assimilation in Berlin*. New Haven: Yale University Press, 2007.

Herzberg, Arno. "A Town in Eastern Germany: The Story of Filehne—A Memoir." *Leo Baeck Institute Yearbook* 42 (1997): 327–36.

Heschel, Abraham Joshua. *God in Search of Man: A Philosophy of Judaism*. 1955. Reprint. London: Souvenir Press, 2009.

Hey Hey It's Esther Blueberger. DVD. 2008. Pinewood: High Flyers Films, 2009.

Hezser, Catherine. *Jewish Literacy in Roman Palestine*. Texts and Studies in Ancient Judaism, 81. Tübingen: Mohr Siebeck, 2001.

Hilton, Michael. *The Christian Effect on Jewish Life*. London: SCM Press, 1994.

Hobsbawm, Eric, and Terence Ranger, eds. *The Invention of Tradition*. 1983. Reprint. Cambridge: Cambridge University Press, 2012.

Hoffman, Justin. "The Organization and Administration of Schools in Classical Judaism." *Religious Education* 87.3 (1992): 416–34.

Hoffman, Lawrence A. *Covenant of Blood: Circumcision and Gender in Rabbinic Judaism*. Chicago: University of Chicago Press, 1996.

Holm, Jean, and John Westerdale Bowker, eds. *Rites of Passage*. London: Pinter Publishers, 1994.

Holzer, Isaak. "Aus dem Leben der alten Judengemeinde zu Worms: Nach dem 'Minhagbuch' des Juspa Schammes." *Zeitschrift für die Geschichte der Juden in Deutschland* 5.2–3 (1934): 169–81.

Horaot meiRabbanei Tzarfat. In *Piskei Rabbeinu Yehiel MiParis*, edited by Eliyahu Dov Pines. Jerusalem: Mekhon Yerushalayim, 1973.

Hsia, R. Po-Chia. *The Myth of Ritual Murder*. New Haven: Yale University Press, 1988.

Hsia, R. Po-Chia, and Hartmut Lehmann, eds. *In and Out of the Ghetto: Jewish-Gentile Relations in Late Medieval and Early Modern Germany*. Publications of the German Historical Institute. Washington DC: Cambridge University Press, 1995.

Hyamson, Albert M. *The Sephardim of England: A History of the Spanish and Portuguese Jewish Community, 1492–1951*. London: Methuen, 1951.

Hyman, Paula E. *Gender and Assimilation in Modern Jewish History: The Roles and Representation of Women*. Seattle: University of Washington Press, 1995.

———. "The Introduction of Bat Mitzvah in Conservative Judaism in Postwar America." *Yivo Annual* 19 (1990): 133–46.

Hyman, Paula, and Dalia Ofer, eds. *Jewish Women: A Comprehensive Historical Encyclopedia*. Online publication. Shalvi, Jerusalem, 2006. http://jwa.org/encyclopedia (accessed February 6, 2012).

Ingall, Marjorie. "Bat Mitzvahs Get Too Glitzy." *Tablet Magazine*, March 27, 2012. Online publication. www.tabletmag.com (accessed February 20, 2014).

Ingber, Judith Brin. *Seeing Israeli and Jewish Dance*. Detroit MI: Wayne State University Press, 2011.

Isaacson, Judith, and Deborah Rosenbloom. *Bar and Bat Mitzvah in Israel: The Ultimate Family Sourcebook*. [Bethesda MD]: Israel Info-Access, 1998.

Israelite (Cincinnati). Newspaper. Weekly since 1854 (*American Israelite* since 1874). Online archive. www.israeliteonline.com.

Jacob ben Asher. *Tur: Orach Chayyim*, Vol. 1. Warsaw: Bi-defus ha-ahim bene Shemuel ben Hayyim Orgelbrand, 1882.

Jacobs, Joseph. *The Jews of Angevin England: Documents and Records from Latin and Hebrew Sources Printed and Manuscript for the First Time Collected and Translated*. English History by Contemporary Writers. London: David Nutt, 1893.

Jagel, Abraham. *Catechismus Judaeorum: in disputatione et dialogo magistri ac discipuli scriptus a Rabbi Abraham Jagel, Monte Silicis oriundo; Et Latinus ex Hebraeo Factus à Ludovico de Compeigne de Veil*. London: A. Godbid and J. Playford, 1679.

Jakimyszyn, Anna, ed. and trans. *Di Takkana Kuf Kuf Krake: Statut Krakowskiej Gminy Żydowskiej Z Roku 1595 I Jego Uzupełnienia tłumaczenie sporządzone na podstawie odpisu Majera Bałabana wstęp*. Kraków: Księgarnia Akademicka, 2005.

Jeffay, Nathan. "Rainbow Flags Aflutter, Orthodox Groups Enter a Float in Gay Pride Parade." *Jewish Daily Forward*, June 24, 2011. www.forward.com/articles/138719/#ixzz1nxJbVRn9 (accessed March 1, 2012).

Jellinek, Adolf. *Die erste Confirmations-Feier in der Leipzig-Berliner Synagoge am zweiten Tage Des Wochenfestes 5607 (22. Mai 1847)*. Leipzig: C. L. Fritzsche, 1847.

Jewish Chronicle (London). Newspaper. Weekly since 1840.

Jewish Encyclopedia, The. 12 vols. New York: Funk and Wagnalls, 1901–6.

Jewish Legal Heritage Society. "Takkanot neged Motarot." Online publication. www.mishpativri.org.il/motarot/motarotindex.htm (accessed December 31, 2007).

Jewish Life Cycle. DVD. Or Yehuda: Doko Entertainment, 1996.

Jewish Standard. Newspaper. London, 1888–91.

Jewish Virtual Library. Online publication. American-Israeli Cooperative Enterprise. www.jewishvirtuallibrary.org (accessed June 23, 2013).

"Jewish Witness to a European Century: An Interactive Database of Jewish Memory." Online Oral History Project. Vienna: Study Center of Jewish Life in 20th Century Central Europe, since 2000. www.centropa.org (accessed June 23, 2013).

Jews' Free School Magazine. London: Jews' Free School, 1910–39.

Joseph, Norma Baumel. "Bar Mitzvah, Bat Mitzvah." *Encyclopedia Judaica.* 2nd ed. (2007): 3:164–66.

——— . "Bat Mitzvah: Historical and Halachic Aspects." *JOFA Journal* 9.1 (Fall 2010): 4–5.

——— . "Ritual, Law and Praxis: An American Response to Bat Mitzvah Celebrations." *Modern Judaism* 22 (2002): 234–60.

Josephus. *The Works of Josephus Complete and Unabridged.* Translated by William Whiston. Peabody MA: Hendrickson Publishers, 1987.

Juspa Schammes (R. Jousep). *Minhagim di-K.K. Vermaisa: Wormser Minhagbuch.* Edited by Jair Chajim Bachrach, Benjamin Salomon Hamburger, and Erich Zimmer. Vol. 1. Jerusalem: Mekhon Yerushalayim, 1988. Vol. 2. Jerusalem: Mekhon Yerushalayim, 1992.

Kabakoff, Jacob. "Some Notable Bibliographers I Have Known." Rosaline and Meyer Feinstein Lecture Series, 1999. Online publication. www2.jewish culture.org/jewish_scholarship/jewish_scholarship_feinstein_kabakoff.html (accessed October 15, 2007).

Kadden, Barbara Binder, and Bruce Kadden. *Teaching Jewish Life Cycle: Traditions and Activities.* Denver: A.R.E. Publishing, 1997.

Kahn, Ellie. "Centenarian Celebrates Fourth Bar Mitzvah." *JewishJournal.com,* November 13, 2008. Online publication. www.jewishjournal.com/bar_and_ bat_mitzvahs/article/centenarian_celebrates_fourth_bar_mitzvah_20081113 (accessed May 15, 2012).

Kanarfogel, Ephraim. *The Intellectual History and Rabbinic Culture of Medieval Ashkenaz.* Detroit MI: Wayne State University Press, 2013.

——— . *Jewish Education and Society in the High Middle Ages.* Detroit MI: Wayne State University Press, 1992.

——— . *"Peering through the Lattices": Mystical, Magical and Pietistic Dimensions in the Tosafist Period.* Detroit MI: Wayne State University Press, 2000.

Kaplan, Marion A., ed. *Jewish Daily Life in Germany, 1618–1945*. Oxford: Oxford University Press, 2005.

Katz, Jacob. "Halakhah and Kabbalah as Competing Disciplines of Study." In *Jewish Spirituality from the Sixteenth-Century Revival to the Present*, edited by Arthur Green, 34–63. London: Routledge and Kegan Paul, 1987.

Keeping Up with the Steins. DVD. Los Angeles: Miramax/Winsome, 2006.

Kerner, Samuel. "Le Règlement de la communauté juive de Metz de 1769 d'après un manuscript inédit." *Annales de l'Est* 24 (1972): 201–53.

Kessner, Carole S. "Kaplan and the Role of Women in Judaism." In *The American Judaism of Mordecai M. Kaplan*, edited by Emanuel S. Goldsmith, Mel Scult, and Robert M. Seltzer, 335–56. New York: New York University Press, 1992.

Keyser, Jason. "Mass Bar Mitzvah Lifts Violence-Weary Israelis." Online publication. Beliefnet, 2001. www.beliefnet.com/News/2001/04/Mass-Bar-Mitzvah-Lifts-Violence-Weary-Israelis.aspx?p=1 (accessed May 14, 2012).

Kimmel, Eric A. *Bar Mitzvah: A Jewish Boy's Coming of Age*. New York: Puffin Books, 1997.

Kirchner, Paul Christian. *Jüdisches Ceremoniel. 1717*. Reprint. Hildesheim: Olms, 1974.

Klagsbrun, Francine. "How the Bat Mitzvah Has Changed: A Grandmother Reflects." *Jewish Week* (New York), February 8, 2011.

Klapheck, Elisa. *Fräulein Rabbiner Jonas: The Story of the First Woman Rabbi*. San Francisco: Jossey-Bass, 2004.

Klapper, Melissa R. *Jewish Girls Coming of Age in America, 1860–1920*. New York: New York University Press, 2005.

Klein, Daniel M., and Freke Vuijst. *The Half-Jewish Book: A Celebration*. New York: Villard, 2000.

Kley, Eduard. *Predigten in dem Neuen Israelitischen Tempel zu Hamburg*. Erste Sammlung. Hamburg: Ben Hoffmann und Campe, 1819.

Kober, Adolf. "Emancipation's Impact on the Education and Vocational Training of German Jewry (Concluded)." *Jewish Social Studies* 16.2 (April 1954): 151–76.

———. "150 Years of Religious Instruction." *Leo Baeck Institute Yearbook* 2.1 (1957): 98–118.

Kranson, Rachel. "More Bar than Mitzvah: Anxieties over Bar Mitzvah Receptions in Postwar America." In Greenspoon, *Rites of Passage*, 9–24.

Krasner, Jonathan, and Joellyn Wallen Zollman. "Are You There God? Judaism and Jewishness in Judy Blume's Adolescent Fiction." *Shofar: An Interdisciplinary Journal of Jewish Studies* 29.1 (2010): 22–47.

Leavy, Patricia. *Oral History*. Oxford: Oxford University Press, 2011.

Lebendiger, Israel. "The Minor in Jewish Law." *Jewish Quarterly Review* NS 6.4 (April 1916): 459–93.

Leeser, Isaac. *Catechism for Jewish Children, Designed as a Religious Manual for House and School.* 4th ed. 1839. Reprint. Philadelphia: Sherman and Co., 1873.

Lehrer, Leibush. *Camp Boiberik: The Growth of an Idea.* Pamphlet. [New York]: Boiberik, [1959].

Leigh, Michael. "Women in the Synagogue." *Synagogue Review* (London) (December 1961): 103–6.

Leneman, Helen, ed. *Bar/Bat Mitzvah Basics: A Practical Family Guide to Coming of Age Together.* 2nd ed. Woodstock VT: Jewish Lights Publishing, 2001.

———, ed. *Bar/Bat Mitzvah Education: A Sourcebook.* Denver: A.R.E. Publishing, 1993.

Levine, Chaim. "Understanding the Bat Mitzvah Attack." Online publication. Aish HaTorah, Jerusalem, 2002. www.aish.com/jw/id/48892032.html (accessed February 18, 2012).

Levy, Harold. *Becoming and Remaining Barmitzvah.* Pamphlet. London: United Synagogue, 1971.

Liberles, Robert. "Leopold Stein and the Paradox of Reform Clericalism, 1844–1862." *Leo Baeck Institute Yearbook* 27.1 (1982): 261–79.

Lilker, Shalom. *Kibbutz Judaism: A New Tradition in the Making.* East Brunswick NJ: Cornwall Books, 1982.

Lipstadt, Deborah E. "Feminism and American Judaism." In *Women and American Judaism: Historical Perspectives,* edited by Pamela Susan Nadell and Jonathan D. Sarna, 291–308. Hanover NH: University Press of New England, 2001.

Loewe, Raphael. "Solomon Marcus Schiller-Szinessy, 1820–1890: First Reader in Talmudic and Rabbinic Literature at Cambridge." *Transactions of the Jewish Historical Society of England* 21 (1968): 148–89.

Lohmann, Ingrid, ed. *Hevrat Hinukh Nearim: Die jüdische Freischule in Berlin (1778–1825) im Umfeld preussischer Bildungspolitik und jüdischer Kultusreform: eine Quellensamlung.* 2 vols. Münster: Waxmann. 2001.

London. *Laws of the Congregation of the Great Synagogue, Duke's Place, London.* London: J. Wertheimer, 1863.

———. *Takkanot HaKehilla deKahal Kadosh Ashkenazim deBeit HaKnesset HaGedolah beLondon.* London: Yehuda Leib ben Alexander, 1791.

———. *Takkanot LeAdat Yeshurun deKehilla Kedosha deBeit HaKnesset HaGedolah Duks Pleihs beLondon.* London: Joseph Wertheimer, 1827.

———. *Takkanot miHevra Kadisha Gemilut Hasadim deBeit HaKnesset HaGedolah miLondon.* London: Galabin and Marchant, 1810.

Löw, Leopold. *Die Lebensalter in der Jüdischen Literatur. Von Physiologischem, Rechts-, Sitten-u. Religionsgeschichtlichem Stankpunkte Betrachtet.* Vol. 2. of *Beitrage zur Jüdischen Alterthumskunde.* Szegedin: Druck von S. Burger, 1875.

Lowenstein, Steven M. *The Mechanics of Change: Essays in the Social History of German Jewry.* Atlanta: Scholars Press, 1992.

Lowther Clarke, W. K., and Charles Harris, eds. *Liturgy and Worship: A Companion to the Prayer Books of the Anglican Communion.* London: SPCK, 1932.

Luria, Solomon. *Sefer Yam shel Shelomoh: Al Massekhet Bava Kamma.* New York: LeHasig Be'Artzot Ha'Brit and Hotzeit Idishkit, 1985.

Lyons, Alexander. *At Sinai: A Manual of Confirmation.* New York: Bloch Publishing Co., 1922.

Maag, Christopher, "Having a Bat Mitzvah in Their 90s Because It's a Hoot." *New York Times,* March 21, 2009. www.nytimes.com/2009/03/22 /us/22batmitzvah.html (accessed January 3, 2012).

Maccoby, Hyam. *Judaism on Trial: Jewish-Christian Disputations in the Middle Ages.* Littman Library of Jewish Civilization. East Brunswick NJ: Associated University Presses, 1982.

Macdowell, Mississippi Fred (pseud.). "The Bar Mitzvah of the Child Soldier Grandson of Rabbi Shmuel Salant." Online blog, August 29, 2010. onthemainline.blogspot.co.uk/2010/08/bar-mitzvah-of-child-soldier -grandson.html (accessed May 22, 2012).

——. "An 18th Century Chanukah Pastime—Going to the Opera." Online blog, December 2, 2010. http://onthemainline.blogspot.co.uk/2010/12 /18th-century-chanukah-passtime-going-to.html (accessed May 25, 2012).

——. "On Reverend's Handbooks and Bar Mitzvah Speeches for American Boys of a Century Ago." Online blog, December 26, 2011. onthemainline .blogspot.com/2011/12/on-reverends-handbooks-and-bar-mitzvah.html (accessed February 16, 2012).

Magida, Arthur J. *Opening the Doors of Wonder: Reflections on Religious Rites of Passage.* Berkeley: University of California Press, 2006.

Maharil. *Sefer Maharil: Minhagim Shel R. Yaakov Moellin (The Book of Maharil).* Edited by Shlomo Spitzer. Jerusalem: Mekhon Yerushalayim, 1989.

——. *Sefer She'elot uTeshuvot.* Krakow: Fischer and Deutscher, 1881.

Malkiel, David, ed. *The Lion Shall Roar: Leon Modena and His World.* Jerusalem: Hebrew University, 2003.

Mann, Jacob. "The Responsa of the Babylonian Geonim as a Source of Jewish History." *Jewish Quarterly Review* NS 7.4 (April 1917): 457–90.

Marcus, Ivan G. *The Jewish Life Cycle: Rites of Passage from Biblical to Modern Times.* Seattle: University of Washington Press, 2004.

———. *Piety and Society: The Jewish Pietists of Medieval Germany*. Leiden: Brill, 1981.

———. *Rituals of Childhood: Jewish Acculturation in Medieval Europe*. New Haven: Yale University Press, 1996.

Marcus, Jacob Rader. *The American Jewish Woman: A Documentary History*. New York: Ktav, 1981.

———. *Israel Jacobson: The Founder of the Reform Movement in Judaism*. 2nd ed. Cincinnati: Hebrew Union College Press, 1972.

Marks, D. W. *Sermons Preached on Various Occasions, at the West London Synagogue of British Jews*. London: R. Groombridge and Sons, 1851.

Marmorstein, A. "Sur un auteur français inconnu du treizième siècle (Or. Brit Mus. 2853)." *Revue des Études Juives* 76 (1923): 113–31.

Marrus, Michael R. *The Politics of Assimilation: A Study of the French Jewish Community at the Time of the Dreyfus Affair*. Oxford: Clarendon Press, 1971.

Marx, Alexander. *Studies in Jewish History and Booklore*. New York: Jewish Theological Seminary of America, 1944.

Massekhet Soferim. Edited by Michael Higger. New York: Debe Rabbanan, 1937.

Matthews, Karen. "Convict Stages Son's Bar Mitzvah in NYC Jail." Online publication. Jewish Federations of North America, 2009. central.ujcfedweb.org /page.aspx?id=201800 (accessed May 14, 2012).

McDonald, Nicola F., and W. M. Ormrod, eds. *Rites of Passage: Cultures of Transition in the Fourteenth Century*. York: York Medieval Press, 2004.

Mead, Margaret. *Coming of Age in Samoa: A Psychological Study of Primitive Youth for Western Civilisation*. 1928. Reprint. New York: Morrow, 1961.

Melabev. "Intergenerational Bar-Mitzvah Project in Beit Shemesh: Bar Mitzvah Boys Learn to Care for Others, Including the Elderly." Online publication. Jerusalem. melabev.org/intergenerational-bar-mitzvah-project-beit -shemesh-bar-mitzvah-boys-learn-care-others-including-elderly/ (accessed June 23, 2013).

———. "Melabev Bat-Mitzvah Outreach-the Twilight Years and the Teens." Online publication. Jerusalem. http://melabev.org/800/ (accessed June 23, 2013).

Mendelson, Yaakov Ben Tzion HaCohen. *Mishnat Yaavetz*. Vol. 3. Newark: Y. Ben Tsiyon ha-Kohen Mendelson, 1925.

Mendes, Abraham P. *Sermons*. London: John Chapman, 1855.

Meyer, Michael A. *The Origins of the Modern Jew: Jewish Identity and European Culture in Germany, 1749–1824*. Detroit MI: Wayne State University Press, 1967.

———. "The Religious Reform Controversy in the Berlin Jewish Community, 1814–1823." *Leo Baeck Institute Yearbook* 24.1 (1979): 139–55.

———. *Response to Modernity: A History of the Reform Movement in Judaism.* New York: Oxford University Press, 1988.

———. "Women in the Thought and Practice of the European Jewish Reform Movement." In *Gender and Jewish History*, edited by Marion A. Kaplan and Deborah Dash Moore, 139–57. Bloomington: Indiana University Press, 2011.

Meyers, Ruth A. "Christian Rites of Adolescence." In *Life Cycles in Jewish and Christian Worship*, edited by Paul F. Bradshaw and Lawrence A. Hoffman, 55–80. "Two Liturgical Traditions" series, vol. 4. Notre Dame IN: University of Notre Dame Press, 1996

Miccoli, Dario. "Moving Histories: The Jews and Modernity in Alexandria, 1881–1919." *Quest: Issues in Contemporary Jewish History* 2 (October 2011). Online journal. www.quest-cdecjournal.it/focus.php?id=223 (accessed February 27, 2012).

Michaelson, Tzevi Yehezkel. *Sefer Pinot HaBayit.* Petrikov, USSR: Isaiah Zev Palman, 1925.

"Minyanim Worldwide." Online listing. www.shirahadasha.com (accessed February 8, 2012).

Mishnah. *Mishnayot Mevoarot.* Edited by Pinchas Kehati. 12 vols. Jerusalem: Heichal Shelomoh, 1977.

Mitchell, Claudia, and Jacqueline Reid-Walsh. *Girl Culture: An Encyclopedia.* Westport CT: Greenwood Press, 2008.

Modena, Leon. *The History of the Rites, Customs, and Manner of Life, of the Present Jews, throughout the World, Translated into English by Edmund Chilmead.* London: Printed for J. Martin and J. Ridley, 1650.

———. *Igrot Rabbi Yehudah Aryeh MiModena Letters of Rabbi Leon Modena.* Edited by Yacob Boksenboim. Tel Aviv: Chaim Rosenberg School of Jewish Studies, Tel-Aviv University, 1984.

———. *Midbar Yehudah MiDerashot Yehudah Aryeh.* Venice: Daniel Zanetti, 1602.

Momigliano, Arnoldo. "A Medieval Jewish Autobiography." In *History and Imagination: Essays in Honour of H. R. Trevor-Roper*, edited by Hugh Lloyd-Jones, Valerie Pearl, and Blair Worden, 30–36. London: Duckworth, 1981.

Monypenny, William Flavelle. *The Life of Benjamin Disraeli Earl of Beaconsfield.* Vol. 1: *1804–1837.* London: John Murray, 1910.

Mordecai HaCohen. *Sefer Siftei Cohen, Ki Siftei Cohen Yishmeru Daat ve Torah Yevakshu MiPihu.* Venice: Daniel Zanetti, 1605.

Morgan, David T. "Judaism in Eighteenth-Century Georgia." *Georgia Historical Quarterly* 58.1 (1974): 41–54.

Morosini, Giulio. *Derekh Emunah. Via delle fede mostrata agli ebrei.* Rome: Nella Stamparia della Sacra Cong. de Prop. Fide, 1683.

Morrison, Karl F. *Conversion and Text: The Cases of Augustine of Hippo, Herman-Judah, and Constantine Tsatsos.* Charlottesville: University Press of Virginia, 1992.

Muir, Edwin. *Ritual in Early Modern Europe.* Cambridge: Cambridge University Press, 1997.

Mussafia, Hayyim Yitshak. *She'elot uTushuvot Hayyim VeHesed.* Vol. 2. Jerusalem: HaKatav Institute, 1987.

Naftali Ashkenazi. *Imrei Shefer.* Venice: Daniel Zanetti, 1601.

Neusner, Jacob. *Judaism and Christianity in the Age of Constantine.* Chicago: University of Chicago Press, 1987.

——— . *Understanding Rabbinic Judaism: From Talmudic to Modern Times.* New York: Ktav, 1974.

"New York Architecture." Online publication, 2004. www.nyc-architecture.com (accessed April 15, 2012).

Occident, The. Chicago, 1843–69, monthly. Online archive. theoccident.com /Occident/index.html.

Olitzky, Kerry M., and Ronald H. Isaacs. *Rediscovering Judaism: Bar and Bat Mitzvah for Adults.* Hoboken NJ: Ktav, 1997.

Olitzky, Kerry M., and Marc Lee Raphael, eds. *The American Synagogue: A Historical Dictionary and Sourcebook.* Westport CT: Greenwood Press, 1996.

Oppenheimer, Mark. *Thirteen and a Day: The Bar and Bat Mitzvah across America.* New York: Farrar, Straus and Giroux, 2005.

Orme, Nicholas. *Medieval Children.* New Haven: Yale University Press, 2001.

Orsborn, Carol Matzkin. "The Initiation of Confirmation in Judaism: A Psychohistorical Study of a Jewish Ritual Innovation." PhD diss., Vanderbilt University, 2002.

Oxford English Dictionary. 20 vols. Oxford: Clarendon Press, 1989.

Pärdi, Heiki. "The Crumbling of the Peasant Time Concept in Estonia." *Pro Ethnologica* 9:61–82. Tartu: Publications of Estonian National Museum, 2000.

Paterson, Moira, ed. *The Bar Mitzvah Book.* London: W. H. Allen, 1975.

Paz, David, Oz Almog, and Shay Rudin. "Bar Mitzvah Celebrations in the Secular Sabra Community." *People Israel,* 2008. Online publication. www .peopleil.org/details.aspx?itemID=7574 (accessed February 28, 2012).

Perlmutter, Leila Herman. "Coming of Age in Remarried Families: The Bar Mitzvah." *Journal of Jewish Communal Service* 59.1 (1982): 58–65.

Philipson, David. *Confirmation in the Synagogue* [Cincinnati]: Bloch Printing Co., [1891].

——— . *The Reform Movement in Judaism.* New York: Macmillan, 1931.

Philipson, David, and Louis Grossman, eds. *Selected Writings of Isaac Mayer Wise.* Cincinnati: Robert Clarke, 1900.

Philadelphia Jewish Exponent. Newspaper. Philadelphia. Weekly since 1887.

Phillips, Helen. "Rites of Passage in French and English Romances." In *Rites of Passage: Cultures of Transition in the Fourteenth Century*, edited by Nicola F. McDonald and W. M. Ormrod, 83–107. York: York Medieval Press, 2004.

"Phlichten der Israelitischen Syndiken." *Sulamith* 2.2 (1809): 305–12. www.compactmemory.de (accessed June 23, 2013).

"Phlichten der Rabbiner." *Sulamith* 2.2 (1809): 300–305. www.compactmemory.de (accessed June 23, 2013).

Pilch, Judah. "Leading Jewish Educators of Blessed Memory." *Journal of Jewish Education* 40.4 (1971): 9–19.

Pinkas Hakehillot Germanyah: Encyclopaedia of Jewish Communities, Germany. Jerusalem: Yad Vashem, 1992.

Plain Dealer (Cleveland OH). Newspaper. Daily since 1842.

Plaut, W. Gunther. *The Rise of Reform Judaism: A Sourcebook of Its European Origins*. New York: World Union for Progressive Judaism, 1963.

Pleck, Elizabeth H. *Celebrating the Family: Ethnicity, Consumer Culture, and Family Rituals*. Cambridge MA: Harvard University Press, 2000.

Pollack, Herman. *Jewish Folkways in Germanic Lands (1648–1806): Studies in Aspects of Daily Life*. Cambridge MA: MIT Press, 1971.

Pool, David, and Tamar de Sola. *An Old Faith in the New World: Portrait of Shearith Israel, 1654–1954*. New York: Columbia University Press, 1955.

Preschel, Tuvia. "Isaac Rivkind (1895–1968)." *Proceedings of the American Academy for Jewish Research* 37 (1969): xxxii–xxxiv.

Raphael, Marc Lee. *The Synagogue in America: A Short History*. New York: New York University Press, 2011.

Rappaport, Jill. *Mazal Tov: Celebrities' Bar and Bat Mitzvah Memories*. New York: Simon and Schuster, 2007.

Rayner, John. "From Barmitzvah to Confirmation." Sermon at the Liberal Jewish Synagogue, London, 1961. MS. Leo Baeck College Library, London.

"Reform Movement's Resolution on Patrilineal Descent (March 15, 1983): The Status of Children of Mixed Marriages." Final text of the Report of the Committee on Patrilineal Descent adopted on March 15, 1983. Online publication. Jewish Virtual Library, American-Israeli Cooperative Enterprise, 2002. www.jewishvirtuallibrary.org/jsource/Judaism/patrilineal1.html (accessed March 31, 2012).

Reilly, Joan, and Bert Metter. *Bar Mitzvah, Bat Mitzvah: The Ceremony, the Party, and How the Day Came to Be*. New York: Clarion Books, 2007.

Resnick, David. "Confirmation Education from the Old World to the New: A 150 Year Follow-Up." *Modern Judaism* 31.2 (2011): 213–28.

Richler, Mordecai. *The Apprenticeship of Duddy Kravitz*. 1959. Reprint. Toronto: Penguin, 1995.

Richmond, Charles. "Disraeli's Education." In *The Self-Fashioning of Disraeli, 1818–1851*, edited by Charles Richmond and Paul Smith, 16–41. Cambridge: Cambridge University Press, 1998.

Rigal, Lawrence, and Rosita Rosenberg. *Liberal Judaism: The First Hundred Years*. London: Liberal Judaism, Union of Liberal and Progressive Synagogues, 2004.

Rivkind, Isaac. *Le-Ot u-le-Zikkaron: Toledot "Bar Mitzvah" VeHitpat-huto BeHayyei HaAm Ve Tarbuto: Bar Mitzvah: A Study in Jewish Cultural History with an Annotated Bibliography*. New York: Shulsinger Bros., 1942.

Romain, Jonathan, ed. *Great Reform Lives: Rabbis Who Dared to Differ*. London: Movement for Reform Judaism, 2010.

Rose, Alison. *Jewish Women in Fin de Siècle Vienna*. Austin: University of Texas Press, 2008.

Rosenbaum, Judith. "Jewish Feminist Leaders: What Drove Jewish Women into the Feminist Movement?" *MyJewishLearning.com*. Online publication. www.myjewishlearning.com/history/Modern_History/1948-1980/America/Liberal_Politics/Feminism.shtml (accessed June 5, 2012).

Ross, Tamar. "Modern Orthodoxy and the Challenge of Feminism." In *Jews and Gender: The Challenge to Hierarchy*, edited by Jonathan Frankel. Studies in Contemporary Jewry XVI. Oxford: Published for the Avraham Harman Institute by Oxford University Press, 2000.

Roth, Cecil. "Bar Mitzvah: Its History and Its Associations." In *Bar Mitzvah Illustrated*, edited by Abraham I. Katsh, 15–22. New York: Shengold Publishers, 1955.

———. "Forced Baptisms in Italy: A Contribution to the History of Jewish Persecution." *Jewish Quarterly Review* NS 27.2 (October 1936): 117–36.

———. "Sumptuary Laws of the Community of Carpentras." *Jewish Quarterly Review* NS 18.4 (April 1928): 357–83.

———. *Venice*. Philadelphia: Jewish Publication Society of America, 1930.

Ruben, Bruce L. *Max Lilienthal: The Making of the American Rabbinate*. Detroit MI: Wayne State University Press, 2011.

Rubin, Nissan. "Coping with the Value of the *pidyon ha'ben* Payment in Rabbinic Literature: An Example of a Social Change Process." *Jewish History* 10.1 (Spring 1996): 39–61.

Rubinstein, Aryeh. "Isaac Mayer Wise: A New Appraisal." *Jewish Social Studies* 39.1–2 (1977): 53–74.

Sales, Amy, Nicole Samuel, and Alexander Zablotsky. *Engaging Jewish Teens: A Study of New York Teens, Parents and Practitioners*. Waltham MA: Maurice and Marilyn Cohen Center for Modern Jewish Studies, Brandeis University, 2011.

Salkin, Jeffrey K. *Putting God on the Guest List: How to Reclaim the Spiritual Meaning of Your Child's Bar or Bat Mitzvah*. Woodstock VT: Jewish Lights Publishing, 1992.

Saperstein, Marc. *Jewish Preaching, 1200–1800: An Anthology*. Yale Judaica Series, vol. 26. New Haven: Yale University Press, 1989.

Satten, Sandra C. *In the Thirteenth Year*. Los Angeles: Alef Design Group, 2000.

Schacter, Jacob Joseph. "Rabbi Jacob Emden: Life and Major Works." PhD diss., Harvard University, 1988.

Schacter, Naomi. "The Changing Status of Orthodox Jewish Women." Online publication. Institute for Jewish Ideas and Ideals, 2009. www.jewishideas.org/ articles/changing-status-orthodox-jewish-women (accessed June 4, 2012).

Schapiro, Yerachmiel. "Birthdays in Halacha." *Journal of Halacha and Contemporary Society* 51 (2005): 66–84.

Schauss, Hayyim. *The Lifetime of a Jew throughout the Ages of Jewish History*. New York: Union of American Hebrew Congregations, 1950.

Schiller-Szinessy, S. M. *Confirmation—A Genuine Jewish Institution: A Sermon, Delivered on* שבועות של ראשון יום *5612 (24th May, 1852) at the Solemnization of the First Ceremony of Confirmation in the Halliwell-Street Synagogue, Manchester*. Manchester: Cave and Sever, 1852.

Schneerson, Menachem M. *I Will Write It in Their Hearts: A Treasury of Letters from the Lubavitcher Rebbe: Selections from Igros Kodesh*. Brooklyn NY: Sichos in English, 1999.

Schneider, Moira. "South Africa's 'Blind Chazzan,' 96, Just Held His 3rd Bar Mitzvah." *JWeekly*, April 25, 2003. Online edition. www.jweekly.com/article/ full/19780/south-africa-s-blind-chazzan-96-just-held-his-3rd-bar-mitzvah (accessed May 12, 2012).

Schoenfeld, Stuart. "Changing Patterns of North American Bar Mitzvah: Towards a History and Sociological Analysis." MS. Department of Sociology, Glendon College, York University, Ont., December 1984. www .policyarchive.org/handle/10207/bitstreams/10138.pdf (accessed February 16, 2012).

———. "Integration into the Group and Sacred Uniqueness: An Analysis of Adult Bat Mitzvah." In *Persistence and Flexibility: Anthropological Perspectives on the American Jewish Experience*, edited by Walter P. Zenner, 117–36. Albany: State University of New York Press, 1988.

———. "Recent Publications on Bar/Bat Mitzvah: Their Implications for Jewish Education Research and Practice." *Religious Education* 89.4 (1994): 593–604.

———. "Too Much Bar and Not Enough Mitzvah? A Proposed Research Agenda on Bar/Bat Mitzvah." *Journal of Jewish Education* 76.4 (2010): 301–14.

Scholem, Gershom. *Major Trends in Jewish Mysticism*. New York: Schocken Books, 1961.

——— . *Sabbatai Sevi: The Mystical Messiah, 1626–1676*. London: Routledge and Kegan Paul, 1973.

Schorsch, Ismar. "From Wolfenbüttel to Wissenschaft: The Divergent Paths of Isaak Markus Jost and Leopold Zunz." *Leo Baeck Institute Yearbook* 22.1 (1977): 109–28.

Schroeder, H. J., ed. and trans. *Canons and Decrees of the Council of Trent*. 1941. Reprint. Rockford IL: Tan Books and Publishers, 1978.

Schudt, Johann Jacob, ed. "Neue Franckfurter Jüdische Kleider-ordnung." In *Jüdischer Merckwürdigkeiten*, vol. 4. Frankfurt am Main: M. C. Multzen, 1717.

"Seder Chazzanut Amsterdam." Online publication. Amsterdam Portuguese Community, 2005. www.chazzanut-esnoga.org/Life_Cycle/bar_mitzwah/bar-mitzwah.htm (accessed February 15, 2008).

Seeliger, Herbert. "Origin and Growth of the Berlin Jewish Community." *Leo Baeck Institute Yearbook* 3.1 (1958): 159–68.

Selikovitch, P. G., ed. *Der Idish-Amerikaner Redner. The Jewish-American Orator: Containing 517 Choice Speeches, Toasts and Sermons in Yiddish, English and Ancient Hebrew, Written Expressly by the Most Famous Orators and Writers*. New York: Hebrew Publishing Co., 1907.

Sered, Meir Maynard. "The Bar Mitzvah Speech: History and Decline, 1575–1970." Master's thesis, Northwestern University, 1971.

Serious Man, A. DVD. Los Angeles: Focus Features, 2010.

Shabtai Sofer. *Siddur HaMedakdeik HaGadol Baki bekhol hadrei haTorah mi-ha-R. Shabtai Sofer be-R. Yitzhak mi-Premishla*. Baltimore MD: Yeshivat Ner Yisrael, 2002.

——— . *Tefilah Nekhonah Zakhah uM'usheret BeTakhlit Hashelemut M'uteret*. London: Talmud Torah veHinukh Yeladim, 1827.

Shahar, Shulamith. *Childhood in the Middle Ages*. London: Routledge, 1990.

Shalom Center. "Guide to an Eco-Bar/Bat Mitzvah Observance." Online publication, 2009. www.theshalomcenter.org/node/1620 (accessed March 1, 2012).

Shellnutt, Kate. "Sharing Good Fortune with a Second Mitzvah." *Houston Chronicle*, June 24, 2010. Online edition. www.chron.com/life/houston-belief/article/Sharing-good-fortune-with-a-second-mitzvah-1706950.php (accessed May 10, 2012).

Sherwin, Byron L. *In Partnership with God: Contemporary Jewish Law and Ethics*. Syracuse NY: Syracuse University Press, 1990.

Siddur Tefilat Yaakov HaShalem, Nusah Ashkenaz. Vilna, 1911.

Siegel, Danny. *Danny Siegel's Bar and Bat Mitzvah Mitzvah Book: A Practical Guide for Changing the World through Your Simcha*. Pittsboro NC: Town House Press, 2004.

Signer, Michael A., and John Van Engen, eds. *Jews and Christians in Twelfth Century Europe*. Notre Dame IN: University of Notre Dame Press, 2001.

Silberman, Melvin L., and Shoshana R. "From Bar/Bat Mitzvah through the Teen Years: Challenges to Parent and Community." In *Celebration and Renewal: Rites of Passage in Judaism*, edited by Rela M. Geffen, 53–70. Philadelphia: Jewish Publication Society, 1993.

Silver, Harold. "The Rabbi and His Congregation: 'Today I Am a Woman!'" *CCAR Journal* 9.4 (1962): 39–42.

Silverstein, Alan. *Alternatives to Assimilation: The Response of Reform Judaism to American Culture, 1840–1930*. Hanover NH: Published for Brandeis University Press by University Press of New England, 1994.

Skinner, Patricia, ed. *The Jews in Medieval Britain: Historical, Literary and Archaeological Perspectives*. Woodbridge NY: Boydell Press, 2003.

Solomon, H. N., ed. *Daily Prayers Read in Synagogue and Used in Families According to the Custom of the German and Polish Jews*. 6th ed. Published for the Use of the Jews' Free School. London: Samuel Solomon, 1854.

Sommer, Allison Kaplan. "In Israel, Bat Mitzvahs Where Torah Is Read Remain Rare." *Jewish Daily Forward*, June 24, 2010. Online publication. Forward Association, New York. blogs.forward.com/sisterhood-blog/128994/in-israel-bat-mitzvahs-where-torah-is-read-remain (accessed May 14, 2012).

Sperber, Daniel. "Congregational Dignity and Human Dignity: Women and Public Torah Reading." *Edah Journal* 3.2 (2002): 1–13. Online publication. www.edah.org/backend/JournalArticle/3_2_Sperber.pdf (accessed June 23, 2013).

Stanislawski, Michael. *A Murder in Lemberg: Politics, Religion and Violence in Modern Jewish History*. Princeton: Princeton University Press, 2007.

Staub, Jacob J. "A Reconstructionist View on Patrilineal Descent." *Judaism* 34.1 (1985): 97–106.

Stein, Regina. "The Road to Bat Mitzvah in America." In *Women and American Judaism: Historical Perspectives*, edited by Pamela Susan Nadell and Jonathan D. Sarna, 223–34. Hanover NH: University Press of New England, 2001.

Strassfeld, Michael, and Sharon Strassfeld. *The Second Jewish Catalog*. Philadelphia: Jewish Publication Society of America, 1976.

Sulamith (Leipzig/Dessau). Periodical. 1806–48. Online archive. www.compactmemory.de (accessed June 23, 2013).

Swarsensky, Manfred. Interview in "Oral Histories: Wisconsin Survivors of the Holocaust." Madison: Wisconsin Historical Society, 1980. www.wisconsinhistory.org/HolocaustSurvivors/Swarsensky.asp.

Swartz, Sarah Silberstein. *Bar Mitzvah*. New York: Doubleday, 1985.

Synagogue Review, The. Periodical. London: Reform Synagogues of Great Britain, 1934–66.

Talmud. *Talmud Bavli*. 37 tractates. Vilna: Romm, 1886 and reprints.

Tananbaum, Susan L. "Jewish Feminist Organisations in Britain and Germany at the Turn of the Century." In *Two Nations: British and German Jews in Comparative Perspective*, edited by Michael Brenner, Rainer Liedtke, and David Rechter, 371–92. Tübingen: Mohr Siebeck, 1999.

Ta-Shma, Israel M. *Creativity and Tradition: Studies in Medieval Rabbinic Scholarship, Literature and Thought*. Cambridge MA: Harvard University Press, 2006.

———. "The Earliest Literary Sources for the Bar-Mitzva Ritual and Festivity" (Hebrew). *Tarbiz* 68.4 (July–September 1999): 587–98.

———. *Ha-Nigle She-BaNistar: The Halachic Residue in the Zohar: A Contribution to the Study of the Zohar*. Tel Aviv: Hakibbutz Hameuhad, 2001.

———. "Ivan Marcus, Rituals of Childhood: Jewish Acculturation in Medieval Europe" (review). *Jewish Quarterly Review* 87.1–2 (July–October 1996): 233–39.

———. "On Birthdays in Judaism" (Hebrew). *Zion* 67 (2002): 19–24.

Temkin, Sefton D. *Creating American Reform Judaism: The Life and Times of Isaac Mayer Wise*. Littman Library of Jewish Civilisation. London: Vallentine Mitchell, 1998.

Teter, Magda. *Jews and Heretics in Catholic Poland: A Beleaguered Church in the Post-Reformation Era*. Cambridge: Cambridge University Press, 2006.

Tropper, Amram. *Wisdom, Politics, and Historiography: Tractate Avot in the Context of the Graeco-Roman Near East*. Oxford: Oxford University Press, 2004.

Turner, Victor. *Dramas, Fields, and Metaphors: Symbolic Action in Human Society*. Ithaca: Cornell University Press, 1974.

———. *From Ritual to Theatre: The Human Seriousness of Play*. New York: PAJ Publications, 1982.

———. *The Ritual Process: Structure and Anti-Structure*. 1969. Reprint. New York: Aldine de Gruyter, 1995.

Union for Reform Judaism. "Adult B'nei Mitzvah." Online publication. urj.org/worship/wisdom/adult_bnei_mitzvah (accessed May 22, 2012).

L'Univers Israélite. Periodical. Paris, 1844–1937.

Van Gennep, Arnold. *The Rites of Passage*. Translated by Monika B. Vizedom and Gabrielle L. Caffee. 1908. Reprint. London: Routledge and Kegan Paul, 1960.

Vinick, Barbara, and Shulamit Reinharz, eds. *Today I Am a Woman: Stories of Bat Mitzvah around the World*. Bloomington: Indiana University Press, 2012. Also additional material not in the book from www.brandeis.edu/hbi/publications/directors/morestories.html (accessed June 23, 2013).

Waddington, Arthur H., and Raymond B. Williamson, eds. *The Expulsion of the Jews: 1492 and After*. New York: Garland, 1994.

Waskow, Arthur Ocean, and Phyllis Ocean Berman. *A Time for Every Purpose under Heaven: The Jewish Life-Spiral as a Spiritual Path*. New York: Farrar, Straus and Giroux, 2002.

Weidenthal, Bud. "Confirmations in Cleveland." Online publication. Cleveland Jewish History, Cleveland OH, 2010. www.clevelandjewishhistory.net/events/confirmation.htm (accessed May 22, 2012).

Weil, Ernest. "About the Author." *Love to Bake Pastry Cookbook*. Online publication, 2006. www.lovetobakecookbook.com (accessed February 29, 2012).

Weil, Gotthold. "A Copenhagen Report concerning 'Reform' Addressed to Rabbi Meir Simha Weil." *Journal of Jewish Studies* 8 (1957): 91–101.

Weinstein, Ronni. "Rites of Passage in Sixteenth-Century Italy: The Bar-Mitzva Ceremony and Its Sociological Implications" (Hebrew). *Italia* 11 (1994): 77–98.

Weintraub, Stanley. *Disraeli: A Biography*. London: Hamish Hamilton, 1993.

Wertheim, Aaron. *Law and Custom in Hasidism*. Hoboken NJ: Ktav, 1992.

Wertheimer, Jack, ed. *The American Synagogue: A Sanctuary Transformed*. Cambridge: Cambridge University Press, 2003.

West London Synagogue Archives. Anglo-Jewish Archives University of Southampton.

Wice, David Herschel. "Bar Mitzvah and Confirmation in the Light of History and Religious Practice." Rabbinic thesis, Hebrew Union College, 1933.

Wieseltier, Leon. *Kaddish*. London: Picador, 2000.

Williams, George Huntston. *The Radical Reformation*. 3rd ed. Kirksville MO: Sixteenth Century Journal Publications, 1992.

Wise, Isaac Mayer. *Selected Writings*. Edited by David Philipson and Louis Grossman. Cincinnati: R. Clarke, 1900.

Wolff, Ferida. *Pink Slippers, Bat Mitzvah Blues*. Philadelphia: Jewish Publication Society, 1989.

Woocher, Jonathan, Kate O'Brien, and Leora Isaacs. "Driving Congregational School Change to Enhance 21st Century Jewish Learning." *Journal of Jewish Education* 76.4 (2010): 334–57.

Wouk, Herman. *Marjorie Morningstar*. 1955. Reprint. London: Hodder and Stoughton, 2008.

Wurtzel, Yehuda, and Sara Wurtzel. *The Mitzvah Machine*. Video. Jerusalem Media Workshop, 1987.

YadVaShem. "To Live with Honor and to Die with Honor." Online publication. YadVaShem, Jerusalem, 2010. www1.yadvashem.org/yv/en/exhibitions/live_with_honor/index.asp (accessed May 14, 2012).

Yisrael ben Binyamin of Belzec. *Yalkut Hadash . . . mi kol sefer Zohar Haggadol veZohar Hadash ve-Tikkunei Zohar.* Lublin: Tsevi bar Avraham Kalonymos Yafeh, 1648.

Yoffie, Eric H. "Sermon by Rabbi Eric H. Yoffie at the San Diego Biennial, December 15, 2007." Union for Reform Judaism. Online publication. http://urj.org//about/union/leadership/yoffie//?syspage=article&item_id=6079 (accessed February 20, 2012).

"Your Bat Mitzvah / Bat Chayil." Online publication. United Synagogue, London. www.theus.org.uk/lifecycle/bat_mitzvah/your_bat_mitzvah_bat_chayil (accessed March 11, 2012).

Zalman, Shneur, ed. *Siddur Rabbeinu HaZakein Al Pi Nusah HaKadosh HaAri.* Brooklyn NY: Otzar HaHasidim, 2004.

Zegans, Susan, and Leonard S. Zegans. "Bar Mitzvah: A Rite for a Transitional Age." *Psychoanalytic Review* 66.1 (1979): 115–32.

Zohar. *Sefer Zohar Hadash.* Edited by Reuven Moshe Margoliot. Jerusalem: Mossad Ha-Rav Kook, 1978.

Zohar, Zion. "Oriental Jewry Confronts Modernity: The Case of Rabbi Ovadiah Yosef." *Modern Judaism* 24.2 (2004): 120–49.

Zunz, Leopold. *Die gottesdienstlichen Vorträge der Juden, historisch entwickelt.* Frankfurt: J. Kauffmann, 1892.

———. *Gessammelte Schriften, Zweiter Band.* Berlin: Louis Gerschel Buchhandlung, 1876.

———. "Zunz: Mein erster Unterricht in Wolfenbüttel." *Jahrbuch für Jüdische Geschichte und Literatur* 30 (1937): 131–38.

INDEX

Page numbers in italics indicate illustrations.

Aaron, 4
Aaron of Luntshits (Łęczyca), 48
Aaron son of Jacob HaCohen of Narbonne, 21
Abimelech, 2
Abraham, 1–3, 12, 26, 28–29, 31, 33, 184
Acre (now Akko, Israel), 16, 66
Adar, month of, 41–42, 263
Adelaide Hebrew Congregation, 150
Adler, Hermann, 98, 154
Adler, John, 184, 254n76
Adler, Juraj, 172
Adler, Nathan Marcus, 115, 171
Adler, Samuel, 87
adolescence, 120, 158, 201, 210, 218
adult bar mitzvah. *See* bar mitzvah: adult
adult bat mitzvah. *See* bat mitzvah: adult
Afikim, Kibbutz, 144
Africa. *See* North Africa
age. *See* correct age for bar/bat mitzvah
Agnon, Shmuel Yosef, 148
agnostic celebrates confirmation, 104
Ahasuerus, 2
AIDS, 185
Akiva, Rabbi, 28
Albany NY, 92, 118
Alexander, Levy, 137, 239n46

Alexandria (Egypt), 88, 106, 117–18, 198
Algeria, 117, 135
Alliance Israelite Universelle (Egypt), 117
Alsace, 41, 57
Altona, 43–46, 54, 57, 61, 63, 71, 88–89, 178
American Joint Distribution Committee, 168
American Psychological Association, 162
Amichai, Yehuda, 145
Amsterdam, 43–47, 62, 64–66, 70, 137; rules and restrictions in, 43
Ana Kurdi, 137
Ancona, 54, 57, 62, 88, 245n39
Anshe Chesed (Cleveland), 94
Anshe Chesed (New York), 92
Anshe Emes (Brooklyn NY), 123
anthropology. *See* historical anthropology
Antiochus, 2
Apple, Raymond, 251n75
Arabs: and circumcision, 3
Aramaic 33, 129, 227n4, 262, 264–65; speech in, 132
Are You There God? It's Me Margaret (Blume), 165
Areyvut Charity (New Jersey), 185
Argentina, 247n81
Ariès, Philippe, 202, 214
ark in synagogue, 44, 84, 94, 132, 138

Aron, Arnaud, 87

Aron, Isa, 180

Artom, Benjamin, 67

Aschaffenburg, 57

Ascher, Benjamin, 96

Ashkenaz, 39, 205, 215, 256n37, 261–63; medieval, 8, 196

Ashkenazic: Altona 63–64, America, 63, 65; Amsterdam, 44, 46, 65; Britain, 43, 138, 154; circumcision, 214; Eastern, 182; form of blessing, 25; innovation, 32; maftir, 46; party, 33, 37, 64; *pinkasim*, 57, 62; prayer books, 24, 203, 227n7; shabbat, 135; spread of ceremony, 57; traditions and customs, xii, 14, 22, 25, 31–37, 135, 138, 146, 182, 193, 196, 233n132; Venice, 65; women, 215

assimilation, 62, 189

aufruf, 55, 261

Augsburg, 193, 218

Auschwitz, 117, 123, 140

Australia, 88, 119, 150

Austria, 24–25, 261

Avigdor (Avigdor Kara), 257n75

Avigdor son of Elijah HaKohen, 207

Avigdor Tzarfati (Avigdor the Frenchman), 17–20, 28–29, 31, 33, 34, 206–10, 213, 215

Babylon, 21, 261

Bader, Jerzy, 140

Baeck, Leo, xiv, 122

The Balkans, 116–17

Bamberg, 86

baptism, xi, 27–28, 36, 82–83, 113, 210–11, 216–221

Bar and Bat Mitzvah Mitzvah Book (Siegel), 185

Bar/Bat Mitzvah Hesed programs, 186

Barcelona, 14, 206

Barda, Racheline, 118

bark mitzvah, 148

Barling, Mrs. S., 142

bar mesimah, 144

bar minyan, 65, 69, 108, 114, 217

bar mitzvah: abolished, 95, 99, 160, 173, 188; adult, 168–70; decline in standards of, 69, 152–54; first use of the term, 22–23; minimum standard for, 155, 186; reintroduced, 74, 100, 102, 173

Bar Mitzvah Lessons (Elsant), 175

"The Bar Mitzvah Party" (Amichai), 145–46

bar onsha, 29, 31

Baruch of Rothenburg. *See* Maharam

barukh she-petarani, xii, xvii, 1, 12, 13, 16–17, 21, 22–25, 30, 45, 151, 203. *See also* father's blessing

Barukh son of Zekli, 41

Basel, 67

Baskin, Nora, 168

bat chayil, 126

bat minyan, 108, 114

bat mitzvah, 101–2, 106–34; adult, 129–32, 248–49; age for, 109; contemporary extravagance of, 177; first in American Reform, 123; first use of the term, 114, 245; Judith Kaplan's (1922), 106–8; Judith Kaplan's second (1992), 129; parties more restrained and tasteful for, 173

bat Torah, 132

Bavaria, 59

Bayswater Synagogue (London), 97, 115, 247n91

Beer, Amalie, 110

Beer, Jacob Herz, 83, 110

Beer Temple (Berlin), 83, 85, 106, 110–12

Beit HaKnesset HaGedolah (Venice), 65

Beit Shemesh, 186

Belgrade, 117

Belzer Hasidim, 177

Benei Yeshurun (Cincinnati), 92
Ben Ish Hai, 116, 127
Benjamin, Israel Joseph, II, 136
Berehovo, 51
Bereshit Rabbah, 12, 13, 17, 22–26, 30,
    203, 205
Bergman, Henriette (née Wahls), 122
Berlin: assimilation in, 82, 85, 221; bat
    mitzvah in, 107, 121–23; Berlin Tem-
    ple, 85, 110; Charlotte Salamon in,
    121; confirmation in, 83, 86; girls cel-
    ebrate in, 106, 107, 247n77; guests
    restricted in, 54, 57, 59–60; Jewish
    Museum, 200; Jewish population of,
    245n24; Nazi era in, 121, 122; Reform
    congregation in, 110–14; schools in,
    77, 78, 83, 109–10
Berlin, Lob Mayer, 82
Berliner Synagogue (Leipzig), 114
Bernsdorf, Demoiselle, 106, 111
Bernstein, Stephen, 135, 140
Bertram, Daniel, 52
Beth-El Zedeck (Indianapolis), 237n66
betrothal, 28–29, 33, 214
Bevern, Demoiselle, 106, 111
Bialik, Haim Nahman, 250n24
Bible, 1–10, 18–20, 29, 36, 65, 81–82, 102,
    123, 140–42, 214, 229n28, 261–65
bimah, 102, 119, 122, 124, 162–63, 179,
    185, 261
Birkenstein, Elias, 84
Birmingham (UK), 88
birthdays: awareness of, 36, 214; cake,
    142–43, 199; candles, 141–42, 199; of
    kings, 2; as a marker, xv, 36, 188; par-
    ties, 1, 2, 30, 116, 127, 183, 187, 199; pro-
    hibited, 214; special birthdays, 127;
    thirteenth, 2, 15, 30, 31, 33–34, 41, 63,
    64, 137, 141, 150, 236n47; twelfth, 116
Black Death, 35
Blackheath (London), 66
black mitzvah, xi

Blackpool (UK), 248n101
blessing: given by parents, xiii; given by
    rabbi, xiii, 136. See also father's blessing
Block, Richard, 104
Blueberger, Esther, 150
Bluhm, Vera, 117
Blum, Ida, 106, 121, 223
Blume, Judy, 165
B'nai B'rith, 121
B'nai Mitzvah Revolution (Project), 159
B'nai Or Tallit, 183, 254n72
Bock, Moshe Hirsch, 77, 110, 240n5,
    244n16
Bohemia, 92
Boiberik, Camp, 142
Bologna, 88
Bonder, Evelyn, 131
Bordeaux, 87, 112
Borough Synagogue (London), 247n91
Boskovitz, 57
Boston, 100, 147
Boteach, Shmuley, 176
Breslau, 79, 87, 109, 112
bridal chamber, 31, 32, 261
bride, 32–33, 58, 220, 233n139
bridegroom, 32–33, 45, 55, 148, 220,
    233n139, 235n36, 261
Britain, 43, 95–98, 149, 185, 229n33. See
    also England
Brixton Synagogue (London), 247n91
Brondesbury Synagogue (London),
    247n91
Brooklyn NY, 123, 126, 147, 149
Brunswick, 87
Brussels, 132
Burns, Barney, 185
Buxtorf, Johannes, 67

California, 130–31, 179
Calumet MI, 106, 121, 223
Calvin, John, 218
Calvinism, 219

Cameo, Joseph M., 87, 113

Canada, 7, 63, 128, 143–44, 176, 222–23

Canadian Expeditionary Force, 139

candles, 36, 52, 83, 135, 138, 141–43, 146, 172, 178, 199, 205, 262; Shabbat, 36, 122–24, 148

cantor (hazzan), 42–45, 55, 60, 64–66, 79, 126, 169, 179, 262

Cape Town Hebrew Congregation, 126

Cardiff (Wales), 125, 132

Caribbean, 63, 91

Carillon, Benjamin, 87

Caro, Joseph, 10, 25, 264

Caro, Yehezkel, 119

Carpentras, 59

catechism, 68, 74, 76–77, 91, 95–97, 100, 104, 110, 113, 220, 240n3, 244n16

Catholics, 17, 55, 68, 76, 113, 197, 210, 217–19, 224, 265

celebrities' celebrations, 147

census, 4, 72, 152

Central Conference of American Rabbis, 99–100, 160, 166–67, 173

Central Synagogue (London), 247n91

Central Synagogue (Nassau County), 130

Chabad, Lubavitch, 25, 128, 138, 158, 168, 234n19, 261

Chapin, Richard, 105

charity: Abraham and, 26, 184; donations and pledges, 55, 56, 68, 99, 136, 138, 176, 184–86; projects, xvi, 128–29, 145, 158, 184–87; twinning, 185

Charleston SC, 74, 86, 90–91

Chaver Le'Torah, 169

Chicago IL, 118, 122–23, 156, 158; Board of Jewish Education, 156; Chicago Temple, 123

chief rabbi, 43, 98, 115, 125, 154, 171

childhood, xvi–xvii, 3–4, 6, 38–39, 51, 69, 71, 141, 149–51, 162, 197, 202, 204, 210–12, 221, 234n141

child marriages, 31, 33, 72, 234n141

Chile, 132

Chilmead, Edmund, 69

Chmelnitzky, Bohdan, 49

Christian Hebrew scholars, 67

Christianity: American, xi; baptism in, 67, 82; birthdays and, 36, 214; catechism in, 68, 76; Christian Hebrew scholars, 67; Christians celebrate bar/bat mitzvah, xi; Christians in Jewish schools, 78; Christians visit synagogues, 67–69, 82–83, 110; confirmation in, 82, 103; influence of, 19; Jesus's bar mitzvah and, 4; Jewish converts to, 27, 67–68, 85; laying on of hands in, 7; liminality and, 201; medieval, 19; missionaries and, 70; Pentecost in, 74, 78, 82, 113, 211, 240; Reformation and, 218

Christmas, 121

chuppah (wedding canopy), 32, 36, 40–41, 132, 183, 220, 233n139, 261

Church of England, 83

Cincinnati OH, 88, 92, 155

circumcision, 3, 26, 37–39, 55, 58, 60, 65, 152–53, 184, 211, 214–16, 229n32, 232n108, 261

Cistercian, 196

civic religion, 94

Cleveland OH, 75, 88, 94, 104, 131, 244

clothes: collars, 60, 61, 251n75; fine, 148; gloves, 113, 116, 118; new, 60, 70, 116, 216; shirts, 60, 144. *See also* tallit

Coen Brothers, 163

Cohen, Francis Lyon, 88, 119

Cohen, Rev G. M., 88

Columbus platform, 222

coming of age, xii, xiv, 11, 74, 83, 85, 98, 154, 215, 220, 244n16

communion (Christian), xi, 196, 211, 217: first, 114, 211, 217;

communion (Jewish), term for girls' confirmation, 118

comparative studies, 210, 224

concentration camps, 140

confession (Christian), 78, 205, 217

confirmands, 77, 92–94, 96, 99–100, 104, 112, 197

confirmation (Christian), 17, 78, 82, 114, 192, 197, 211, 216–18

confirmation (Jewish), xiii–xv, 74–105, 109–15, 118–20, 130; as a ritual of conversion, 166; decline of, 104; raising the age for, 98; research on, 197; special prayers for, 100; used as English translation for the term "bar mitzvah," 80, 101, 171

consecration ceremony for girls, 125–26, 142, 247n89

Conservative Judaism: adult bat mitzvah in, 131; bat mitzvah in, 109, 123–27, 190; ceremonies for girls in, 100; confirmation in, 76, 95, 100, 154; divorce and, 160, 162; extravagance in, 172–73; parent's speech in, 53; parties in, 176; return to tradition in, 222; setting of standards and, 156; women's role in, 123

Consistoire or Council of the Jews of Westphalia, 81

converts, ceremonies for, 130, 191

Copenhagen, 79, 83, 86, 109

correct age for bar/bat mitzvah, 3, 5–6, 10, 42, 101, 107, 109, 117

correct age for confirmation, 99, 105

Cossacks, 49

Council of the Four Lands, 43, 57

Counter-Reformation, 217, 219

Cowan, Lionel, 169

Creizenach, Michael, 87

criminal responsibility, age of, 144, 205

Croatia, 116–17

Cromwell, Oliver, 69

Crusades, 9, 19

Crystal, Is, 170

Czechoslovakia, 140

Danon, Rachel, 117

darush, 64, 137, 261

dating the evidence, principles of, 206, 256n37

Davis, Alexander Barnard, 120

day school, Jewish. See school

deafness, 4, 164–65

dedication of a new house, 37, 262

delinquency, 71–72, 189

Denmark, 83, 91, 109

derashah. See speech

Dessau, 79, 80, 86, 109, 112

devar Torah, 49, 128

Dinah, 7

disabilities. See special needs

disputations, 14, 18, 207–8

Disraeli, Benjamin, 54, 66–67, 83, 238n46

D'Israeli, Isaac, 67

divorced parents, 160–63, 190, 225

DIY celebrations, 181

dog collars, 82, 157, 171, 251n75

dogs. See bark mitzvah

Donin, Nicholas, 18

Don Quixote (Cervantes), 214

Douglas, Kirk, 169

Douglas, Mary, 202

Dresden, 87

Dreyer, Deana Baum, 142

Durkheim, Émile, 200

durna, 137

Dutch, 69

dyslexia, 148

Eastern Ashkenazic tradition, 182

East London Synagogue, 247n91

Eber, 2

egalitarian prayer group, 120

Egers, Samuel, 87

Egypt, 3, 51, 106, 117, 198, 263

Ehrenberg, Samuel Meyer, 79–80, 86

Eimer, Colin, 157

Einhorn, David, 112

Einsegnung, 79, 122, 247n77

Eisenstein. *See* Kaplan, Judith

eitzei-hayyim, 225

Ekbert of Münster, Bishop, 27

Elazar, Rabbi, 12, 13, 30–31, 40, 211, 230n62

Eliahou Navi Synagogue (Alexandria), 118

Elsant, Martin, 175

Emden, Jacob, 70

England: adult bar mitzvah in, 169; bar mitzvah in medieval, 20, 208; catechism and, 96–97; child marriages in, 33; confirmation in, 95, 114; First World War and, 139; girls' celebrations in, 100–101, 115, 121, 125–26; immigration to, 222; medieval, 20, 28, 207–9; in nineteenth century, 83; scholars in, 207–8; in seventeenth century, 69, 76; test of knowledge in, 156; in thirteenth century, 20; Whitsun in, 113

Eperies (now Prešov, Slovakia), 87

Erasmus, Desiderius, 218

Esau, 1, 12–13

eshet chayil, 126

Esther, 2, 34, 263

Estonia, 234

ethnographies, 239n50

Ettlinger, Jacob, 88–89

Europe: bar mitzvah origin in, 16; birthdays in, 36, 214; central, 59, 70, 125, 200, 208, 214; Christian influence on, 197, 221; cultural studies about, 199–200; eastern, 52, 117, 138, 153, 154, 170, 172, 182, 222, 249n16, 262; education in, 117, 217; expulsions from, 35; gifts in, 136; haftarah in, xii; Holocaust in, 140; medieval,

8–10, 18, 22, 28, 78, 202, 205, 210, 219; persistence of bar mitzvah in, 188; records available in, 222; regulations from, xiv, xvi, 54–62; Sephardim in, 63–64; in sixteenth century, 37; small parties held in, 170; social theory in, 200; sources from, 11; southern, 14; spread of celebration in, xiv, 54, 62, 84–85, 92, 116, 125; standards decline in, 70; universities in, 200; western, 49, 70, 73, 152, 189, 211, 222; white dresses worn in, 113; women in, 118, 215

evening dress, 171

evil inclination, 3, 26, 31

examination. *See* test of knowledge

expulsions of Jews, 19, 21, 35, 207, 209, 218

extravagance of the celebration, 33, 55–58, 71, 73, 114, 124, 133, 155, 160–61, 170–80, 188, 220

Ezekiel, 141

Falaise (Normandy), 207–8

Falk, Joshua, 8

Fasanenstrasse Synagogue (Berlin), 122

father of bar/bat mitzvah: and daughter, 107, 121, 127, 134; death of, 66, 79, 138, 150, 198; divorced, 162–63; feelings of, xvii, 151; gives party, 1, 28–29, 63, 138, 155, 171–72, 178; kaddish for, 20; leads prayers, 138–39; makes donations, 27, 136, 184; makes speech, 53, 140; neglects son, 90, 155; with non-Jewish partner, 165–68; and origin of bar mitzvah, xi, xiv, 12–26; pays fee, 43; places hands on son's head, 17–20, 29, 205, 213–14; pressure from, 164; and son, 1, 3–4, 8, 140, 148, 150, 157, 165, 169, 175, 196, 210, 215–16; teaches son, 186; testifies to age of son, 67–68; in war, 139

father's blessing ("who has freed me"),
xii, xiv, xvii, 1, 12–18, 21–22, 24–25,
30, 34, 41–42, 45, 53, 67–69, 137–38,
143, 151, 203, 205, 208, 220, 238n43,
244n14, 249n6, 249n16; for a girl, 127;
longer form of, 22, 24, 45
feast. *See* party
Federation of Reconstructionist Congregations and Havurot, 166
Feinstein, Jerome Tov, 123
Feinstein, Moshe, 126, 173, 188
Feldman, Dayan Asher, 126
Ferrara, 64, 207
festivals, Jewish, xiii, 4, 8, 29, 44–45,
74, 78, 80, 90, 93–94, 103, 112–13, 116,
122, 158, 187, 210, 225, 235n35, 240n8,
245n39, 262–64
fictional sources, use of, 223
Filehne (Germany), 139
Fineberg, Louis, 121
fines, 44, 46, 71, 154
Fink, Alice, 106, 122–23
floral prayer, 77
flowers, 77, 93–94, 113, 117, 132, 141, 148,
172, 176, 181
folk customs and traditions, 121, 167,
195, 198
foods: alcoholic drinks, 178; beef, 61;
biscuits, 54; brandy, 61; brunch, 147;
cakes, 54, 60, 135, 139, 141–43, 155,
172, 176, 196, 199, 211; carp, 55, 61;
chicken, 170; chocolate, 176; coffee,
54, 61–62, 145, 157; eggs, 196, 211; *ein
gemakht*, 56; fish, 55–56, 61, 176; herring, 37, 172; honey, 54, 60, 196, 211;
ice cream, 172; international menus,
176; kichels, 172; mead, 56; meat, 61,
127; *melida*, 132; nuts and sweets, 45;
poultry, 61; salad, 27, 176; sandwiches,
147; Savoy biscuits (sponge fingers),
62; schnapps, 172; sugared almonds,
61; sweets, 45, 62. *See also* wine

fountain pens, 8, 143, 145
fourth bar mitzvah, 160, 170
France: bar mitzvah declines in, 153;
bat mitzvah in, 108, 116–17; birthdays in, 214; childhood rituals in,
210; child marriages in, 33; confirmation in, 90; customs of, 16–21, 31,
206–8; expulsions from, 19, 21, 207;
German customs in, 15; immigration
to, 222; *initiation religieuse* in, 90,
112–13, 117; medieval, 20, 28, 34, 105,
208, 213; Napoleon and, 81; northern,
1, 11, 14, 17, 192, 206, 208–10, 261, 263,
265; origin of bar mitzvah in, 13, 16–
21, 214; scholars in, 201, 206, 208–9,
213; sources from, 18; southern, 13, 21;
spread of celebration in, 27; in thirteenth century, 14–18, 206, 209; in
twelfth century, 8, 11; white dresses
worn in, 113. *See also* Avigdor Tzarfati (Avigdor the Frenchman)
Francolm, Isaac Asher, 86
Frankel, David, 80, 84, 110
Frankel, Jacob, 88
Frankfurt am Main (Germany), 54, 57,
60, 68, 87, 89, 109, 135, 140
Frederick William III (Prussian king), 110
Friday night ceremonies, 123, 125, 131–
32, 144–46
Friedländer, David, 78
Friedmann, Meir, 119
fringes. See *tzitzit*
Fulda (Germany), 41
full formula for blessing. *See* father's
blessing: longer form of
Fürth (Germany), 43–44, 49, 57, 59, 62, 87

Gabbai, 43
Gaster, Moses, 170
Geiger, Abraham, 87
Genesis, 7, 12, 29, 71, 265
Georgia, 142

Germany: assimilation in, 80–83, 110–12, 221; bar mitzvah after the Nazis in, 135, 140; bat mitzvah in, 110–12, 121–22; birthday cakes from, 142; catechism in, 77; child marriages in, 33; childhood rituals from, 210; confirmation in, 78–83, 89, 197–98; customs of, 15, 22, 37, 45, 206; day schools in, 78, 109; *Einsegnung* in, 79, 122, 247n77; emancipation in, 78; emigration from, 154; First World War in, 139; in fourteenth century, 23; medieval, xiv, 205; Napoleon in, 81; northern, 43; origin of confirmation in, 74; origin of the party in, 27, 35–37; orphans in, 44; Orthodox in, 153; Reformation in, 218–19; Reform Judaism in, xv, 82, 188; scholars from, 200, 208; in sixteenth century, 192; speech at bar mitzvah in, 65; spread of celebration in, 22, 37, 57; in twelfth century, 16; wedding customs of, 45; Westphalia, 81–83, 98
Gershom, Rabbeinu, 14, 212
Gettleman, Eugene, 160, 170
Gibraltar, 238n31
gifts: books, 141, 144, 157; duplicate, 144; fountain pens, 8, 143, 145; horse, belt, and purse, 27; lists of, 143, 223; money, 136, 143–44; mother's story as, 161; origin of, 136; practical, 143, 145; reading list as, 71; reservations about, 145; restrictions on, 183; sent by the child, 61; sent by the host, 55–56; substitutes for, 160; table laden with, 143; twinning and, 185; useful, 143; in the Zohar, 32
gifts to the poor or to charitable funds. *See* charity
Ginsberg, Reuben, 135, 139
girls: first ceremony for, 111, 244n16, 245n37; given boy's certificate, 122; origin of ceremonies together with boys, 74; read from Torah Scroll, 120. *See also* bat mitzvah
Glanz, Leib, 148
Głogów (Poland), 57, 59
Glückel of Hameln, 70
Golb, Norman, 209
Golders Green Synagogue (London), 247n91
Goldman, Matan, 183
Goldstein, Elyse, 164
gold worn by women, 58
Goldziher, Ignaz, 49, *50*
Golinkin, David, 198
Gombiner, Avraham, 40–41
good deeds, 68, 149, 184, 214
Gottschalk, Benno, 122
grace after meals, 38–39, 60, 216, 229n50
graduation ceremony, 74, 79, 95, 103, 152
grandfather, 53, 63, 67, 137, 178, 183, 206, 231n90, 251n61
grandmother, 63, 107
grandparents, xiii, xvi, 52, 101–2, 138, 166, 187
Gratz, Rebecca, 91
Great Depression, 172
Great Synagogue (Brussels), 132
Great Synagogue, Dukes Place (London), 43–45, 96, 125, 154
Gries, Moses, *75*
Grossman, David, 160
group ceremonies, xiii, 76–105, 108–120, 122–23, 125–26, 133, 142, 168, 170, 191, 198; criticisms of, 120
Grunwald, Charlotte, 121
Gryn, Hugo, 51
Guatemala, 133
guests, restrictions on number of, 55–61, 63, 177
Guttman, Fred, 105

Habonim Congregation (Manhattan), 148

Hadassah, 130–31

Hadera (Israel), 129

haftarah, xii–xiii, 8, 25, 35, 46–47, 66, 69, 70, 107, 123, 131, 137–41, 145–49, 156–57, 164, 172, 179, 236n46, 250n23, 252n76, 262, 263; minimum age for, 8, 25, 47

Hagar, 2

The Hague (Netherlands), 44

haham, 64, 136

halakhah, 158, 193, 261–62

Halliwell Street Synagogue (Manchester UK), 97

Halperin, Abraham, 48

Hamburg, 43–46, 54, 61, 64, 71, 77, 83, 86, 109, 111–12, 178, 206–7

Hampstead Synagogue (London), 97, 247n91, 251n75

hands on head in blessing, 17, 120, 205, 210

Haninah, Rav, 38

Hannah and her son Samuel, 29

Hanover (Germany), 218

Hanukkah, 2, 119, 125–26, 262

hanukkat habayit, 216

Haredi, 128

Hart, Walter, 223, 247n93

Hartman, Tova, 128

Hasidei Askenaz, 16, 205, 256n34, 262

hasidic, xiii, 37, 49, 158, 177, 262–64

Hasidim, 37, 158, 188

havdalah ceremonies, 132, 169, 262

havurah movement, 181

Hazan, Eliahu, 88, 117

head coverings, 182, 193

Hebrew: blessings, xii, 16, 25, 66, 203; book, 141, 194; calendar, 42; learning and studying of, 8, 55, 66–67, 69–70, 73, 78, 84, 113, 118, 122, 131, 148, 152, 156, 164, 189–91, 196, 211, 222; name, 132, 141, 167; novel, 160; people, 2, 97; revival of, 100; school, 91, 156

The Hebrew Observer, 97

Hebrew Union College–Jewish Institute of Religion, 159, 195

Heidelberg (Germany), 87

Heinemann, Jeremiah, 82

Hen, Joseph, 167

henna, 136

Henry V (Roman emperor), 27

Herman (Hermannus Quondam Judaeus), 27–28, 32–33, 171

Hermanitz (Valašské Meziříčí) (Czechoslovakia), 70

Herod, King, 2

Hershman, Abraham, 121

Hertz, Joseph, 125

Herzberg, Arno, 139

Heschel, Abraham Joshua, 103

Hey Hey It's Esther Blueberger (movie), 150

High Holydays, 44 45, 96, 153

Hillel, School of, 4

Hispanic American, 143, 224

historical anthropology, 202

Holdheim, Samuel, 88

Horaot MiRabbanei Tzarfat, 14

Horowitz, Shabbatai Sheftel, 65

Hoshaiah, Rabbi, 12, 26

hotels, parties in, 170–71, 174

Hugh of St. Victor, 17, 213

Hull (UK), 125

humanist celebrations, 147

humanist education, 214

Hungary, 49, 51, 88, 97, 115, 117, 193

"I am a man." *See* "Today I am a man"

identity, doubts about, 149, 161

Immerman, Abe, 169

Indian Jews, 132

initiation, 90, 94, 112, 117–18, 196, 198, 210–11

initiation ceremonies into Jewish education, 186, 210–12

initiation religieuse, 90, 112, 117
interfaith families. *See* mixed faith families
invented tradition, 224
inviting, xiii, xvi, 2, 26, 30, 37, 40, 45, 55–56, 59, 61–62, 64, 67, 71, 83, 89, 107, 116, 120, 129, 133, 149, 153, 162–63, 170–71, 177–78, 181, 183, 220
Iran, 130
Iraq, 21
Isaac, 1–3, 12, 17–18, 26, 29–31, 184
Isaac father of Avigdor Tzarfati, 18, 207
Isaac of Joigny, 209
Isaac son of Abba Mari of Marseilles, 13
Isaiah, 97, 141
Ishmael, 2, 3, 30, 32
Ish Shalom, 119
Israel: allegiance to, 190; bar mitzvah in, 137, 142, 144–47; bat mitzvah in, 127–29, 144–47, 160–61, 223; bonds, 52; customs and traditions, xii, 127–29, 132, 137; immigration to, 106, 118, 132, 135; influence of, 109, 199, 222; mass ceremonies in, 168; mitzvah projects in, 185–86; secular, 128, 129, 144, 147; Shavuot in, 113; special needs children in, 164; terrorism in, 129; twinning with, 185; visiting for the celebration, 147, 161, 174–76, 187
Isserles, Moses: chuppah described by, 220; correct age for bar mitzvah given by, 10, 39; father's blessing mentioned by, 24–25; role of women mentioned by, 215; tefillin mentioned by, 10, 40, 42, 211–12
Italy, xiv, 57, 65, 68, 90, 108, 117, 208; bar minian unique to, 65, 108, 114, 217; bat mitzvah in, 108; confirmation in, 90; restrictions on party in, 61–62; role of women in, 215; white dresses worn in, 113
Itzig, Isaac Daniel, 78

Jacob of London, 20
Jacob son of Moshe Moellin. *See* Maharil
Jacobs, Joseph, 208
Jacobson, Israel, 80–82, 85–86, 110, 198, 221, 241n19
Jagel, Abraham, 76
Jamaica, 132
Jean, Laura, xi
Jefferson Airplane, 163
Jellinek, Adolf, 88, 106, 114–15
Jérôme Bonaparte, King of Westphalia, 81
Jerusalem, 66, 115, 141, 145, 177, 185, 212; bat mitzvah in, 129; fasting in, 11; feminist, 128; Jerusalem Talmud, 8, 9, 264; Jesus in, 4; mitzvah projects in, 185; pilgrimage to, 4; tefillin used in, 137; Western Wall, 147, 168, 174–75
Jesus, 4
Jewish Catalog, The Second (Strassfeld and Strassfeld), 130, 181, 183
Jewish Chronicle (newspaper), 87–88, 164
Jewish Cultural Studies, 199
Jewish Free Schools. *See* school
The Jewish Life Cycle (Marcus) 196–97, 212
Jewish status, bar/bat mitzvah as a marker of, 166–68
Jewish Theological Seminary, 196; Alumni Association, 194
Jews' Free School (London), 25, 125–26, 142, 168, 223
Joan of Arcadia, 133
Job, book of, 71, 84
Johannesburg, 88, 125, 138
Johannisstrasse Synagogue (Berlin), 122
John the Baptist, 2
Jonah, 71
Joseph, 2
Joseph Bekhor Shor, 208

Josephus, 3, 228
Joshua, 17, 97, 141
Jost, Marcus, 221
The Journey (movie), 149
Judah of Metz, 207–8
Judah son of Barukh, 14, 16, 21, 31, 33, 206
Judah son of David the Levite. *See* Herman
Judah son of Temah, 6
Judah son of Yakar, 14, 230n64
Juspa Shammash of Worms, 41–43, 70, 72, 151–52, 189, 216

Kabbalah, 29, 235n21, 262
Kabbalat Torah, 103–4, 167
Kaddish, 9–10, 20, 23, 36, 66, 138, 229, 238n42, 262
Kaplan, Judith, 106–9, 121, 123, 129–30, 133, 198
Kaplan, Mordecai, 106–8, 172, 199, 222
Kardashov, Nina, 129
Karlsruhe, 86
Kasher, Menachem Mendel, 26
Kassel, 81–82, 86, 110
Kedoshim, 107
Keeping Up with the Steins (movie), 160, 178
Keneseth Israel (Philadelphia), 100
Khabarovsk (Siberia), 168
Kibbutz, 128, 135, 144–46
Kiddush, 127, 139, 181, 262
Kimmel, Morris N., 155
King, Larry, 147
Kinloss Gardens, Finchley United Synagogue (London), 254n76
Kley, Eduard, 83, 86, 91, 111–12
klezmer, 61
kneeling in synagogue, 94
Kohler, Kaufmann, 99, 155, 194, 229n28
Kohn, Abraham, 88
Kol Nidrei, 5, 122

Königsberg, 86, 89
Krakow, xvi, 26, 43, 45, 52–60, 184, 235n30
Kravitz, Duddy, 143, 223
Krohn, Nikolai, 149
Krusty the Clown, 8, 169
Kudelka, Tana, 101
Kuperstein, Isaiah, 237n66
Kurdistan, 132, 137
Kyjov, 140

Lashkowitz, 148
Lateran Council, 217
Latin, 27, 76–77, 175, 213
Latin America, 175
Lauderdale Road Sephardi Synagogue (London), 126
lavish parties. *See* extravagance of the celebration
laying on of hands, 17, 197, 213, 218
Lazarus, Harris M., 247n89
leap year, bar mitzvah and, 42
leaving for school, ceremony for, 18–19, 209–10, 213
Lebendiger, Israel, 194
Łęczyca. *See* Luntshits
Leeser, Isaac, 91
Lehrer, Leibush, 142
Leibling, Mordecai, 165
Leibman, Charles, 198
Leigh, Michael, 101, 113
Leipzig, 88, 106, 108, 114, 193
Leiter, Robert, 171
Lemberg (now Lviv, Ukraine), 8, 88, 119, 138
Leningrad, 149
Leo Baeck College (London), xiv
lesbians, 147
Levi, 7
Levinas, Emmanuel, 200
Levinthal, Israel, 126
Lévy-Bruhl, Lucien, 200
Lewin, Raphael, 94

Liberal Jewish Synagogue (London), ix,
74, 101
Liberal Judaism: in Britain, xiii, 100–
101, in Denmark, 83
Libya, 135, 249n5
Liebman, Joshua, 100
Liegnitz, 87
lighting décor, 176
Lilienthal, Max, 87–88, 92
liminality, 201–4
Lindberg, Paula, 121–22
Lithuania, 49, 56–57
Livorno, 64–65
London: bar mitzvah in, 45, 74, 154, 184;
bat chayil in, 126; bat mitzvah in, 101,
115, 125; compulsory bar mitzvah in,
154; confirmation in, 87, 95–97, 100–
101, 114–15; consecration ceremonies for girls in, 125–26, 142, 168, 223;
East London, xiv, 247; Gaster archive
from, 170–71; Isaac D'Israeli in, 67,
82; manuscripts in, 206–7; medieval,
20, 209; objections to bar mitzvah
from, 101–2; priority of bar mitzvah
in 45; resettlement in, 69; rules and
restrictions in, 43–45, 143; Sephardim
in, 64, 66–67, 156, 239n46; special
needs bar mitzvah in, 164; standards
decline in, 154; test of knowledge in,
156, 158; white dresses worn in, 113
Los Angeles, 130, 160, 162, 170
Löw, Leopold, 87–88, 90, 193–97, 210
Löwi, Isaac, 87
Lublin, 55
Lugos (Hungary), 88
Luke the Evangelist, 4
lunch party, 118, 132, 170, 172, 174
Luntshits (Łęczyca), 48
Luria, Solomon. See Maharshal
Lustig, Branko, 140
Luther, Martin, 68, 217–19
Lviv. See Lemberg

Lvov. See Lemberg
Lwow. See Lemberg

Maccoby, Max, 173
Machzor Vitry, 8–9, 210
Madrid, 132
maftir, xii, 8–10, 25, 35, 46–47, 138–39,
149, 227n5, 236n46, 251n76, 262
Magnes, Rabbi Judah, 99
Maharam (Meir of Rothenburg), 208,
211, 232n97, 232n99
Maharil, 22–25, 46
Maharshal (Solomon Luria), 35–40, 46–
48, 54–56, 164, 193
Maimonides, 6, 29, 33, 80, 209
Mainz, 14, 22
Majorca, 21
mamar (shorter speech), 49
Manchester Reform Synagogue, 97, 100
Manchester (UK), 88, 97, 100, 115, 125,
169–70
Mannheimer, Isaac Noah, 84, 86
Mantua, 57, 61
manuscripts, 7, 9, 13–14, 15, 18, 20, 28, 30–
31, 61, 91, 200, 206–8, 228n22, 230n59,
230n65, 231n80, 232n109, 240n69
Mapu, Abraham, 141
Marcus, Ivan, 86, 196–97, 205, 210–14,
246n63
Marjorie Morningstar (Wouk, novel and
movie), 171–73
Marks, David Woolf, 87, 95–96, 114
Marmorstein, Arthur, 206
Marranos, 64, 262
marriage. See weddings
Marseilles, 13, 88, 206
matrilineal principle, 166, 252n15
meal: to celebrate bar mitzvah, xiii, xiv,
2, 10, 26–31, 33, 35–41, 50–64, 116,
138–39, 141, 170–72, 175–76, 184, 193,
195, 216, 220; to celebrate bat mitzvah, 116, 127–28, 132–33, 145, 186

medieval era, xiv, 2, 8–10, 16, 19–20, 28–29, 34, 78–79, 105, 194–97, 199, 202–6, 208–16, 219, 230n65, 264
Mediterranean area, 116
Meir of Rothenburg. *See* Maharam
Melammed, Shira, 129
Menasseh son of Israel, 69
Mendelssohn, Felix, 82
Mendelssohn, Lea and Abraham, 82
Mendelssohn, Moses, 78, 81
Mendes, Abraham Pereira, 88, 97
Menorah Park (Cleveland), 131
Messiah, 91
Methodist celebrates bat mitzvah, xi
Metz, 54, 57–58, 71–73, 95, 152, 189, 207–8
Mexico, 133
Meyerbeer, Giacomo, 244n22
Miami Beach, 131, 176
Mickve Yisrael (Savannah), 63
Middle Ages. *See* medieval
midrash, 1, 20, 26, 30, 33–34, 203, 232n109, 261–62, 264
Midrash Aggadah, 26, 34, 232n109
Minhag America, 93
Minhagbuch of Juspa Shammash of Worms, 41, 70
minyan, 65, 67, 69–70, 108, 114, 137
misbehavior at the celebration, 45–46, 54, 71, 178, 180
Mishnah, 4–8, 30, 65, 109, 214, 228n9, 229n28, 234n141, 262–65
Mishnah Berurah, 8
Mishpatim, 31
mishteh. *See* parties
mishteh gadol (big party) 2, 26, 34
mishteh livno (party for his son), 28, 34
The Mitzvah Machine (cartoon), 150
mitzvah projects, xvi, 128–29, 14, 158, 184–87
mixed faith families, 119, 147, 160–61, 165–68

mixed-race families, 147
Modena (Italy), 57
Modena, Leon, of Venice, xvi, 48, 61, 65, 68–70, 109, 217, 244n8
Momigliano, Arnoldo, 233n117
monastery, 196, 211–12
Monday, celebrations on, xiii, 64, 126, 136–37, 146, 164
Montevideo, 133
Montreal, 139, 143
Mordecai HaCohen of Safed, 151
Mordecai HaGadol (Mordecai son of Hillel HaCohen), 22–23, 25, 232n99
more bar than mitzvah, 173–74
Morel, Sir, 208
Morel of Norwich, 209
Morgenstern, Seth, 171
Morocco, 135–36, 249n7
Morosini, Giulio, 68, 152, 217
Morteira, Saul Levi, 64
Moses, 3, 17
mothers 2, 26, 52, 58, 61, 63, 70, 79, 110, 121, 126, 128, 130, 137–38, 148, 152, 161, 165–66, 169–70, 173, 215–16, 252n11
Mount Zion Temple (St. Paul MN), 100
movies, 133, 146, 149–51, 160, 165, 173, 178, 192, 223–24, 253n42
Munich, 87, 112
musaf, 108
music, 45, 47, 54, 61, 77–78, 81, 84, 90, 94, 132–33, 137, 143, 146, 149, 170, 176, 181, 185 238n42
musicians, 94, 172, 178
music signs. *See* trope
Muslims, 36
Mussafia, Avraham (son of Hayyim Yitzhak Mussafia), 115
Mussafia, Hayyim Yitzhak, 66

Napoleon, 81
Narbonne, 21–22
Natronai Gaon, 9

Nazarian, Soraya, 130
Nazis, 52, 85, 106, 121–23, 139–40, 142, 200, 221
Ndembu tribe, 201
Neolog Movement, 193
Neuberger, Julia, 101
New Congregation (Johannesburg), 125
New Haven CT, 8
New Historicism, 199
New Synagogue (Prinzregentstrasse, Berlin), 106, 122
New West End Synagogue (London), 247n91
New York: adult bar mitzvah in, 168; bar mitzvah in, 65, 95, 101, 147–48; bat mitzvah in, 106, 121, 129, 147; confirmation in, 74, 88, 92, 95, 100, 104; early settlement in 63, 65; educational requirements from, 156; manuscript from, 240n69; mixed seating in, 118; research from, 192, 194–96; Sephardim in, 65, 175; speeches from, 51; Yiddish camps near, 142
Niddah, 5, 214
Nieto, David, 64
Nikolsburg, 57
Nissenson, Hugh, 164
Nobel, Israel, 140
Nof, Edgar, 164
non-Jewish bar/bat mitzvah celebrations, xi, 1, 190
non-Jewish parents, prayer to be read by, 181
non-Jewish sources, 67–69
non-Jews in Synagogue, 220
Normandy, 18–20, 207–9
North Africa, 135
North London Synagogue, 247n91
Northwestern University, 196
Numbers, Book of, 3

oath. *See* pledge of obedience

objections to bar mitzvah, xiii, 84–85, 95, 101–2, 124
oblation, 196, 211–12
The Occident (journal), 87–88, 91–93
oral history, 117, 223
Or Hadash (Haifa), 164
orlah, 32
Orléans, 208
orphans, 23, 43–44, 49, 62, 138, 161, 185, 238n42
Orthodox Judaism: adult bat mitzvah in, 131; age for bat mitzvah in, 109, 128; bar mitzvah referred to as confirmation by, 171; bat mitzvah in, 109, 123, 126, 128, 133, 168, 190; ceremonies for girls in, 107–9, 113–15, 119, 121, 125–26; circumcision and, 152; confirmation in, 76, 85, 90, 96–98, 100, 189; criticisms of bar mitzvah in, 102; German, 153; group bar mitzvah in, 133, 168; lesbians and, 147; liminal moment in, 203–4; *maftir* and, 8; Paris and, 153; parties for girls in, 116; speech in, xiii; special needs and, 164, 175; test of knowledge and, 156; white dresses and, 113
Orvieto, Alberto, 88
Osijek (Croatia), 117
Oxford, 14, *15*, 18, 231n80

padrinhos, 66
Palestine (British Mandate), 121, 145, 264
Palestine (Roman), 3, 228n9, 264
Palestinians, 129
Panama City, 133
Pardo, Joseph, 64–65, 238n33
Pardo, Saul, 65
parents: African American, xi; aspirations of, 187; in the Bible, 2–3; boy's speech and, 49, 51; charity and, 184; confirmation and, 78, 91, 93, 99,

152; delinquent children and, 72; divorced, 162–63; emotions of, xvi–xvii, 155; gifts by, 143; of girls, 111, 115, 126; gratitude for, 100; guidebooks for, 223; invitations from, 89; of Jesus, 4; materialism of, 175; mitzvah projects and, 186; mixed-faith, 165–66, 181–82; neglectful, 79; parties and, 136–37, 141, 147, 149, 173–76, 181, 204; popularity of bar/bat mitzvah among, xiv; pressure from, xiv, 98, 125–26, 154, 158, 197; separation from, 19–20, 209; special needs children and, 165; speech by, 53; stories about, xi, 117; toasts for, 139; Torah ceremony and, xiii; tuition arranged by, 42, 153, 186

Paris, 14, 16, 18, 23, 87, 114, 118, 153, 206–9, 222

parishes (Christian), 217

parnas. See warden of Synagogue

parties: absence of, 61, 70–71, 148; adult bat mitzvah, 132; ancient, 1, 3, 26; bat mitzvah, 115–16, 127–29, 147, 177, 223; betrothal, 28; birthday, 1–2, 36, 116, 127, 199; black mitzvah, xi; breakfast, 170; brunch, 147; Canadian, 143; Chabad, 138; circumcision, 216; cocktail, 62; confirmation, xiii, 89, 100; disco, 174; DIY, 181; doubts about, 38–39; eco, 181, 183; economical, 172; as essential, xiii, xv; farewell, 29; French, 28, 34; German, 37; guidebooks for, 176; hosted by mother, 138; increasing popularity of, 37; invitations for, 170; Israeli, 137; Italian, 61–62, 68; in jail, 148; justification for, 37, 39–41; kibbutz, 144; Kurdish, 137; medieval, 34; midweek, 171; misbehavior at, 71, 178; *mishteh*, 2, 26, 28–29, 33–34; missing evidence for, 35; modern, xi, 204; music prohibited at,

61; non-Jewish, 28; origin of, 1–3, 18, 26–30, 33–34; for orphans, 62; *pinkasim* and, 56; for the pious, 36; prohibition of, 54, 71; as reason for the ceremony, xiv–xv; refusal to attend, 71; regulation of, xvi, 55–59, 65, 155; restrictions on, 59, 215, 220; as rite of passage, 204; Saturday afternoon, 60, 216; secular, 141, 144; for Sephardim, 64; speech for, 35, 39, 51–52, 139; spread of, 54–73, 213; Sunday, 60; taxes payable on, 61; tea, 142; themed, 176; in Theresienstadt, 140; Ukrainian, 138; weaning, 2; wedding, 2, 4, 28, 33–34, 72–73; weekday, 137; in the Zohar, 29–30. *See also* extravagance of the celebration; meal

Passover, 3–4, 37, 92, 113, 170, 262–64

patrilineal Jews, 166

Pentecost, 74, 78, 82, 113, 211, 240n8

Peretz, Isaac Leib, 141

performance, bar/bat mitzvah as, 159, 179–80, 202–3

perushim, 18, 19

Pesinok (Slovakia), 172

Pest (Hungary), 193

Pezinok. *See* Pesinok

Pharaoh, 2

Philadelphia, 63, 88, 91, 93, 100, 120, 171, 183

Philip Augustus, King, 19

Philipson, David, 77, 98 99

photographs, 49, 50, 113, 117, 123, 142, 146, 147, 170–71, 174, 194

pietists, German. *See* Hasidei Ashkenaz

pilpul, 48, 193, 220

Pinkasim. See rules and rule books

Pink Slippers, Bat Mitzvah Blues (Wolff), 102

Pirkei Avot, 6, 193, 263

Pittsburgh Platform, 222

Pleck, Elizabeth, 224–25

pledge of obedience, 91–94, 97
Poland: bat mitzvah in, 119; education in, 47, 110; in eighteenth and nineteenth centuries, 31, 72, 110, 203; origin of speech in, 39, 220; Reformation in, 217, 219, 258; regulations from, 43, 55–56, 59; in seventeenth century, 49, 54, 55, 59; in sixteenth century, 25, 36–37, 43, 47–48, 215, 217, 219–20; spread of celebration in, 25, 54, 57, 72; in twentieth century, 52, 119, 139–40, 167
Polk, Grace, 133
popular culture and music, 133, 143, 146, 149, 170, 174–76, 200
popularity, xi, xiv–xvii, 35–53, 158, 160, 186–89; of adult bar mitzvah, 168; of adult bat mitzvah, 130, 224; of bar mitzvah, xv–xvi, 25, 35–53, 73, 213–17; of bat mitzvah, 74, 102, 108, 112–29, 132, 181, 190–91; of birthdays, 36, 214; breadth of, 158; of candles and cakes, 135, 142, 172; of charity projects, 27; of confirmation, 76, 80, 84–98, 111, 210; of first communion, 114; future, 187; of group ceremonies, 168; growth of, 47; implications and problems of, xvi, 71, 73, 159, 186; of Jewish history, 200; of quinceañera, 224; of the speech, 7, 49; reasons for, xi, 11, 154–55, 186–89, 191, 202, 213, 220; of tallit, 183; threats to, 188; of *tikkun leyl Shavuot*, 29; today's, 11, 142, 158, 178, 186–89, 191; of trips, 147; unplanned, 189; of women attending services, 118
population, 72, 111, 130, 153, 162
portion, incorrect, 41
Portland Street Synagogue (London), 164
Portuguese. *See* Spanish and Portuguese Jews

Posen, 45, 57, 59, 86
post-confirmation classes, 95
postmodern families, 160–61, 225
postsentimental ritual, 225
poverty, 26, 43, 49, 59–60, 70, 90, 109, 118, 136, 148, 172, 184
Prague, 45, 54, 57, 61, 87, 237, 257n75
Prato, David, 118
prayer: for bar/bat mitzvah, xiii, 45, 67, 112, 123, 156; for confirmands, 80–81, 94, 100; for girls' consecration, 126; for non-Jewish parents, 181–82; for rabbi, 67. *See* father's blessing
prayer shawl. *See* tallit
Praying with Lior (DVD), 160, 165, 252n11
presents. *See* gifts.
Priesand, Sally, 125
privatized religion, 179
processions, 46, 93–94, 113, 115, 136
projects: charity and mitzvah projects, xvi, 128–29, 145, 158, 184–87
Protestants, 74, 76, 78, 82, 192, 197, 210, 217–21, 224
Provence, 13–14, 21, 29, 210
Proverbs, book of, 126
Prussia, 85, 110, 145
Psalms, 51, 84, 169
pseudepigraphic literature, 206
puberty, 5–6, 10–11, 33, 38–39, 40, 47, 109, 151, 194, 203–4, 218–19, 234n141
Purim, 2, 36, 263
Putting God on the Guest List (Salkin), xvi, 181

Queen Louise Award, 111
quinceañera, 133, 143, 224
quorum. *See* *minyan*

Rabbinical Assembly (Conservative), 123
Rabbinic Conference of the British Liberal Movement, 253

Rabbinic Ordination, 17
Radus, Joshua Leib, 138
Rambam. *See* Maimonides
Randall, Cathy, 150
Rapaport, Aaron Cohen, 48
rap style, 146
Rashbam, 213
Rashi, 2–3, 10, 14, 18, 39, 212–13, 230n66, 262–63, 265
Rava, 6, 39, 234n17, 236n42
Rayner, John, 101
Rebekah, 2
The Reconstructionist (journal), 174
Reconstructionist Judaism, 155, 165–66
redemption of the first-born, 3–8
Redlich, Alice. *See* Fink
The Reformation, 76, 213, 216–19
Reformed Society of Israelites, Charleston, 90
Reform Judaism: Adolph Jellinek and, 114; adult bat mitzvah in, 131; American, 94–95; assimilation and, 221; baptism discouraged by, 82; bar/bat mitzvah dropout from, 159; bar mitzvah abolished by, xiii, 74, 95, 99–100, 189; bar mitzvah controversies in, 154–56, 180; bar mitzvah reintroduced by, 99–100, 173, 224; bat mitzvah, age for in, 109; bat mitzvah and, 84, 106, 111, 123–25, 190; bat mitzvah, objections to, 124; in Berlin, 110, 114; in Charleston, 90; in Cleveland, 104; Columbus platform of, 222; confirmation and, 74, 76, 84–85, 89, 104, 111, 152, 154, 193; confirmation, age for in, 99; David Frankel and, 80, 84, 110; day schools and, 79; in Dessau, 80; Eduard Kley and, 77; extravagance criticized by, 172–74; in France and Italy, 90; in Germany, xv, 153; group ceremonies and, 125–26; in Guatemala, 133; guidebooks for parents in, 223; Isaac Mayer Wise and, 93; Israel Jacobson and, 85, 110; Israel visits and, 175; Jewish status and, 166–67; in Leipzig, 193; Leopold Stein and, 89; in Lvov (Lemberg), 119; in Manchester, 97; Michael Meyer and, 222; in Montreal, 143; Orthodox influenced by, 126; parties and, 176; post-confirmation classes in, 95; privatized ceremonies and, 179; prohibition of, 85; Protestant models and, 221; return to tradition in, 182, 222; *Sulamith* (journal) and, 84, 110; Torah scroll passing through the generations in, 143; values of, 112; in Vienna, 84; West London Synagogue and, 95–96, 113–14; Yehezkel Caro and, 119; in Youngston OH, 156; Zionism and, 190
Rehfuss, Karl, 87
remarried families, 162
Remember Us Foundation, 140
Renewal Movement, 130, 160, 183
requirements, minimum, 72, 155–56, 166, 189, 222
responsibility: age of, xi–xii, 1, 5–6, 12–13, 23–24, 103, 114, 127, 129, 178, 183, 202–5, 244n14; legal and financial, 205
Revolutionary War, 63
Rhinebeck NY, 142
Richler, Mordecai, 143
Riga, 87, 92
rites of passage, xi, 201–4
ritual: ancient, 200, 202; bat mitzvah, 116, 124, 125, 190; childhood, 4, 11, 196, 210–12; Christian, 218–20; comparative studies of, 224; of confirmation, 76–77, 90, 93–94, 111, 216; criticisms of, 90, 124, 174, 177; demarcation, boundaries

ritual (*continued*)
and liminality, 40, 66, 157, 167, 201,
202–3, 212–14; empty, 84, 90, 124, 133;
ethnic, 192, 225; father's role in, 205;
field observations of, 202; for girls, 116,
124–25; home, 116, 195; murder, 219;
new, 20, 25, 204–5, 213; of Ndembu,
201; as performance, 68, 202, 225; postmodern, 225; as rite of passage, 11, 203;
subversive, 201, 203, 205; among Sephardim, 63, 66; synagogue and prayer,
11, 63, 69, 143, 157, 167, 195, 201, 205,
211; in Thailand, 132; of Torah scroll,
passing through the generations,
143; transformative, xv, 202; women
excluded from, 190, 214–15, 221; of the
word, 220
The Ritual Process (Turner), 201
Rituals of Childhood (Marcus), 196, 210
Rivkind, Baruch Daniel, 194
Rivkind, Isaac, 192, 194–96, 210
Rodef Shalom (Philadelphia), 93
Rodom (Rouen), 209
Rokeah, Yissahar Dov, 177
Roman Catholics, 17, 55, 68, 76, 113, 197,
210, 217–19, 224, 265
Roman Empire, 3, 27, 36, 58, 228n9
Rome, 58, 61, 108
Rosen, Sherry, 124
Rosenfeld, Samson Wolf, 86
Rosenthal, Jack, 149
roses, 116, 132
Rosh Hashanah, 96, 263–64
Rosh Hodesh, 146, 250n23; adult bat
mitzvah on, 131
Rosh Yeshivah, 19
Rotterdam, 218
Rouen, 19–20, 209–10
rules and rulebooks for communities,
55–56, 72, 87, 152, 222, 263
Runkel, 57, 60
Russia, 117, 149, 168

Ruthenia, 235n27
Rwanda, 185

Sabbath. *See* shabbat
Sachs, Michael, 87
Sackter, Bill, 168
Safed (Tzefat), 31, 151, 185, 236n58
Saint Bede, 211
Salkin, Jeffrey, xvi, 181
Salome, 2, 228
Salomon, Charlotte (Lotte), 121
Salomon, Fränze, 121
Salomon-Lindberg, Paula, 121–22
Sammter, Asher, 87
Samson Free School (Wolfenbüttel), 79
Samuel of Chateau-Thierry, 208
Samuel of Falaise, 208–9, 231
Samuel son of Meir, 213
San Francisco, 88, 94
Saperstein, Harold, 173
Saperstein, Marc, 173–74
Saqui, Moses, 66
Sarah, 2, 26, 184
Sarajevo, 66
Satan, 26, 184
Savannah GA, 63, 65
Saxony, 81, 218
"Sayings of the Fathers." *See* Pirkei Avot
Schachter-Shalomi, Zalman, 183
Schiller-Szinessy, Solomon, 87–88, 97–
98, 115, 242n79, 245n45
Schnaittach, 57, 59
Scholem, Gershom, 205, 257
school: Altona, 89; ancient, 228n9; Bre-
slau, 79, 109; boarding, 66; bullying
in, 83; Cincinnati, 92; confirmation
in, 74, 79–80, 85, 94–95, 166, 193, 199;
Copenhagen, 79, 83–84, 109; drop-
ping out from after bar/bat mitzvah,
53; Egypt, 117–18; Esau and Jacob
attend, 12; Freischule Berlin, 78–
79, 109–10; German Jewish School,

Riga, 92; girls', 77, 109–10; graduation from, 94, 105, 117, 221; *haredi*, 128; Hebrew, 53, 100; Hebrew content in, 100; humanist education in, 214; in *Esther Blueberger* (movie), 150; initiation into, 196, 210–11; Israel Jacobson and, 80; Jewish day, 74, 78–80, 83, 89, 111, 113, 133, 150–52, 193, 221, 241n25; Jewish Free (Dessau), 80, 109; Jewish Free (Frankfurt), 89, 109; Jewish Free (Hamburg), 109, 111; Jewish Free (Seesen), 79, 81, 86; Jewish Free (Wolfenbüttel), 79, 86; Jewish Free Schools, 78–80, 111; Jews' Free (London), 25, 125–26, 142, 168, 223; kibbutz, 146; leaving age from, 71, 76; Leopold Zunz and, 79; Metz innovations about, 71; Montevideo, 133; origin of bar mitzvah and, 1, 18–19, 29, 34, 66, 210, 212–13; Panama City, 133; payment for, 43; Philadelphia, 91; rabbinic supervision of, 81; Rouen, 18–20, 209–10; Sabbath, 95, 99; Samson Free, 79; supplementary, 104, 118, 154, 156, 159, 166; tefillin ceremony held in, 26; truancy from, 72; twinning and, 185; Vologda, 149; Winchester UK, 214; year groups in, 6, 36, 214; in Zohar, 32

Schudt, Johann Jacob, 60, 68

Schwerin, 88

second bar mitzvah, 169

second bat mitzvah, 130, 190

secular bar mitzvah, 128–29, 140, 144, 146

secular education, 81, 105, 115, 190

secular Israelis, 147

Seder Rav Amram, 9

Seesen, 79, 81–82, 86

Sefer HaIttur, 13, 16

Sefer HaRokeah, 211

Sefer Huqqei HaTorah, 18, 210, 231n80

Sefer Minhagim, 24

Sefirot, 32, 233n137

Selikovitch, George, 51

Sephardic, xiii, 25, 46–47, 62–67, 117, 126–27, 135, 137, 156, 175, 227n7, 238n43, 239n46, 249n2, 249n6, 261–63

Serbia, 116, 123

Seridei Eish, 127, 248

A Serious Man (movie), 163

sermons, 48, 78, 83–84, 86, 88–89, 92, 95, 98, 111, 118, 157, 173, 236n58

service booklets for confirmation, 98, 197

se'udah. See meal

Sex and the City, 133

sexuality, 11; precocious, 177–78, 203–4

Shaarey Shomayim (Lancaster PA), 100

Shabbat: afternoon, xiii, 47, 60, 66–67, 138, 151, 169, 216, bat mitzvah on, 106; candles, 36, 122–23, 148; certificates presented on, 126; clothes for, 60, 116, 216; confirmation on, 79, 91; creation and, 7; in girls' school, 110; life-cycle events on, 55; meals for, 37, 60, 132, 216; more than one bar mitzvah on, 44; music on, 137; observance and non-observance of, 77, 93, 160, 173, 187–88; preaching on, 48; school, 99; School Committee, 95; services and Torah reading for, xii, 8–9, 40–47, 61, 67, 69, 70, 107–8, 110, 128, 131–32, 135, 138, 142, 146, 157, 170, 172, 179–80

Shabbat Bemidbar, xiii, 261

Shabbat Ki Tissa, 41, 262

Shabbat Nahamu, 70, 263

Shabbat Parah, 157

Shabbat Re'eh, 116, 263

Shabbat Tetzaveh, 41, 264

Shabbat Vayera, 28, 265

Shabtai Sofer, 232

Shakespeare, 36, 214

Shammai, School of, 4

Shavuot: bat mitzvah on, 114; ceremonies for girls on, 116, 126; childhood rituals on, 210; confirmation on, xiii, 29, 74, 75, 78, 80, 82–83, 90–97, 101, 103–4, 113–16, 122, 126, 210, 245n39, 263–64; development of, 240n8; studying on, 29; wearing white for, 113

Shearith Israel (New York), 65, 238n37

Shechem, 7

Sheftall, Benjamin, 63

Sheftall, Mordecai, 63, 65, 238n28

she-heheyanu blessing, 108, 116

Shekhinah, 32, 264

Shem, 2

Shema, 9, 150, 264

Sherwin, Byron, 196

Shimon son of Elazar, 7

Shimon son of Yohai, 30–31, 33, 40

Shimshon son of Tzadok, 22, 208, 215

Shoah Foundation Institute, 122

shofar, 96, 215, 263

Shulchan Arukh, 10, 24–25, 46, 264

Silver, Abba Hillel, 104

Silver, Daniel Jeremy, 104

Silver, Harold, 124

Silverman, Morris, 123

Simchat Torah, 8, 36, 264

Simeon, 7

Simpson, Homer, 8

The Simpsons, 8, 169

Sinai, 3, 103, 113, 204, 264

Slobodka, 138

social occasion, bar/bat mitzvah as, xv, 54, 132, 170–73, 188–89, 224

Society for Humanistic Judaism, 147

Society for the Advancement of Judaism (New York), 106

Soferim, Tractate, 9, 11, 229n46

Sola, David Aaron de, 66

Solomon, Henry, 232n106

son of the commandment, xi, 23, 69

Sorek, Zehorit and Limor, 147

Soviet Jewry, 184

Soviet Union (and former Soviet Union), 149, 185

Spain, 10, 29–31, 132, 214, 233n132, 262–63, 265

Spanish and Portuguese Jews, 47, 63–66, 137, 170, 261

Spanish and Portuguese Synagogue (Withington, Manchester), 170

special needs, 38, 148, 163–65, 168, 175, 190, 191

speech: bar mitzvah 7, 61, 68, 220, 229n33; bat mitzvah, 122, 127–28; confirmation, 77, 82, 112; criticism of, 179; father's, 140; Israeli, 145–46; of thanks, 27; parents', 53; rabbi's, 132; teacher's, 80; at Yiddish ceremony, 141. See also speech of Torah

speech of Torah (derashah), xiii, xv–xvi, 35, 39, 41, 47–53, 128, 136, 138–39, 188, 213, 216, 236n51, 261; common lines from, 52; earliest surviving, 48; given in synagogue, 61, 65; heyday of, 48; occasion for, 41; origin of, xv, 47, 213, 220; payment for, xvi, 35, 48–49, 51, 188; photo of, 50; reason for, xiii, 39; as ritual, 220; Sephardic darush, 64, 137, 261; shorter, 49; standardized, 35, 49; teacher of, 63; tests and rehearsal of, 68; thesis on, 196; training for, 47; written by teacher, 188

Split (Spalato) (Croatia), 66

St. Andrew's Holborn (London), 67

status issues, 166–67

Stein, Leopold, 89

Stern, Tuvia, 148

St. John's Wood Synagogue (London), 247n91

St. Petersburg, 111

Strasbourg, 87

street celebration, 137

St. Simon's Island, 63

St. Thomas (Caribbean Island), 87, 91, 130

St. Victor, Abbey of (Paris), 18

Subotica (Serbia), 123

suffrage for women, 107

Sugenheim, 57

Sukkot, 91, 264

Sulamith (journal), 86, 110, 112

sumptuary laws, 58–59, 65, 177, 181, 222

Sunday, 60, 78–79, 91, 104, 113, 118, 126, 131, 137, 149, 156, 170

supplementary Jewish schools. *See* school

Sura, 21

survivors remember, 122

Swarsensky, Manfred, 106, 122

Sydney (Australia), 88, 119

syllabus and curriculum, 7, 78–79, 95, 126, 144, 157–58

Syrian Jews of New York, 175

Szold, Henrietta, 120

Takkanot, 55, 264

tallit, 264; choice of, 182; as chuppah, 32; for bar mitzvah, 45, 53, 135–36, 139, 147, 150, 163, 182–83, 185; for bat mitzvah, 45, 121, 130, 132, 143, 147, 163, 182, 185; for dog, 148; home-made, 181; for women, 130, 215, 257n75

Talmud, 6–7, 23, 30, 38, 45, 51, 65, 79–80, 92, 114, 194, 208, 227n4, 228n9, 234n141, 264–65; Babylonian, 6, 39, 229n28, 263–65; Jerusalem, 8, 9, 264

Talmud Torah, Venice, 64

Talmud Torah, Wolfenbüttel, 79

Tam, Rabbeinu, 11, 18

Tashbetz Katan, 22

Ta-Shma, Israel M., 197, 203, 210, 212, 214, 233n132, 233n140

taxes, 55–56, 61

teachers: of Avigdor Tzarfati, 18, 206–8, 231n90; of children, 70, 110, 211, 228n9; compulsory, 72, 189; for confirmation, 77, 79, 80–83, 91, 98, 189; fees for, 48–49, 51–52, 70; for bar/bat mitzvah, xiv, 35, 41–42, 48–49, 51–52, 62–63, 67–68, 70–72, 112, 136, 150–51, 153, 175, 183, 186–89, 222; of Hugh of St. Victor, 18, 213; of Jesus, 4; of Rabbi Meir of Rothenburg, 208; of Rashi, 230n66; scarcity of, 70, 140

Tedeschi, Isaac Refael, 88

tefillin, 264; after bar mitzvah, 51, 146; cake shaped like, 143; first wearing of, xiii, 10, 25–26, 40, 42, 47, 49, 51, 64, 121, 136–38, 194, 204, 211–12, 215; for girls and women, 121, 215, 257n75; gift of, 143–45; learning about, 64, 67; lost at sea, 63; speech about, 52; worn outdoors, 136

Temple, the Ancient, 2, 4, 29, 75, 100–102, 163, 180, 262

Temple Beth-El (Great Neck NY), 168

Temple Emanu-El (New York), 95, 101

Temple Israel (Boston), 100

ten commandments, 77–78, 84, 91, 106, 120

Tent of Meeting, 3

Terah, 1

Terezin, 140

terror attack at bat mitzvah, 129

test of knowledge, xv, 6, 9, 67–68, 72, 76, 78, 83–84, 89–90, 95–96, 111, 125–26, 152–53, 156–58, 192, 207, 218–19; written exam, 157

Thanksgiving, 131

Theresienstadt, 140

third bar mitzvah, 169

Third Reich. *See* Nazis

third Sabbath meal, party at, 60, 216

thirteen and a day, xii, 5, 9, 30, 38, 39, 41, 46, 69, 151, 182 thirteen for the commandments, 6, 7, 193

thirteen tasks, 135, 144

Thomas Aquinas, 211, 216

"three towns" (*Der Drei Gemeinden*), 43, 61

Thursday, celebrations on, xiii, 45, 55, 64, 129, 137, 146, 164

Tifereth Israel (Cleveland), 75, 104

tikkun leyl Shavuot, 29

tikkun olam, 186, 264

tish, 177

"Today I am a man," 7–8

Torah blessings, xii, 108

Torah scroll, passing through the generations, 143

Torah Shelemah, 26

tosafists, 16, 18, 20, 207, 216, 265

traditional Eastern European bar mitzvah, 138

Trent, Council of, 68, 217

Trope for chanting, 47, 129

Troyes, 18

The Truth About My Bat Mitzvah (Baskin), 168

Tuck, Desmond, 154

Tuck, Raphael, 251n61

Tunisia, 135, 249n5

the *Tur*, 211

Turner, Victor, 201

tutors for bar mitzvah. *See* teachers

twelve tasks, 128

twinning, 184–85

twins, 12, 42, 104

two boys celebrating on the same day, 47

two years or more minimum study requirement, 72, 155–56

Tyrnau, Isaac, 24–25

tzedakah. *See* charity: projects; mitzvah projects

Tzefat. *See* Safed

Tzitzit (fringes), 10, 30, 67

UJIA Charity UK, 254

Ukraine, 117, 138, 185

Ullmann, Salomon, 87

Ulm, 218

ultraorthodox, 128–29, 139

Ungar, Samuel David, 117

Union for Reform Judaism, 159, 179

Union of Jewish Women (UK), 121, 125

United States: adult bat mitzvah in, 130; colonial era of, 63; bar mitzvah an anachronism in, 99; bar mitzvah as a social occasion in, 170; bar mitzvah reintroduced in, 100–101, 173; bar mitzvah speeches in, 7, 51, 53; bat mitzvah in, 106–8, 120–21, 123–24, 133, 177, 198; celebrities in, 147; comparative studies about, 224; confirmation declines in, 104; confirmation for girls in, 118, 120; confirmation in, 89, 90–95, 98–100, 104, 118, 120; curriculum for, 158; divorce in, 162; extravagance in, 176; first bar mitzvah in, 63; first bat mitzvah in, 106–8; girls reading the scroll in, 106, 120; immigration to, 222; Orthodox Judaism in, 127, 175; parties in, 176; post–bar mitzvah courses in, 104; prayer books in, 93, 94; records available in, 222; Reform and Conservative Judaism in, 53, 95, 99–100, 104, 106, 124–25, 132, 166–68, 173, 175, 223; scholarship in, 197, 199; Sunday Schools in, 91; women in, 118, 125

United Synagogue, London (Orthodox), 43, 45, 125–26, 156–58, 236n46

United Synagogue of America (Conservative), 121

Valley Beth Shalom (Los Angeles), 160, 162

Van Engen, John, 204

Van Gennep, Arnold, 202, 210

veil, 113, 118

Venezuela, 133

Venice, xvi, 48, 61, 64–65, 68–70, 76, 108–9, 152, 217

Verona, 87, 113, 207

Versailles, Treaty of, 139

Vienna, 84, 86, 115, 119, 207–8

village bar mitzvah, 45, 148

Vine, Barry, 8

Vladivostock, 168

Volhynia, 235n27

vow, taking a, 4

Wandsbeck, 43, 61, 239n66

war, 4, 59, 63, 117, 121, 124, 126, 128, 135, 139, 140, 142, 156, 166, 169–72, 195, 223–24

warden of Synagogue, 64, 66, 154

Warsaw, 87; Ghetto, 127

Waskow, Arthur, 183, 203

Wasserzug, David, 88, 125

weaning, 2, 26

wedding of the soul, 32

weddings, 2, 6, 28–29, 31–34, 36, 40–41, 45, 55, 58–59, 61, 65, 143, 171, 176, 183–84, 213, 220, 254n69, 261, 263

weddings held with bar mitzvah. See child marriages

weekday ceremonies, 9, 47, 64, 135, 138. See also Monday; Thursday

week-long celebration, 135, 137

Weidenthal, William, and family, 104

Weil, Ernest, 142

Weinberg, Yehiel Yaakov, 127

Wells, H. G., 144

Wembley Liberal Synagogue (London), xiii

Western Synagogue (London), 44

Western Wall (Jerusalem), 147, 168, 174–75

West London Synagogue, 95–96, 100–101, 113–14

Westphalia, Kingdom of, 81–83, 98

Westwood Horizons (Los Angeles), 160, 170

Weyl, Max, 121

Wheeling WV, 124

white dresses, 93–94, 112–13, 116, 118, 125, 132

Wice, David Herschel, 195, 197

Wielún (Poland), 139

wigs, 54, 60, 225

William and Sarah (ship), 63

Winchester School, 214

wine, 29, 56, 139, 155, 181, 205, 211, 262

Wine, Sherwin, 147

Winkler, Henry, 148

Wise, Isaac Mayer, 77, 93–94

witness, 18, 44, 64, 67–68

Wittenberg, 217

WIZO (Women's International Zionist Organization), 133

Woburn House (London), 157

Wolf, Joseph, 110

Wolfenbüttel, 79, 86

Wolff, Ferida, 102

women, exclusion of, 60–61, 63, 215

women, tefillin and, 215

Woolf, Mrs. Daniel, and Miriam, Rebecca, and Alexander, 130

World War I, 135, 169, 170

World War II, 117, 121, 124, 126, 128, 142, 156, 166, 223–24

Worms (Germany), 14, 18, 41, 42, 60, 70–71, 87, 151–52, 188, 211, 216, 220, 239n66

Wouk, Herman, 171

Wurtzel, Yehuda and Sara, 149–50

Yachad, Kehillat, 147

yahrzeit, 36, 55, 265

Yale University, 196

Yalkut Hadash, 40

Yehiel of Paris, 14, 16, 18, 23, 206–8, 230n70, 232n97

Yehudai Gaon, 21, 206, 232

Yemen, 129, 135

Yeshivah, 19, 43, 56

Yetzer HaRa (Evil Inclination), 26

Yetzer HaTov (Good Inclination), 26

Yiddish, 43, 46, 49, 51–52, 55–57, 71, 81, 140–42, 170, 237n3, 261, 265

Yitzhak, Rabbi, 31

Yoffie, Eric, 179–80, 188

Yom Hashlamat HaMinyan, 137

Yom HaTefillin, 137

Yom Kippur, 5, 11, 16, 122, 265

Yomtov of Joigny, 206, 231

York Massacre, 206

Yosef, Ovadiah, 127

Yosef, Rav, 38, 40, 164

Yosef Hayyim of Baghdad, 116

Yosef son of Natan Official, 207

Youngston OH, 156

Ypres, Battle of, 139

The Zigzag Kid (Grossman), 160–61

Zionism, 100, 117, 119–20, 140, 142, 158, 174, 190, 222

Ziv Tzedakah Fund, 186

Zohar, 26, 29–34, 40, 184, 188, 195, 233n132, 235n21, 265

zola (music), 137

Zunz, Leopold, 74, 79–80, 92, 196

Zwingli, Huldrych, 218

Other works by Rabbi Michael Hilton

The Gospels and Rabbinic Judaism: A Study Guide
with Fr Gordian Marshall, OP
(SCM Press, London, 1988)

The Christian Effect on Jewish Life
(SCM Press, London, 1994)